D0617101

Normandy 1944

The Road to Victory

BY THE SAME AUTHOR

Wall of Steel: The History of 9th (Londonderry) HAA Regiment, RA (SR)
North-West Books, Limavady, 1988
The Sons of Ulster: Ulstermen at war from the Somme to Korea
The Appletree Press, Belfast, 1992
Clear the Way! A History of the 38th (Irish) Brigade, 1941–47
Irish Academic Press, Dublin, 1993
Irish Generals: Irish Generals in the British Army in the Second World War
The Appletree Press, Belfast, 1993
Only the Enemy in Front: The Recce Corps at War, 1940–46
Spellmount Publishers, Staplehurst, 1994
Key to Victory: The Maiden City in the Second World War
Greystone Books, Antrim, 1995
The Williamite War in Ireland, 1688–1691
Four Courts Press, Dublin, 1998
A Noble Crusade: The History of Eighth Army, 1941–1945
Spellmount Publishers, Staplehurst, 1999
Irish Men and Women in the Second World War
Four Courts Press, Dublin, 1999
Irish Winners of the Victoria Cross
(with David Truesdale)
Four Courts Press, Dublin, 2000
Irish Volunteers in the Second World War
Four Courts Press, Dublin, 2001
The Sound of History: El Alamein 1942
Spellmount Publishers, Staplehurst, 2002
The North Irish Horse: A Hundred Years of Service
Spellmount Publishers, Staplehurst, 2002

NORMANDY 1944

THE ROAD TO VICTORY

by

Richard Doherty

SPELLMOUNT
Staplehurst

British Library Cataloguing in Publication Data:
A catalogue record for this book is available
from the British Library

ISBN 1-86227-224-7

Published in the UK in 2004 by
Spellmount Limited
The Village Centre
Staplehurst
Kent TN12 0BJ

Tel: 01580 893730
Fax: 01580 893731
E-mail: enquiries@spellmount.com
Website: www.spellmount.com

1 3 5 7 9 8 6 4 2

Typeset in Palatino by MATS, Southend-on-Sea, Essex
Printed in Great Britain by
TJ International Ltd, Padstow, Cornwall

Contents

To the memory of
14301033 Trooper Leonard A Kemp
22nd Dragoons, Royal Armoured Corps
Who fell on D-Day 6 June 1944

Greater love has no man than this,
that he lay down his life for his friends.

At the British War Cemetery, Bayeux

I walked where in their talking graves
And shirts of earth five thousand lay,
When history with ten feasts of fire
Had eaten the red air away.

I am Christ's boy, I cried, I bear
In iron hands the bread, the fishes.
I hang with honey and with rose
This tidy wreck of all your wishes.

On your geometry of sleep
The chestnut and the fir-tree fly,
And lavender and marguerite
Forge with their flowers an English sky.

Turn now towards the belling town
Your jigsaws of impossible bone,
And rising read your rank of snow
Accurate as death upon the stone.

About your easy heads my prayers
I said with syllables of clay.
What gift, I asked, shall I bring now
Before I weep and walk away?

Take, they replied, the oak and laurel.
Take our fortune of tears and live
Like a spendthrift lover. All we ask
Is the one gift you cannot give.

Charles Causley

List of Maps

Acknowledgements

As ever I am indebted to a range of individuals and organisations for advice, assistance and cooperation along the road that led to this book. Without them the book might have been written but it would have been a much poorer work. My gratitude is due to them but they are exonerated from any errors that appear in the book; for these I accept full responsibility.

Several years ago my good friend, WO I Mick Kemp of the Royal Logistic Corps, asked me if I could find out anything about his great-uncle who was killed in France during the invasion. My research led to Trooper Leonard Kemp who served in 22nd Dragoons and who was killed on D-Day. It also increased greatly my interest in the operations to liberate Europe and helped me decide that I would write about Normandy. For that reason, this book is dedicated to the memory of Leonard Kemp and to all his comrades who died for our freedom. Thank you, Mick, for the incentive that your request provided and I hope that this book is of some interest and consolation to the Kemp family.

Special thanks are due to Captain Ian Hammerton MBE CdG, Honorary Secretary of 22nd Dragoons OCA for his assistance with information on the operations of the Flail tanks of 22nd Dragoons and the loan of the regimental history. Mr Harry Bacon, also 22nd Dragoons, provided photographs of the Regiment as it prepared for Operation OVERLORD. Dr Stephen Pannell, Honorary Secretary of 24th Lancers OCA, provided information on 24th Lancers and a photograph. Major Tony Hughes FTPD MIMgt, who served in Normandy with 24th Lancers, also provided valuable information on his Regiment and on his own experiences in Normandy.

The staff of the Departments of Printed Books and Documents and of the Photograph Archive at the Imperial War Museum were helpful and courteous in their dealings with me and I am most grateful to them for all their help. Likewise the staff of the Reading Room of the National Archives at Kew, the National Army Museum, Chelsea and the Central Library, Londonderry. A special word of thanks is due to the staff of the Linenhall Library, Belfast for their help in tracking down and obtaining several out-of-print books during the course of my research. At the National Army Museum I was able to study the Lummis Files on the Victoria Crosses of the Normandy campaign and I acknowledge the assistance of the Military Historical Society and, especially, of Mr Dennis Pillinger, as custodians of those files.

A special word of thanks is due to David Rowlands for permission to use his painting Operation OVERLORD, depicting 9 (Irish) Field Battery, 7th Field Regiment, Royal Artillery firing on the run-in shoot of the morning of D-Day.

I would also like to thank Sean McMahon for his assistance on the life of John Desmond Bernal, the genius behind Mulberry; Major Roy Walker MBE of the Royal Ulster Rifles Museum, Belfast; Captain Henshall, Home Headquarters, Royal Dragoon Guards; Colonel James T Eaton CBE TD; David Truesdale, for information on the Royal Ulster Rifles in Normandy; and Mr Joe McCready AFM, for his support throughout the project.

Throughout the book I have used quotations from various published works and I wish to thank: Mr Francis Bennett, for permission to quote from *Ultra in the West,* by his late father, Ralph Bennett; Chrysalis Books Group, for permission to quote from *Montgomery as Military Commander* by Ronald Lewin, published by B T Batsford and *Decision in Normandy* by Carlo D'Este, published by Robson Books, an imprint of the Chrysalis Books Group; Colourpoint Books, Newtownards, for permission to quote from *Boyd's War* by George Boyd; Dell & Bredon Publishers and Major Bill Close MC for permission to quote from *A View From The Turret* by Bill Close MC; Four Courts Press, Dublin, for permission to quote from *Irish Volunteers in the Second World War* by Richard Doherty; Greenhill Books/Lionel Leventhal Ltd, for permission to quote from *The Desert Rats: The 7th Armoured Division in World War II* by Major-General G L Verney DSO MVO; HarperCollins Ltd for permission to quote from *The Struggle for Europe* by Chester Wilmot and *Watery Maze* by Bernard Fergusson; David Higham Associates for permission to quote from *Engage The Enemy More Closely* by Correlli Barnett, *Out of Step: The Memoirs of Field Marshal Lord Carver* by Michael Carver and for permission to use the poem 'At the British War Cemetery, Bayeux' by Charles Causley, from *Collected Poems,* published by Macmillan; John Murray for permission to quote from *Deception in War* by John Latimer; Orion Books Ltd for permission to quote from *The History of The Green Howards* by Geoffrey Powell and *Rommel: Battles and Campaigns* by Kenneth Macksey, both published by Arms and Armour Press; Pen and Sword Books Ltd for permission to quote from *The Times of My Life* by Sir John Gorman and *Forrard, The Story of the East Riding Yeomanry* by Paul Mace; Penguin Group (UK) for permission to quote from *Overlord* by Max Hastings, published by Michael Joseph; Lynne Reiner Publishers, Boulder, CO, USA, for permission to quote from *Tank Tactics from Normandy to Lorraine* by Roman Johann Jarymowycz; Robson

Books Ltd, for permission to quote from *Decision in Normandy* by Carlo D'Este; Spellmount Ltd for permission to quote from *Steel Inferno: I SS Panzer Corps in Normandy* and *Sons of the Reich: II SS Panzer Corps* by Michael Reynolds and *Only the Enemy in Front: The Recce Corps at War 1940–1946* by Richard Doherty; Sutton Publishing Ltd for permission to quote from *Roads to Falaise* by Ken Tout; A P Watt Ltd on behalf of Viscount Montgomery of Alamein for permission to quote from the *Memoirs of Field Marshal Montgomery.*

Quotations from documents in the National Archives are reproduced by courtesy of the National Archives while Crown Copyright material is reproduced by courtesy of the Controller of Her Majesty's Stationery Office.

In some cases, and in spite of best endeavours, it has not been possible to trace current copyright holders. However, the publisher and author are prepared to make the necessary arrangements to rectify this at the earliest opportunity. Photographs appear by kind permission of the copyright holders.

Jamie Wilson and his team at Spellmount were their usual helpful, encouraging and friendly selves and I thank them for all their support and friendship.

As always I thank my wife, Carol, and children, Joanne, James and Catríona, for their patience and support.

Richard Doherty
May 2004

Foreword

With each passing year their numbers grow fewer for they are old men now, most of them past their eightieth birthday. Sixty years ago they were young with all the hopes and fears of young men at war. Some had become soldiers, sailors or airmen straight from school. Most would never have chosen to do so in peacetime. But they all had one thing in common: they took part in the greatest military operation of all time.

Sixty years ago their ranks were much greater. The thinning of those ranks began in earnest in early-June 1944 when the blood of many of their numbers stained the sand and the waters of the Normandy beaches. Today Normandy is studded with military cemeteries that hold the remains of young men from many nations, or are home to memorials to those with no known resting place. Walk through those cemeteries today and you will see the graves and memorials to youths who had barely begun to live and you will find them equal in death. One German grave holds the remains of a senior NCO born in 1904 and those of a teenaged soldier. Both died in the opening hours of the fighting for Normandy. In the British cemetery at Bayeux the same story can be found. Those barely out of school may be found lying alongside men with long and meritorious service. But it is the young who are in the majority, emphasising that war's ghastly harvest is usually of the young.

It is difficult to walk through any of those cemeteries without being moved by compassion for the men who made the ultimate sacrifice that war can claim, for their families who paid such a price in pain and suffering, for their comrades who saw them die and wondered when their own turn might come. But there is another feeling that comes to the visitor to those cemeteries: that of peace. For those men died for peace and their sacrifice helped bring an end to the bloodiest war that humanity has ever known. And with that feeling of peace comes a sense of pride in these men who gave their lives that we might live in peace.

More than a quarter of a century has passed since I first walked through a war cemetery in Normandy. I have been back many times and have never failed to be moved by those neat ranks of headstones and I have often wondered about the stories of the individuals who rest or are commemorated in those peaceful graveyards. Those walks have also made me feel humble and indebted to a generation of young men, and some not quite so young, who were never again to see family and friends. More than anything else, it is that feeling of humility that has persuaded me to write about the battle of Normandy and, in so doing, pay my own small tribute to those who gave their lives there in 1944.

Richard Doherty
May 2004

CHAPTER I

Britain stands alone

This fortress built by nature

It was six o'clock on the morning of 6 June 1944. Lieutenant George Boyd of No. 885 Naval Air Squadron, Fleet Air Arm, took off in his Supermarine Seafire MkIII from HMS *Daedalus*, Lee-on-Solent, accompanied by Sub-Lieutenant Rollins. The Seafires flew across the English Channel towards France, passing over 'an amazing sight . . . thousands of ships of all sizes and shapes charging . . . towards Normandy'.[1] For the two young airmen their task was to direct the fire of warships onto shore targets. They were not the first from their squadron to make an operational sortie. At the end of his patrol, Boyd flew low over Ouistreham golf course where lay the wreckage of Sub-Lieutenant A H 'Bertie' Bassett's Seafire. Basset had been on the squadron's first sortie and was shot down by anti-aircraft guns; he had been killed in the crash.[2]

Boyd and Rollins were part of the greatest military operation ever undertaken. Airmen of the Fleet Air Arm were part of an aerial fleet that included the Royal Air Force, United States Army Air Force, air forces from the Dominions and from the occupied countries of Europe. In all, over 13,000 aircraft were participating in the invasion of France, supporting naval and land forces; that 'amazing sight' of thousands of ships totalled almost 6,500 vessels from mighty battleships to tiny LCAs (Landing Craft Assault) and midget submarines. Those LCAs, and other landing craft, would disgorge on to the beaches of Normandy the first wave of thousands of assaulting soldiers with their artillery, tanks, lorries and even bicycles. They formed the tip of the spear of some two and a half million British, American and Canadian soldiers.

Unable to identify suitable targets, Boyd and Rollins strafed two German troop-carrying lorries and a despatch rider before heading for home. Boyd had a near miss while jettisoning his auxiliary fuel tank when a Messerschmitt Bf109 dived straight at him out of the clouds. Evasive action by both pilots ensured that no collision occurred, although the fighters passed within a few feet of each other. The Bf109 was not seen again, nor were many German aircraft encountered over the beaches, such was the Allied aerial supremacy.[3]

That had not been the case only four years before when the Luftwaffe dominated the skies over the French coast as the remnants of the British Expeditionary Force, with French and Belgian troops, were evacuated from Dunkirk, and from Brittany. France fell to the Germans and Britain sustained a humiliating defeat. Somehow the British public saw this as an inspiring 'miracle' of deliverance and a shining example of British tenacity in adversity. It fell to Winston Churchill, who had succeeded Chamberlain as Prime Minister on 10 May 1940, to remind the nation that Dunkirk was 'a defeat and wars are not won by evacuations'.[4]

And it was Churchill who encapsulated the spirit of British defiance, expressing determination that Britain would continue to fight Germany with, eventually, British troops again facing Hitler's armies in Europe. On 17 June Churchill told the nation that Britain was 'the sole champions now in arms to defend the world cause. We shall do our best to be worthy of this high honour'.[5]

But the problem facing Britain was huge. With the Army so weakened that it was fit only for defensive purposes, there could be no question of invading the continent. Instead Britain faced the threat of German invasion. That this never occurred was due to the Royal Navy and Royal Air Force, the latter's fighter pilots earning immortal fame by their achievements in the Battle of Britain that broke the German aerial offensive. In so doing they earned Churchill's praise and their place in history as 'The Few'.* Without control of the skies it was impossible to send a seaborne invasion force across the Channel. Of course, such an invasion fleet would also have required mastery of the sea which the Royal Navy was determined to deny the Germans. That they succeeded in doing so is a matter of record but it is worth reflecting briefly on the German plans for invading Britain.

Having conquered most of Europe, Hitler focused attention on Britain. But this 'fortress built by nature for herself against infection and the hand of war' proved too much for him, as it had for Napoleon. Hitler seems to have realised the difficulties inherent in an invasion since, before approving plans, he tried to make peace with Britain, although this may also have been due to his belief that Britain and Germany could co-exist. Whatever the reason for his hesitation, diplomatic feelers were extended through the Vatican and Berne to which Churchill responded by advising the Foreign Secretary to make 'clear to the [Papal] Nuncio' that Britain had no desire to make any enquiries 'as to terms of peace with Hitler' and that British agents were under strict instructions not to entertain any such entreaties.[6] On 19 July Hitler broadcast an offer of peace to Britain,

* They included men from the Commonwealth, including Irish neutrals, the Empire, occupied countries of Europe and volunteers from the United States.

predicting that Churchill would take refuge in Canada.[7] The offer was followed by renewed diplomatic contacts through Sweden, the Vatican and the United States stating Germany's willingness to make peace. But Churchill saw these overtures as not so much an offer of peace as an attempt to have Britain 'accept the surrender' of those principles that she had entered the war to maintain and defend.[8] In a broadcast on 22 July the Foreign Secretary declared that Britain would 'not stop fighting until freedom is secure'.[9] Although German diplomatic efforts did not cease immediately – an address from the Swedish king on 3 August was also rejected – it became clear that invasion preparations were underway.

Following the Battle of Britain the improvised German invasion fleet was withdrawn and the Luftwaffe changed to night bombing. At the same time, the Kriegsmarine's U-boats were exacting a heavy toll from the merchant ships that supplied the United Kingdom, but Churchill was already considering the problems of a British return to the mainland. This may seem fanciful so soon after Dunkirk when the Army was still suited only to defensive operations, but Churchill was determined to prevent a defensive mentality setting in. He proposed raising specially trained units for raids on occupied Europe on a 'butcher and bolt' basis at first and, later, on a much larger scale with the aim of taking and holding Calais or Boulogne for a short time.[10]

These units became the commandos; the first were raised in June 1940.* On the night of 24–25 June their first raid on mainland Europe, Operation COLLAR, took place. There were minor engagements with enemy troops and press reports of the raid had a positive effect on national morale.[12] At much the same time Churchill called for an airborne force of some 5,000 parachutists. Alongside the commandos, these would play an important role in June 1944.

But the creation of such forces was no substitute for invading Europe and, in October 1940, Churchill expressed his desire that plans for an invasion should be included amongst future operational plans.[13] A week later, in Germany, Field Marshal Keitel announced that 'the Führer has decided that from now on until the Summer [of 1941], preparations for landing in England will be maintained purely as a military and political threat'.[14] It is thus possible to identify this period as the time when the plans that would materialise on the beaches of Normandy in June 1944 were conceived.

* Initially, eleven Commandos were to be formed, numbered 1 to 11 but No. 1 Commando was not formed immediately and nor was No. 10 Commando. In August 1940, No. 12 Commando was raised in Northern Ireland but this had a complement of 250 men, only half that of the other units.[11]

Among other ideas fostered at this time, Churchill stressed the need to develop specialist landing craft; German failure to produce such craft, leading to extemporisation with barges, only served to emphasise this requirement.[15] Commando raids might be strengthened by adding tanks and other armoured vehicles if special craft were available to land these. Development of small assault craft had begun before the war, and some had been used in Norway but had been lost there or at Dunkirk. Churchill now saw the need not only for small landing craft that could be transported by large ships to an invasion point but also for seagoing vessels to carry and land tanks, artillery and heavy vehicles. Over the next year this concept would prove to be the seed from which would be born the LSTs (Landing Ships, Tanks) that played such a crucial part in amphibious operations in the second half of the war.[16]

Another development had been the creation of a separate Combined Operations Command, established in July 1940 and responsible to the Chiefs of Staff for the study and practice of amphibious operations. ('Amphibious' implies only land and sea operations but the air element must also be integral and thus combined operations best describes such warfare.) Admiral of the Fleet Sir Roger Keyes became Director of Combined Operations.

It was in July also that Churchill sent a telegram to Roosevelt in which he wrote that 'plans ought also to be made for coming to the aid of the conquered populations by landing armies of liberation when opportunity is ripe. He stressed that this would require large numbers of tanks and the vessels necessary to carry them and land them on the beaches.[17]

Churchill also resurrected an idea that he had had during the Great War, the creation of an artificial island, which he described as the inspiration for the Mulberry harbours of 1944. This idea had appeared in a paper in 1917 in which he also proposed special lighters with shelving bows or drawbridges to land tanks on a defended beach, thus providing assaulting infantry with immediate fire support. In addition, the lighters would be fitted with bow-mounted wire-cutting equipment. Thus a paper prepared in 1917 was to contribute to the large fleet of tank-landing craft (LCTs) available from 1943 onwards as well as to the Mulberry harbours.[18]

Execution of these ideas was still in the future. In the summer of 1940 Britain stood very much on the defensive and even the defeat of the Luftwaffe, and the ending of the invasion threat, did not fundamentally change that situation. U-boats still threatened defeat and Churchill later admitted that they frightened him most during the war. On the evening of 3 September 1939, hours after war broke out, U-39 sank the liner *Athenia* off Ireland's north coast. The Battle of the Atlantic had begun and would rage until the last hours of war in Europe. Although the U-boat menace was never removed, the Allies gained the upper hand from May 1943 after which shipping losses reduced dramatically while losses in the U-boat fleet increased. But, as Wellington said of Waterloo, it was a near-run thing. By the end of 1940 Allied shipping losses exceeded five million tons, a figure that later increased to nine and a half million a year.[19] Although British shipyards were working at full capacity they could not replace all the losses. Fortunately the United Kingdom had entered the war with a large merchant fleet and American shipyards would also to come to its aid with a shipbuilding programme that helped make up much of the loss.

Once again, Hitler had blundered strategically through his lack of appreciation of maritime matters. German submarines had come close to bringing Britain to its knees in the Great War and the head of the Kriegsmarine, Grand Admiral Erich Raeder, and of its submarine fleet, Admiral Karl Dönitz, believed that U-boats could strangle Britain in this new war. However, they needed sufficient boats for this and Hitler's denial of resources to the Kriegsmarine meant that Germany entered the war with fewer than fifty U-boats, not all of them seaworthy. What might have been achieved with the almost 200 boats that Raeder wanted, or the larger fleet preferred by Dönitz, is a question that must have given many naval personnel sleepless nights. Certainly the strategic advantage in the Battle of the Atlantic, which lasted 2,073 days, must have swung to, and remained with, the submariners at a very early stage. In such circumstances it would be hard to conceive of Allied victory in the battle. And yet such a victory was an imperative before Allied troops could invade continental Europe.

Although officially neutral, Roosevelt was anxious to support Britain as far as possible, short of war with Germany. The US Army was expanded as was the Navy and the Army Air Corps, later the US Army Air Force,* and American military observers arrived in Britain. Although conscious of possible war with Japan, those observers concluded, by late-1940, that, should the US become a combatant, the defeat of Germany had to be the Allies' prime objective. As Omar Bradley later described the global strategic situation

> not only was Germany the ringleader in world aggression, but once having digested her conquests, she alone would possess the power to stalemate or defeat us. In the Pacific where Japan grew more and more belligerent, we could be hurt but not destroyed.[20]

That belief ensured that America would play a full part in the invasion of Europe.

* The US Air Force, as an independent service, was not established until 1947.

In early-1941 British and American service chiefs met secretly in Washington in the first of many meetings. Out of this grew the Combined Chiefs of Staff committee, which 'became an Allied board of directors in the prosecution of the war.'[21] During their Washington meetings in March 1941 the 'board' agreed that, should the US become involved in the war, Allied strategy should be 'Germany first' with the knockout blow aimed at that country.

Of course, politicians from both countries were also conferring and Churchill and Roosevelt developed that 'special relationship' which saw much US effort put into ensuring Britain's survival. By March 1941, with reserves all but exhausted, Britain could no longer afford to buy war materials from the US. Roosevelt stepped in with the Lend-Lease Act, which allowed war materials to be provided with no payment due until the war had ended and then only on materials still in service.* Thus American equipment and weapons rolled off the production lines for Britain. American industry had been brought up almost to wartime levels of production before the US entered the war, a growth in which British money, between 1938 and 1941, played a large part. That in no way diminishes the great act of generosity that was Lend-Lease.

As winter's long nights gave way to spring's brighter evenings, the Luftwaffe began withdrawing its bombers from western Europe. The bomber Luftflotten moved east for a new attack and yet another monumental strategic blunder. In spite of the ten-year non-aggression pact with the Soviet Union, Hitler was preparing to attack Stalin. The latter refused to believe the many signs of impending aggression until, on 21 June 1941, Hitler's forces crossed the border into Soviet-held Poland. A new war had begun in the east that would bleed white the Wehrmacht and Germany itself while the Soviet Union would suffer horrendous casualties, the full extent of which have rarely been appreciated in the west.

Britain was no longer alone. The United Kingdom and the Union of Soviet Socialist Republics made unlikely allies, but allies they were. War in the east held out the possibility of Germany becoming exhausted and made British plans for invading Europe much less 'fantastically premature' as Omar Bradley later described them. Although the first invasion plans had been drafted, such an effort would have made the

* The USA did not really want the material returned after the war, as there was already a surplus of military equipment for the post-war US forces. As a result much of the material still in British service was destroyed with, for example, aeroplanes on aircraft carriers being pushed over the side into the ocean. Some material was kept and thus had to be paid for but this was a very small bill in return for the vast amounts of equipment that the United States had supplied.

contest between David and Goliath seem an even match: Britain had fewer than ten divisions at home whereas Hitler, even after launching 165 divisions into Russia, still had sixty-three in occupied western Europe.

Nonetheless, in the summer of 1941 there was some cause for optimism in Britain.

NOTES

1 Boyd, *Boyd's War*, p. 50.
2 Ibid.
3 Ibid; Boyd, interview with author.
4 Churchill, *The Second World War, vol iii*, p. 103.
5 Ibid, p. 191.
6 Ibid, p. 152.
7 Ibid, p. 229.
8 Ibid, p. 230.
9 Ibid.
10 Ibid, p. 217.
11 Messenger, *The Commandos 1940–1946*, pp. 29–30.
12 Ibid.
13 National Archives (NA), CAB44/242, pp. 1–2.
14 Ibid, p. 1.
15 Churchill, op cit, p. 218.
16 NA, CAB44/242, p. 2.
17 Tank Museum website: www.tankmuseum.org.uk
18 Churchill, op cit, pp. 215–17.
19 Bradley, *A Soldier's Story*, pp. 183–5.
20 Ibid, p. 184.
21 Ibid.

CHAPTER II
Defiant in adversity

Then imitate the action of the tiger

At times there seemed little cause for optimism. The Royal Navy, stretched almost to its limit, was now also escorting convoys to Russia. In the Atlantic U-boats continued to take their toll of shipping but the United States, although still neutral, was helping to escort convoys thereby providing valuable assistance to the Royal Navy. Moreover, the US Navy had decided to build an escort base in the United Kingdom and, in spring 1941, opted to locate this at Londonderry in Northern Ireland alongside the Royal Navy's most westerly base.

In North Africa, late-1940's good news had been followed by bad. Lieutenant-General Richard O'Connor's Western Desert Force had destroyed Tenth Italian Army in Operation COMPASS but O'Connor was thwarted in his desire to advance to Tripoli and end Italian rule in Libya by Wavell's order to stop at El Agheila. His command became static and was stripped of troops for an expeditionary force to Greece. Hitler decided to assist his ally and a German formation, Deutsches Afrika Korps, arrived in Libya under Major-General Erwin Rommel.

Against orders Rommel attacked immediately since, after aerial reconnaissance of the front, he realised how weak the British were. Attacking into Cyrenaica, Rommel soon had the British forces retreating into Egypt; the ground gained by O'Connor was lost. Counter-offensives in the summer came to nothing and Churchill decided to relieve Wavell. The new Commander-in-Chief Middle East, General Sir Claude Auchinleck, began preparing a fresh offensive that would take place in November 1941 using the newly formed Eighth Army.

In October 1941 USS *Reuben James* was sunk by a U-boat while escorting an Atlantic convoy; USS *Kearney* was damaged severely. Both incidents illustrated the extent of United States involvement in the European war. Although US ships were also attacking German submarines, there was no retaliation by Germany except in the form of U-boats attacking American ships or, in German eyes, defending themselves against those ships. Thus Hitler's behaviour less than two months later is all the more surprising.

On the morning of Sunday 7 December 1941 most of America's Pacific

Fleet was at anchor at Pearl Harbor in Hawaii, although its aircraft carriers were at sea. In the lazy hours as the sun rose in the sky, the peace was shattered when Japanese dive-bombers and torpedo bombers struck at anchored ships and aircraft on the ground. Devastation was widespread; 2,403 servicemen and civilians were killed. Declaring that Sunday a 'day that will live in infamy' Roosevelt asked Congress to approve a declaration of war on Japan. The Japanese had also attacked British interests in the Far East, as well as those of The Netherlands, thereby declaring war on several countries. But this did not bring America into the European war; there were two separate wars on two sides of the world. This continued until 11 December when Hitler added yet another to his increasing catalogue of strategic blunders by declaring war on the USA. Hitler was followed by his Italian counterpart, Benito Mussolini. Two wars had become one.

Winston Churchill greeted news of the Japanese attack on Pearl Harbor with the comment 'so we have won after all',[1] in contrast to Hitler's view that Germany could not lose, even though his armies were bogged down before Moscow with Russia's oldest general, Winter, coming to Stalin's aid. But Churchill saw that the full weight of American industry and manpower would now join Britain with Allied victory the ultimate outcome. (Churchill's view was echoed by Japan's Admiral Yamamoto who told his superiors that he could run amok in the Pacific for some months but that eventually Japan would be defeated. His reason? He had seen Detroit.)

Within days Churchill had arranged to meet Roosevelt, and his political and military advisers in a conference codenamed ARCADIA, in Washington. The Prime Minister was to be accompanied by Admiral Pound, First Sea Lord, and Air Marshal Portal, Chief of the Air Staff and by the outgoing Chief of the Imperial General Staff, General Sir John Dill, soon to be promoted to Field Marshal. Dill's successor, General Sir Alan Brooke, was to stay in Britain to get to grips with the 'tremendous problems that awaited him'.[2] Churchill's party also included Lord Beaverbrook and his personal physician Sir Charles Wilson, later Lord Moran.

The party left London for the Clyde on 12 December to board HMS *Duke of York*, a westbound air journey being considered much too risky in winter. *Duke of York* was a new battleship and the voyage would allow her to work up to full efficiency.[3] During eight days at sea Churchill and the chiefs drafted strategy papers and plans for presentation to their American counterparts as discussion documents.[4]

Churchill believed that the first Allied aim for 1942 ought to be the clearing of enemy forces from North Africa. The second was regaining control of the Pacific, which, he considered, could be achieved by May

1942.* Liberating Europe through an invasion ranked as his third aim, not in terms of overall importance but as a matter of chronology; he considered such a landing impracticable before 1943.[5]

In October 1941[6] Churchill had noted Army strength in the UK as twenty-six infantry divisions, plus the Polish Division, with its armoured element. Each division disposed about 15,500 troops with ten corps headquarter organisations to control them. In addition, eight county divisions were deployed on coast defence, each with about 10,000 men but little transport and no artillery other than some coastal guns. Armour was represented by five divisions and four army tank brigades.** There were some additional elements as well as 100,000 men in Home Defence and Young Soldiers battalions; the latter would eventually become fully-fledged front-line troops. To improve the Army's quality, it was proposed to re-organise these formations into twenty-seven field divisions, plus the Polish Division, with armoured forces increased to seven divisions and eight army tank brigades; county divisions would be formed into additional brigades and battalions. It was thus hoped to increase the home army to forty-five divisions in 1942. In the Middle East were another sixteen divisions while the Indian Army provided seventeen in India itself and in Persia/Iraq. Fortress garrisons accounted for seven divisions and African forces another two while, at home and overseas, there were twelve anti-aircraft divisions. Thus the overall strength of British ground forces in 1942 was planned to be ninety-nine divisions.[7] The number in home forces, at forty-five, was still much below the strength of the German garrison in occupied Europe but was a considerable improvement on what had been available in the aftermath of Dunkirk. This increasing strength was one factor that encouraged Churchill to believe that an invasion might be launched in 1943; the planners estimated that this would require forty armoured divisions and a million other troops in its opening phase.[8]

The ARCADIA conference resulted in a series of strategically important decisions. Churchill thought that historians might consider the creation of the Combined Chiefs of Staff Committee as its most important legacy. This

* It is interesting to note that the tide of Japanese expansion in the Pacific was halted by the US Navy at the Battle of Midway in June 1942.

** An army tank brigade was equipped with Infantry tanks, or I-tanks, and was intended to support the infantry. Armoured brigades deployed cruiser tanks. This splitting of the armoured role into two discrete elements was one of the major flaws in British military thinking and led to two basic types of tank being produced. Not until the closing days of the war in Europe was the Army equipped with a truly good British tank in the shape of the Centurion and even then only a small number of Centurions arrived in Germany, too late to be committed to action.

body proved a most valuable tool in the successful prosecution of a coalition war. Since the Combined Chiefs headquarters was to be in Washington, the British chiefs had to be represented there and senior officers were appointed to this role. Chief among them was Field Marshal Sir John Dill who became the senior British service representative in Washington. Dill gained the confidence and trust of Roosevelt and of General Marshall, chairman of the US Chiefs, with whom he established a close personal friendship that would prove a key element in the alliance.[9]

British representatives in Washington were in regular contact with London on an hourly and daily basis.[10] Both nations' chiefs met at the various conferences in venues as far apart as Washington itself, Teheran, Casablanca, Malta, the Crimea and Quebec. There were eighty-nine such meetings at which the greatest number of the most important decisions were taken.[11] Although defeat of Germany as the Allied primary strategic objective had been agreed in February 1941 in London, the British ARCADIA delegation worried that the savagery of the Japanese attack at Pearl Harbor might have changed American views. Churchill was pleased, therefore, when, at the conference's first meeting, General Marshall set out a memorandum stating:

> Notwithstanding the entry of Japan into the war, our view is that Germany is still the prime enemy and her defeat is the key to victory. Once Germany is defeated, the collapse of Italy and the defeat of Japan must follow.[12]

It was recognised that only Germany could defeat the Allies or bring the war to a stalemate; Japanese resources would reduce and, while the Allies could be hurt by the Japanese, they could not be destroyed by them. On 12 January 1942 there was 'complete agreement' on the wider strategic canvas of the war and Allied aims; the Combined Chiefs agreed that 'only the minimum of forces necessary for the safeguarding of vital interests in other theatres should be diverted from operations against Germany'.[13] Disagreement was confined to the priorities accorded some targets and the emphasis on different theatres. Much, of course, was ruled by the availability of shipping and this, especially the availability of landing craft, was later to cause problems.

There was also agreement on production rates for war material, on which Beaverbrook and his American counterpart, Donald Nelson,* found much common ground. With American production already increased by British spending, Beaverbrook persuaded Nelson that targets for 1942 should be set even higher 'to cope with a resourceful and determined enemy'.[14] For example, Beaverbrook suggested that American

* The US Executive Director of War Production.

tank production in 1942 should be 45,000 vehicles against the existing estimate of 30,000. Additional targets set for the following year called for even greater increases in production; tank output rose to 75,000 in 1943.

Another vital element of the production schedule was shipbuilding; US shipyards would seek to build eight million tons, deadweight, of merchant ships in 1942, increasing this by a further two million tons in 1943. Such ambitious targets demanded innovative building techniques and programmes, with non-shipbuilding firms as sub-contractors. Although the 1942 figure was not met, total US tonnage built that year being 5,339,000, the figure for the following year was exceeded by 2,384,000 tons.[15]

Churchill later wrote that the documents prepared by himself and the Chiefs of Staff for ARCADIA bore a 'very close correspondence' to the outworking of the war in 1942 and 1943, but this is not completely accurate. British strategic philosophy was threefold: closing the ring on Germany; liberating the captive populations; and invading Germany itself. On the first of these British and American strategic thinking diverged. 'Closing the ring' did not appeal to American generals who preferred direct offensive action through a single major offensive, whereas Britain's chiefs believed that Germany could be weakened incrementally in a series of campaigns dictated by military logic and fortune. Thus Britain wished to see American forces committed to finishing off the Axis in North Africa followed by further operations in the Mediterranean, a theatre that the Americans regarded as a sideshow to the main business of defeating Germany and in which they saw Britain putting imperial interests first.

Nor was General Sir Alan Brooke, Britain's new CIGS who had not gone to Washington, enamoured of all that Churchill was doing in Washington. Brooke confided some of his misgivings to his diary, noting on 27 December that there had been a long, weary Chiefs of Staff meeting with a series of difficult problems arising principally from the Prime Minister's party 'brewing up a series of discrepancies with what we are preparing here'.[16] Nonetheless, ARCADIA's overall tenor was harmonious and set the pattern for subsequent cooperation.

ARCADIA did not include the Soviet Union, although Churchill and Roosevelt had been very conscious of the campaign in eastern Europe with the Americans concerned about the possibility of Russia collapsing. The Americans therefore urged an Allied contingency plan to invade western Europe in 1942 to relieve pressure on Stalin. This operation – SLEDGEHAMMER – was not something for which Churchill, or the British Chiefs, showed great enthusiasm; Brooke noted that neither Home Forces nor Combined Operations thought it possible with the landing craft available.[17] British agreement was given reluctantly after considerable American pressure. Omar Bradley noted that the operation could hope only to seize a bridgehead with the aim of reducing pressure on Russia[18] and that Churchill was adamant that 'there should be no substantial landing in France unless we intend to remain'.[19] On reflection, Bradley considered that Churchill was probably correct since the effect of an Allied force being ejected from the mainland would be disastrous for morale in the occupied nations. Above all, he wrote, it was vital to maintain morale in Europe by sustaining the belief that the Allies were certain to mount an operation leading to liberation. Other Americans were less sanguine. On 22 July the British rejected SLEDGEHAMMER in favour of an invasion of Northwest Africa, which coincided with Churchill's belief that the first objective for 1942 should be clearing Axis forces from Africa. To Americans this appeared as a diversion that would not assist the Russians in any way. Eisenhower commented that this might become 'the blackest day in history'. Three days later, Roosevelt committed the United States to the African venture, Operation TORCH, to take place no later than 30 October. Marshall and Admiral King, Chief of the US Navy, unsuccessfully tried to change the President's mind.

Plans for a cross-Channel assault were postponed to 1943 under the codename ROUNDUP. Large numbers of American troops were to be sent to Britain; Bradley noted that the figure of a million by spring 1943 was quoted.[20] Meanwhile, American troops were being moved to the United Kingdom in Operation BOLERO* to relieve British formations for deployment to operational theatres. Events in North Africa in 1942 meant that those Americans went to Tunisia alongside their British and French counterparts. The Tunisian campaign reduced the Allied forces available for an invasion in 1943 since not only had large numbers of American troops been committed but a new British army – First Army – was created for the campaign and was reinforced throughout the fighting in Tunisia, which did not end until May 1943. Thus the likelihood of an invasion in 1943 receded, with British planners arguing that any invasion force would be outnumbered heavily and could have only a slight influence on the land battle for the continent. In addition, the strategic situation was changing dramatically with British victory at El Alamein and the German Sixth Army threatened at Stalingrad. The urgency felt by Allied planners only a few months before no longer existed.

British planners were also influenced by Operation JUBILEE, the raid on Dieppe carried out by a Canadian/British force in August 1942, which also seems to have helped convince Roosevelt of the wisdom of abandoning SLEDGEHAMMER.[22] This raid involved 10,000 Canadian and

* The original plan for BOLERO was for 1,147,000 men to be sent to the UK but this was reduced to 427,000 following Operation TORCH.[21]

British personnel with the Canadians providing almost 5,000 infantrymen. Churchill had foreseen commandos moving on to larger operations that might include taking and holding Calais or Boulogne for a short time. Substitute Dieppe and the genesis of the raid may be traced back to Churchill's concept. There was the added advantage that it might draw some German forces away from the eastern front to bolster the defences of France.

Why Dieppe? The port was close to England – less than seventy miles – which fulfilled two important considerations: the attack force could cross in darkness; and British-based fighter aircraft could provide cover, although with a time over the area of only ten minutes. Lord Louis Mountbatten, now Chief of Combined Operations, and a Chief of Staff, also considered seizing a port essential to any successful invasion; the raid would therefore provide a dress rehearsal for a major assault. Against this, topography favoured the defenders with headlands overlooking the sea approaches to Dieppe, unscaleable bluffs and steep shingle beaches with many large and slippery rocks. And the considerable German forces included a panzer division. Mountbatten's headquarters had estimated the defence as being weak, with the town held by a battalion of low-category troops. But the defenders were good quality and von Rundstedt had recently ordered their reinforcement; a three-battalion regiment rather than one battalion held Dieppe. Not far away were veteran divisions from the Russian front, including three SS and a parachute division while 10th Panzer Division was but forty miles away and up to full strength.[23] Opposition to the raiding force was formidable.

Although the larger part of the attacking force was Canadian, British, American and Free French troops were also involved. But, even before the first soldiers went ashore, there were setbacks with the eastern landing force meeting an escorted German convoy. The ensuing battle caused losses on both sides and disrupted the landing force's plans. Worse still, German land forces were alerted, thereby depriving the attackers of any element of surprise. In the ensuing battle over 4,000 Allied servicemen were killed, wounded or captured. The Canadians lost over 900 dead and almost 1,900 captured[24] while the US Army lost its first soldier in land fighting in Europe in this war: Second Lieutenant Edward V Loustalot, 1st Ranger Battalion, was one of three Americans killed.[25] (A small group of Rangers took part alongside British and Canadian Commandos.[26]) Much equipment was also lost including over 100 RAF aircraft against fewer than fifty Luftwaffe. The Royal Navy lost a destroyer and thirty-three landing craft and its covering fire proved inadequate against the powerful shore batteries. Ten LCTs landed twenty-seven tanks, all of which were lost, as were ten landing craft. This was the new Churchill I-tank's debut and it was far from auspicious; the tanks could not get off the beach due to large concrete obstacles emplaced by the Germans, which the Sappers were unable to destroy, and were subjected to heavy fire. However, the Churchill would play a major role in Normandy in 1944.

Dieppe was a disaster due to inadequate planning, faulty communications and poor support. The planning stage was the responsibility of several senior figures, most of whom distanced themselves from the operation once it had taken place, including Lieutenant-General Bernard Montgomery, who had been posted to Egypt as commander of Eighth Army only days before JUBILEE. Mountbatten and others share some responsibility for the failure but Denis and Sheelagh Whitaker suggest that the decision to go ahead, even when it was appreciated that losses could be heavy, was made by Churchill, who, they note, assured Stalin that the operation was about to take place and that casualties might be very heavy. Both he and Brooke, they comment, were determined to sell JUBILEE and TORCH, the invasion of Northwest Africa, as a substitute for the second front that Stalin was demanding. They could not, therefore, cancel the Dieppe raid. The Whitakers also quote Mountbatten's biographer, Philip Ziegler, who told them that Churchill had made a commitment to Stalin and that the operation would go ahead even in the face of the anticipated heavy casualties.[27]

There were other reasons for mounting the operation. It would persuade Americans that the British were prepared to act against the Germans on the mainland and would also, as Brooke noted, convince them of the difficulties of trying to open a second front. In addition, it would cause Hitler sufficient unease to divert more troops from the Russian front to protect the Channel coast. Finally, with SLEDGEHAMMER a memory and plans for TORCH coming to the fore, it would help divert German attention from the preparations for the latter. Thus Dieppe served as a deception for TORCH.

But Dieppe was also an important lesson for Allied planners. With the difficulties of taking a port demonstrated so clearly, minds now turned to other tactics. Relatively small numbers of defenders had pinned down the attackers and this could be guaranteed to happen to an even greater extent at a more strategic port. More men was not the answer. In what might be described as typical British fashion, some way of working round the flank was necessary. Dieppe was an important milestone in amphibious operations, simply because it was a disaster. The reason for that is best summed up by John Keegan when he compares the lessons of Dieppe to those in maritime safety from the *Titanic* episode, or those about state intervention in the economy gleaned from the *ateliers nationaux* of the 1848 revolutions.[28]

With SLEDGEHAMMER abandoned, attention turned to plans for an invasion of France in 1943 but TORCH made this more and more unlikely. American opinion favoured invasion in 1943 but British planners argued for further Mediterranean operations following TORCH in the working out of the British 'closing the ring' policy. The British won the argument with the next phase of operations being mounted in the Mediterranean theatre. Such strategy fitted British philosophy and the experience of the British Army which had never been strong enough to take on a foe as powerful as Germany unless as part of an alliance. By contrast, the United States was building the largest army in US history and American philosophy, based on manpower and material superiority, was to tackle the enemy head on.

Marshall's lack of enthusiasm for TORCH was one main reason for the operation being delayed until 8 November; US planners had already delayed drafting plans and there was marked lack of support from Admiral King until Roosevelt ordered him and his fellow Chiefs to cooperate fully. TORCH failed to end the North African war in 1942 through lack of boldness: US planners, keen to mount a cross-channel attack in 1942 or 1943, were reluctant to sanction landings as far east as possible on the Mediterranean coast. Allied forces failed, but only just, to take Tunis by December. Had they been landed farther east, they could have succeeded.

Time lost through hesitation and argument over TORCH, that uncharacteristic lack of boldness from the Americans in the choice of landing areas, and the reluctance of the British Chiefs meant that ROUNDUP would not happen.

JUBILEE and TORCH were significant. Many lessons were learned from the Dieppe operation, which allowed the tragedy to be recast in much more positive light, while TORCH led to the ultimate surrender of over 250,000 Axis troops, 150,000 of them first-class German fighting men. Jodl might claim moral victory for the Germans in Tunisia by stating that the campaign won Germany a 'certain gain in time'[29] that was worth the sacrifice but this was nonsense; the opinion of OKW*, that it was a disaster for German arms second only to Stalingrad, was a more realistic assessment.

NOTES

1 Churchill, *The Second World War, vol. vi*, p. 205, although since this was written post-war, the first verb is in the past tense.
2 Ibid, p. 222.
3 Ibid, p. 221.
4 Ibid, pp. 238–9.
5 Ibid, pp. 248–51.
6 Directive by the MoD, 9 Oct 41, Churchill, op cit, p. 118.

* Oberkommando der Wehrmacht or High Command of the German forces.

7 Churchill, op cit, p. 119.
8 Ibid, p. 247.
9 See Danchev, *Very Special Relationship*, p. 32.
10 Churchill, op cit, p. 274 .
11 Ibid.
12 Quoted in Wilmot, *The Struggle for Europe*, p. 100.
13 Quoted in Churchill, op cit, p. 290.
14 Nelson, quoted in Churchill, op cit, p. 276.
15 Churchill, op cit, p. 277–8.
16 Brooke, *War Diaries*, p. 215.
17 Ibid, p. 255–6.
18 Bradley, *A Soldier's Story*, p. 188.
19 Ibid, p. 190.
20 Ibid, p. 187.
21 Ibid, p. 191.
22 Whitaker & Whitaker, *Dieppe. Tragedy to Triumph*, p. 218.
23 Ibid, p. 16.
24 Ibid, p. 271.
25 Ranger Training Brigade website: www.benning.army/rtb/rtbmain.htm.
26 Ibid.
27 Whitaker & Whitaker, op cit, p. 285.
28 Keegan, *Six Armies in Normandy*, p. 124.
29 Wilmot, op cit, p. 114.

CHAPTER III
Preparing the second front

Stiffen the sinews, summon up the blood

As operations continued in Tunisia, Allied leaders met at Casablanca in January 1943. Stalin declined to attend, due to pressure of military business, but urged Churchill and Roosevelt to hold true to their promise of opening a second front in Europe, with that offensive beginning in spring 1943. Although Churchill was still keen for ROUNDUP to take place in 1943, the British Chiefs were reluctant, citing inadequate numbers of men, ships and landing craft for TORCH, further Mediterranean operations and invading France in July. Since it was realised that the Tunisian campaign could last until May, a cross-Channel invasion was unlikely before September, too late in the year to allow successful operations to develop.

The Casablanca conference, SYMBOL, became a largely Anglo–American affair with differences on strategy between these allies dominating proceedings. British reluctance to undertake ROUNDUP in 1943 was eroding American support for the Germany-first strategy. King wanted a shift of emphasis to the Pacific and his less-than-wholehearted enthusiasm for European operations meant that American naval support would never reach its full potential, especially in the allocation of landing craft, which King wanted for the Pacific. The presence of Sir John Dill at the conference was a tremendous boon to the British for Dill's diplomacy ensured continued American commitment to the Germany-first strategy. Brooke subsequently wrote that achieving an agreement with the US delegation 'was for the greater part due to Dill'.[1] SYMBOL tends to be remembered for several reasons – including the declaration that only Germany's unconditional surrender would be acceptable – but this saving of the strategy agreed a year earlier was probably the most important outcome.

The final plenary session took place on 23 January when the Combined Chiefs presented their report on 'The Conduct of the War in 1943' which emphasised the strategic imperative of defeating the U-boats. By now Axis submarines – including Italians – had destroyed over 17,000,000 tons of Allied shipping, equivalent to one and half times the tonnage of the pre-war American merchant fleet or 1,500 Liberty ships.[2] Since submarines in the Atlantic threatened the US build-up in Britain it was small wonder that defeating the U-boats so exercised the minds of the Combined Chiefs.

The next priority was sustaining Stalin's forces, with all the risks involved in running Arctic convoys. Then came the objective of European operations to defeat Germany in 1943; this would be achieved by using the strongest forces that the Allies could deploy against Germany.

The British continued to propose operations in the Mediterranean and the Americans had agreed that, following the campaign in Tunisia, Allied forces should invade Sicily. Eisenhower was directed to carry out this operation – HUSKY – during the period of the July full moon. According to Churchill, occupying Sicily would make the Mediterranean lines of communication more secure, divert German pressure from Russia and intensify pressure on Italy.

The 'heaviest possible' bombing offensive, codenamed Operation POINTBLANK, was to be mounted against Germany's war effort. While, in the main, this would involve bases in the UK, Mediterranean bases would allow further air operations against targets in southern Germany and Austria; this element was Operation STRANGLE.[3] Limited offensive operations would continue from Britain with the amphibious forces available. And the build-up of Allied forces in Britain would continue so that the 'strongest possible' force might be ready to re-enter the mainland as soon as German resistance was weakened sufficiently.

Both Churchill and Roosevelt approved this strategy but emphasised to their respective Chiefs that the build-up of US forces in Britain should be accelerated to allow some form of SLEDGEHAMMER during favourable weather in August. This was not to be: the Combined Chiefs calculated that the invasion would require at least forty divisions to be assembled in Britain and as many as a hundred in subsequent operations, the bulk of which would have to come from the United States. It would be at least spring 1944 before this force could be assembled and the intervening time would be needed to secure the Atlantic sea-lanes by defeating the U-boats and to gain air supremacy over Europe, as well as reducing Germany's ability to wage war through POINTBLANK. Moreover, the Combined Chiefs believed that, for 1943, the Allies had accepted that there would be a 'defensive, encircling line of action' for mainland Europe, the only exceptions being air operations and blockade.[4] But the Chiefs were determined that the invasion would go ahead in 1944. Among measures aimed at ensuring no further slippage in the date for invasion, orders were issued to transfer four US and three British divisions from the Mediterranean to Britain; these were to move in late-1943. One unfortunate side effect of this was that the US Chiefs were not convinced of Britain's commitment to the operation; this led to the United States making greater allocations of manpower, aircraft and shipping to the Pacific than might otherwise have occurred.

For a time it looked as if the U-boats might make redundant the Allied plans for the continuation of BOLERO and the invasion of northern France. In March 1943 the Allies suffered their worst-ever period for shipping losses: in three weeks they lost ninety-seven ships totalling over 500,000 tons, of which three-quarters had been in convoy. During the entire month, 120 ships were lost, with a tonnage of almost 700,000; most to U-boats – 627,377 tons – but the Luftwaffe had also sunk twelve ships totalling about 65,700 tons.[5] Most worrying of all was that the proportion of ships sunk in convoy had risen by almost seventy per cent over February. How had the Germans achieved this? Several factors had combined: improved command allowed greater concentrations against convoys; communications had improved and new weapons, including acoustic torpedoes, made attacks more effective. New U-boats were also being planned that could travel as fast underwater as on the surface and did not have to surface to recharge batteries.

But the Allies were also making advances. Within two months the U-boat menace had been tamed and Dönitz was ordering his boats out of the north Atlantic. May 1943 saw the U-boats suffer their worst casualties. They had lost the initiative for several reasons: better Allied intelligence through ULTRA decrypts; interception of German radio signals through High Frequency Direction Finding (HF/DF or 'Huff-Duff'); better anti-submarine training in which the Londonderry bases in Northern Ireland were pivotal; new weapons, including the forward-firing 'Hedgehog' which supplemented the depth-charges fired over the stern of a ship; and, perhaps most critical of all, the small escort aircraft carriers that provided air cover for all convoys. The Battle of the Atlantic had turned in favour of the Allies and the build-up of fortress Britain could continue so that, by the end of 1943, it was home to almost 1,500,000 American servicemen.

Following the invasion of Russia, the Germans had reduced their forces in occupied Europe. The garrison of France was composed largely of low-grade divisions with soldiers who were either too old for front-line duties, unfit for such duties or foreign nationals. Among nations represented in the divisions in France were Rumanians, Poles and Russians. Although some Russians who had been captured on the Eastern Front had thrown in their lot with their captors, others were anti-communist exiles. A typical German battalion could include Russians, Georgians, Cossacks, Armenians, Poles, Tartars and even Turcoman Muslims, providing a nightmare for administration and command in battle. France also provided a rest area for divisions from the Eastern Front, and the presence of such formations helped seal the fate of the Dieppe operation.

In early July 1943 Germany disposed 186 divisions on the Eastern Front and forty-four in western Europe with another seven in Italy. Occupying

Vichy France increased the strain on German resources in France. The burgeoning threat from the west, including the bombing offensive, resistance movements in occupied countries and Allied success in the Mediterranean all led Hitler to issue his Directive No. 51 on 3 November 1942, which referred to a greater danger than that from the east: an Anglo-Saxon landing in the west. According to Hitler, if such a landing broke through German defences on a wide front the results would be unpredictable. He expected such a landing perhaps even before spring 1944, which he considered the latest date for an offensive by the western Allies, and ordered no further weakening of defences and formations in the west in favour of the Russian front.

In spite of this, Hitler continued to believe in the strength of what he called the Atlantic Wall. He had ordered the construction of this on 14 December 1941 to defend the coastline from Norway to the Spanish border. By the end of 1942 Hitler was worried about landings in areas as far apart as Norway and Spain and Portugal, strangely mirroring Churchillian ideas for Allied offensives. But the Atlantic Wall was never the bulwark that Hitler wanted; even when Rommel took command the wall was still a long way from completion. Nor could even Rommel's energy ensure its completion in the most likely areas for invasion by summer 1944; in Normandy only eighteen per cent was complete on 6 June 1944.[6]

So, although the garrison in France was being strengthened in principle, German forces there continued to be a source of reinforcement for other fronts. Even when a division was ordered to France from the east, the move could be frustrated by OKH and battle groups that included the best elements of those divisions might be left behind, allowing only a cadre to travel west. It could be even less than this, as von Rundstedt noted:

> often I would be informed that a new division was to arrive in France direct from Russia, or Norway, or Central Germany. When it finally made its appearance in the west it would consist, in all, of a divisional commander, a medical officer, and five bakers.[7]

None of this could have helped morale in France and only a commander with the inspiring qualities of Rommel could have raised morale in the garrison of that country in the pre-invasion months.

Hitler was certainly right in believing that the western Allies were planning to invade France. A planning organisation had been established following SYMBOL to prepare for the invasion. That organisation was COSSAC, from the initials of the Chief of Staff to the Supreme Allied Commander (designate), based in Norfolk House in London's St James' Square with officers drawn from all three services of both Britain and the

USA.* Heading COSSAC was a British officer, Lieutenant-General Sir Frederick E Morgan, whose deputy was Major-General Ray W Barker, US Army. Morgan had commanded I Corps before being asked to study work previously carried out for an Allied cross-Channel assault and develop a plan for the future.

However, it was 26 April before Morgan was given his responsibilities from the Combined Chiefs and official designation as COSSAC. He was told that the Allies intended to 'defeat the German fighting forces in North-West Europe'[8] and to prepare plans for a full-scale assault on the mainland at the earliest possible date in 1944. In addition, he was to prepare an 'elaborate camouflage and deception scheme' over the summer of 1943 with the aim of convincing the Germans that the invasion might yet come in that year and thereby pin down German forces in the west. Finally, Morgan was to plan for an immediate return to Europe, with the forces available at the time, should Germany begin to collapse. This latter plan was Operation RANKIN.

Morgan had only recently received his brief when the Combined Chiefs met again at the TRIDENT conference in Washington in May 1943 and set a target date for the invasion: 1 May 1944. To enable that target to be met, the necessary forces and material for a cross-Channel assault would be built up in Britain as quickly as possible. Morgan was given a further directive and a list of forces expected to be available. Twenty-nine divisions were identified with nine for the initial assault and the remainder subsequently moving into the lodgement area. Of the assault divisions, five infantry divisions would land from the sea as the first wave, with a further two infantry divisions following up, and two airborne divisions dropping. Provision was to be made to capture and clear ports for the subsequent build up; further divisions would disembark at the rate of three to five a month. Naval forces for the invasion would include about 3,300 assault ships and landing craft while there would also be some 11,400 aircraft, of which 632 were to transport airborne forces.[9]

In the first week of June Morgan was told to submit an outline plan by 1 August 1943. One matter was already settled: the invasion had a new codename, OVERLORD.[10] The US commitment to BOLERO included a target of 1,340,000 men by the following spring, a figure that soon increased to 1,460,000.[11]

Meanwhile Mediterranean operations continued. D-Day for HUSKY, the invasion of Sicily, was to be 10 July and following the occupation of the island Eisenhower was to plan further operations that might cause Italy to surrender. This was to lead to the invasion of Italy in September.

* Strictly speaking, the US had only two services, the Army and the Navy, at this time as the air arm, the US Army Air Force, as its title implies, came under Army command. Not until 1947 was a discrete US Air Force established. Nonetheless, USAAF officers were appointed to COSSAC alongside their RAF counterparts.

Morgan's task must have appeared daunting, if not almost impossible. Morgan was enthusiastic and energetic and had the fruits of work already carried out by the planners of SLEDGEHAMMER and ROUNDUP, some of whom were on his staff. There were also British staff studies on a cross-Channel assault that had been undertaken since Dunkirk. Added to these was the knowledge and experience built up from raiding the enemy coast. Combined Operations had, by mid-1943, amassed considerable skill and experience in seaborne assaults and had cooperated with the service ministries in producing appropriate training manuals, as well as creating specialised training areas with highly-professional instructors. Mountbatten's headquarters had been involved in developing the landing craft needed for a major cross-Channel assault while Mountbatten was also responsible for the Commandos, eight of which were to take part in OVERLORD with their American cousins, the Ranger battalions. Thus the task set General Morgan was not so daunting as it may first have appeared. Even so, it was demanding and, although there were major changes to Morgan's plans, he deserves much credit for his contribution to OVERLORD.

Among the material upon which Morgan was able to draw were the lessons from Dieppe. Encompassing all three services, these emphasised the difficulties to be overcome. Sir Bernard Fergusson, of Chindit fame, wrote

> Though there are still some that dispute the value of what was learned on the beaches of Dieppe, they are not to be found among informed persons, or among any who bore high responsibility in the later stages of the war, except for Lord Montgomery.[12]

The Official History supports Fergusson and notes that

> outstanding among the lessons learnt was the importance of overwhelming fire-support in the initial stages of a seaborne landing.[13]

Captain John Hughes-Hallett, Mountbatten's Naval adviser before Dieppe, took part in the operation. Although impressed by the RAF air cover, Hughes-Hallett concluded that many other factors had to be improved. Chief among these was the need for much heavier firepower, which he described as 'overwhelming fire support, including close support, during the initial stages of the attack'.[14] For OVERLORD, therefore, a new bombardment technique was created in which weapons from all three services would participate, with the Army's artillery firing at shore targets while still afloat. On the day itself, the Army's first shots came from the self-propelled equipments of 9 (Irish) Field Battery, 7th Field Regiment, on the run-in to Queen Beach.

The naval element of the bombardment was to be much heavier than at Dieppe where the floating firepower of four destroyers with sixteen 4-inch guns proved inadequate and ineffective against heavy coastal artillery in strengthened positions. Subsequent operations, especially OVERLORD, would benefit from much heavier firepower, including the guns of battleships and monitors; the latter mounted guns of battleship size. Such weapons would stun an enemy into inaction. Their gunners would have the benefit of airborne spotters while heavy and medium bombers from the Allied air forces would supplement their terrifying power. Dieppe had also suggested to the planners that, rather than rely on surprise, they should instead rely on firepower. Many other lessons from Dieppe would be applied to OVERLORD. In August 1943 an inter-service committee, under Air Vice Marshal Graham, was established to look at the problems of fire support in an assault.[15] Subsequently, Exercise PRIMROSE demonstrated that seaborne field artillery could be fired effectively in the support role and this led to artillery units firing on the run-in to the landing beaches on D-Day.[16]

Hughes-Hallett ensured that even more work went into developing specialised landing craft whose crews would have to rehearse assault operations. That would mean keeping a permanent force in being and this was done, with the organisation taking its title – J Force – from the codename of the Dieppe operation – JUBILEE.

Dieppe had also shown a need for specialised armoured vehicles to overcome beach obstacles, mines and soft sand, and deal with other problems as the battle progressed, including blown bridges and cratered roads. Such vehicles became the responsibility of 79th Armoured Division under Major-General Percy Hobart and were known as 'Hobart's Funnies'. They were an invaluable asset to British and Canadian forces in OVERLORD but, unfortunately, were not employed by the Americans. One other specialised armoured vehicle was used by the US Army: the Duplex-Drive, or DD, Sherman tank, an amphibious adaptation of the Sherman, capable of swimming to the beach and, therefore, not dependent on port facilities or LCTs. Thus tanks would be able to give support to the infantry in the very first stages of the landing.

Before moving on to look at these aspects in more detail, we should consider the logistical needs of an invading army. Soldiers needed food, ammunition, clothing and all the basic necessities. Each day the British soldier required twenty pounds of supplies to keep him in action while his American cousin needed half that figure again. Thus daily needs for the Allied armies would reach a staggering 26,000 tons of supplies.[17]

Medical support was essential with some form of basic accommodation for medical and other services. Field ambulances of the RAMC were to land with the assaulting formations on D-Day 'with a self-contained medical organisation comprising two field dressing stations, two field surgical units and a field transfusion unit supported by small surgical teams' assigned to each beach group.[18] Field hospitals would begin arriving from D+2, to be followed by general hospitals.[19] Casualty Evacuation Points (CEPs) were to be established on each beach on D-Day, although the CEP on Sword was forced to close down because of heavy shelling; its casualties were transferred to another CEP.[20] Arrangements were also made for the air evacuation of casualties and this began on 13 June. For sea evacuation, DUKWs were used as water ambulances and some LSTs were converted for casualty evacuation; hospital carriers were also used.[21]

The first field transfusion units to land were to be provided with supplies sufficient for two days. Transfusion fluids were included in the maintenance supplies that would be brought ashore from D-Day onwards while two Advanced Blood Banks would also land in the early stages – they came ashore on D+3 – with one allocated to each corps front. Supplies of whole blood would be sent from the UK by naval dispatch launch, supplemented by air transport as soon as possible; air carriage of blood began on D+16.[22]

The medical plan for OVERLORD also had to include hygiene arrangements. Although flies were not considered a nuisance, precautions had to be taken to prevent their breeding. Thus latrines on the beaches were essential 'no matter how shallow' and foul areas were designated for these. Two types of latrine were to be used: the Middle East 'squatting' type and the 'box' latrine.[23] Flies might also breed where there were animal carcasses and arrangements were made for the disposal of these; carcasses were to be sprayed with waste oil or petrol and then burned or buried. The problem proved to be much greater than estimated and the provisions for dealing with flies using sprayers and muslin were later described as 'ridiculously inadequate'.[24]

Highly mobile armies required adequate supplies of fuel and spares for their vehicles which had to be shipped to France so that they might then carry all the armies' requirements from disembarkation points to the various formations and units. On D-Day alone some 15,000 vehicles would be put ashore with thousands more on each successive day. Their enormous thirst for fuel, oil and lubricants was to be met by the ingenious use of floating and underwater pipelines.

In planning OVERLORD it was calculated that each division of about 16,000 men would require another 25,000 men in the theatre in corps, army, GHQ and Lines of Communication troops. For the British/Canadian 21 Army Group – Second (British) and First (Canadian) Armies – this increment would include about 41,000 men and some 8,000 vehicles with RAF personnel adding another 4,000. By August 1944, 21 Army Group included some 660,000 personnel, about fifty-six per cent of them fighting soldiers and the remainder 'services'.[25] This gives some small idea of the effort needed to place the Allied armies in France and sustain them thereafter.

Much of the burden of meeting all these requirements would fall on the Royal Army Service Corps (RASC),* which had already been preparing for a British return to the mainland. The RASC provided the Army's main logistic sinews and OVERLORD was to be one of its finest achievements. One function was to ensure adequate provisions of POL (petrol, oil and lubricants) for the Army at home and in each theatre of war. Pre-war Britain had drawn some forty-three per cent of its oil from Venezuela, Colombia and Trinidad, a further twenty-four per cent from the Persian oilfields and the balance from the United States.[26] Fortunately, these sources continued to be available, although tankers had to undertake hazardous journeys under threat of submarine and air attack to deliver the oil. During 1941 and 1942 the War Office increased bulk petroleum supplies in Britain and established six petrol reserve depots to hold 50,000 liquid tons of packed stocks, as well as building tin-making plants to produce containers. Two large filling plants were also created for filling returnable containers. The Petroleum Board administered further military reserves in civilian installations – with fuel rationing there was less demand from the public than before the war – and, from less than a quarter million liquid tons of bulk storage in 1941, military holdings increased to almost a million liquid tons by 1945. Experience in North Africa, Italy and other theatres proved invaluable for OVERLORD. By D-Day the skills of laying pipelines and erecting storage tanks to provide supplies over both short and long distances were such that these facilities could be created very quickly. So, too, could the system for bulk distribution on lines of communication.[27]

Morgan and his staff had to arrange the transporting of the expeditionary force to France. A large tonnage of shipping was necessary and many ships would need somewhere to discharge cargoes. Mountbatten considered a port essential and initial studies had considered landing at a port. But that was before Dieppe, which proved the difficulties of such an operation, not least because the Germans would expect the Allies to try to

* In 1965 the Corps shed its supply functions when the Royal Corps of Transport (RCT) was formed, taking on additional transport and movement responsibilities. As a part of the Government's Options for Change defence review, a Logistic Support Review was conducted and it was decided that a new logistic support corps would be formed to take over the roles of the RCT, Royal Army Ordnance Corps, Royal Pioneer Corps, Army Catering Corps and the postal responsibilities of the Royal Engineers but the other logistic corps, the Royal Electrical and Mechanical Engineers (REME), was not to be included. The new organisation, the Royal Logistic Corps (RLC), came into being in 1993.

capture a port in the initial phase of any invasion. The planners' minds turned to alternatives but Morgan had first to consider shipping and, then, how those ships could unload.

The Combined Chiefs had considered the size of force to be deployed: twenty-nine divisions would be available but only nine would make the initial assault; the remainder would move subsequently into the lodgement area. Two of those nine would be airborne divisions and the remainder infantry, with five landing from the sea in the first wave and the others following up. That scale of forces dictated the size of fleet needed to transport men, equipment, vehicles and supplies. Although the supply of assault ships and landing craft was growing, there were many demands on them with the US Navy, especially, needing large numbers for the Pacific. Admiral King was not disposed to releasing further craft for the cross-Channel assault, particularly as he was probably the American who was most sceptical of British intentions. And there were other calls on available shipping, including the Mediterranean and South-East Asia while, as Omar Bradley noted, landing-craft production lagged behind demand as late as 1944.[28] Indeed the Italian campaign became bogged down in a long slogging match since sufficient landing craft could not be allocated to allow amphibious outflanking manoeuvres. At Quebec, Churchill had asked for an increase of twenty-five per cent in landing craft for OVERLORD but both Marshall and King had argued against this, saying that there were not enough vessels available and that OVERLORD's allocation could only be increased at the expense of operations in the Pacific, to which they would not agree.[29]

The number of ships available was Morgan's greatest restraining factor. His predicament was that of a tailor, given cloth sufficient only to produce a two-piece suit, who is asked to produce not only a three-piece but also a spare pair of trousers and an overcoat. It was an impossible equation. But, although he could not get enough vessels for the larger force he would have preferred, Morgan had the consolation of knowing that he had the right types of vessels. This lesson had been learned early in the war and the Allies were to benefit from it in the second half of the war. In Britain and the United States work had begun on developing a range of landing craft before the end of 1940, with the first LCT under trial in October 1940.[30] Prior to that the US Navy had no landing craft while the Royal Navy began the war with a paltry half-dozen. No one had foreseen a need for large numbers of landing craft but Dunkirk and the threat of invasion had changed all that: the former because it meant that an opposed landing would have to be made in Europe, the latter because it had been recognised in Britain that the improvised invasion barges employed by the Germans were unsuitable for a cross-Channel assault.

The range of landing craft began with small vessels to bring infantry inshore up through a series of different sizes to the very largest, known as

Landing Ships, Tanks, or LSTs, that could be run ashore to allow their cargo to drive onto the beach. Those LSTs included British- and US-built vessels that were specially designed and constructed to land tanks and other heavy equipment,* plus adaptations of existing vessels that were not quite so versatile as the custom-built ships. More detail on the range of landing craft can be found in Appendix 2.

Almost all these vessels were designed and built, or adapted, during the war, often from specifications drawn up by the Admiralty in the early years of war, and proved invaluable in OVERLORD and other major operations. Without them the task of landing an attack force, with artillery and armoured support, would have been almost impossible. Those who designed the specialist craft used in OVERLORD contributed greatly to its success.

Although the British Army had long experience of expeditionary force warfare, it was generally believed, before the war, that a port was needed to disembark forces. The Germans, with little experience of such warfare and the abandoned SEELÖWE plan, remained convinced that any Allied invasion force would be directed on a port so that its facilities could be brought into early use. Thus German thinking focused on defending ports and, should their capture seem likely, destroying their facilities to deny these to the invader. Even after Dieppe, the Germans concluded that the Allies would land near a port and then envelop that port, thus concentrating German defensive thinking on such lines. But Allied thinking changed dramatically after Dieppe. Churchill's Great War idea now came into its own as a possible solution to the problem of needing a harbour but not trying to seize one as the first objective of an invasion. From the idea of an artificial island it was not much of a leap of imagination to that of an artificial harbour.

By late-1943 work was underway on constructing two prefabricated, floating harbours. As far back as 30 May 1942, almost three months before Dieppe, Churchill had written a 'Secret' minute on the subject of 'Piers for Use on Beaches' in which he outlined some problems that would be met. In his own hand, at the foot of the minute, he noted that such piers would have to float up and down with the tide, the anchor problem had to be mastered and that those receiving the minute were not to argue the matter since 'the problems will argue for themselves. Let me have the solution worked out'.[31] Solving those problems was the remit of a group headed by Brigadier Bruce White of the War Office, a civil engineer. But it was Professor John Desmond Bernal who conceived the idea of a floating harbour.

* The author's father served in a heavy anti-aircraft (HAA) battery which went ashore at Salerno on D-Day + 6 from an LST which carried the battery's full complement of eight 3.7-inch HAA guns, vehicles and personnel.

Bernal, born in Nenagh, County Tipperary in 1901, and known as 'The Sage' at Cambridge, is one of the forgotten figures of the Second World War, receiving much less credit than is his due from historians. Part of that may have stemmed from his political beliefs; he became a Communist Party member for a time but, although he eschewed that philosophy, he remained a convinced socialist and founded Scientists for Peace, forerunner of the Campaign for Nuclear Disarmament. But his relegation to the footnotes of the war's history may also be due to his having been a philosopher who thought of *solutions* to problems, such as that of supplying the invading armies. Mountbatten thought highly of him and he played a major part in planning OVERLORD; he was awarded the US Medal of Freedom in 1947* and was also decorated by the Soviet Union in 1953 with the Lenin Peace Prize.[32]

With the difficulties resolved Mulberry became part of the story of OVERLORD with two harbours being built, one for the British and Canadian forces and the second for the US forces.

At Casablanca it had also been decided that the 'heaviest possible' bombing offensive should be mounted against Germany's war effort. Much of this was carried out from bases in Britain, but there would also be operations against targets in southern Germany and Austria from bases in the Mediterranean area, especially following the invasion of Italy. This offensive was intended to gain air supremacy over Europe and reduce Germany's fighting capacity through bombing the Reich's principal industrial centres. Such a policy appealed to the airmen, who believed that the war might be won by bombers alone, without landing troops on the continent. Brooke noted that Portal, Chief of the Air Staff, was convinced that this was the winning strategy, that through building up large bomber forces in England, success could be 'assured through the bombing of Europe'.[33] This belief persisted in the USAAF long after the war had ended – and probably only came to an end with Vietnam – although many in RAF Bomber Command were questioning its effectiveness, and its cost in lives, before then.

* In the era of McCarthyism in the USA, Bernal was not permitted to enter that country.

NOTES

1 Brooke, *War Diaries*, p. 362.
2 Bradley, *A Soldier's Story*, pp. 192–3.
3 NA, CAB44/295, p. 143.
4 Quoted in Grigg, *1943, The Victory That Never Was*, p. 62.
5 Barnett, *Engage the Enemy More Closely*, p. 597.
6 Cooper, *The German Army*, p. 494.
7 Quoted in Cooper, p. 495.
8 Morgan, *Overture to Overlord*, p. 64.
9 Ellis, *Victory in the West, vol i* (hereinafter *Victory in the West*), pp. 10–11.
10 Ibid, p. 11.
11 Bradley, op cit, p. 194.
12 Fergusson, *Watery Maze* p. 181.
13 Ellis, op cit, p. 13.
14 Keegan, *Six Armies in Normandy*, p. 125.
15 NA, CAB44/295, p. 163.
16 Ibid, p. 198.
17 Hastings, *Overlord*, p. 197.
18 NA, CAB44/271, p. 2.
19 Ibid.
20 Ibid, p. 4.
21 Ibid, p. 5.
22 Ibid, pp. 8–9.
23 Ibid, p. 9.
24 Ibid, p. 30.
25 Forty, *Handbook of the British Army*, p. 44.
26 Sutton, *Wait for the Waggon*, p. 166.
27 Ibid, p. 179.
28 Bradley, op cit, p. 212.
29 Wilmot, *The Struggle for Europe*, pp. 137–8.
30 NA, CAB44/295, p. 6.
31 Churchill, *The Second World War, vol. ix*, between pp. 77 & 78.
32 Website http://www.gnometech.freeserve.co.uk/html/mulberry_harbour.html; DNB; Sean McMahon.
33 Brooke, op cit, p. 409.

CHAPTER IV
The plan is refined

Disguise fair nature with hard-favour'd rage

In May 1943 Allied leaders met again in Washington for the TRIDENT conference. Churchill's party sailed from Britain on 5 May on *Queen Mary* which, Brooke noted,[1] was 'almost empty' with only 3,000 servicemen on board; the liner had been converted to carry 15,000 as a troopship. Brooke was concerned about shipping, which he discussed with the Chiefs, the Commanders-in-Chief in India – Admiral Somerville, General Wavell and Air Marshal Peirse – as well as the Minister of Transport and Director of Movements. His prime concern was that the Americans had sent larger forces to the Pacific than to Europe which seemed to be against the spirit of 'Germany first'. Allied strategy in Europe might be affected adversely unless the United States was prepared to transfer more shipping from the Pacific to Europe.

With the fortnight-long conference failing to clarify strategic and political issues, Brooke later noted that he went through 'a phase of deep depression' at this time.[2] There was not even agreement on Mediterranean strategy after Sicily, although an off-the-record meeting of the Combined Chiefs on 19 May agreed that operations should continue without agreeing their form. Churchill was unhappy to learn that the Sicilian invasion would almost certainly rule out a 1943 cross-Channel operation; but he did become a convert to the British Mediterranean strategy.[3] Further disagreement occurred over Far East strategy; the Americans wanted operations aimed at keeping China in the war. King again lent his weight to the Pacific campaign.

Morgan had not long had his brief for OVERLORD when TRIDENT took place. One of the few positive decisions was setting the date of 1 May 1944 for the invasion. Morgan was given an indication of the forces that should be available (see Chapter III) and of shipping; the latter dictated the size of the first assault force. In the end Brooke considered that an acceptable compromise had been reached at TRIDENT, which was almost exactly what he had wanted – continuing the war in the Mediterranean to eliminate Italy and disperse German forces in southern Europe under 'strategically bad conditions.'[4]

Morgan now had two months to prepare his plans for the next conference, QUADRANT, scheduled for Quebec in August. Once again the British party crossed the Atlantic on *Queen Mary* which had been repainted and looked much smarter.[5] During the conference the Combined Chiefs studied COSSAC's preliminary plan, which Brooke considered as 'very over optimistic in places'.[6] But what exactly had Morgan and his staff suggested?

Working from information gathered by the Combined Commanders,* who had carried out studies for SLEDGEHAMMER and ROUNDUP, and from Mountbatten's staff, Morgan's people had been busy. Every possible landing beach and port from The Netherlands to the Bay of Biscay had been assessed.

> From their intelligence archives the British had culled volumes of patient research on subsoils, bridges, moorings, wharfage, rivers, and the thousands of intricate details that went into this appraisal of the OVERLORD plan.[7]

Thus it was that, on all the beaches, there existed considerable detailed information, including factors such as the nature of the beaches, tides and winds, exits for vehicles and men, the land abutting the beaches, and its susceptibility to flooding, and the seaward approaches. Much information was gathered by aerial photographic reconnaissance, some by seeking holiday photographs of the entire Belgian and French coast, and some from the raiding parties that were creating such a nuisance in occupied Europe. Highly detailed information was gathered by Combined Operations Pilotage Parties (COPPs) who brought back samples of sand and shingle, as well as data on tidal flows and the flooding carried out by the Germans. As OVERLORD drew closer these parties became even more important and their work proved vital. (Bradley was amazed when he sought information on the subsoil at Omaha Beach and was briefed some days later by a Royal Navy officer who produced 'a thick glass tube' which had been obtained during a 'visit to Omaha Beach to drill a core in the shingle'.[8]) Another COPP operation, using two miniature submarines, known as X-Craft, allowed the construction on the Norfolk coast for

* The Combined Commanders included General Sir Bernard Paget, C-in-C, Home Forces, with the Air Officer Commanding-in-Chief RAF Fighter Command – Sir Sholto Douglas who was succeeded by Sir Trafford Leigh-Mallory – and Vice Admiral Sir Bertram Ramsay, or his representative, joined as necessary by Lord Louis Mountbatten of Combined Operations. In his role as Commanding General European Theater of Operations of the US Army (ETOUSA), General Dwight D Eisenhower was also associated with this group, as was his successor in that post, Lieutenant-General Frank M Andrews.

training and experimentation of a mock stretch of the German-held coast complete with defences.[9]

As well as these factors the planners had to consider the distance of the beach from Britain, critical for air cover, and the suitability of nearby land for the early construction of airstrips, or the presence of airfields that might be captured in the breakout.

The possibility of taking a port, or ports, at an early stage was studied, as was the possibility of assaulting at or near a port. Assessment had to be made of the strength and nature of coastal defences and the numbers and quality of forces manning them. Among other factors considered were enemy naval strength, offshore minefields and the naval support needed for the operation. Morgan and his planners then had to decide how suitable an area was for building up the assault force so that it could meet the threat of the enemy's reserves.

The Combined Commanders had concluded that the most suitable location for a landing on the scale anticipated was in Normandy, close to Caen. But that was conditional upon including in the assault area the eastern beaches of the Cotentin peninsula so that the port of Cherbourg, at the head of the peninsula, might be taken quickly. COSSAC staff examined all the material available and reached a conclusion not far removed from that of the Combined Commanders: the choice came down to the Caen sector of Normandy, or the Pas de Calais.

To the layman, the latter was the obvious choice being closer to Britain and thus allowing the best air cover while the sea crossing would be short and a landing there would put the Allies on the shortest route to Germany. But these factors were also obvious to the Germans, who had made the Calais locale the fulcrum of their anti-invasion defences; nowhere on the long coastline would an invader meet such strong opposition. And local topography presented disadvantages. High cliffs, narrow beaches and restricted beach exits would make the maintenance of an invading force very difficult. Using the Pas de Calais would mean extending the lodgement area eastward or westward to include either Belgian or Seine ports; this would be extremely hazardous against the known opposition in the area. Even before a landing could be made, the Pas de Calais suffered another disadvantage: the invasion fleet would be too large to be accommodated in ports in the Dover area. All these factors drew the COSSAC planners to the same conclusion as the Combined Commanders: the Caen area was the best choice. Fortunately, the layman dictating German strategy would be convinced until too late that the invasion would come in the Pas de Calais.

The problems attending the Pas de Calais did not apply to Normandy. The area was less heavily fortified, having been a backwater for the German garrison and a home for lower quality forces. Its beaches, largely sheltered from the prevailing westerly winds by the Cotentin, were more suitable for landing troops, as well as vehicles and supplies. Normandy had one principal disadvantage: landing there meant a sea crossing of some 100 miles, which also reduced the time that British-based fighters could spend over the beachhead. However, this was a disadvantage that both naval and air force staff considered acceptable, since so many other positive factors outweighed it.

Although Morgan and his staff also accepted the need to capture Cherbourg as quickly as possible, their proposal differed in one major respect from that of the Combined Commanders. The latter had concluded that landings should also be made on the eastern shores of the Cotentin to place Allied forces within striking distance of Cherbourg. COSSAC decided to exclude those beaches from the invasion plan. Why? Did COSSAC consider the early capture of Cherbourg did not require the eastern Cotentin beaches? This was not the case, but COSSAC was restrained by the manpower limits set by the Combined Chiefs.

COSSAC proposed a short air bombardment of the defences, followed by the initial assault by three divisions from the sea, supported by commandos and two airborne divisions; the assault divisions would be followed by 'the equivalent of two tank brigades and a regimental combat team'.[10] Given certain conditions

> *if the enemy's fighter forces were reduced; if his reserve troops in France and the Low Countries as a whole did not exceed twelve full-strength, first-quality divisions on the day of the assault; and (since maintenance would have to be carried out over beaches for some three months) if improvised sheltered waters were provided for use till adequate ports were available* .[11] (Italics in original)

then an assault on these lines might have a 'reasonable chance of success'.[12] Nonetheless, Morgan recommended that, if possible, the forces for the assault should be increased so that the follow-up might be strengthened while the assault frontage should also be widened. It is clear that Morgan was aware of his plan's shortcomings and of how to resolve them. Neither Eisenhower nor Montgomery was being fair to Morgan when each claimed to have identified these weaknesses in COSSAC's plan. The truth is that they inherited a sound basic plan that needed adjustments, which they implemented, since they carried the weight to ensure those adjustments were made.

Nor were Eisenhower and Montgomery alone in suggesting changes. Churchill did likewise. At QUADRANT he urged an increase of at least twenty-five per cent in attacking forces and the inclusion of the Cotentin's eastern beaches. Independently, both British and American Chiefs studied the outline plan, which was then considered by the Combined Chiefs who recommended its adoption to Churchill and Roosevelt at QUADRANT.

The Combined Chiefs also agreed to make stronger forces available, if possible, but not the necessary additional shipping.

Thus Morgan had the satisfaction of having his outline plan approved, leading to an order to work on detailed planning with the Combined Chiefs' full authority to take the necessary executive action to implement those plans, but also the frustration of not knowing if the size of the attacking force would be increased. Nor did he know if additional shipping would be allocated, although he considered that insufficient ships, and aircraft, had been assigned, even with the modest forces to be deployed. There still remained, for example, an allocation of landing craft sufficient only for the three assault and two immediate follow-up divisions; the movement of further divisions would depend on the speed at which the turnaround of shipping and landing craft could be achieved, and the number of the latter that survived the initial assault.

General Morgan and his staff went ahead with putting flesh on the skeleton they had created. When Sir Alan Brooke had first given Morgan his brief he had been fully aware that the Combined Commanders had concluded that success could be guaranteed only if ten divisions could be landed in the first assault. But with shipping for only half that number Brooke had told Morgan that the basic plan would not work but that Morgan and his staff would have to 'bloody well make it work'.[13] What Morgan and his staff were now doing was drawing up two discrete plans: as well as OVERLORD, the assault, there was NEPTUNE, the naval plan covering the shipping needed to transport, support and supply the invasion force.

The COSSAC team decided that the assault should be made between the Vire and Orne rivers, the former on the inside 'corner' of the Cotentin and the latter to the east along the coast, north by north-east of Caen, and just east of the coastal town of Ouistreham. Grandcamp, to the east, and Courseulles, to the west, were the two 'outer markers' of a front of about thirty miles. As Morgan's staff came to grips with detail they found that the shipping situation was even worse than they had thought. The landing craft allocated could only carry three infantry divisions ashore with fully-equipped, combat-ready soldiers; in other words the immediate follow-up divisions could not be loaded at the same time as the assault divisions. Nor could the aircraft allocation carry two combat-ready airborne divisions. The planes could lift only two airborne brigades, far short of the numbers needed on the ground. Until the end of the year, Morgan and his staff suffered many headaches as they reworked their plans, tailoring them to the men, ships and planes available. They must have felt especially frustrated, but also somewhat relieved, when their final plan was presented to Eisenhower and Montgomery in January 1944 and immediately rejected.

Thus COSSAC's proposals were for a three-division assault from the

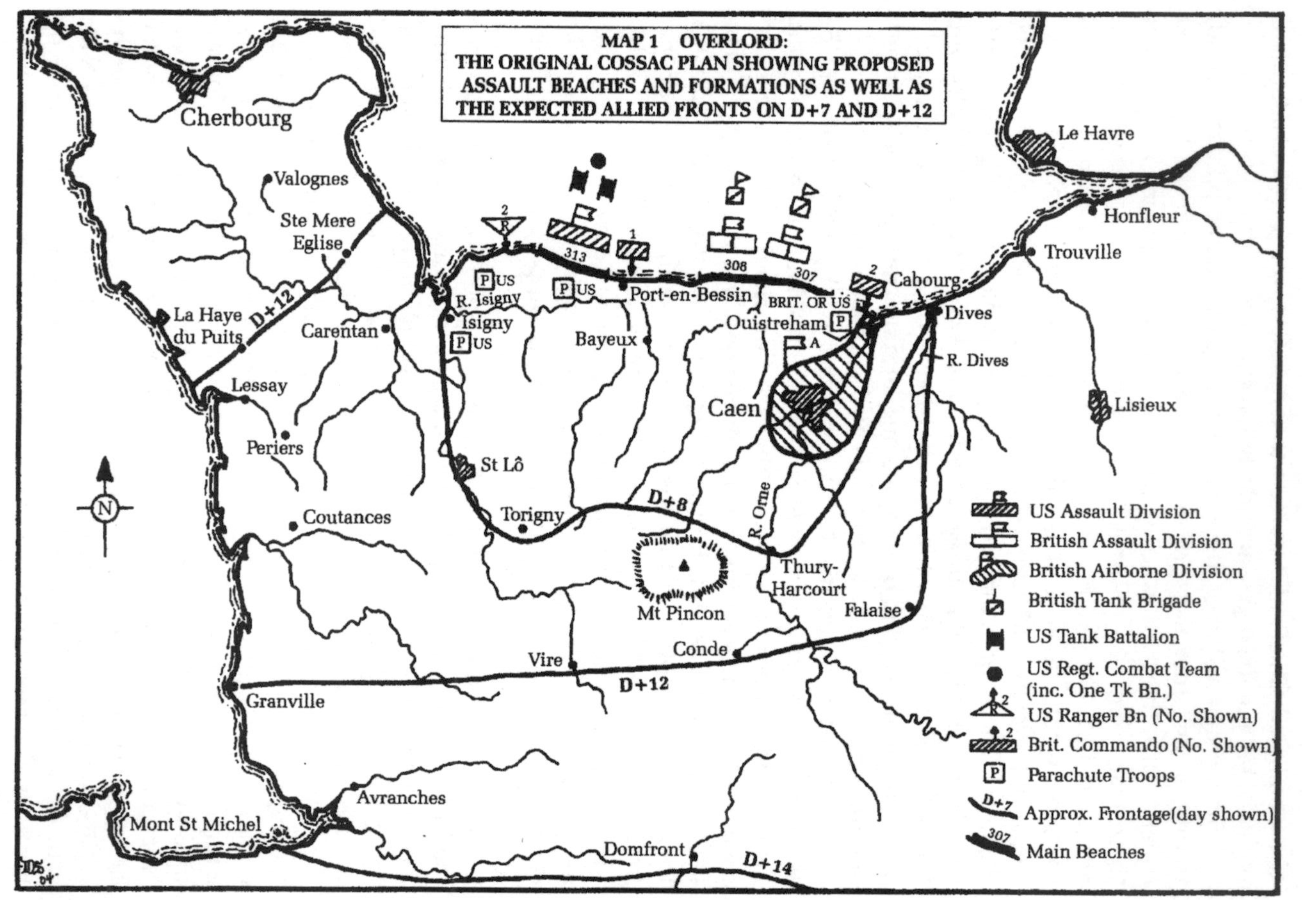

MAP 1 OVERLORD:
THE ORIGINAL COSSAC PLAN SHOWING PROPOSED ASSAULT BEACHES AND FORMATIONS AS WELL AS THE EXPECTED ALLIED FRONTS ON D+7 AND D+12

sea and an airborne *coup-de-main* to seize Caen. Thereafter a thrust would be made south and south-westwards to take airfield sites and create the depth needed for the right-wheeling move towards the Cotentin, leading to the capture of Cherbourg. It was planned to have the port in Allied hands within two weeks of D-Day, by which time some eighteen divisions would be fighting in France, supported by up to thirty-three fighter squadrons in Normandy. Thereafter, the Supreme Commander would decide how the campaign would develop. Until now, however, there was no Supreme Commander.

One firm decision taken at QUADRANT had been to appoint Eisenhower as Supreme Allied Commander; Morgan now knew to whom he was Chief of Staff. On 12 February 1944 Eisenhower received his 'job description' from the Combined Chiefs. This told him:

> You are hereby designated as Supreme Allied Commander of the forces placed under your orders for the liberation of Europe from Germans. Your title will be Supreme Commander Allied Expeditionary Force.[14]

Inter alia, the directive told Eisenhower that he was to enter the continent and, 'in conjunction with the other United Nations', conduct a campaign that would lead to the destruction of the German armed forces. The campaign was to begin in May 1944; it was to take advantage of a possible Soviet offensive about the time of OVERLORD that would prevent the transfer of German forces from the Eastern Front; offensive action in the Mediterranean would also 'assist your operation'.[15] This latter was to include Operation ANVIL.

Eisenhower's appointment was a disappointment to Brooke who had been promised the job by Churchill. But circumstances had changed and Churchill recognised that, whereas an invasion in 1943 would have been carried out with a majority of British troops, OVERLORD was now to have a majority of US forces which, as the campaign progressed, would assume an ever greater burden. Logic dictated, therefore, that the overall commander should be American. According to Brooke,[16] the Prime Minister had given in to Roosevelt and Harry Hopkins who wanted George Marshall for the job, with Eisenhower succeeding Marshall in Washington while Alexander would succeed Eisenhower in the Mediterranean. Bradley wrote that Churchill suggested Marshall to Roosevelt but the President decided to keep Marshall in Washington with Eisenhower commanding the European forces. And Bradley went on to note that

> in the army hierarchy of command the appointment of General Marshall as Supreme Commander would have entailed a stepdown

> from his post as Army Chief of Staff. But stepdown or no, had General Marshall left Washington to go to Europe, no one – not even Eisenhower – could have taken his place.[17]

In exchange for his agreement to an American supreme commander for the Allied expeditionary force, Churchill secured Roosevelt's agreement that Mountbatten should be appointed Supreme Allied Commander, South-East Asia.

In his history of the Second World War Churchill wrote that Brooke 'bore the great disappointment with soldierly dignity'.[18] At no time does Churchill appear to have realised how deep was Brooke's disappointment, from which it took him several months to recover.[19] Mountbatten's new appointment could have done nothing to assuage Brooke's hurt. Under Eisenhower would be three British commanders: Admiral Sir Bertram Ramsay* for the Allied Naval Expeditionary Force, General Sir Bernard Montgomery for 21 Army Group – which would include First (US) and Second (British) Armies – and all ground forces, while Air Chief Marshal Sir Trafford Leigh-Mallory commanded the Allied Expeditionary Air Force. These appointments ensured that British national pride would not be hurt; but there was some resentment among Americans that the top three jobs had gone to Britons. Ramsay's appointment was logical since most naval forces involved would be British. Montgomery was considered the most experienced Allied field commander and his appointment was also seen as logical, although he would surrender command of all Allied ground forces when Eisenhower moved his headquarters to France while 21 Army Group would become a Commonwealth formation and 12 US Army Group would form alongside it. Leigh-Mallory was also a sound choice as an experienced airman who knew the continent and what was required of the air forces. The fact that another British airman, Air Chief Marshal Sir Arthur Tedder, became Eisenhower's Deputy made the command structure appear even more biased to the British and rankled with a few Americans. But, in the spirit of inter-Allied cooperation, the planners got down to their job.

Although Eisenhower knew that he was to be Supreme Allied Commander Allied Expeditionary Force as early as 6 December 1943, the appointment was not official until 12 February 1944 and his headquarters – SHAEF, or Supreme Headquarters Allied Expeditionary Force – did not come into being until the following day. (At SEXTANT in Cairo in November and early December, the question of the Supreme Commander

* In August 1943 Admiral Sir Charles Little, C-in-C, Portsmouth, had been nominated as the naval commander but it was subsequently recognised that the Portsmouth Command should be maintained as a separate entity and the OVERLORD/NEPTUNE command went to Ramsay. [20]

had been discussed. SEXTANT was 'interrupted' by EUREKA, held in Teheran, at which Stalin was present, and it was Stalin's urging that led to the appointment being made.) Between December and February Eisenhower began work on OVERLORD and NEPTUNE. Before travelling to London he discussed the COSSAC plans with Montgomery who left Eighth Army at the end of December to return to London and his new command. That meeting took place on 27 December and also present was Lieutenant-General Walter Bedell Smith, known as 'Beetle', Eisenhower's chief of staff in North Africa who would remain in that position for OVERLORD. All three agreed that the frontage of the seaborne assault was too narrow and should be widened to include five divisions.

Eisenhower moved his headquarters out of London, reasoning that 'a Headquarters located in the heart of a great city would not be as unified as one located elsewhere'[21] and so SHAEF settled at Bushey Park near Hampton Court Palace. But he had already begun to change the OVERLORD plan before that move. In his report on the invasion, Eisenhower wrote:

> I had felt when I originally read the Overlord plan that our experiences in the Sicilian campaign were being misinterpreted, for . . . it was my conviction that had a larger force been employed against the island beachheads our troops would have been in a position to overrun the defenses more quickly. Against the better prepared defenses of France I felt that a . . . minimum of five divisions should assault in the initial wave.[22]

None of this would have surprised Morgan who had been adamant that stronger forces were necessary; Churchill had made the same point. In his *Memoirs* Montgomery, who arrived in London on 2 January 1944, also claims the credit for changing the plan, writing that the more he examined the 'proposed tactical plan of 21 Army Group, based on Morgan's outline plan, the more I disliked it'.[23] Montgomery's main disagreements were that the assault frontage was too narrow; that only one corps headquarters was to control the landing; and that the beachhead would soon become 'very congested'. However, Montgomery noted that Morgan had done a good job, given the restraints placed on him, and that his plan provided a sound basis for further work. Montgomery also claims that he was first shown the plan by Churchill at Marrakesh on 1 January 1944.[24] This is not true; he had seen and discussed it with Eisenhower and Bedell Smith five days earlier, which casts a different light on the detailed appreciation of the plan that he submitted to Churchill on the morning of the 2nd.

Montgomery noted one significant major weakness that, in the view of his supporters, illustrates why he was a sound choice to command the assault forces: there was no clear vision of how operations should develop once the lodgement had been made. In Montgomery's view the first priority was to decide how land operations on the mainland would develop and then 'work backwards from that to ensure that we landed on the beaches in the way best suited to the needs of the master plan'.[25] That 'master plan' involved destroying the enemy's forces and occupying Germany. But it is interesting to note that Admiral Ramsay had made the very same point in late-1943 in a paper for a lecture on Combined Operations, which, for security reasons, the Admiralty did not permit him to deliver; it was published in 1948.[26] Since Montgomery and Ramsay were in close contact, might the latter have shared the contents of his paper? Certainly Montgomery had thus far demonstrated no remarkable capacity for thinking beyond the next battle. His handling of El Alamein had fallen down for that very reason.

In the short term, Montgomery also felt that the assault forces might be facing six German divisions by the end of D-Day and he had no illusions about German fighting qualities. To ensure success, Montgomery considered that the Allies needed a secure lodgement before enemy reserves arrived on the scene: 'We must gain space rapidly and peg out claims well inland.'[27] At the same time, Allied air forces would have to prevent the incursion of enemy aircraft while also hindering the movement towards the beachhead of German reserves. The lessons of the desert war, in which ground and air forces had worked in close harmony, were obviously uppermost in his mind. Montgomery's considered conclusion was that the assault force should include at least five divisions, with airborne divisions providing flank protection as the ground forces moved quickly inland. He recommended that there should be eight divisions, including airborne, on shore by the evening of D-Day, a further four by the following evening and eighteen in total before the end of the first week.

Eisenhower commented that Montgomery agreed completely with his proposed changes to the plan, as also did Ramsay and Leigh-Mallory, 'even though a larger assault force raised great new problems from both the naval and air points of view'.[28] Churchill's suggestion that a landing should also be made on the eastern coast of the Cotentin was echoed by Eisenhower. OVERLORD was now to include this area while, to the east, the beaches at Ouistreham would also be included. Airborne divisions were to be deployed to either flank; two would support troops assaulting the Varreville beaches of the Cotentin while a third would secure bridges over the Orne and Dives rivers north-east of Caen. Thus the equivalent of an airborne corps would be employed, rather than the two brigades envisaged in the outline plan. Although Montgomery and Ramsay supported this deployment of airborne forces, Leigh-Mallory feared problems with the drops in the Cotentin area with losses of up to eighty per cent in both troops and aircraft. Eisenhower considered the airborne landings essential since only one division would land at Varreville where exits from the beach were difficult and restricted by a lagoon; those would have to be secured from the rear to assist seaborne troops off the beach and that could only be achieved by airborne soldiers. The Varreville landing was also an imperative to ensure the swift capture of Cherbourg, 'vital to the support and maintenance of our land forces', since otherwise the Germans might be able to seal off the Cotentin's marshy neck.

Eisenhower arrived in Britain on 15 January and, eight days later, communicated the proposed changes to the Combined Chiefs, while broaching the subject of the date for OVERLORD, which had been set as 1 May. But the need to bring in additional landing craft put that date in doubt. Eisenhower therefore asked for a month's delay to ensure the success of the operation should the Combined Chiefs endorse his changes and approve the greater allocation of vessels. The Supreme Commander was confident that an additional month's production of landing craft 'would go far toward supplying the deficiency [my planners] then foresaw for the earlier date'.[29]

There were advantages to be gained from such a delay. For the air forces it gave more time to wear down German air strength and disrupt enemy communications. For the naval forces, it would allow more time for training and delivery of additional craft. The naval planners favoured a delay to early June to have tides suitable for the operation. On a strategic scale a month's delay would allow for Soviet operations on the Eastern Front to assist OVERLORD while, by then, the picture in the Mediterranean might be clearer and a diversionary operation there might not be necessary.

This diversion, Operation ANVIL, was an American proposal that was not supported by the British. ANVIL was to coincide with OVERLORD, thereby increasing pressure on the Germans and drawing off forces that might be ordered to Normandy; it would also open up a logistic support line, especially from the United States. The British view was that Allied armies in Italy were already drawing off many German divisions and that increased pressure on the Italian front would have better strategic results than pulling experienced divisions out of Italy to invade southern France; ANVIL would also take many landing craft from Normandy. Montgomery thought that the success of OVERLORD depended on whether ANVIL could be reduced to a threat, thereby releasing more landing craft for the cross-Channel assault. The Americans would win the argument and ANVIL went ahead, but not until August, thus alleviating Montgomery's concern, and renamed DRAGOON,

The Combined Chiefs approved Eisenhower's new proposals and OVERLORD was put back to June. Detailed planning could go ahead on the basis that the date for the invasion was now 5 June. Cherbourg was the port that the Allies intended to take as soon as possible so that it could then be used to support the expeditionary force in Europe. It was known that the Germans would sabotage the port's facilities, the restoration of which would take some time. With the experience of Dieppe fresh in everyone's mind, there would be no assault from the sea on Cherbourg and thus the concept of a temporary harbour had loomed large in the planners' minds. So it was that Mulberry came into being.

We saw in Chapter III that two Mulberry harbours were constructed, one for the Americans and the other for the British and Canadian forces. Some writers have criticised Mulberry as being unnecessary – although the American harbour was wrecked by a storm the Americans were able subsequently to unload over the open beach at much the same rate as the British at Port Winston, the Mulberry at Arromanches – but, as Max Hastings points out,[30] it was the insurance provided by this imaginative project that convinced those with doubts that OVERLORD was possible. And among the doubters was Winston Churchill, haunted by the spectres of Gallipolli and Dieppe. Mulberry, therefore, was crucial to the morale of those responsible for undertaking OVERLORD; Omar Bradley later described the project as 'one of the most inventive logistical undertakings of the war'.[31] Details of Mulberry are included in Appendix 1.

As SHAEF refined the invasion plans, its staff were able to draw on the experience of several landings. There was Dieppe, which had ensured that OVERLORD would not have a port as its target and that naval gun support much heavier than that of destroyers was needed. The Salerno landings in September 1943 had also confirmed the need for heavy naval fire support and for fighter cover over the beachhead as well as having a cohesive front on the beaches – the gap between British and American troops at Salerno had almost caused disaster. Another lesson from earlier operations, and battlefield experience, was the requirement for armour to support the infantry as early as possible and for specialised armoured vehicles to overcome battlefield obstacles. Montgomery was to show that he had learned this particular lesson when he decided to send in his armour in the first wave on D-Day, preceding the infantry. From that lesson, also, came the 'Funnies' of 79th Armoured Division. Commanding 79th Armoured Division was Major-General Percy Hobart, one of Britain's foremost thinkers on armoured warfare but who had been forced into retirement in 1940 following an adverse report by his superior, General Wilson, even though Hobart had formed and trained to a high level of efficiency the first British armoured division in the Middle East – 7th Armoured, soon to be known as the Desert Rats. Following a spell as a volunteer in the Home Guard, Hobart was called back to command a division on Churchill's orders. Initially he was asked to raise and train 11th Armoured Division, which he did with considerable success, but when this division was assigned to overseas service he was asked to raise yet another formation. This was 79th Armoured, which had been, at first, a standard armoured division but was reprieved from disbandment to become the formation to operate a range of specialised tanks that soon became known as 'Hobart's Funnies'. Hobart only accepted command of the Division when Brooke told him that he would also command it in action rather than being left behind in Britain.

Following Dieppe there had been a clear understanding that armour must assist infantry in any opposed landing with a particular need for armoured vehicles to overcome or destroy the obstacles that the Germans were creating to pin down invading forces. These obstacles were part of the defences that Hitler had ordered to be constructed from the Dutch coast to Biscay, the 'Atlantic Wall', to keep the Allies out of Fortress Europe. Although the 'Wall' was never completed, such elements as were finished were formidable and many exist to this day as a demonstration of their strength. In one sense, the 'Wall' was a throwback to siege warfare, using engineering skills to defeat an enemy. But, just as engineers built siegeworks, so they were also skilled at identifying and exploiting their weaknesses and overcoming them. It was no surprise that Hobart had begun his military career as an engineer. And his specialised armour would show how the siegeworks of the Atlantic Wall could be overcome.

The first tanks ashore on D-Day were Shermans adapted as amphibians. These were the DDs, or Duplex Drive Shermans, fitted with two propellers to drive them through the water, in which mode they could travel at 4.5 knots. A canvas buoyancy screen around the hull was raised before the tank entered the water. The theory was that DD Shermans could be 'launched' offshore to precede the infantry on to the beach, thereby providing immediate close support. DD Shermans were also used by US Army armoured units and were the only 'Funnies' used by the Americans on D-Day. Their experience was far from good; many tanks were lost with their crews when they were launched too far from the shore and swamped by choppy seas.

The other 'Funnies' were all British. Although offered to the Americans the offer was declined, to the detriment of American soldiers, and their use was restricted to British and Canadian assaulting formations. Among the defences expected on any beach were mines, creating a need for a tank to clear them. In 1942 such a tank had been developed in Egypt for use at El Alamein. Using obsolescent Matildas, engineers had created 'flail' tanks, dubbed Scorpions, by fixing to the sides of the tank two steel jibs between the front ends of which was a roller turned by an auxiliary engine. As it revolved, the roller flailed lengths of chain to thrash the ground and detonate any mines in the tank's path. The Scorpions had not been entirely successful but one reason for that was the use of the well-worn Matildas with the need for an auxiliary engine. The concept had been refined since with a variant of the ubiquitous Sherman, the Crab, being produced. As with the Scorpion, the Crab mounted a rotating roller with flails to clear mines from its path; it could clear a gap ten-feet wide at a speed of 1.5 mph and could also destroy barbed-wire obstacles. But the Crabs would not work singly.

> The width of ground flailed by one tank was insufficient for following vehicles and so it was necessary for the flailed path to be at least two tanks wide. This necessitated the following tank or tanks to drive with one track in a track print of the tank in front – by night and under fire. This formation was known as echelon to the right, or left. With the aid of some rear-facing lights mounted on long arms, we began to acquire the necessary skills.[32]

Other 'Funnies' were based on the British Churchill, a reliable, well-armoured vehicle suitable for adaptation to various roles. One such variation was the 'Bobbin', designed to assist tanks and other vehicles pass over soft sand by laying a canvas carpet from a roller on the tank's front; this carpet was an inch short of ten feet in width and thus capable of carrying most military vehicles. One Churchill AVRE (Assault Vehicle Royal Engineers) was the ARC (Armoured Ramp Carrier) adapted to carry a bridge that could be dropped over a thirty-foot-wide gap in as many seconds. Alternatively the equipment could be used to surmount a fifteen-feet high wall. In either case the bridge could support forty tons, allowing all but the heaviest vehicles to cross. Other Churchill-based AVREs carried fascines – bundles of wooden rods – to fill anti-tank ditches, or Spigot Mortars firing Petards, explosive-filled canisters to tackle heavily-fortified strongpoints. Among other weaponry that could be deployed on AVREs was Snake, a four-inch explosive-filled metal tube that could be fired 400 feet into a minefield to clear a lane for tanks. Then there was Crocodile, a conversion of the Churchill Mk VII, with a flame gun in place of the hull-mounted machine gun and towing a trailer carrying 400 gallons of fuel that was forced from trailer to gun by compressed nitrogen. Crocodile was a terrifying weapon in action when its gun spewed forth a long tongue of flame and many German soldiers thought it an unfair weapon.* As well as these, there was an armoured version of the Caterpillar Company's heavy-duty bulldozer that could be used on a battlefield for a variety of tasks. Before long, dozer-bladed Churchills and Shermans would also appear.

* At a Fallschirmjäger reunion in Germany in 1990, German veterans told the author that they would have executed immediately the crews of any Crocodiles who fell into their hands, such was their anger at the use of flamethrowers. Nonetheless, the German army itself used flamethrowers.

Hobart's task was to develop all these specialised fighting vehicles to the highest standards of reliability, train their crews to similar levels and advise on their use on the battlefield. And this had to be achieved in a year, or less. But the task did not end there: the Royal Navy would have to ferry the vehicles in their landing craft and so methods of deployment and employment had to be worked out with the Navy. Once ashore 'Funnies' would support infantry, armour and other arms and appropriate operational procedures had to be devised; the close cooperation of all arms was crucial to OVERLORD's success.

The wartime order of battle for an armoured division varied but in April 1943 such a division deployed 278 tanks,[33] including thirty-four anti-aircraft (AA) tanks, in its headquarters, armoured reconnaissance regiment and armoured brigade. In the latter were three armoured regiments plus a motor battalion of infantry, usually provided by a Green Jackets regiment. Alongside the armoured brigade would be an infantry brigade of three battalions, plus a support group, while Royal Artillery and Royal Engineers would also be represented in strength, the Gunners with two field regiments, one towed and one self-propelled, as well as an anti-tank regiment and a light anti-aircraft regiment, and the sappers with two field squadrons and a field park squadron. In March 1944 the tank complement of an armoured division increased to 343 tanks,[34] including twenty-five AA tanks and eight observation post (OP) tanks but the organisation remained as an armoured brigade and an infantry brigade. Although 79th Armoured adopted the April 1943 organisation, this was inappropriate for the division's new role and a unique order of battle ensued. For D-Day the division included 30 Armoured Brigade, 1 Tank Brigade and 1 Assault Brigade and Assault Park Squadron, RE, plus divisional signals. In turn, for OVERLORD, these brigades included 22nd Dragoons, Westminster Dragoons and 1st Lothians and Border Horse in 30 Armoured Brigade,* 11th, 42nd and 49th Royal Tanks in 1 Tank Brigade and 5th, 6th and 42nd Assault Regiments, Royal Engineers, in 1 Assault Brigade.[36] Finally the division also deployed 1st Canadian Armoured Personnel Carrier Regiment.

Hobart's division had its own operating procedures; each brigade used one type of specialised armour with brigade headquarters commanding and administering its units in the usual fashion. In action units were assigned to other formations while the brigade commander acted as adviser to the formation concerned. This required a high level of training and professionalism and Hobart was ruthless in ensuring that his division achieved such standards. Nor was 79th Armoured Division controlled by a corps headquarters as were conventional divisions. Since it came under

* During the Normandy fighting 141st Regiment, RAC would join the brigade, serving with it from 2 July to 4 September.[35]

direct command of 21 Army Group its formations and units could be assigned to support an army for a specific operation or series of operations. Hobart was entirely successful in achieving his aims. The specialised armour of his division played an invaluable role in Normandy from the very first day and many units had cause to be grateful to the 'Funnies' for their support.

The Allied Expeditionary Force would be the most mechanised military force ever assembled with an enormous thirst for fuel. In the subsequent advance through France an infantry division consumed six times the weight of petrol that it used in food, while for an armoured division the ratio went up to eight.[37] Not for nothing did the French dub petrol *le sang rouge de la guerre*. Since the force to be assembled in Normandy would be about two million strong, its requirements for supplies and stores can be imagined. Petrol was among the most important of these and much thought had been given to ensuring that sufficient fuel was always available when and where it was needed. The problem was addressed in three ways. Supplies of cased petrol were to be offloaded over the beaches, through Mulberry or small ports within the lodgement area in the normal manner. More novel was the concept of mooring tankers offshore with buoy-supported pipes to carry fuel from the ships to storage tanks at Port-en-Bessin and Ste Honorine. This concept, codenamed TOMBOLA, proved very successful, with a maximum daily capacity of 8,000 tons reached on one day in July and another in August.[38] By the end of August more than 175,000 tons of fuel had been pumped ashore through TOMBOLA. But it was the third method of supplying fuel that became, probably, the best known. As with Mulberry, this was an innovative approach to a problem: pump the fuel under the sea through a pipeline. Known as PLUTO – PipeLine Under The Ocean – this involved pumping fuel from England through an armoured submarine pipeline from the Isle of Wight to Querqueville, west of Cherbourg. Obviously, PLUTO would not be in use in the early stages of the operations but it was planned that there would be four lines delivering a daily total of 2,500 tons of fuel to the Expeditionary Force. It was almost six weeks after D-Day before PLUTO became operational. By then the Normandy battles were over.

Between D-Day and the end of August, over two million men, almost 500,000 vehicles and some 3,000,000 tons of stores and supplies would be landed in Normandy. That achievement required huge effort on the part of Allied naval forces and their Merchant Navy comrades, an effort that would continue until the end of the war. The final naval plan – NEPTUNE – included over 5,000 ships and a further 4,000 ship-to-shore craft in the assault and build-up phase.[39] By 16 April 1944 the Combined Chiefs had decided on the naval forces for the invasion. Chief among those forces, which would support and protect the invasion fleet as it crossed the Channel and provide firepower for the assaulting forces, were to be six battleships, two monitors, twenty-two cruisers and ninety-three destroyers.[40] The naval force for NEPTUNE would operate in two elements: Western Task Force for the American zone and Eastern Task Force for the British/Canadian zone. As the armada crossed the Channel, twelve minesweeping flotillas would clear the seas ahead of them with other naval forces securing the flanks. To the west an anti-submarine screen would deter U-boats from the Atlantic coast bases. From the battleships and monitors, heavy guns would strike at enemy shore batteries and strongpoints to neutralise them as the assaulting forces landed.

In carrying out that task, the ships' guns would augment the work of the Allied air forces. Two Tactical Air Forces had been created to provide direct support to the armies: the British 2nd Tactical Air Force and the US Ninth Air Force. These could deploy almost 2,500 fighter and fighter-bomber aircraft plus 700 light and medium bombers to hit targets such as bridges, railways, radar sites and coastal batteries. The programme of attacks on railway targets, especially stations, junctions and marshalling yards as well as bridges, was to begin sixty days before D-Day and be spread over a wide geographical area so as to give no clue to the intended assault area. As D-Day drew closer attacks would become more focused but not so as to indicate Normandy as the invasion site. This plan was intended to deprive the Germans of the means of reinforcing rapidly their front-line formations, to disrupt movements of fuel and supplies, to prevent concentration of German forces and to make the Germans use roads to a greater extent, thereby wasting fuel and transport and increasing vulnerability. Strategic bombers would also participate in this disruption programme in one of their most successful employments during the war, although it was not met with great enthusiasm by the most senior airmen.

On 21 November 1943 Field Marshal Erwin Rommel left Italy for leave at home before undertaking an inspection of the defences in Western Europe, on which he was to report his findings directly to Hitler. Rommel's inspection began in Denmark and continued down the coast to the Pyrenees and then along France's Mediterranean coast. Too often, in his view, defences were defective or even non-existent while many local commanders showed a lack of urgency. Rommel's visits had an electrifying effect and there was a subsequent marked improvement in the speed of construction. The Desert Fox wanted a system of defences as strong as it was possible to make them in the time and with the material and manpower available. He was determined that the invasion, when it came, should be defeated on the beaches; that would mean that it would be a long time before the British and Americans tried again, if ever, and would allow Germany to concentrate on the Eastern Front to stop the Soviet advance and perhaps even allow a limited offensive there. Given such a situation, Rommel believed that a negotiated peace settlement might be possible. Meeting and defeating the invasion on the beaches was vital. Should the Anglo–Americans be allowed to make ground they would increase their lodgement area in an expanding torrent and a Western Front would be created to swallow up forces that could have been deployed to meet the Soviets.

Much of the work that Rommel wanted done had to be performed by German soldiers; he did not want slave labour, preferring that any Frenchmen used in the work should be volunteers and rewarded for their efforts. The defences he envisaged were impressive, beginning offshore with four belts of underwater obstacles, the first under six feet of water, the next at low tide mark, another at the midway point between low and high tides and the fourth at the mean high tide mark. Onshore would be minefields, fortified strongpoints and artillery while ground on which gliders might land was to be sown with stakes that were soon dubbed *Rommelspargel*, or Rommel's Asparagus, by his soldiers. Rommel intended the stakes to be topped by mines but this never happened because of the shortage of mines; the stakes were insignificant impediments to the glider forces. The minefields demanded millions of mines since Rommel wanted a five-mile-deep zone including several parallel belts, each of great depth. Such zones would be created anywhere a seaward landing was possible and would be swept by fire from fortified strongpoints, which demanded huge quantities of concrete and steel, and static tanks. A deception plan allowed for dummy positions that might deter an invader, as well as fictitious formations and staffs with movement tables, communications traffic and all the panoply needed to present a picture of defence forces at the ready.

Rommel's visits were inspirational and motivated soldiers and commanders to a level of zeal that had probably not been seen before in occupied Europe. The urgency of the situation was impressed upon them, the aura of the Desert Fox took the sting from Rommel's ruthless driving of his forces and something of his own determination passed to them. Some commentators suggest that the Rommel of this period was not the same man who had led Italo–German forces in North Africa, that he was tired and disillusioned, and not fully recovered from the ill health that had plagued him in the desert. That was certainly not the impression he left on his visits. His engineer commander, General Meise, thought Rommel the 'greatest field engineer of the Second World War' while one of his biographers, General Sir David Fraser, a veteran of north-west Europe, wrote that 'Everywhere he went [Rommel] produced new ideas and experimentation.'[41] Over four million mines were laid along with thousands of obstacles on beaches and potential glider landing areas, many of them booby-trapped, and Rommel's own genius for camouflage came into its own in the form of dummies and decoys to mislead enemy airmen and intelligence analysts.

Siegework principles also came into play in siting coast defence artillery; this could be seen clearly in the batteries around the Bay of the Seine (see Map 4). The Bay is a three sided re-entrant on the Normandy coast with a clear field of fire for the coastal gun batteries that were one of the main lines of defence in the region. Twenty batteries were located from Barfleur on the north-east of the Cotentin down into the main coastal strip of the bay and then up to Grand Clos, just above le Havre as the coast begins to arc north-eastward towards Dieppe. Rommel's guns could cover most of the waters of the bay and present a major threat to Allied vessels. Such was the strength of their emplacements that it would take the powerful fire of heavy surface ships, rather than destroyers as deployed at Dieppe, to neutralise them.

Having made his mark on the Atlantic Wall programme, Rommel took command of the sector including northern France and the Low Countries. This was done at his own request and became the area of Rommel's Armeegruppe (Army Group) B from 15 January 1944; it covered the French coast from north of the Loire estuary, as well as the Belgian and Dutch coasts as far as the Zuider Zee. (Army Group B had been Rommel's command in Italy and, therefore, this was simply a relocation of his headquarters.) Within the sector, Army Group B included Fifteenth Army, under General von Salmuth, and Seventh Army, under General Dollmann. The inter-army boundary was west of the Seine and ran south towards le Mans; Fifteenth Army therefore covered the Pas de Calais and eastern Normandy with Seventh Army overseeing the rest of Normandy and neighbouring Brittany. Army Group B's command also included General Christiansen's command in The Netherlands, Wehrbereich Nederlande. Within Fifteenth and Seventh Armies there were, in January, thirty-two infantry divisions including eight Luftwaffe divisions; the former army had seventeen divisions with the balance in the latter. Needless to say, both were reinforced as the months passed and Army Group B in the Normandy campaign was to include fifty-one divisions, including thirteen Panzer or Panzer Grenadier divisions.[42]

Rommel's commander was Field Marshal Gerd von Rundstedt with whom he disagreed on the anti-invasion plans. As well as the two army groups, all armoured forces were under command of General der Panzertruppen Baron Geyr von Schweppenburg who wished to keep his armour concentrated and gained Generaloberst Heinz Guderian's support for this plan. Rommel considered this strategy flawed, believing, from his experience of Allied air power, that he should have strong reserves, including armour, close to the beaches. Should the Allies gain a foothold, argued Rommel, it could prove impossible to stem the flow of the invasion.

That could be done only if they were defeated on the beaches. The eventual compromise, from Hitler, was for four Panzer divisions to be held as an OKW reserve, a solution that made no one happy.

With Rommel commanding Army Group B and Montgomery at the helm of 21 Army Group, the two rivals of El Alamein would meet again.

NOTES

1 Brooke, *War Diaries*, p. 399.
2 Ibid, p. 406.
3 Grigg, *1943. The Victory That Never Was*, pp. 88–9.
4 Brooke, op cit, p. 411.
5 Ibid, p. 436.
6 Ibid, p. 435.
7 Bradley, *A Soldier's Story*, p. 214.
8 Ibid, pp. 214–5.
9 Barnett, *Engage the Enemy More Closely*, p. 777.
10 Eisenhower, *D-Day to VE Day*, pp. 16–7.
11 Ellis, *Victory in the West*, p. 16.
12 Ibid, p. 17.
13 Brooke, op cit, p. 395n.
14 Eisenhower, op cit, p. 1.
15 Ibid, p. 4.
16 Brooke, op cit, p. 441.
17 Bradley, op cit, p. 205
18 Churchill, *The Second World War, vol v*, p. 76.
19 Brooke, op cit, p. 442.
20 Ellis, op cit, p. 19.
21 Eisenhower, op cit, p. 20.
22 Ibid, p. 21.
23 Montgomery, *Memoirs*, p. 219.
24 Ibid, p. 211.
25 Ibid, pp. 219–20.
26 Barnett, op cit, p. 763.
27 Montgomery, op cit, p. 220.
28 Eisenhower, op cit, p.22.
29 Ibid, p. 25.
30 Hastings, *Overlord*, p. 197.
31 Bradley, op cit, p. 302.
32 Hammerton, *Achtung! Minen!* p. 51.
33 Joslen, *Orders of Battle, Second World War*, p. 8; Forty, *Handbook of the British Army*, p. 152.
34 Joslen, p. 9; Forty, p. 152.
35 Joslen, p. 181.
36 Ibid, p. 181 & p. 195; Hastings, op cit, p. 335.
37 Bradley, op cit, p. 245.
38 Ellis, op cit, p. 480.
39 Eisenhower, op cit, p. 37.
40 Ibid.
41 Fraser, *Knight's Cross*, p. 456.
42 Ibid, p. 457.

CHAPTER V

Lies and tank parks

I see you stand like greyhounds in the slips

As the opposing armies prepared for the coming battle, plans were being finalised for measures to deceive the Germans about the landing area. At Casablanca Winston Churchill uttered the axiom that, in war, truth is so important that it must be defended by a bodyguard of lies. His comment was especially true in the months before the invasion. To the Germans, invasion was inevitable but they knew neither *when* nor *where* it would come. Misleading them on both points was vital. Thus was born a series of deception plans and measures to be implemented prior to invasion and after the first landings so that these might be regarded as a diversion.

The strategic deception plan was Operation BODYGUARD which included schemes to create the impression that the invasion could come in any of several locations, the best known of which was Operation QUICKSILVER. This featured a fictitious US Army Group, apparently preparing for an assault on the Pas de Calais, under General George Patton, who was highly regarded by German generals, although Hitler called him the 'cowboy general'. Operation FORTITUDE had two elements: FORTITUDE NORTH included a fictitious British force, Fourth Army, in Scotland, making ready to invade Norway; FORTITUDE SOUTH tied in with the deception involving Patton's fictitious army group, which the Germans referred to as Armeegruppe Patton, to suggest that the Normandy landings were a diversion to draw German reserves away from the Pas de Calais where Patton would make the real attack six weeks later. BODYGUARD represents 'probably the most complex and successful deception operation in the history of warfare'[1] with over forty plans that would take a book to detail. Since NEPTUNE/OVERLORD was the biggest military operation in history the deception plans had to be of comparable magnitude.

In almost every respect the deception worked. The sole exception was on the highest strategic level where attempts were made to convince the Germans that the main invasion could come somewhere other than the western seaboard of Europe. Operationally, however, the plan was hugely successful and a tribute to those who worked on it. The Germans did not believe that the main assault would come anywhere other than France because of its sheer scale. They could not believe that the Allies, with their huge base in Britain, would do anything other than cross the Channel. Also high on the list of reasons for believing that the attack would come through north-western France was Hitler's Directive No. 51, of 3 November 1943, in which he declared the area to be his chief priority for 1944, although he highlighted the Pas de Calais as the focus of Allied effort. Another factor in German reasoning came from their own lack of experience of amphibious warfare. Von Rundstedt suffered from this lacuna, believing that similar conditions would apply to an Allied cross-Channel assault as had applied to SEELÖWE in 1940. He considered that the Allies would also opt for the shortest cross-Channel route but, in 1940, German forces had been constrained by lack of sea and air power, factors not affecting the Allies in 1944. Most German senior officers simply did not understand that and were also misled by the Dieppe raid, which, to them, confirmed that the Allies would try to seize a major port in any invasion. That the Allies had drawn exactly the opposite lesson from Dieppe seems not to have entered their thinking. Even Rommel believed in the 'target a port' theory, and thought, initially, that the Allies would land at the Somme estuary to flank and seize le Havre.[2]

The deception plans were designed to gain maximum surprise for the invasion itself and the subsequent build-up in the beachhead. This latter would be easier if the Germans could be persuaded not to rush reinforcements to Normandy but to hold back lest the real invasion had yet to come. This would remove the one real advantage that the defenders might enjoy: the ability rapidly to reinforce the battle area. If German reinforcements could be held back then Allied forces in the bridgehead would be able to increase their strength to the point at which they could break out. This would be the critical element of the battle and deception could play a pivotal role.

Thus was born FORTITUDE SOUTH, to suggest that the true effort would come in the Pas de Calais some six weeks after the Normandy 'diversion'. The success of this plan would be measured by the extent of Fifteenth Army's involvement in Normandy. On that basis the plan must be considered one of the best examples of wartime deception since it succeeded in convincing the majority of the German command, at all levels, that the Pas de Calais was the Allies' real target. We have already seen that FORTITUDE SOUTH placed Patton at the head of a fictitious First US Army Group, or FUSAG, including Ninth and Fourteenth Armies, in south-east England. Within FORTITUDE SOUTH, the plan involving this ghost army group was QUICKSILVER, of which there were six parts: the supposed assault was QUICKSILVER I; radio traffic deception was QUICKSILVER II while a display of landing craft, a bombing programme – covered by two numerical designators – and false lighting schemes along the south coast represented the other parts.

From 24 April 1944 QUICKSILVER II provided a skilfully crafted programme of radio traffic simulating an army group preparing for a major operation. The US Army's 3103rd Signals Service Battalion arrived in Britain in February and began studying signals patterns and analysing information so that they could better reproduce a large formation signals network. The battalion simulated the army group headquarters, an army, three corps and nine divisions as their trucks moved through the countryside. Also involved was 5th Wireless Group, Royal Signals, which showed some ingenuity by recording all traffic in advance and deploying equipment that allowed a single transmitter to simulate six. This Group could provide the traffic of a division and its component brigades with a single wireless truck. A measure of the skill and success of the signallers is that their deception was never suspected, even though the German radio intelligence service was experienced in analysing patterns and rhythms of operators and through such analysis tracked 82nd Airborne Division from Italy to England, in spite of a radio deception scheme to hide the move. Radio traffic was backed up with visual displays, landing craft for QUICKSILVER III, in the eastern ports of the Thames estuary and Kent, and lighting schemes for QUICKSILVER VI. But, since the RAF controlled the skies over southern Britain, there was little Luftwaffe reconnaissance and thus little need for large-scale camouflage and physical deception programmes.

FUSAG included genuine formations, among them Third US and First Canadian Armies, as well as many US divisions that were still training at home. The cover plan suggested that twelve divisions would land at Calais with another thirty-eight to follow, supported by Ninth Air Force. So this plan not only aided the Pas de Calais deception but also helped disguise the build-up for the real landing. Another adjunct to the deception plan was the use of double agents, British intelligence having succeeded in turning almost the entire German spy network in the United Kingdom.[3]

From March 1944 an Allied bombing campaign appeared to be concentrated on the Pas de Calais for, although bombers appeared over Normandy's defences, the concentration of ordnance dropped on the former was double that in Normandy. Likewise, reconnaissance missions were flown on a ratio of two-to-one between the Pas de Calais and Normandy. An even greater proportion of the bombing of railways was concentrated in the Pas de Calais. Disrupting enemy rail communications was vital for OVERLORD since a badly damaged railway system would frustrate the movement of German reinforcements; Eisenhower believed that the Allied build-up in the beachhead could not otherwise outpace the enemy. This bombing programme, the Transportation Plan, was adopted on the recommendation of a team under Professor Solly Zuckerman, a scientific member of Tedder's staff, who had convinced both his own chief and Eisenhower that this was the most effective way for strategic bombers to contribute to OVERLORD.[4] Elsewhere the response was not as enthusiastic. Churchill opposed it since Lord Cherwell had suggested the possibility of up to 40,000 French casualties. Both Harris of Bomber Command and Carl Spaatz of the US Army Air Force* were also opposed, since they were convinced of the efficacy of the strategic bombing campaign and saw the Transportation Plan as an unnecessary diversion; neither man really believed in OVERLORD, believing that their bombers would bring Germany to collapse.[5]

Although Churchill continued to oppose the Transportation Plan until May, Roosevelt and Marshall persuaded him that it was the best use of the big bombers in the preparatory phase. At Churchill's suggestion, both Bomber Command and the US Eighth Air Force were placed under Tedder's command, which meant that 'Spaatz could take his orders from Eisenhower' and a similar arrangement could exist between Tedder and Harris.[6] From the night of 31 March–1 April, therefore, Bomber Command switched to bombing railway targets; it had already made several small-scale precision raids with some success. During the day, Eighth Air Force also switched to similar targets. In most cases bombing was much more accurate than anyone had anticipated. Harris had considered it impossible to achieve sufficient accuracy against railway goods yards, junctions and similar targets in France and Belgium to keep civilian casualties to a minimum, even writing about a possible toll of 200,000.[7] He could not have been inspired by the first major operation on the night of 9–10 April against the Lille-Délivrance goods yard. Bomber Command sent out 239 aircraft from four groups, of which the majority – 166 – were Halifaxes and the remainder Lancasters, Stirlings and Mosquitoes. One Lancaster was lost on this raid but the yard was hit by only forty-nine bombs, causing extensive damage to buildings, tracks and rolling stock; 2,124 wagons of the 2,959 there were destroyed. Tragically, most bombs fell outside the yard, killing 456 French civilians. Over ninety per cent of the dead were in the Lomme suburb, where some 5,000 houses were destroyed or damaged. A French eyewitness recalled the resentment the inhabitants felt towards the British at the time.[8] Harris must have considered his misgivings justified, especially as a further ninety-three French civilians died in another raid that same night on railway yards at Villeneuve-St-Georges near Paris. No aircraft were lost from the 225 despatched but there is no accurate record of the damage to the railway yard, although Bomber Command claimed a successfu1 raid; over 400 houses were destroyed or damaged.

The following night railway targets at Tours, Tergnier, Laon, and Aulnoye, as well as Ghent in Belgium were bombed. Serious damage was caused to most targets but there were also civilian casualties, with Ghent

* As well as Eighth Air Force based in Britain, Spaatz also commanded Fifteenth Air Force based in the Mediterranean.

suffering worst; 428 Belgians died. A week later Tergnier was again a target along with Rouen, Juvisy and Noisy-le-Sec. Marshalling yards at Noisy-le-Sec were not repaired until 1951 although a through line was operational a few days later; but there were also considerable civilian casualties at Noisy with 464 people killed. At Tergnier, fifty railway lines were blocked but again there were civilian losses as most bombs fell in residential areas south-west of the target; the death toll is not known.[9]

Two nights later there were raids on la Chapelle and Ottignies yards with a new marking system being used for the first time at the former. No. 5 Group used Lancasters of No. 617 Squadron, the Dambusters, to mark the target from low level and also employed three Pathfinder squadrons recently transferred from No. 8 Group. Of 269 aircraft six were lost but results were good. None of the 196 machines sent against Ottignies was lost and severe damage was caused to the southern half of the railway yards. On the same night the Lens yard and Chambly railway depot were also targeted. Only fourteen Stirlings, using the G-H blind bombing aid, attacked the latter, of which ten aircraft did not bomb; one Stirling was lost. Much damage was done to engine sheds and workshops at Lens by 175 bombers for the loss of one Halifax.[10]

Losses reached five per cent of the attacking force at Laon on the night of 22–23 April, among them one of the Master Bombers, Wing Commander A G S Cousens of No. 635 Squadron. Severe damage was caused to the target area which was struck by 181 aircraft in two waves. Rarely did losses reach even three per cent, although there was one remarkable exception when 8.3 per cent of attacking bombers were lost during raids on Mailly-le-Camp and Montdidier on the night of 3–4 May. At the former, 11.6 per cent of the attackers were lost, largely due to communication problems that caused a delay in the main attack and allowed German fighters to wreak havoc. Considerable damage was caused by the 1,500 tons of bombs that were eventually unleashed with great accuracy. No French casualties occurred through bombing although some people died when a Lancaster crashed on their house. Otherwise, the only casualties were German service personnel.[11]

The level of accuracy increased as the campaign progressed and by the night of 5 June Bomber Command had flown operations against railway targets, explosives factories, military buildings, coastal batteries and motor industry factories, as well as striking at German cities on those nights that they were not required for the pre-OVERLORD programme. In all, strategic bombers made an indispensable contribution to the operation and Harris's doubts about their ability to achieve the high level of accuracy necessary proved unfounded. Subsequent analysis and interviewing of French railway officials indicated that, by June, as many as seventy per cent of locomotives were out of service; the figure had risen from twenty per cent in January.[12]

These attacks reinforced the belief that the invasion would come in the

Pas de Calais. Although attacks were concentrated on targets between the Seine and Meuse rivers, making it seem as if the Allies were trying to cut off the Pas de Calais, the main railway lines into Normandy ran through this area and thus were paralysed every bit as effectively as if they had been hit in Normandy. One estimate of the percentage of the bombing of railways between the Seine and the Meuse puts the figure at ninety-five per cent. The programme was so successful that Rommel reported to von Rundstedt that its emphasis made it more likely that the invasion would come in the Pas de Calais. That report was made only two days before D-Day.[13] Thus Fifteenth Army continued to await an attack that would never come from an army group that did not exist.

Although FORTITUDE NORTH was not as complex as FORTITUDE SOUTH it also involved a bogus formation, in this case Fourth British Army, commanded by Lieutenant-General Sir Andrew 'Bulgy' Thorne, who had been British military attaché in Berlin ten years earlier and was known to Hitler. The cover story for Thorne's command was that it would invade Norway after the main Allied invasion. Since Scandinavia was an area from which the Germans intended to draw reinforcements to meet the invasion, this meant that troops had to be kept in Norway and Denmark to deal with Fourth Army.[14]

Thorne's army was simulated by Headquarters No. 12 Reserve Unit, which also represented II and VII Corps. Those corps included 55th and 61st Divisions, plus 9 Armoured Brigade, in the former and 38th and 45th Divisions in the latter alongside 47 Armoured Brigade. A fictitious 2nd Airborne Division also came under army command.[15] The other divisions did exist but only 55th (West Lancashire) was a full-strength formation; the others were lower-establishment formations relegated to providing reinforcements, although 61st had expected to be an assault division. Of the two armoured brigades, 9 was serving in the Mediterranean and 47 never existed. At times there were other divisions in Fourth Army: 3rd Division, a D-Day assault division, trained in Scotland and assisted the pretence that an invasion of Norway was planned. And a Scottish formation, 52nd (Lowland) Division, also joined Fourth Army, having been trained in mountain warfare (and wearing 'Mountain' and 'Lowland' flashes on uniforms and vehicles) and equipped as if it were ready to descend on Norway.* Also appearing on the army order of battle was 80th Division, a reserve formation.[17]

* Paradoxically, 52nd (Lowland) Division first saw action in the Low Countries, having been re-roled as an air-portable division and assigned to the Allied Airborne Army for Operation MARKET GARDEN in September. Although it was intended that the Division should be flown into Deelen airfield, this did not happen and the only element of the Division to fight at Arnhem was the seaborne echelon, which served under XXX Corps.[16]

Fourth Army's radio deception was provided by elements of II Corps, 9th Armoured Division, Scottish Command and personnel from various other units. Transmissions covered such subjects as footwear and training in skiing while messages emanated from all sorts of minor units, including a film and photographic section.[18] Preparations were carried out as if for a real operation – war diaries of some units indicate that they expected to fight in Norway – with amphibious training taking place, large numbers of ships in the Forth, conspicuous landing craft and the Fleet Air Arm's Operation VERITAS, an aerial reconnaissance of the Narvik area on 26 April. RAF aircraft moved to Scotland from East Anglia and dummy aircraft were placed on several Scottish airfields, along with dummy tanks and gliders.

The Scandinavia deception was carried a little further with an apparent diplomatic initiative to enlist Sweden's assistance in an attack on Norway. Operation GRAFFHAM included raising the cost of Norwegian securities on the Stockholm stock market.[19] Although the Germans accepted Fourth Army at face value, they considered that operations in Scandinavia would be minor, since air support would be limited by distance. Even so, Hitler continued to believe in the possibility of an invasion and a fresh division of first-class troops was posted to Norway in May. FORTITUDE NORTH, although not a complete success, ensured that significant numbers of German troops remained well away from the main battleground at the beginning of June and for some time thereafter. But the Norwegian deception also helped strengthen the belief that the real invasion would be in the Pas de Calais.

Winston Churchill also wanted operations in Norway but was persuaded of their impracticality by Brooke. On the southern flank Brooke supported operations in Italy, as did Churchill, which were seen as another way to tie German troops down well away from Normandy. Thus the Battle of Cassino in May played its part in the subsequent cross-Channel operations. But Italy also provided the opportunity to threaten the Balkans and thereby prevent the transfer of troops from the Mediterranean to northern France. Operation ZEPPELIN played out this bluff, using Ninth and Tenth Armies, which were real but very low in strength, and the fictitious Twelfth Army.* Real and ghost formations were included in ZEPPELIN, which impressed Hitler and even caused OKW to suggest that the Allied emphasis on north-west Europe might be a bluff to draw attention from the Balkans.

In the preparations for OVERLORD British and American formations were transferred from Italy to the United Kingdom. The move of veteran

* It had been proposed to use the title Twelfth Army for the British forces invading Sicily in Operation HUSKY but Montgomery opposed this suggestion and the title Eighth Army was retained. A real Twelfth Army was later formed in Burma.[20]

formations* was masked by Operation FOYNES, which, among other things, suggested that the presence in Britain of so many soldiers with the Africa Star ribbon was due to experienced men arriving to train inexperienced troops for the forthcoming offensive. The Germans knew of the move before long but it was some time before they were able to place any of those divisions in Britain and even longer before they accepted that others were not resting in southern Italy.

Deceptions pointing to further operations in the Mediterranean played on the fear that an attack on the Balkans might be launched from Egypt and Libya. Since it was intended to invade southern France in an operation planned to coincide with OVERLORD – ANVIL – it was essential that such deceptions would not compromise the real operation. Jon Latimer notes that

> In the Mediterranean theatre the overestimation [of Allied forces in Egypt and Libya] was as much as eighty-five per cent and played a major part in preventing the movement of German troops from that theatre to the crucial arena of northern France.[21]

The threat from the south was identified by the Germans as serious enough to maintain strong forces in southern France, none of which moved north until mid-June when a panzer division was transferred. Even then, that formation was not followed by others until mid-July. Another threat, to Bordeaux, was created, mainly through a female double agent who had gained the confidence of the Abwehr,** German naval intelligence. Operation IRONSIDE appears to have kept 11th Panzer Division in the Bordeaux area for most of the week after the Normandy landings.[22]

Montgomery's intelligence chief, Brigadier Bill Williams, estimated that there were over fifty German divisions in the west, including six panzer divisions.[23] A month later fifty-five divisions, eight of them armoured, were identified.[24] That estimate was later revised to sixty divisions, of which ten were panzer and twelve panzer grenadier.[25] But Oberst Baron von Roenne, who commanded Fremde Heere West (FHW), OKH's intelligence branch, did not share Montgomery's high opinion of these formations. Von Roenne was concerned that France was a rest area for formations that had suffered heavy losses on the Russian front and were,

* These included the British 7th Armoured (the Desert Rats), 50th (Northumbrian), 51st (Highland) and 1st Airborne Divisions, as well as some independent brigades. Montgomery had also wanted to take 2nd New Zealand Division but was prevented from doing so by Brooke. The American divisions to transfer included 1st Infantry Division, the 'Big Red One'.

** The Abwehr ceased to exist in February 1944.

therefore, less likely to be effective against an invader. And von Roenne was convinced that an invasion was in the offing. He recognised the threat to Norway as a deception, and did not take seriously the threat against the Balkans. But all his efforts to draw the attention of the high command to what he perceived as the real threat were nullified by several factors. Chief among these was the sycophantic attitude of the high command to Hitler's intuition, which led them to ignore genuine intelligence reports, or downplay the contents of such reports. And rivalry between intelligence agencies also played its part. Von Roenne's reports were passed through the SS security branch, the Sicherheitsdienst, or SD, whose commander, Generalleutnant der Polizei Ernst Kaltenbrunner, amended von Roenne's estimates of Allied strength to suit what Hitler wanted to hear: that the Allies were nowhere near as strong as they were. When von Roenne began submitting overestimates of Allied strength, Kaltenbrunner chose that time to stop scaling down the reports he passed up. Thus a spurious Allied order of battle, showing ninety divisions instead of the thirty-seven that really existed, was accepted as genuine by German generals from May 1944.

For a range of reasons, some almost bordering on farce, Allied deception plans worked, although, on occasions, planners had serious worries about the security of the overall plan. One such occurred when a parcel containing accurate information on the invasion was found in Chicago's main post office. Another occurred in Britain when answers to crossword clues in the *Daily Telegraph* included words related to the plans, including OVERLORD, NEPTUNE, Mulberry, Omaha and Utah. That the enemy might have had good intelligence on the plans was also suggested by reports from France of movements of major German formations, including the arrival from Hungary of Panzer Lehr Division. Other formations were redeployed with 12th SS Panzer Division Hitlerjugend based near Lisieux, almost too close to the landing beaches for comfort, while 21st Panzer Division, a name that African veterans would recognise, moved from Rennes to Caen, on the right flank of the planned British sector. With Panzer Lehr at Chartres and le Mans, and 91st Airlanding Division, plus 6th Fallschirmjäger Regiment, moving into the Cotentin – they had been intended for Brittany – it looked as if the Germans were aware of Allied plans. However, what was happening was that the German commanders were once again accepting Hitler's intuition. The Führer had decided that Brittany and Normandy were potential invasion areas and, on 4 March, pronounced them as 'particularly threatened'.[26] Even earlier, in October 1943, von Rundstedt had pointed to the sensitivity of both regions, especially around Brest and Cherbourg.[27] Then on 6 May, days after the original planned date for D-Day, von Rundstedt was told that Hitler attached 'particular importance to Normandy' and, especially, to the Cherbourg area, which was to be strengthened as much as possible without committing OKW reserves. Von Rundstedt continued to see the area as being threatened, referring on 24 April to the coast from the Scheldt estuary to Normandy and, perhaps, even to Brest in Brittany as being the focus of Allied intentions. On 15 May he sharpened his own focus: le Havre or Cherbourg could be the target for an invasion force and an 'attempt to form a bridgehead rapidly on the Cotentin peninsula in the first phase would therefore seem very natural.'[28] Two weeks later he was stating that the Allied air offensive, including attacks on the Seine bridges, was pointing to 'enemy designs on Normandy (formation of a bridgehead).'[29]

Hitler still insisted that the entire coast be defended and that the main Allied effort would come in the Pas de Calais. Thus Normandy, especially the Bay of the Seine, to which von Rundstedt pointed in his situation report of 5 June, was not reinforced as it might have been. Furthermore, the Kriegsmarine did not believe that the Allies had sufficient shipping for an assault, according to a report from Admiral Theodor Krancke on 4 June. Krancke also wrote that there had been insufficient air reconnaissance during May to give a clear picture of Allied intentions on either the Atlantic or Mediterranean coasts of France; but the Kriegsmarine noted that 'at the present moment a major invasion cannot be assumed imminent'.[30] Allied air superiority was such that German aircraft had little chance of survival over Britain. In late-May the Kriegsmarine presented an analysis based on tide tables that led them to conclude that it would be mid-August before there was any real danger. And so the Germans clung to their long-held belief that invasion, when it happened, would come in the Pas de Calais; any other operation would be a diversion to draw strength from that region.

The Pas de Calais subterfuge was to continue with a tactical deception on the cusp of D-Day as the invasion fleet crossed the Channel. No. 617 Squadron, the unit that had carried out the raid on the German dams in May 1943, deployed with sixteen Lancasters, supported by six G-H-equipped Stirlings of No. 218 Squadron, to drop a dense cloud of 'Window', metallic strips, now known as 'chaff', to simulate a large fleet making for the area between Boulogne and le Havre and thereby threatening the Pas de Calais. At the same time bombers of No. 100 Group,* which specialised in electronic warfare, carried out support operations. The Group flew thirty-four radio countermeasures (RCM) missions, while another twenty-seven 'Serrate' missions were flown. (The latter was a device that homed on to the radar transmissions of German

* This Group was formed in 1944 to carry out electronic warfare duties and it deployed a mix of aircraft that included Lancasters, Stirlings, B17 Flying Fortresses and Mosquitoes to perform its work.[31]

night-fighters.) In addition, twenty-four ABC-equipped* Lancasters from No. 101 Squadron patrolled the likely approaches of night-fighters with German-speaking radio operators who could counter instructions from German ground controllers as well as using the ABC equipment to jam radio transmissions. Finally, twenty-five Mosquitoes flew intruder patrols; two of these were lost together with one ABC Lancaster.

The most difficult operation was that carried out by Nos. 218 and 617 Squadrons, since it required very high navigational standards. Both squadrons had been practising for some time and operating procedures were honed to perfection by D-Day. The 'Window' strips were cut to differing lengths to simulate different types of radar reflections but also, on this occasion, not only did 'Window' have to simulate ships, the 'fleet' had to cross the Channel at a believable speed. Therefore, the bombers had to fly low and in a racecourse pattern that gradually moved across the Channel at the speed of slow-moving ships. This was an outstanding piece of airmanship.

Thirty-six bombers from four squadrons played another part in tactical deception by dropping explosive devices and dummy paratroopers over areas that were not being invaded, thus simulating a series of airborne landings. Two Stirlings from No. 149 Squadron were lost on this mission.

Nor was this the end of the deception programme. The fictitious formations continued in being, 'Army Group Patton' in south-east England and Fourth Army in Scotland with the latter moving from Scotland in mid-July to join FUSAG. Fourth Army now included 55th and 58th Divisions with 35 Tank Brigade in II Corps and 5th Armoured, 61st and 76th Divisions in VII Corps; it stayed in existence as an 'assault' formation until 7 September when it was redesignated as a reinforcing army for any part of the continent, moving north to York in November.[33]

As the NEPTUNE/OVERLORD plan took its final shape in early-1944, it presented a real problem for the Royal Navy, which was to supply the majority of shipping for the invasion. When Ramsay examined Montgomery's revised plan for a five-division assault on a fifty-mile front, he realised that he needed even more ships. As well as additional landing craft and assault ships, he wanted to increase his bombardment force to six battleships or monitors, twenty-five cruisers and fifty-six destroyers, an increase of one battleship, seven cruisers and fourteen destroyers. This, argued Ramsay, was necessary to eliminate shore batteries.[34] The Royal Navy simply could not meet these requirements and deal with all its other commitments since the service was experiencing a manpower shortage arising from the limits created by the United Kingdom population;

* These transmitters were known as Airborne Cigars; the device was used on all major bombing raids after October 1943.[32]

45,000,000 people against almost twice that figure in greater Germany and more than three times it in both the USA and USSR. Ramsay needed help from the United States Navy but it took a month for his request to receive an answer from King. Fortunately, it allowed for even more ships than Ramsay had requested: the Americans offered three battleships, two cruisers and thirty-four destroyers.[35]

The invasion of Europe was, in Winston Churchill's words, 'the greatest thing [the Allies had] ever attempted' and would have been impossible without Britain's resolution in 1940, which allowed the country to become the storehouse for the assaulting forces. In those final months before invasion forces sailed, parts of Britain became a huge military camp while others became the largest quartermaster's store in history. All invasion forces had to assemble in Britain, train in Britain and be accommodated in Britain. Stores of ammunition, food, fuel and all the material necessary were built up. Around the United Kingdom, shipyards and aircraft factories worked to meet the planners' demands. The shipyards, expanded almost beyond belief and with sub-contracted production in places that would never have been dreamt of in peacetime, were building landing craft, repairing and fitting out ships and building new ships and the pieces of the jigsaw that would make up the Mulberry harbours. Such was the strain that British yards were unable to cope with the requirements of the British forces and American production was vital in meeting those demands.

Some idea of the effort being put into OVERLORD/NEPTUNE can be gleaned from considering the number of personnel gathering in Britain. By D-Day more than 3,500,000 men would be stationed in the country. The British Army alone accounted for almost half while Dominions' forces added another 175,000 men. In the United States Army and Army Air Forces there were a further 1,500,000 personnel while other Allied nations, including Poland, Belgium, The Netherlands, Czechoslovakia and France, added almost 44,000 to the total. By the end of May more than 1,500,000 men arrived from North America, the bulk of them in escorted convoys. Almost a third had crossed unescorted in British passenger ships, or passenger ships under British control; Cunard's two great liners, *Queen Mary* and *Queen Elizabeth*, carried more than 425,000 troops, not one of whom had been lost at sea. These liners had relied on speed to evade U-boats and only when they came within range of German aircraft in mainland Europe were they escorted. Each *Queen* was converted to carry 15,000 men – tantalising targets for any U-boat captain.

Such masses needed accommodation. This was provided by building and requisition. More than half the US accommodation needs was provided for by transferred British establishments or requisitioned accommodation, such as hotels and private homes. Of soldiers alone there were twenty American divisions, fourteen British, three Canadian and one each from the French and Polish forces, as well as smaller formations and units from other nations. About two-fifths of the American requirement in accommodation was newly built, just over a quarter of it by British labour. Nissen huts, Quonset huts shipped across the ocean, and tents were home to thousands. Their headquarters, from Army Group down to battalion and regimental levels, were to be found in a variety of buildings from barracks to rambling mansions.

Across the land were tank parks, artillery parks and vehicle parks, crammed with thousands of Sherman, Churchill, Cromwell and Stuart tanks, among others, and guns of all varieties from anti-tank weapons to heavy cannon while vehicles included tiny Willys jeeps, White half-tracks and terrifyingly large American Dodge and GM trucks that dwarfed their British counterparts and appeared, to many British servicemen, to have been designed specifically for war, due to their purposeful and pugnacious appearance. Across the south of England, from Kent to Cornwall, seemed to be one massive military camp with tentacles spreading northward. US air forces had 133 airfields throughout Britain, of which eighty-three had been transferred from the RAF while the remainder were built for the Americans, fourteen with American labour and the rest with British labour. In some areas the civilian population was moved out and the area reserved for military use but this was something the British public had learned to live with since the outbreak of war. The final months of preparation saw huge quantities of material shipped in from the United States. In the five months before D-Day, more than two million tons of stores and equipment arrived by sea. However, almost a third of all materials for US forces were provided from British sources.

As the months, weeks and days wore on towards D-Day, movement of service personnel became more and more restricted. It was vital that the civilian population knew little, and saw less, of what was happening, since this might assist enemy spies. Nonetheless, civilians knew that something major was in the offing but had no idea of when. As part of the security restrictions, travel between Britain and neutral countries was banned in the spring, including travel to southern Ireland where the Germans maintained a legation. This came into effect on 13 March 1944 although exceptions could be made in special circumstances. Even so, many managed to travel to Ireland, including a staff officer of 30 Brigade in 79th Armoured Division who went home to Dublin a fortnight before D-Day. Michael Morris, later Lord Killanin, found that no one tried to stop him even though he was classed as 'bigoted'* and knew everything about the operation, except that it would be postponed by twenty-four hours.[36]

* Those who were involved in the planning for OVERLORD/NEPTUNE were said to be 'bigots'. The code word was derived from a palindrome of 'To Gib', referring to Gibraltar, with which many of the intelligence officers involved with the planning were associated. This was yet another example of deception in practice.

Security became tighter immediately before embarkation and assembly areas were sealed with only the most essential movement in or out allowed.

Before considering the events of D-Day and the battle for Normandy, let us take a look at the plans for the invasion drawn up by the SHAEF staff, based on the work of COSSAC and the Combined Planners. The refined plans consumed such a volume of paper* that it is possible only to summarise them. OVERLORD could succeed only if NEPTUNE, the naval plan, worked and the object of the latter was summarised as

> to carry out an operation from the United Kingdom to secure a lodgement on the Continent from which further operations can be developed. This lodgement area must contain sufficient port facilities to maintain a force of 26 to 30 divisions and enable this force to be augmented by follow-up formations at the rate of three to five divisions in a month.[38]

Achieving this aim committed Allied navies to a project of a scale and nature that they had never before undertaken. There was experience, of course, of amphibious landings – TORCH, HUSKY, AVALANCHE and SHINGLE, to say nothing of the ill-fated JUBILEE. But, other than JUBILEE, all these had been in the Mediterranean with its lack of tides; operating in the Channel, exposed to the Atlantic, posed many more problems. And yet all were overcome by the planners who, in Correlli Barnett's words, achieved something remarkable.

> In scope and thoroughness, in the complexity and scale of the problems solved, they eclipse the renowned performances of the German General Staff from 1866 onwards. They stand to this day as a never surpassed masterpiece of planning and staff work.[39]

The NEPTUNE fleet numbered some 4,000 vessels for the D-Day landings alone; escort, bombardment, minesweeping and other craft would add almost another 3,000 vessels to the list.** Thereafter the navies were to bring in follow-up formations and provide maintenance for the expeditionary force. Of the 4,000 landing ships, landing craft and barges, about half would cross the Channel under their own steam while the remainder would be towed or carried by, and launched from, larger ships.

* Ramsay's plan ran to about 700 foolscap pages, all closely typed. [37]
** The Official History notes that the planned number of ships was 6,939 of which 1,213 were naval combatant vessels, 4,126 were landing ships and craft, 736 were ancillary ships and 864 were merchant ships.[40]

These would be escorted by 221 destroyers, frigates, sloops, corvettes, trawlers and patrol craft while 287 minesweepers would clear a path for the force; another 495 light craft would deploy on a range of essential tasks. Of the escort ships assigned to NEPTUNE, fifty-eight would carry out anti-submarine patrols on the western approaches to the Channel against possible incursions by U-boats. Then there were depot ships, anti-aircraft ships, tugs and other salvage vessels, hospital ships, tankers and store ships of many types. And fifty-nine blockships were to be sunk to create an artificial area of sheltered water off the coast.

In all there would be five naval assault forces, one for each assault area or 'beach'. Each force included transports and landing craft plus bombardment ships, escorts and other vessels. Such numbers made great demands on harbour space with about 750 additional berthing spaces being provided in the Solent and most ports from Felixstowe on the east coast round to Milford Haven on the west being used. Even with that space, the bombardment forces were sent to the Clyde and Belfast Lough, which meant that they would have to sail much earlier than the remainder of the armada. Likewise, the blockships were based at Oban in Scotland and many anti-submarine ships came from the Londonderry Escort Force, based on Lough Foyle in Northern Ireland.

Under cover of Allied fighter aircraft the assault forces were to sail in convoy from assembly points around the coast to a rendezvous point some fifteen miles off the Isle of Wight, known officially as Area Z but soon dubbed 'Piccadilly Circus'. From there they would sail southwards for France, preceded by five fleets of minesweepers, to sweep, and mark with buoys, ten channels, known as the Spout, to where the mother ships would lower their assault craft. From the lowering areas the minesweepers were to search and mark clear anchorages for bombardment ships, and assault ships, before moving on to widen the channels in the Spout, extend the swept waters inshore and create new channels along the coast. Nor would that end their work as these channels had to be kept clear at all times. Small wonder that the commander of the American Western Task Force, Rear Admiral D P Kirk, described the minesweepers as 'the keystone of the arch in this operation'.[41] Meanwhile, the bombardment ships would be hammering their first targets, twenty coast defence batteries that presented particular danger to the assault forces; these included ten that had already received the unwelcome attention of RAF heavy bombers.

The task of the naval forces was to deliver the assaulting troops to the beaches and although their work did not end there it is at this point that NEPTUNE and OVERLORD interlock and we move on to consider the latter part of the operation. Across five landing areas, British, Canadian and American soldiers would come ashore under cover of a heavy bombardment as

> every available weapon would join in a crescendo of fire to plaster the beaches with bombs, shells and rockets so that the defenders could no longer serve their weapons and must seek shelter or be killed.[42]

From west to east the assaulting forces were provided by General Omar Bradley's First US Army in the form of 4th and 1st Infantry Divisions* and General Sir Miles Dempsey's Second British Army, with 50th (Northumbrian), 3rd Canadian and 3rd British Divisions. Each army employed two corps HQs for the operation: VII and V US Corps and XXX and I British Corps. The landing areas have achieved the status of legend and are marked, under their 1944 codenames, on modern maps of Normandy: from west to east, Utah, Omaha, Gold, Juno and Sword. On the British and Canadian beaches – Gold, Juno and Sword – attacking infantry would be supported by armour from 8, 2 Canadian and 27 Armoured Brigades respectively, while 'Funnies' of 79th Armoured Division would also deploy across the sector. In both sectors special forces – Rangers on the American front and Royal Marine and Army Commandos on the British – had roles to play.

The flanks of 21 Army Group were to be secured by airborne forces; elements of 82nd and 101st US and 6th British Airborne Divisions dropped during the hours of darkness. To the airborne soldiers, therefore, fell the distinction of being the first Allied soldiers in France on D-Day. They would be joined on the evening of D-Day by the remainder of their divisions. This element of the assault had two codenames: the drop on the night of 5–6 June was Operation TONGA; that which followed on the evening of the 6th was MALLARD. Montgomery insisted on using airborne troops to secure the flanks of the invasion while Bradley gained approval to deploy two US airborne divisions on the right flank.[43]

Having broken out of the beaches and established the bridgehead, 21 Army Group had two distinct tasks, one assigned to the Americans, the second to the British and Canadians. In his first definition of the roles of the two invading armies, Montgomery foresaw the Americans clearing the Cotentin peninsula to

> capture the port of Cherbourg. They will subsequently develop their operations to the south and west. The British [and Canadian] Army will operate to the south to prevent any interference with the

* The American assaulting forces were Regimental Combat Teams (RCTs), equivalent to British brigade groups and formed from infantry regiments of three battalions and an armoured battalion, with artillery and other support as necessary. On Omaha Beach there were two RCTs, 16 RCT of 1st Division and 116 RCT of 29th Division while on Utah the assault force was 8 RCT of 4th Division, which was followed by the rest of the division with elements of 90th Division in support.

> American Army from the east. It is hoped eventually to get a firm lodgement from Caen to Nantes with the British Army being built up through the [Cotentin] peninsula and the American Army through Brittany.[44]

Thus it was that Montgomery intended First (US) Army to strike out from its bridgehead to take Cherbourg and then push south and west into Brittany while Second (British) Army would push south and south-east from the eastern flank. Both armies would realign as an army group for the thrust to the east to take the Seine crossings, after which further regrouping would be necessary before the offensive continued towards Germany.

It would take some time before SHAEF could reshape completely the plans for NEPTUNE/OVERLORD and obtain the Combined Chiefs' approval. Eisenhower had gone to Washington in early January on leave and to meet the US Chiefs and had argued for a revised plan, using much the same logic as Montgomery. The American Chiefs continued to support Morgan's plan but were unwilling to veto Eisenhower's proposals for change, since to do so would equate to a vote of no confidence in the Supreme Commander. By contrast the British Chiefs supported the proposed revised plan and, on 1 February 1944, the Combined Chiefs approved the revision of the COSSAC plan, as the NEPTUNE Initial Joint Plan.[45] As planning progressed, the invasion was set for the end of May, although Eisenhower was given discretion to set the final date on the basis of weather forecasts.

NOTES

1 Latimer, *Deception in War*, p. 205.
2 Liddell Hart, *The Rommel Papers*, p. 453; Fraser, *Knight's Cross*, p. 462.
3 Latimer, op cit, p. 202.
4 Probert, *Bomber Harris*, p. 291.
5 Hastings, *Bomber Command*, p. 275.
6 Probert, op cit, p. 290.
7 Ibid, p. 292.
8 Middlebrook & Everett, *The Bomber Command War Diaries*, p. 492.
9 Ibid, p. 495.
10 Ibid, pp. 496–7.
11 Ibid, pp. 498 & 505–6.
12 NA, AIR37/719, pp. 3–4.
13 Latimer, op cit, p. 221.
14 Ibid, pp. 210–11.
15 NA, WO199/1325 & 1326.
16 Doherty, *Only The Enemy in Front*, pp. 179–80.
17 NA, WO199/1325 &1326; Joslen, *Orders of Battle*, p. 103.
18 NA, WO219/2221.
19 Latimer, op cit, p. 213.

20 NA, WO201/1812.
21 Latimer, op cit, p. 216; Cruickshank, *Deception in World War II*, p. 197.
22 Breuer, *Operation Dragoon*, p. 60.
23 Montgomery, *Memoirs*, p. 220.
24 Ellis, *Victory in the West*, p. 80.
25 Latimer, op cit, p. 220.
26 Ellis, op cit, p. 128.
27 Ibid.
28 Ibid, p. 129.
29 Ibid.
30 Quoted in Barnett, *Engage the Enemy More Closely*, p. 812.
31 Harvey, *Allied Bomber War*, p. 74.
32 Ibid.
33 NA, WO199/1325 & 1326.
34 Barnett, op cit, p. 770.
35 Ibid, pp. 771–2.
36 Lord Killanin, interview with Miles Dungan.
37 Neillands, *The Battle of Normandy 1944*, p. 69.
38 Quoted in Barnett, op cit, p. 781.
39 Ibid, p. 780.
40 Ellis, op cit, App II, p. 507.
41 Ibid, pp. 68–9.
42 Ibid, p. 71.
43 D'Este, *Decision in Normandy*, p. 65.
44 NA, CAB44/242.
45 D'Este, op cit, p. 68.

CHAPTER VI
From exercises to Normandy

Cry havoc and let slip the dogs of war

While Eisenhower had been in Washington, Montgomery and the planning team had moved into overdrive to revise the plans and provide the greatest chance of success. One problem caused much soul-searching: Operation ANVIL. Montgomery wanted this cancelled or downgraded to a threat, using as little as one division, arguing that ANVIL would take precious landing craft from OVERLORD and weaken the Allies in Italy at a crucial time.[1] By late-February, Montgomery was urging cancellation and Eisenhower was beginning to accept his argument.[2] Finally, Eisenhower decided that ANVIL would be postponed so as not to compromise the allocation of landing craft to OVERLORD. The operation eventually took place in August as DRAGOON.

In his *Memoirs* Montgomery suggests that his team revised the OVERLORD plan, which was approved by Eisenhower on 21 January.[3] Once again this claim is not entirely true. Soon after arriving in London, Montgomery set up Headquarters 21 Army Group in St Paul's School in Hammersmith, where he had once been a pupil. He and Bedell Smith met the COSSAC staff on the 3rd for a detailed briefing on OVERLORD, which Montgomery described as unsound. With Bedell Smith remaining as Eisenhower's Chief of Staff Morgan was now sidelined and his original COSSAC staff found new faces arriving as planning entered its final stage. At 21 Army Group HQ, the previous staff of Home Forces – the foundation of the Group – found the same happening, with Montgomery transplanting much of his Eighth Army team.

After that first meeting Montgomery had many further discussions with planners and naval and air commanders to revise the plan. His opinions were aired at the first Supreme Commander's conference at Norfolk House on 21 January when he urged a stronger assault, to quickly obtain dominance in Normandy, as well as the early capture of a port so that the armies did not have to rely entirely on Mulberry harbours. This demanded including the Cotentin's eastern shore in the landing area to allow the seizure of Cherbourg. In addition, he wanted a wider beachhead to reduce congestion during the build-up and allow more manoeuvre room. (The normally cautious Montgomery also spoke of deep thrusts by armoured formations to take ground that would impede the flow of German reinforcements.) He now proposed a five-division seaborne assault, supported by one airborne division, with two armies, each deploying two corps. On the right flank would be the Americans, simply because the dispositions of American forces in Britain made it simpler to insert them on that flank. The point at which First (US) and Second (British) Armies met was to be near Bayeux.

These modifications did not endear themselves to naval and air commanders, since the former realised that many more landing craft would be needed, as well as escort ships, and the latter were concerned that forward airstrips could not be established in sufficient numbers unless Caen and the surrounding area was captured. Nonetheless, both agreed to the revisions, in spite of these reservations, while the Americans were pleased that the proposals gave US forces a greater role. Although ANVIL remained a problem between Montgomery and Eisenhower, the latter decided to endorse Montgomery's plan to the Combined Chiefs with the recommendation that D-Day be postponed for a month to build up resources for five divisions.

Approval for the revised plan, and date, was given but SHAEF staff had identified serious flaws in Montgomery's plan. Most seriously, there was no concentration of force, with the five divisions spread over some fifty miles. Needless to say, Montgomery argued that there was concentration but it is difficult to see where this could be found. Although Eisenhower had prepared a signal seeking Combined Chiefs' approval for Montgomery's revised plan, the SHAEF Chief of Staff delayed its transmission until after further discussions. At the same time a compromise plan for a four-division assault in the Caen sector only was drafted. The planners considered that Montgomery's wide front would jeopardise operations in the Caen sector but that their compromise would produce the concentration necessary to defeat the enemy in that area in a period of between a week and ten days.[4]

How did the plans differ? The significant difference is that the planners' revision of the Montgomery model concentrated on seizing Caen, defeating German reserves and taking ground south and south-east of the city on which airstrips might be built *before* moving on the Cotentin to take Cherbourg. By contrast Montgomery planned to do it all at the same time. Was he being too ambitious? He considered the early capture of Cherbourg essential for the fastest possible build-up after the landings while operations around Caen were intended to anchor his left flank and take ground for airstrips, as well as for future operations on that flank.

While the planners accepted that Montgomery's proposal would mean the earlier capture of Cherbourg, they were concerned still that British forces might be spread too thinly and susceptible to enemy counter-attack and defeat. In such circumstances, they reasoned, Cherbourg would be of little value, especially as the Cotentin is not suited to constructing airstrips. They also doubted if Cherbourg could handle as many divisions as was being suggested.

Bedell Smith made the final decision without waiting for discussion. After receiving the planners' new proposals and meeting with Montgomery he ordered that Eisenhower's signal be sent to Washington on the night of the 23rd. Although Bedell Smith met Eisenhower that night, there is no evidence that he discussed the matter with him, nor does the record of the following day's conference refer to any compromise plan. What Bedell Smith's action ensured was that Montgomery's plan was the one sent to Washington for approval.[5] As a result, Montgomery could claim that his was the plan used, even though that was still not completely true; it was Bradley who ensured the addition of two airborne divisions to the one that Montgomery envisaged and two American airborne divisions were dropped on the right flank. It is worth remembering the planners' doubts about the Montgomery option, especially when considering the events surrounding the taking of Caen for it was there that they felt that Montgomery's plan was flawed.

With the plan decided there began the final preparations for NEPTUNE/OVERLORD, including the build-up of personnel, supplies and equipment already outlined as well as fine-tuning the plan and its expansion down to all levels necessary. Each assaulting army had to produce its plan, from which the corps headquarters then worked to generate theirs. From corps, detailed planning moved down to divisional level with each D-Day division creating a plan. Within divisions, plans were worked up at brigade level – in British and Canadian forces – and regimental level – in US forces – and then the planning moved down to battalion level. Eventually battalion commanders would brief company commanders who, in turn, would inform platoon commanders of their roles in the assault.

Montgomery's 21 Army Group would control both assaulting armies – First (US) and Second (British) – with each army controlling two corps which, in turn, would command the assault divisions. The British assault divisions were, from right to left flank, 50th (Northumbrian), landing on Gold Beach, 3rd (Canadian), Juno Beach, and 3rd (British), Sword Beach. Commanding Second Army would be Lieutenant-General Sir Miles 'Bimbo' Dempsey, a 'Monty man' who had studied under his commander at the Staff College at Camberley and who had his chief's trust. Dempsey was an intelligent man with a sharp brain, excellent, almost photographic, memory and a talent in mapreading that, to this author's knowledge, was matched only by Gerald Templer; both could absorb the detail of a map and appreciate ground before seeing it. Such a talent is rare; it is also a blessing for a general and would stand Dempsey in good stead in Normandy. Dempsey also shared a trait with Montgomery: a determination not to waste soldiers' lives.

For his corps commanders, Montgomery either chose men he knew and trusted, or accepted War Office appointments on trust, such as John Crocker, a man of little humour but with considerable armoured experience, who commanded I Corps, an appointment Montgomery happily accepted. At the helm of XII Corps was another War Office appointee, Neil Ritchie, sacked as GOC-in-C Eighth Army in 1942 but, since he was a favourite of Brooke, he was rehabilitated with this command. Montgomery did not demur.* That leaves Montgomery's two direct appointees. Paradoxically, both were to be removed by him. The first was Sir Richard O'Connor, who had secured Britain's first victory in North Africa but had subsequently been captured. After escaping from an Italian prisoner-of-war camp, O'Connor came home to be given command of VIII Corps for the invasion. His later removal by Montgomery, often stated to be because he had lost his flair due to the years spent in a PoW camp, occurred because he refused to submit an adverse report on an American armoured divisional commander who was, temporarily, under his command. O'Connor was independently minded with a strong streak of Irish stubbornness that would not allow him to give in to Montgomery, even though they had long been friends.[6] The final corps commander, Gerard Bucknall, Montgomery chose against Brooke's advice. The latter considered Bucknall unsuitable for corps command but Montgomery disagreed. Events proved Brooke to have been correct; Montgomery replaced Bucknall with Brian Horrocks in August.

Training for the invasion was underway with mock assaults taking place around Britain. One British division – 3rd – carried out assault training in Scotland to add to the ruse that Fourth Army was preparing for operations in Norway. Many training exercises were carried out at various levels, from battalion to corps. Guards Armoured Division participated in a series of exercises that began with Exercise SNOW in January, followed by Northern Command's Exercise EAGLE in February, OPTION in April and DRAKE in May. The Guardsmen also learned about some of the opposition they would meet, including 17th SS Grenadier Division Goetz von Berliehnigen, and their weaponry, including the *Panzerfaust* (previously *Faustpatrone*), which fired a 5.5lb projectile in its Mark I version or 7lb in

* The perceived wisdom is that Ritchie was a misappointment for Eighth Army, and that the blame for his failure lay with Auchinleck, whereas Auchinleck appointed him as a stopgap but an announcement that Ritchie was the new army commander was made to the House of Commons and Auchinleck was then stuck with him. He proved a competent commander in Normandy.

its Mark II version, and the *Panzerschrecht* (previously *Panzerbuchse*), an 88mm rocket launcher that fired a 7lb projectile and emitted a sixteen-foot jet of flame that required protective clothing for the user. Estimates of the armour-penetrating qualities of both weapons varied; for the former it was noted the German estimate was 200mm against a British estimate of 165mm while, for the latter, the figures were 180mm and 110mm respectively.[7]

The tankmen of 8 Armoured Brigade Group took part in Exercises SMASH I, II, III and IV, GRAB and FABIUS in April and May. They also attended a demonstration by rocket-firing Typhoons at Corfe Castle on 12 April.[8] GRAB was a divisional exercise, held at Burghead in Scotland, to train the Royal Navy, 8 and 9 Armoured Brigades and No. 6 Beach Group in carrying out an assault landing, the brigade groups in capturing and consolidating their portion of the divisional beachhead, and the Beach Group in their responsibilities within the beach maintenance area.[9] This also gave units the opportunity to land from LCTs; 4th/7th Royal Dragoon Guards noted that they carried out such a landing at Tarbet in January as part of GRAB. In April 49th (West Riding) Division held its Exercise BUMP, in which B Squadron 1st Northamptonshire Yeomanry took part while the Northamptons then participated in 7th Armoured Division's Exercise KELLY'S EYE II before winning 33 Armoured Brigade's waterproofing competition. The units that were to operate the 'Funnies' trained for their specialist roles: Westminster Dragoons carried out Exercise ELK II on 27 January in which A Squadron, with 16 Assault Squadron Royal Engineers and infantry, practised a night assault on a defended locality; Generals Brooke and Eisenhower attended. Exercise SPARKS I, the regiment's first in the flail role, was conducted on 15 February. Another specialist unit was 22nd Dragoons, A Squadron of which took part in the regiment's first exercise in its new role – MOON – in January. This war-raised unit* also took time to have a regimental group photograph taken in February. An infantry battalion converted to armour became 'the first flame-throwing tank regiment in the British Army' on 30 April when 141st Regiment RAC (141 RAC), formerly 7th Buffs, became operational with its full complement of Crocodiles.[11] Another infantry battalion converted to the armoured role was 2nd Irish Guards, which began the year training in Scotland before moving to Yorkshire. The Micks were concerned that the battalion was to lose some fifty drivers and that officers' servants were to be cut down, again, from eight to five per squadron. However, there was some good news with the issue of fresh oranges to the battalion on 26 January; each soldier received a pound of the fruit, 'the first sight or taste of them that we have had since 1939'. The

* The regiment was formed on 30 December 1940 with a cadre of men from 4th/7th Royal Dragoon Guards and 5th Royal Inniskilling Dragoon Guards.[10]

battalion's war diarist demonstrated his sense of humour two days later when he recorded the 'sad news that Major Madden has blown his new tank coat to ribbons, by putting first a thunderflash and then a lighted pipe into his pocket'. In February the Micks participated in Exercise RHINO, followed by a divisional exercise – SNOW – from which they went into Exercise EAGLE, in which British forces were represented by VIII Corps with 4 and 8 Army Groups, Royal Artillery (AGRAs) while the Germans were represented by 49th Division, 9th Armoured Division and 2 AGRA. During this exercise there was a panic about Norwegian paratroopers, all of whom were rounded up later at Divisional HQ. One Norwegian commented that he would 'much rather be dropped over Oslo than try to find his way around this damned Division, chased by Drill Sergeants and Security Officers'.[12]

Gunners and infantry were also preparing for D-Day through the same exercises. Among the Gunner regiments that would fire on the run-in to Sword Beach was 7th Field, which took part in landing exercises in February and then in shooting from LCTs in March; regimental concentrations were fired for AMBLE, a divisional artillery exercise. In May the regiment played its part in the major pre-invasion Exercise FABIUS and was also inspected by both Eisenhower, who commented that he was impressed by them, and King George VI.[13] Exercises BURGHER, PRECIPITATION, and FIZZLE all included 1st Royal Norfolk Regiment, the last of these being a combined services exercise 'to practise synchronisation of all three services in a combined operation'. The battalion was involved in a series of exercises during February and March. In April it took part with Staffordshire Yeomanry in Exercise YEOBOY before going on to FABIUS in May.[14] A similar story is told by the war diary of 7th Norfolks which included Exercises FORD, UPSTREAM and LINNET in its routine in January and February; the battalion also took part in Exercises WAPAS III and FIDO IV in March. WAPAS III was based on two panzer divisions moving from the general direction of Cambridge and 'likely to gain contact with forward brigades of 59 Div tonight [5 March]'. Exercises HONEY, DIVE III and HICKUP followed in April; Lieutenant-Colonel Ian Freeland took over command on 22 April.[15] For 2nd King's Shropshire Light Infantry there were three days on board SS *Empire Battleaxe* in January during which the battalion practised the drill for landing from an LSI in LCAs while HQ Support and Z Companies had a lecture on handling prisoners on 21 April.[16] Both 2nd KSLI and 2nd Warwicks' war diaries note that the battalions took part in Exercises CROWN and ANCHOR in February and that all soldiers received inoculations against typhus.[17] This experience was also recorded by the war diarist of 1st Queen's Own Rifles of Canada.[18]

Every effort was made to make training as realistic as possible and exercises were conducted with live ammunition. Inevitably this led to casualties, some of them fatal. On 3 February soldiers of 7th Duke of Wellington's Regiment were attending a Mines Course at Yarmouth racecourse. During the afternoon, while watching the detonation of a British Mark V anti-tank mine, Private Robert Baxter was killed by the blast. Private Baxter, aged twenty, had joined the battalion a year before and was 'well respected by all ranks'. He was the runner for Support Company and a native of Coleraine in County Londonderry,[19] where he was subsequently buried.* Robert Baxter was one of many who lost their lives during the preparation for OVERLORD.

During the training period Irish and Welsh units found time to celebrate their national saints' days in March. St David's Day was marked in some style by 1/5th Welch Regiment while, on St Patrick's Day, 2nd Irish Guards had Mass at Ampleforth Abbey, which was attended by the commanding officer and some 300 guardsmen. This was followed by a presentation of shamrock and Major-General Adair, commanding Guards Armoured Division, was entertained to lunch. Sadly, the Micks' Catholic padre, Father Curran, later died in his sleep of heart failure and was succeeded by Father Stonor who accompanied the battalion to France.[21]

The training regime was intended to 'render the troops proficient in the handling of many novel weapons . . . but also to ensure that the individual soldier should become to some extent battle-hardened in the course of his training rather than the hardening process should be deferred until he came into actual contact with the enemy as had been the practice in earlier wars'.

> Credit for the many advances in training methods adopted in this country and which produced such satisfactory results belongs in the main to ideas advanced by Lieut-General The Hon. H. R. L. O. Alexander; by General Sir Alan Brooke; by General Sir Bernard Paget; by Major General J. E. Utterson-Kelso and others. For the most part it fell to Sir Bernard Paget to give effect to the various ideas. This he did during his term as Commander-in-Chief, Home Forces. As he has stated 'the need for intensive training was realised and applied by Field Marshal Lord Alanbrooke (as he now is) when he became Commander-in-Chief, Home Forces in 1940. It was developed by me.'[22]

Not all training could be described as realistic. Many units trained at Thetford battle area in Norfolk but East Anglia was no substitute for Normandy's bocage. In spite of all the painstaking preparation, minute analysis of photographic reconnaissance pictures, and information from

* Pte Baxter is buried in Grave No. 282 in St John's Church of Ireland graveyard, Killowen.[20]

individuals who had holidayed in the area, insufficient account was taken of this unique feature of the Norman countryside. For centuries local farmers had enclosed their small fields by building earth banks and hedgerows while stock was moved on narrow tracks. Over time the hedge roots had become part of the banks, creating what was almost a new substance, a reinforced earth barrier that was probably the most frustrating tank obstacle ever met by the Allies. Between the fields the tracks had been worn down by rain and the passage of many hooves and wheels over hundreds of years so that the tracks were lower than the fields, thereby increasing the height of hedges and banks.

> Large areas . . . are 'bocage' – pasture land divided by hedges, banks and ditches into many small fields and meadows. In some places the roads are sunken and lined by steep banks. Movement by vehicles may therefore be difficult off the roads.[23]

This intelligence report understated the problem. The word *bocage* means, literally, copse or thicket and the area was once entirely thus until the first farmers, probably Celts, claimed it from the wild. Later farmers built very solid houses for defence that still made formidable obstacles in 1944. But the bocage's origins were of little interest to those who fought there. They were more concerned that the area was murderous for tanks; every bank and hedgerow provided an ideal ambush spot for anti-tank gunners or infantrymen carrying the German answers to the bazooka and PIAT, the *Panzerfaust* and *Panzerschreck*. Measured against that reality, armoured warfare training at Thetford was no preparation for Normandy. Matters were no better for the infantry, who would find the countryside equally difficult and would learn to curse every bank, hedgerow and farmhouse of the area.

Training and planning was refined until every individual understood his part in the operation. There were exercises in which assaulting troops went ashore from landing craft against beaches chosen to represent as closely as possible those they would be storming. All that was missing in many cases was the thunder of the naval bombardment. One such exercise resulted in tragedy when German fast patrol boats attacked US forces carrying out a full-scale rehearsal for the Utah landing. That rehearsal was held at Slapton Sands in Devon, not far from Dartmouth, and the attack resulted in the loss of more than 700 men when two LSTs were sunk.[24] US losses on Utah were lower than in the rehearsal.

Similar exercises were held for each assaulting division until the time came for troops to move into concentration areas in their first move towards the embarkation ports. In those areas vehicles were waterproofed, specialised equipment collected and the administrative tails of formations left behind. Some armoured units beefed up the protection of their tanks. This usually consisted of adding additional armour plating. East Riding Yeomanry's tanks were sent to Glasgow in batches to have extra armour panels welded on by shipyard staff. But it did not end there. In the same regiment

> a great deal of ingenuity [was] shown to provide additional protection around the turrets. Sergeant Lyon of A Squadron was once asked by the Brigadier . . . what he was busy with, so the Sergeant demonstrated that with a few metal bars welded to the turret, he could hang another ten track plates around it. It says much for the Brigadier's attitude that Sergeant Lyon's modification was to be applied throughout the Brigade and a Brigade order to this effect was issued the following morning, with the inventor's name quoted too.[25]

Such recognition was a positive contribution to morale and helped weld East Riding Yeomanry and its fellows of 27 Armoured Brigade* into a determined fighting formation. A similar strengthening of armour was taking place in 8 Armoured Brigade; on 3 April the war diary notes 'Shermans now held by Brigade being fitted with additional armour 'Quick-fix' at rate of 8 per day by Brigade Workshops.'[27]

From the concentration areas, the attacking elements moved again, this time into forward areas, dubbed 'sausages' from the markings designating them on maps.[28] This was the penultimate move: from the 'sausages' the troops would embark for France. In the 'sausages', which were camouflaged to prevent detection from aerial reconnaissance, troops would receive final briefings and their task would become completely clear. Operational maps were issued in craft loads, sealed with orders that packages could be opened only after sailing.

> Each officer had fourteen and each section leader eleven. Each officer also had two folders of aerial photographs showing a 'wave-top view' of the coast, the Assembly area, the immediate area of the beachhead, the anti-tank ditch and the town of Caen.[29]

Briefing was carried out using bogus maps that were correct in every detail save that code names had been substituted for the real ones; Caen became 'Poland' while maps also included 'Japan', 'Mexico', 'Dublin' and 'Belfast'.[30] On 18 May Westminster Dragoons were supplied with aerial photographs of the coastal area to be attacked together with 'maps less place names'.[31]

* For the invasion, 27 Armoured Brigade included 13th/18th Hussars and the Staffordshire Yeomanry as well as East Riding Yeomanry and it was commanded by Brigadier G E Prior-Palmer who remained in command until the brigade was disbanded in France on 30 July 1944.[26]

Since this meant that every man had been let into the secret of D-Day, the 'sausages' were cut off by barbed-wire cordons and civilian traffic into coastal areas was banned. Checkpoints were strung across the countryside and hundreds of security personnel deployed to prevent any leaks that might compromise NEPTUNE/OVERLORD. This was the greatest security operation ever mounted in Britain. It was also probably the most successful. The integrity of NEPTUNE/OVERLORD was not compromised.

While most civilians appreciated the need for the disruption of their lives, some regarded the presence of soldiers as an inconvenience. On 7 May 2nd Irish Guards, based at Hove on the south coast, received a complaint from the mayor of Brighton that 'our tanks were spoiling his promenade'. The war diary notes that he got the answer 'he deserved'.[32]

During this time, also, personnel received anti-gas protection, including a new suit of battledress

> as stiff as planks and [with] a white residue . . . We were informed that they had been soaked in a solution to prevent lice . . . I read after the war that they expected the Germans to use a liquid gas . . . Our battledress was soaked in a solution to counteract this gas. I must admit that I believed the story about the lice.[33]

That battledress was not the sole gas countermeasure. A Royal Navy officer recalled that

> the Allies were expecting gas at Normandy because I was equipped with special socks and a tube of something or other to cover all my shoes with . . . the holes where the laces go, and a cape, and of course you had your gas mask.[34]

While the assaulting troops carried out their final rehearsals and moved to embarkation areas, Montgomery was finalising his plans. Already, on 7 and 8 April, he had held a two-day exercise for all general officers of the field armies during which senior commanders were acquainted with the general plan as it affected naval, land and air forces and possible problems were discussed. Both Eisenhower and Churchill put in appearances at this exercise, thus underlining its importance. Then, on 15 May, SHAEF convened a conference at which the final plan was presented. This was held in St Paul's School, although Montgomery had now moved 21 Army Group's headquarters to Southwick House near Portsmouth, and was attended by King George VI, Churchill, Eisenhower and Field Marshal Jan Smuts of South Africa. In his *Memoirs*, Montgomery noted that Eisenhower was 'quite excellent' and that the King made a short impromptu speech that was 'exactly right' while both Churchill and Smuts also spoke. 'Altogether this was a very good day.'[35]

Needless to say, Montgomery also spoke, presenting the plan for the invasion and subsequent battle. He made this presentation 'with rare skill . . . as he tramped about like a giant through Lilliputian France'.[36] That unlikely reference to Montgomery as 'a giant' was prompted by his method of presentation: a relief map of Normandy, as wide as a city street, covered the floor of a large room and over this Monty strode.[37] During his presentation Montgomery outlined the progress that he hoped to make after the landings. This he did by means of three phase lines, each indicating a possible extent of advance on specific dates. Before looking at those phase lines, and the subsequent controversy surrounding them, let us consider Montgomery's broad plan.

Each assaulting army was to field four divisions – one airborne and three seaborne in Second (British) Army and two airborne and two seaborne in First (US) Army – with the airborne securing the flanks. Having obtained a lodgement both armies would 'knit' their own beaches together and then make contact with each other to create a single front. That achieved, First Army was to cut off the base of the Cotentin to isolate Cherbourg prior to seizing that port while Second Army was to seize Caen and expand onto the flat lands beyond, thereby providing space for airfields. The Americans would then 'pivot on the British position' ready for an advance towards Paris in a movement that would isolate Brittany and its ports and Third Army, under Patton, would take the field to liberate Brittany.

Once the American pivot was complete, the Allied line would be facing eastwards on a front almost 150 miles long, its left flank on the British beaches and the right on the Loire. It was believed that the enemy would defend along the Seine, the Allies' next objective. As the Americans fought for the Cotentin and Brittany, British and Canadians would draw German reserves onto their front in the east of the bridgehead. Thus, while British and Canadians held the enemy at Caen, the Americans would begin the sweep towards Paris. By this stage, of course, Patton's Third Army and First Canadian Army would have arrived and 12 US Army Group would be activated under Bradley's command, with 21 becoming a British/ Canadian formation, although Montgomery would still exercise overall command of Allied ground forces.

> When reckoned in terms of national pride, this British decoy mission became a sacrificial one, for while we tramped around the outside flank, the British were to sit in place and pin down Germans. Yet strategically it fitted into a logical division of labours, for it was towards Caen that the enemy reserves would race once the alarm was sounded.[38]

The Germans had every reason to defend Caen. Not only was the city a nodal transport point, but from there to the Seine was not even fifty miles while the ground beyond the city was relatively flat, its gentle undulations offering little obstacle to armoured forces. Therefore, Caen was the ideal jumping-off point for an armoured advance to the Seine from where it was but seventy miles to Paris and a further 180 to the Siegfried Line and the Reich itself. To the Germans an attempt to take Caen as soon as possible was logical and made the city vital in defending the routes to the Reich. Thus the Germans would do exactly what the Allies wanted: throw their reserves against Montgomery while Bradley advanced from the right against lighter opposition.

This then was the plan, clearly expounded by Montgomery at St Paul's School. Monty had a gift for simplifying complex issues and certainly did so on this occasion. Perhaps it was because he was making the entire operation sound so straightforward that he became increasingly optimistic and even talked of his armour breaking clear on D-Day to 'knock about a bit' down at Falaise. This was over thirty miles from the beaches. In reality, it took Montgomery sixty-eight days to get there. The phase lines also simplified the operational plan for the campaign. In the years since they have given ammunition to Montgomery's many critics who say that he failed to achieve what he set out to do. But phase lines are only tools used by commanders to illustrate how they will conduct operations and the possible dates by which they will complete their various phases. As Ronald Lewin, a Montgomery biographer who served under him, wrote:

> such maps . . . are essentially professional tools which, if misused, can do damage. They have two sound purposes. Every commander planning an operation must have a rough idea, at the least, of where – taking into account all possible mischances – he may get to as his attack progresses. Phase maps are thus useful for a commander (with all the possible mischances in his mind) as a diagrammatic representation of his hopes. But they can obviously mislead those unaware of the many possibilities of things not going to plan which are daily present in the commander's head. . . . A phase line map in fact represents a rational estimation of a possibility, rather than the committal of a cast-iron guarantee. As such it is of great value for those responsible for the difficult task of logistical forecasting.[39]

There have been those who have interpreted the phase lines as cast-iron guarantees, while Montgomery's own air of confidence has also helped his critics. A man who planned set-piece battles, as Montgomery was reputed to do, left himself open to such criticism, whether justified or not. On the other hand, Bradley did not favour the use of phase lines, since such was not contemporary US military doctrine, and so Montgomery removed

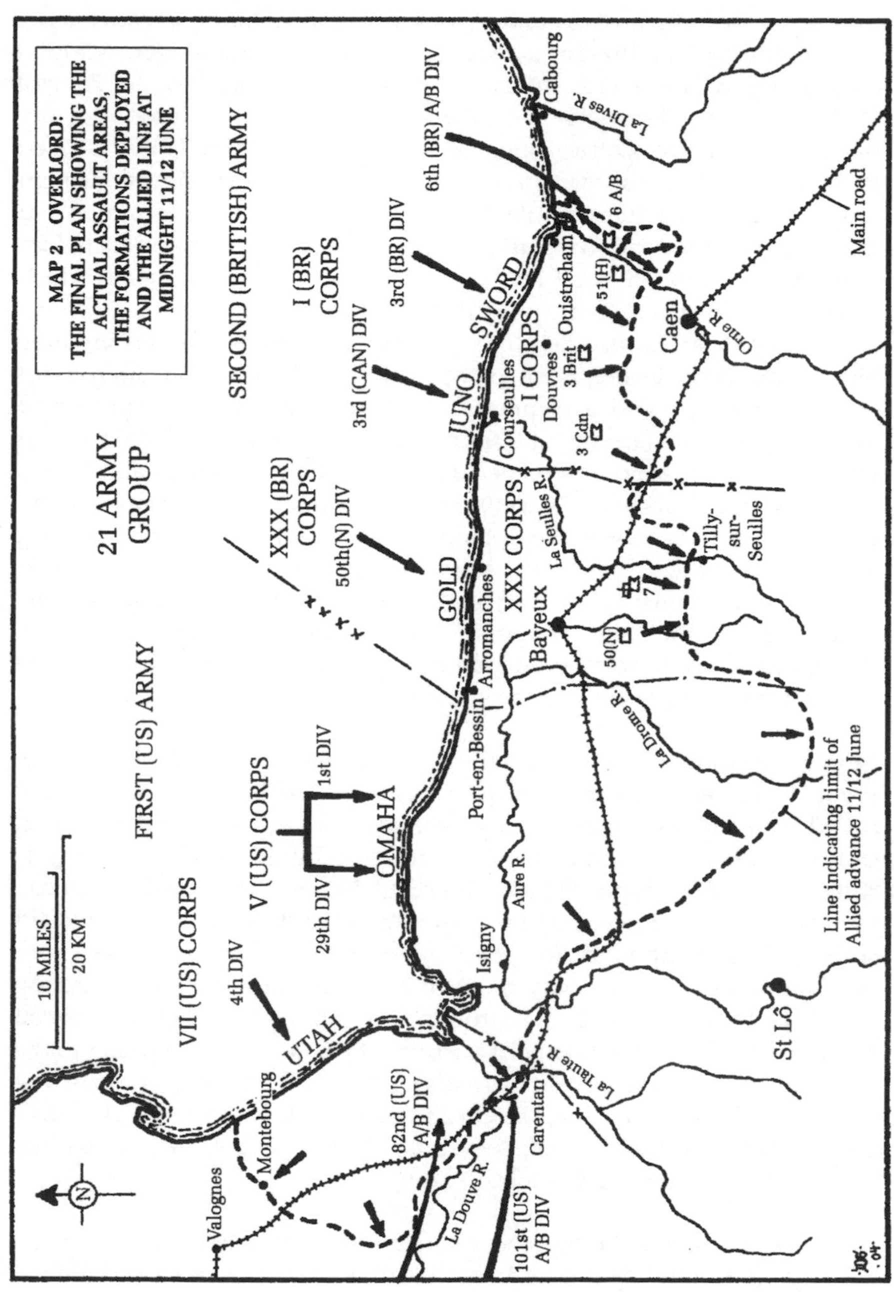
MAP 2 OVERLORD:
THE FINAL PLAN SHOWING THE ACTUAL ASSAULT AREAS, THE FORMATIONS DEPLOYED AND THE ALLIED LINE AT MIDNIGHT 11/12 JUNE
10 MILES
20 KM
21 ARMY GROUP
SECOND (BRITISH) ARMY
FIRST (US) ARMY
VII (US) CORPS
V (US) CORPS
XXX (BR) CORPS
I (BR) CORPS
4th DIV
29th DIV
1st DIV
50th(N) DIV
3rd (CAN) DIV
3rd (BR) DIV
6th (BR) A/B DIV
82nd (US) A/B DIV
101st (US) A/B DIV
UTAH
OMAHA
GOLD
JUNO
SWORD
Valognes
Montebourg
Carentan
Isigny
Port-en-Bessin
Arromanches
Courseulles
Douvres
Ouistreham
Cabourg
Bayeux
Caen
Tilly-sur-Seulles
St Lô
XXX CORPS
I CORPS
50(N)
7
3 Cdn
3 Brit
51(H)
6 A/B
La Douve R.
La Taute R.
Aure R.
La Drome R.
La Seulles R.
Orne R.
La Dives R.
Main road
Line indicating limit of Allied advance 11/12 June

these from the US area of operations on the map at St Paul's, but only at the last minute and at Bradley's request. The presentations were supplemented by a document entitled *'Overlord – Appreciation on Possible Development of Operations to Secure Lodgement Area'*, produced by Montgomery's Plans Officer, Brigadier Charles Richardson. This was given to Bradley and Dempsey with a covering letter noting that the outline plan represented Montgomery's 'intentions as far as they can be formulated at this stage' and the proviso that the development of operations on such lines depended not only on the Allied but also on the 'enemy situation which cannot be predicted accurately at the present moment'.[40]

The Appreciation included four discrete sections: OVERLORD mission; terrain analysis; development of operations, including an analysis of enemy resistance; and a summary of conclusions. It thus represented Montgomery's plan for operations in Normandy and included a map on which were marked four possible courses of action. That map also shows one phase line, marked D+14, defined as the bridgehead, an area bounded by the line from Lessay on the Cotentin's west coast to Thury Harcourt on the Orne and then west to just above Falaise before swinging towards Argences and thence to Cabourg on the Bay of the Seine, west of the Orne estuary. While the Allies would take a large portion of that ground by D+14, much would remain outside their hands, especially Caen, as the Germans threw reserves into the struggle for the city.

Montgomery also made visits to the forces under his command so that he would be known to as many of his soldiers as possible. In a special train, called 'Rapier', he visited every formation that would take part in OVERLORD. This took him to many locations in Britain, making as many as three visits a day, inspecting parades of 10,000 men or more. At each site he would conduct the visit in his own inimitable style, which 'astonished some of the generals who did not know me well'.[41] Troops were drawn up in a hollow square and Monty spoke to unit commanders before ordering the ranks to turn inwards with the men standing easy. He then paced through the files before taking to the bonnet of a jeep and speaking to the assembled men, explaining to them his plan and emphasising the care that he was taking to ensure success. On 28 February he inspected 1st Queen's Own Rifles of Canada where he spoke of his pride in the Canadian division that had served in Eighth Army in Italy.

> All in all General Montgomery made a very favourable impression on the men, and they appear to hold him in very high esteem, which of course is the way it should be.[42]

Since he was confident of success, stated Monty, his soldiers should be equally confident. Visiting 7th Duke of Wellington's Regiment on 16

February he 'asked them to have confidence in him and together they would see it through'.[43] By mid-May Montgomery had visited all his formations and spoken to men of many nationalities. Although an immense undertaking he believed it would pay dividends in morale. It was a typical Montgomery performance; and it worked. Soldiers felt that he was confiding in them, that he was giving them his trust in return for theirs. And, of course, that was true. He had to ensure that morale was high, that his soldiers were confident that he could deliver on his promises, that success would reward their efforts. A letter from Bedell Smith confirmed that he had this effect on American troops as well as British; one American source stated that 'confidence in the high command is absolutely without parallel' and that Montgomery's visits left 'a warm and indelible impression'.[44] Monty's visits were not restricted to military formations. At the behest of the Ministry of Supply he visited factories to emphasise the team nature of the war: soldiers and workers united to 'destroy German domination of Europe and of the world'.[45] He addressed gatherings of railway workers and London dockworkers, delivering the same message. From his visits he took away another message: that since the British civilian was war weary it was vital to bring the European war to an end in 1944. Montgomery was later asked to desist from such visits but ignored the request, pointing out that he had been asked to make them by government departments.[46]

Finally everything was in place, troops in their assembly areas, ships and landing craft ready to collect their cargoes, naval vessels to slip anchor and aircraft waiting for the order to move. On 29 May Eisenhower received favourable weather reports for the first week in June from his chief meteorologist, Group Captain J M Stagg, RAF. The Navy's requirements for NEPTUNE were visibility not less than three miles and surface winds not exceeding Force 3 (8–12mph) onshore or Force 4 (13–18 mph) offshore in the assault area during D-Day to D+2, mounting to a maximum of Force 5 in open seas but only for short periods.

> In the days preceding D-Day, there should be no prolonged periods of high winds of such direction and in such Atlantic areas as to produce any substantial swell in the Channel.[47]

With all seemingly going as well as could be expected, Eisenhower moved to his invasion headquarters at Portsmouth on 2 June as men began boarding. The following day brought a setback: Stagg reported that a depression was moving in and D-Day would be overcast and stormy with clouds down to 500 feet. These were not favourable conditions. But already some elements of the fleet had sailed. These were the vessels with the greatest distances to travel, including those from Northern Ireland,

Scotland and some of the westernmost ports. At 4.30am on the 4th Eisenhower and his senior commanders met Stagg for an updated weather report, probably the most critical such report in history. Stagg brought some good news – sea conditions would be slightly better than expected – but the overall forecast was still gloomy, both metaphorically and literally. D-Day would be very overcast, making conditions very difficult, especially for the airmen who might not be able to deliver the support required. Montgomery argued for the invasion to go ahead but was opposed by Tedder and Leigh-Mallory; Ramsay was non-committal. Only Eisenhower could make the final decision. He opted to postpone the operation. There would be a delay of twenty-four hours.

However, two vessels could not be recalled. Two Royal Navy midget submarines, or X-craft, X20 and X23, reached the Normandy coast just before daybreak on the 4th. These were the first Allied vessels involved in NEPTUNE/OVERLORD to arrive off France and they were to guide the incoming craft, which they would do by surfacing and showing lights. Having positioned themselves on the 4th, the X-craft anchored and submerged to await D-Day. At 1.00am on the 5th they received a wireless message notifying them of the postponement; they would have to spend another twenty-four hours on the bottom.

NEPTUNE/OVERLORD was a battle that would be fought in all three elements of sea, land and air and, certainly more than any land battle in history, weather was critical. The timing of the operation had to take account of favourable tides, which occurred only at intervals. For the original planned date – 1 May – conditions were ideal with a full moon, the Channel calm and cloudless skies.[48] The next full-moon period, in the first week of June, saw overcast skies, days of rain and choppy seas. For the landing a low tide was necessary 'to enable the initial assault elements to land and prepare lanes through the heavy obstacles which were above water only at or near a low tide'.[49] Good light conditions were vital so that beach defences might be attacked by aircraft and engaged by naval bombardment. All of these factors made 5, 6 and 7 June suitable dates for the invasion but a postponement beyond these days would mean waiting until 19 June when tides would be favourable, but there would be no moon. Thus a postponement until 19 June was not desirable. The commanders awaited Stagg's next forecast with some anxiety. When it came, the forecast opened up a possibility of going ahead on the 6th. Eisenhower recorded that Stagg's forecast for 6 June 'contained a gleam of hope'.[50] Late on the 5th and lasting until the next morning fair conditions would prevail with the wind easing and broken clouds with a base not lower than 3,000 feet but, towards the evening of the 6th, the winds would pick up again with a resultant rougher sea. Such conditions were likely to continue for some time. Eisenhower considered a further twenty-four-hour postponement to be out of the question since the bombardment

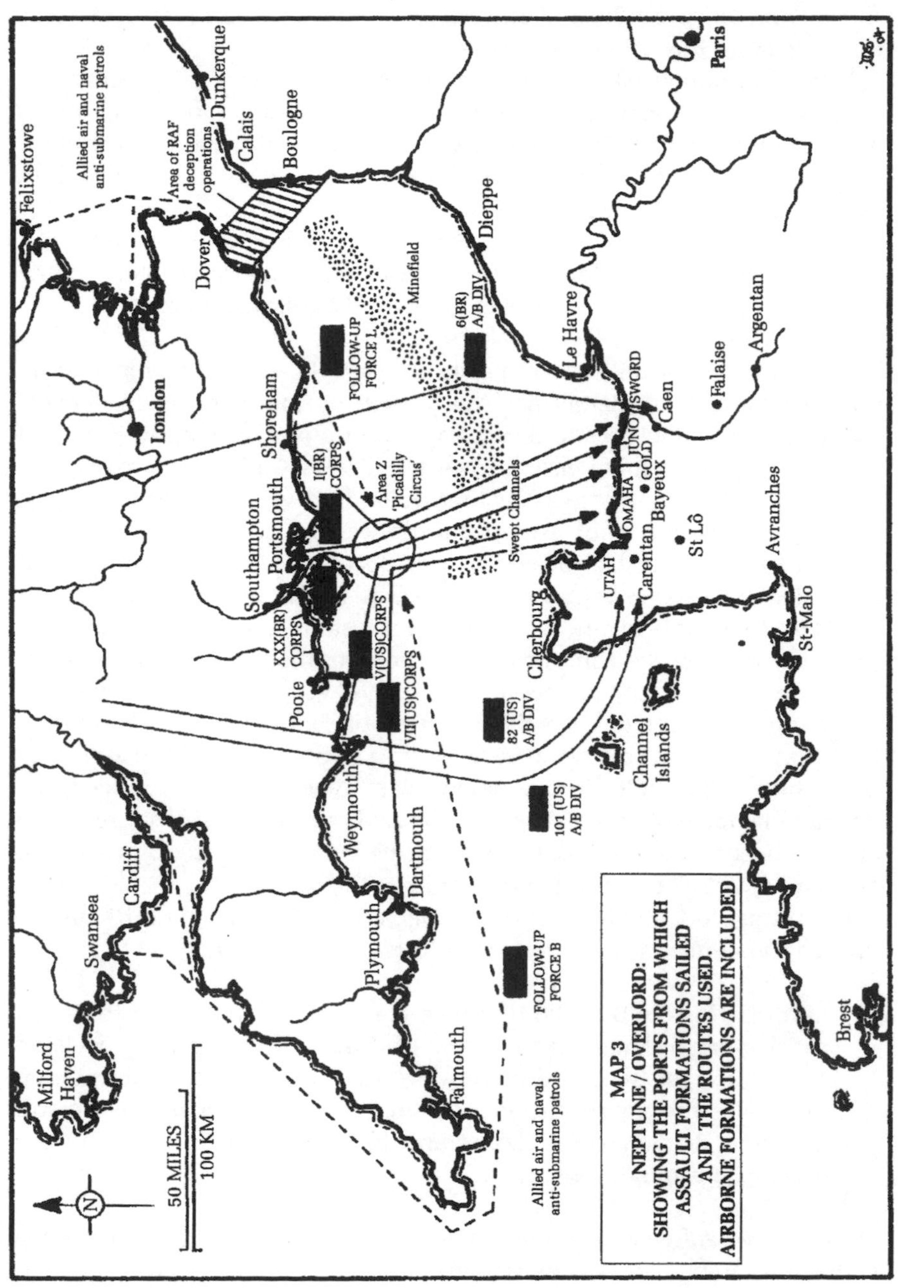

Felixstowe
Allied air and naval anti-submarine patrols
Area of RAF deception operations
Dunkerque
Calais
Boulogne
Dover
Dieppe
Minefield
London
Shoreham
Southampton
Portsmouth
FOLLOW-UP FORCE L
6(BR) A/B DIV
Le Havre
SWORD
Caen
JUNO
GOLD
Bayeux
OMAHA
Falaise
Argentan
Paris
I(BR) CORPS
Area Z 'Picadilly Circus'
Swept Channels
UTAH
Carentan
St Lô
Avranches
XXX(BR) CORPS
V(US)CORPS
VII(US)CORPS
Poole
Cherbourg
82 (US) A/B DIV
101 (US) A/B DIV
Channel Islands
St-Malo
Weymouth
Dartmouth
Plymouth
Cardiff
Swansea
Milford Haven
Falmouth
FOLLOW-UP FORCE B
Allied air and naval anti-submarine patrols
50 MILES
100 KM
N
Brest
MAP 3
NEPTUNE / OVERLORD:
SHOWING THE PORTS FROM WHICH
ASSAULT FORMATIONS SAILED
AND THE ROUTES USED.
AIRBORNE FORMATIONS ARE INCLUDED

forces from Northern Ireland and Scotland would have to return to port for refuelling, thus upsetting the overall schedule.

What alternative was there to going ahead on the 6th? Eisenhower concluded that a delay until tide and moon would again be favourable – in early July – would damage morale. It could also mean losing tactical surprise and, in the longer term, stall the subsequent battle to break out, perhaps through the following winter. And so

> At 0400 hours on 5 June I took the final and irrevocable decision: the invasion of France would take place on the following day.[51]

Eisenhower's decision took immense courage. It was a decision that no one else could take. Rarely has the burden of command been demonstrated so emphatically and in a manner so pivotal to history. If he had never achieved anything else in his lifetime, this American soldier, who would serve his country twice as President, deserves his place in history, and in the pantheon of American heroes, for that single decision. Eisenhower's courage is placed in perspective by the difficulties that presented themselves and the weak points in the overall plan. Brooke noted the latter as being the weather, and it is significant that he places this first, followed by the complexities of the operation that could produce confusion that could 'degenerate into chaos' very quickly if something went wrong. Then there was the difficulty of control, once the operation was launched, maintaining secrecy as long as possible and the strains of command.[52] Churchill, Brooke noted, was 'over optimistic'; indeed, the Prime Minister had 'done his best to be on board a cruiser that night' to observe events at close hand.[53] Instead, he was touring the Portsmouth area and making 'a thorough pest of himself'.[54]

In contrast to Churchill's enthusiasm, Eisenhower still had doubts; he drafted a statement for the press should the operation fail.

> Our landings in the Cherbourg–le Havre area have failed to gain a satisfactory foothold and I have withdrawn the troops. My decision to attack at this time and place was based upon the best information available. The troops, the air, and the Navy did all that bravery and devotion to duty could do. If any blame or fault attaches to the attempt it is mine alone.[55]

Of course, Eisenhower never had to issue that statement. He kept it in his wallet until July before giving it to his naval aide, Captain Harry Butcher. The statement, and the fact that it came into the public realm, speaks volumes about Eisenhower. It is difficult to imagine Montgomery ever drafting such a statement, let alone allowing it to become public once it was redundant. The suspicion must always linger that Monty would have

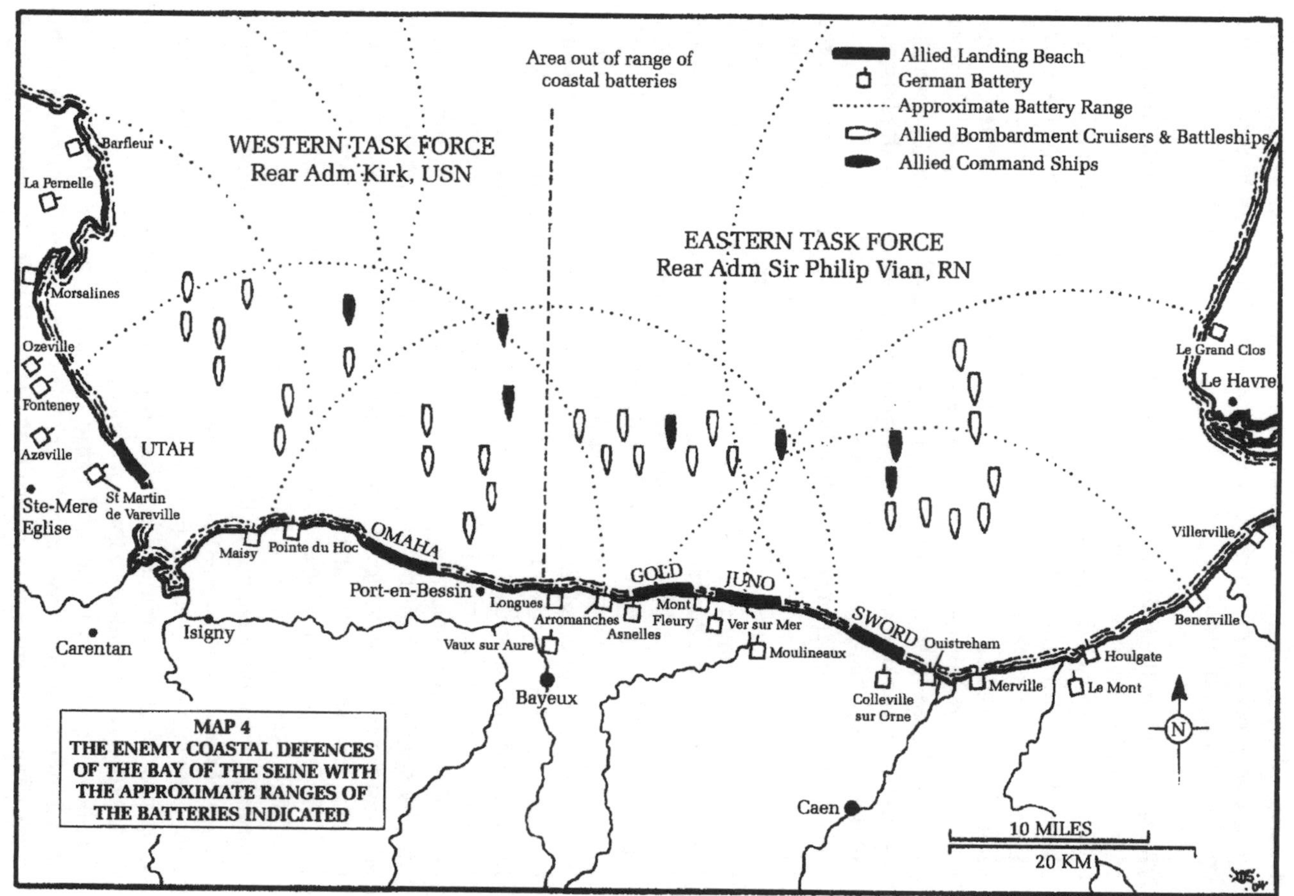
Area out of range of coastal batteries
Allied Landing Beach
German Battery
Approximate Battery Range
Allied Bombardment Cruisers & Battleships
Allied Command Ships
WESTERN TASK FORCE
Rear Adm Kirk, USN
EASTERN TASK FORCE
Rear Adm Sir Philip Vian, RN
Barfleur
La Pernelle
Morsalines
Ozeville
Fonteney
Azeville
UTAH
Ste-Mere Eglise
St Martin de Vareville
Maisy
Pointe du Hoc
OMAHA
Port-en-Bessin
Longues
Arromanches
Asnelles
GOLD
Mont Fleury
JUNO
Ver sur Mer
Moulineaux
SWORD
Ouistreham
Colleville sur Orne
Merville
Houlgate
Le Mont
Benerville
Villerville
Le Grand Clos
Le Havre
Carentan
Isigny
Vaux sur Aure
Bayeux
Caen
N
10 MILES
20 KM
MAP 4
THE ENEMY COASTAL DEFENCES OF THE BAY OF THE SEINE WITH THE APPROXIMATE RANGES OF THE BATTERIES INDICATED

tried to place the blame on shoulders other his own. In this case there would have been no Auchinleck to blame but Monty would surely have tried to find a substitute.

The order given, the invasion vessels cast off, and slowly made their way to sea, joining convoys that would merge into the greatest armada in history south of the Isle of Wight. For some, it was their second time to sea; others had endured an additional twenty-four hours on board the ships that would carry them across the Channel. Inland, paratroopers and gliderborne soldiers made ready on the airfields of Nos 38 and 46 Groups while, at other airfields in bomber country, the heavies of Bomber Command were loaded with massive bomb loads that would shortly be cascading on the defenders of the Normandy coast. And on the bases of Eighth Air Force, similar preparations were underway.

As part of the softening-up process before the seaborne landings, over a thousand aircraft – 551 Lancasters, 412 Halifaxes and forty-nine Mosquitoes – of Bomber Command were despatched to bomb coastal batteries on the night of 5–6 June. Some 946 machines hit targets at Fontenay, St Martin de Varreville, Merville, la Pernelle, Maisy, Pointe du Hoc, Longues, Mont Fleury, Ouistreham and Houlgate.[56] The batteries were bombed in two waves, the first three having to be hit shortly after midnight before airborne troops dropped nearby.[57] More than 5,000 tons of bombs fell, an average of 500 tons on each battery, most bombing being carried out with 'Oboe', a blind-bombing system using signals from two ground stations to indicate when the aircraft was over the target. 'Oboe' was necessary since cloud covered all targets except la Pernelle and Ouistreham.[58] The weight of bombs dropped that night was the highest for any single night in the war to date, since the relatively short range allowed bombers to trade fuel for additional bombs. According to the Official History, eleven aircraft and seventy men were lost[59] but the *Bomber Command War Diaries* state that only three aircraft were lost, two Halifaxes over Mont Fleury and a Lancaster over Longues.[60] The latter cannot be accurate since one of the first bombers over the Merville battery was shot down. The bombing of the last seven targets was timed so that defenders could not recover fully before the naval bombardment began; and, in spite of the weight of bombs dropped, it was the naval guns that were expected to neutralise the coastal batteries.

Following Bomber Command came Eighth Air Force's heavies. More than a thousand Fortresses and Liberators arrived shortly after daylight, as the naval guns were already firing and the first landing craft making for shore; they were to drop their bombs – almost 3,000 tons[61] – fifteen minutes before the first landing craft touched ground. But it was still cloudy and the heavy bombers were instructed to delay their drop by thirty seconds, an order authorised by Eisenhower, to reduce the danger of hitting landing craft. Unfortunately, the bombs, of which Bradley reckoned there were 13,000, fell not on the coastal defences but into fields and hedges up to three miles inland. 'This margin of safety had undermined the effectiveness of the heavy air mission.'[62] As a result, American infantry approaching Omaha Beach suffered many casualties. There was another result. Hundreds of cattle were killed and the stench of rotting flesh was something that survivors of Normandy would never forget. Normandy is famed for its dairy produce – milk, butter and cheeses, among them Camembert, from the eponymous village – and so there were many cattle in the region. These were not to be the sole four-legged casualties of the campaign. Since German forces relied to a great extent on horse-drawn transport, horses would also die in great numbers over the next weeks, among them many Percherons, that fine Norman breed of sound-tempered plough and draught horses that were also pressed into German service.

One Royal Navy officer recalled that his LCT had sailed from Plymouth on 4 June and had been eight hours at sea when the order to return was received. LCT 796, loaded with six Shermans and a command car, returned to Plymouth, another eight-hour journey, dropped anchor and awaited the order to sail again. When this came the vessel put back to sea for the rendezvous area, Piccadilly Circus, off the Isle of Wight whence it made for Normandy. The LCT was off Omaha Beach soon after dawn on D-Day and anchored offshore to await its turn to run in to the beach. As dawn broke the crew gazed out on an unforgettable sight.

> There were ships as far as you could see. From where we were to the horizon nobody could navigate a ship and take their eyes off what they were doing for more than a minute or two. It looked as if you could walk back to England across ships.[63]

There were some 2,700 vessels with another 1,897 landing craft carried on landing ships and 195,000 sailors, marines and merchant seamen, over half of them British, manning the vessels transporting some 130,000 soldiers, 12,000 vehicles, 2,000 tanks and almost 10,000 tons of stores.[64] As the invasion fleet made its steady way across the Channel, other parts of the jigsaw were falling into place. These included the deception operation by the RAF and a small number of surface ships that represented a major invasion fleet making for the Pas de Calais, the Bomber Command and Eighth Air Force attacks and airborne landings to secure the flanks of the invasion area and prevent enemy reinforcements menacing the first assault waves.

Probably the first Allied troops to set foot on French soil on D-Day were men from 22nd Independent Parachute Company, the pathfinders for 6th

Airborne Division.* Their task was to mark drop zones (DZs) for paratroopers and landing zones (LZs) for gliders with Eureka beacons that transmitted a signal to Rebecca receivers in the aircraft carrying paratroopers or towing gliders; this allowed pilots to home in on the LZ or DZ. The pathfinders also set lights or flares to mark out LZs and DZs. For the gliders it was especially important that landing areas be clear of obstructions, whether natural or placed by the Germans; these were flimsy machines and could not hope to win an argument with any major obstruction.

Following the pathfinders came the first troops from 3 and 5 Brigades** of 6th Airborne Division. Their tasks were, for 3 Brigade, to cut enemy reinforcement routes over the bridges on the Dives, secure the high ground commanding those routes and seize the Merville battery. Meanwhile 5 Brigade was to seize and hold the Orne crossings. Thus would the left flank of 21 Army Group be secured. Sixth Airborne's objectives were all east of the Orne.

There were three main dropping zones: Ranville (N) and Touffreville (K) for 5 Brigade and Varaville (V) for 3 Brigade. Pathfinders and advance parties were to land at twenty minutes past midnight; the first wave of assault troops, with the main bodies of each brigade, would take about twenty minutes to land, beginning at 12.45am. Finally, the third wave would come in at 3.20am with divisional headquarters, anti-tank guns, jeeps, bulldozers and other heavy engineering equipment and various stores. The remainder of the division would arrive on the evening of D-Day.

A reinforced company – five platoons – of 2nd Oxfordshire and Buckinghamshire Light Infantry, with thirty members of 249 Field Company Royal Engineers, commanded by Major John Howard, were to seize bridges over the Caen canal at Bénouville and the Orne river at Ranville; river and canal run northwards on parallel courses no more than 1,000 yards apart. Howard's command landed in five Horsa gliders at DZ/LZs X and Y between the canal and the river with a sixth glider landing off target some distance away near Varaville. At the same time, three parties from 22nd Independent Parachute Company dropped to perform their marking role at DZ/LZs K, N and V. Howard's party was to take the bridges intact so that seaborne reinforcements could move quickly into the airborne bridgehead to consolidate and exploit 6th Airborne Division's work. Once Howard and his men had seized the

* Pathfinders from the two US airborne divisions may also claim to have been the first Allied troops into Normandy but, considering the flight paths and timings, it seems most likely that the British pathfinders took that distinction.

** 3 Brigade included 8th (Midland Counties), 9th (Home Counties) and 1st (Canadian) Parachute Battalions while 5 Brigade included 7th (Light Infantry), 12th and 13th Parachute Battalions.

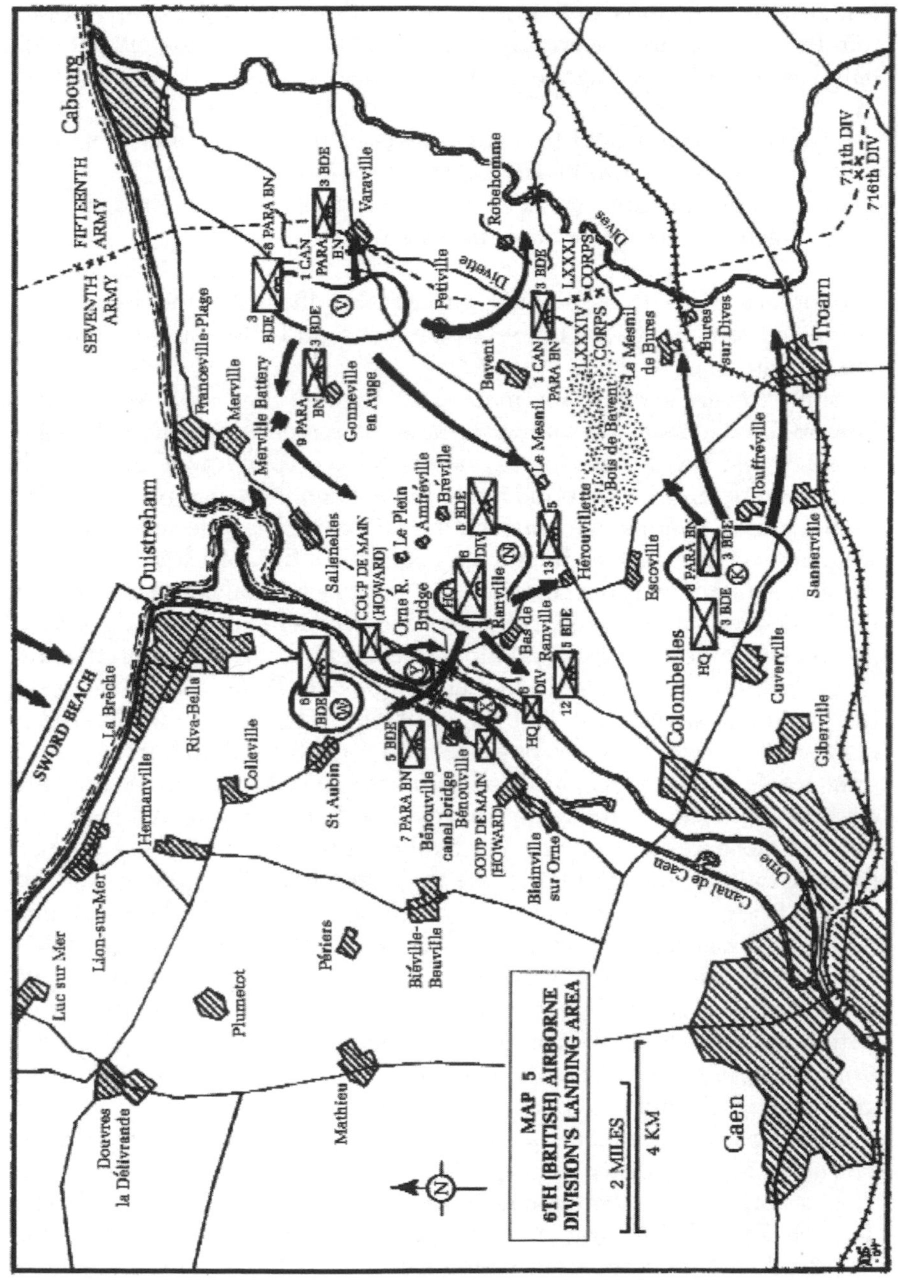
MAP 5
6TH (BRITISH) AIRBORNE
DIVISION'S LANDING AREA
2 MILES
4 KM
SWORD BEACH
Ouistreham
Cabourg
SEVENTH ARMY
FIFTEENTH ARMY
Franceville-Plage
Merville
Merville Battery
Varaville
Robehomme
Petiville
Dives
Divette
Gonneville en Auge
Bavent
Le Mesnil
Bois de Bavent
Bures sur Dives
Troarn
Touffréville
Sannerville
Escoville
Hérouvillette
Ranville
Bas de Ranville
Bréville
Amfréville
Le Plein
Sallenelles
Orne R. Bridge
COUP DE MAIN (HOWARD)
Bénouville canal bridge
Bénouville
Blainville sur Orne
Colombelles
Cuverville
Giberville
Caen
Canal de Caen
Orne
St Aubin
Colleville
Riva-Bella
La Brèche
Hermanville
Lion-sur-Mer
Luc sur Mer
Plumetot
Périers
Biéville-Beuville
Mathieu
Douvres la Délivrande
LXXXI CORPS
LXXXIV CORPS
711th DIV
716th DIV
9 PARA BN
1 CAN PARA BN
8 PARA BN
7 PARA BN
3 BDE
5 BDE
6 BDE
6 DIV
HQ

bridges, the main force of 5 Brigade, under Brigadier Nigel Poett, would reinforce and secure the area around both bridges until the arrival of a battalion of 8 Infantry Brigade from 3rd (British) Division. Poett's task was

(a) to seize and hold the crossings over the CANAL and R ORNE at BENOUVILLE 098748 and RANVILLE 104746.
(b) secure the area BENOUVILLE – RANVILLE – LE BAS DE RANVILLE against infantry or armoured assault.[65]

The orders for 5 Para Brigade Group also included the injunction: 'Infantry positions will be fought to the last round and anti-tank guns to the muzzle.'[66]

John Howard's coup de main has become the stuff of legend, immortalised in many books and on the silver screen, especially in the film 'The Longest Day', based on Cornelius Ryan's eponymous book. Both bridges were seized, and found not to have demolition charges fitted. The local German commander, Major Hans Schmidt, had decided that the weather was such that he did not have to order a full alert since there was no chance of an invasion; charges were not placed in their chambers lest the French resistance set them off.[67] Once in British hands the bridges were given new names: Pegasus and Horsa Bridges instead of Bénouville and Ranville. More recently Robin Neillands' book *The Battle of Normandy 1944* has included an account that suggests that Howard's role has been exaggerated over the years and that 7th Parachute Battalion played a greater role in seizing the bridges.[68] However, it is difficult to see how the traditional version of the battle survived so long without challenge if it was not close to the truth of what really happened. The waters are also muddied a little further by the fact that Bénouville Bridge was dubbed Antrim Bridge for a short time before becoming Pegasus Bridge, the name by which it has been known ever since. Why Antrim? This suggests that men of 591 (Antrim) Parachute Squadron, Royal Engineers may have helped capture the bridge but that squadron was with 9th Parachute Battalion while Howard's company was supported by men of 249 Field Company. A detachment of Antrims did reinforce the *coup de main* force at Bénouville bridge.[69] Whatever the sequence of events and the exact *dramatis personae* the fact remains that both bridges were in Allied hands. The battle for Normandy had begun and fierce fighting continued around Pegasus bridge with the regimental aid post being overrun at one stage. The Medical Officer was reported missing while the chaplain, the Reverend George Parry from Essex, was killed. Although fighting continued into the daylight hours, the bridgehead was held.

One Bomber Command target that night had been the coast defence battery at Merville, north-east of Ranville. This battery, believed to hold four 150mm guns, faced north-west to threaten Sword Beach and, since it was heavily defended by a 20mm dual-purpose gun, six machine guns, a minefield, anti-tank ditches and barbed wire,[70] its capture was assigned to a battalion of 3 Parachute Brigade – 9th Parachute Battalion, commanded by Lieutenant-Colonel Terence Otway, from County Tipperary. (Otway's parent regiment was the Royal Ulster Rifles, which had the distinction of being the only regiment with both regular battalions in action on D-Day.) Also dropping into the Ranville area were the men of 2 Troop, 591 (Antrim) Parachute Squadron.[71]

The men of 2 Troop did not enjoy the success of their comrades in 1 and 3 Troops, whom we shall meet later. One glider broke its tow rope and landed in Britain while the other two, without the benefit of flares on the ground, landed about two hundred yards off target; one landed in an orchard near the battery having been struck and damaged badly by anti-aircraft fire but the other made a safe landing. The original plan had called for all three gliders to land inside the perimeter of the battery in a *coup de main* assault as the main body of the battalion attacked. Few Antrim sappers, who were to demolish the Merville battery, reached that objective. However, the battery was put out of action, largely by the efforts of Otway's battalion.[72]

Otway had trained his battalion rigorously, rehearsing for almost a week in a training area in rural Berkshire near Newbury that simulated the ground around the Merville battery; his soldiers knew the layout of the area from many hours of briefings.[73] They were as well trained as soldiers could be, every company knew its part in the operation and morale was very high. The bombing raid that should have softened up the battery went disastrously wrong when one of the first bombers was shot down near its target, crashed onto a nearby village and exploded. Following crews assumed the resultant flames and explosions were marking the target and dropped their bomb loads there as well. Merville battery suffered no damage.

When the transport aircraft with Otway's men arrived over Merville there was another disaster as jumpmasters prematurely gave the order to jump. Many soldiers drowned before they could discard their parachutes and heavy equipment as they came to earth in swampy ground or in areas that had been flooded deliberately.

Otway reported what had happened.

> By 0250 hrs the Battalion had grown to 150 strong, with 20 lengths of Bangalore torpedo. Each company was approximately 30 strong. Enough Signals to carry on. No 3″ mortars; one machine gun; one half of sniping party; no 6pdr guns; no jeeps or trailers, or any glider stores; no sappers; no field ambulances but six medical orderlies; no mine detectors, one company commander missing. The commanding officer decided to advance immediately.[74]

Some of his men recalled later that Otway called: 'Everybody in, we're going to take this bloody battery.'

And take it they did, although Otway's battalion could muster only a quarter of its strength. But those survivors, with those of the reconnaissance troops, blasted holes in the barbed wire surrounding the battery and charged in with guns blazing. Initially the very audacity of this attack may have knocked the defenders off balance but they regained their composure and put up ferocious resistance. At the end of the battle 9th Parachute Battalion had lost about seventy men while the defenders had 178 dead or wounded from 200. Some of the garrison surrendered with apparent enthusiasm; these were Russians who had been forced into fighting for the Germans.[75] In the dying stages of the battle Lieutenant Mike Dowling, Otway's acting second-in-command, reported to his commanding officer that the battery had been captured. Having saluted his commanding officer and made his report, Dowling was killed by a mortar shell.[76]

Two of the battery's four guns were reported destroyed with the others damaged sufficiently to put them out of action for some time. Otway fired a yellow flare to let the Royal Navy know that the battery was in British hands; that flare went up only fifteen minutes before bombardment of the site was due to begin. The battalion's signals officer also released a carrier pigeon to take the news to England. With no orders to hold the battery, Otway then withdrew his eighty survivors to make for le Mesnil and their next objective, some men of 1st Canadian Battalion providing a rearguard. Although the Germans later retook the Merville battery and the damaged guns were brought back into action to shell the landing beaches, they were unable to fire at the critical time on 6 June.[77]

The assault on the Merville battery proved costly in lives, both British and German. It 'was a fine feat of arms, [but] rendered anti-climactic by the discovery that the casemates mounted only 75 mm guns with slight capacity to harass the beaches'.[78] In at least one case the gun mounted in a casemate was a 100mm field piece on a platform[79] although it seems, from German accounts, that all four guns were 105mm pieces.[80]

Otway was awarded the DSO for his 'conspicuous bravery and outstanding leadership' during the assault on the Merville battery, described as the Sallenelles battery in the citation which also included Otway's leadership of the battalion during subsequent operations over several days around le Mesnil where it beat off 'two major enemy attacks of several hours duration'. On this occasion his leadership of a 'very weak and tired' battalion was described as 'magnificent'.[81] On 12 June Otway and some of his officers were inspecting his positions when a shell landed nearby; the explosion killed Lieutenant Christie, wounded Sergeant McGeever and concussed Otway and two others. Some days later, when he began suffering after effects from the explosion, Terence Otway was examined by a doctor who declared him unfit for further service; Major Napier Crookenden succeeded him in command of 9th Battalion.[82]

The third principal task given to the airborne soldiers was to destroy four bridges over the Dives and another over a stream at Varaville to slow the progress of enemy reinforcements from the east. Of the bridges over the Dives two were at Bures and one each at Robehomme and Troarn. Assigned to these tasks were 1st Canadian and 8th Parachute Battalions, commanded by Lieutenant-Colonels George Bradbrooke and Alistair Pearson respectively, with 3 Parachute Squadron Royal Engineers under Major Tim Roseveare to carry out demolitions. Pearson's battalion was to land near Touffreville, in zone K, and cover the engineers as they blew the Troarn and Dives bridges but the battalion was dispersed in the early drops with some landing on zone N, about three miles to the north. Pearson landed in the correct location but could assemble only some 160 of his men. Information from local residents and reconnaissance established that Escoville, Sannerville and Troarn were occupied by enemy troops, from whom there was considerable fire. Pearson considered that he did not have the strength to attack Troarn and so took his little force to high ground south-west of Bavent woods to cover the sappers destroying the bridge at Bures.[83]

The men who had landed in zone N had gathered into two parties, one of sixty men of 8th Battalion under the mortar officer and another of a similar number of sappers under Major Roseveare. Subsequently the latter was joined by between twenty and thirty men of 8th Battalion as they moved to Bavent woods. Roseveare's group also had a sizeable quantity of explosives and demolition equipment as well as a jeep and trailer with medical stores. Both parties met on the high ground west of Bavent woods where the infantry remained to hold a firm base while Roseveare's sappers, less Roseveare, another officer and seven men, moved off to blow Bures bridge. Reloading the jeep and trailer with demolition equipment, Roseveare and his eight companions set off to destroy the Troarn bridge. In an action that might appear as the work of an overactive imagination were it to feature in a Hollywood movie, the nine men drove through Troarn village, and a hail of fire from the Germans, to reach the bridge where they demolished the centre span. Their sole casualty was one soldier who had been on the trailer, giving rear-covering fire from a Bren gun. Having accomplished their task the sappers abandoned the jeep and made their way across country to join their fellows who had blown the bridge at Bures.[84]

Difficulty also beset the men dropping at zone V, at Varaville. The advance party included a company of 1st Canadian Parachute Battalion who were to take an enemy headquarters and signals station before the main body arrived. Although most landed west of the Dives there were exit problems in the aircraft and 'other misfortunes'. One pathfinder party landed accurately to place its beacon but the other was some thousand yards away. Some men later reached the area but lost much equipment in flooded areas close to the Dives. No better fortune met the main body. If anything, they had even more misfortune as their drop was timed shortly after Bomber Command's attack on the Merville battery. The raid created great clouds of dust and smoke to add to the natural cloud already obscuring the area and only one of eleven gliders landed accurately while more than half the aircraft carrying paratroopers dropped their loads more than a mile away. Some men fell into flooded ground astride the Dives, more than two miles from their DZ. Nonetheless, the Canadian advance party, with some sappers, destroyed Varaville bridge and moved on to the German headquarters in a nearby chateau. Following a fierce fight that lasted into daylight the Canadians were successful but at heavy cost. Some local people assisted with medical care for the wounded while at least one Frenchman donned a red beret and took part in the action; he was credited with shooting three enemy snipers.[85]

At much the same time, another group of about sixty Canadian paras were making for Robehomme where, although explosive charges for the bridge had not arrived, they were able, with the help of a sapper sergeant and explosives carried by the paras, to put the bridge out of action. The group then took up positions on a hill overlooking the river and road and established an observation post in the church tower.

As airborne soldiers fought their isolated battles the invasion fleet steamed steadily towards the Bay of the Seine. The two X-craft awaited the moment to surface and guide in the first assault vessels and the gun crews on bombardment vessels prepared for the task ahead. In Britain the airmen who would provide cover over the beaches were making ready for the day ahead. USAAF heavy and medium bombers were already en route to add to the pounding that Bomber Command had given the coastal batteries. On the assault craft, soldiers waited anxiously for dawn. Many suffered from seasickness as their vessels fought the choppy Channel seas in the final two hours before the landing. Some were so ill, in spite of anti-seasickness tablets, that they would have preferred to face enemy fire than remain on the assault craft, the floors of which were treacherous with the evidence of their occupants' sickness. Others, in spite of being sick, managed to sing as their landing craft pounded through the waves and a bugler of 2nd East Yorkshire Regiment even sounded 'General Salute' as his craft passed its command ship on its way to Sword Beach.[86]

At 5am on 6 June X20 and X23 rose from the seabed some three miles off the strips of coast now become better known as Juno and Sword and began flashing their green lights out to sea to guide the approaching assault vessels.[87] They also put out radio beacons in dinghies to mark the assault beaches.[88] Already American assault craft were making for Utah and Omaha beaches, the US command having decided that its H-Hour should be 6.30am, an hour earlier than the British and Canadian, and that their lowering area should be about eleven miles offshore, some three to four miles farther out than the British and Canadians. This latter precaution, intended to keep attack transports out of range of German coastal guns, was considered unnecessary by Admiral Ramsay due to the weight of Allied naval gunfire that could be directed on those guns.[89]

By 5.30am it was light enough for aircraft to spot for the naval bombardment force. From the ships of the Eastern Task Force guns unleashed their storm of steel upon the coastal defences. The Western Task Force opened fire twenty minutes later, although the US H-Hour was an hour before the British; Admiral Kirk had decided upon a bombardment of only thirty to forty minutes against Ramsay's preferred two-hour bombardment. Kirk had hoped to gain surprise by this tactic but failed. The shells raining down upon the defenders ranged from the 16-inch rounds of the battleship HMS *Rodney*, with nine such weapons, and 15-inch rounds from the battleships *Ramillies* and *Warspite*, each of which could bring four guns of this calibre* to bear on its targets, and the monitor *Rob*erts,** with two such weapons, through the 6-inch projectiles of the cruisers – and secondary guns of the battleships – to the 4-inch shells of the destroyers. Bombarding Force K, covering Gold Beach, included four Royal Navy cruisers, the Dutch gunboat HNLMS *Flores*, twelve Royal Navy destroyers and the Polish destroyer ORP *Krakowiak*. Juno was covered by Bombarding Force E, including two Royal Navy cruisers, *Belfast* and *Diadem*, seven RN destroyers, two Royal Canadian Navy destroyers, *Algonquin* and *Sioux*, the Norwegian destroyer HNMS *Glaisdale*, and the French destroyer FFS *La Combattante*. At Sword, Bombarding Force D included the battleships *Warspite* and *Ramillies*, the monitor *Roberts*, four RN cruisers, the Polish cruiser ORP *Dragon* and a baker's dozen of destroyers, mostly British but including Poland's ORP *Slazak*, and the Norwegian *Stord* and *Svenner*. The reserve element of Eastern Task Force included the battleship *Rodney*, two British cruisers, one of which, *Scylla*, was the Task Force Flagship and a number of destroyers that were otherwise assigned to escort duties. In all, a massive weight of fire could be brought to bear on targets in the British and Canadian sector: nine 16-inch guns, ten 15-inch guns, seven 7.5-inch guns, ninety-six 6-inch guns,

* The 15-inch gun, which weighed 100 tons, could fire a round weighing 1,938 pounds at a muzzle velocity of 2,458 feet per second to a distance of 33,550 yards at an elevation of 30 degrees. [90]

** All three vessels were of Great War vintage. *Warspite* had carried out a similar role at Salerno in September 1943 when the ship was struck by a German FX-1400 radio-controlled bomb; it still had a turret and a boiler room out of action as a result. *Ramillies* had been due to be laid up in 1943 together with her sister ship *Revenge* but both had been reprieved.

twenty-eight 5.25-inch guns, three 5.9-inch guns and a multitude of 4.7- or 4-inch guns. The latter weapons – the 4- and 4.7-inch guns – were those of the destroyers, which accompanied landing craft groups as they made for the shore; fleet destroyers with their 4.7s engaged enemy positions behind the beaches while the smaller Hunt-class destroyers closed as far inshore as possible to provide support with their 4-inch guns.[91]

That firepower was supplemented by landing craft intended to provide close-support in each assault force. In Eastern Task Force, 242 landing craft mounted weapons ranging from 4.7-inch naval guns through 5-inch explosive rockets to 60-pound spigot bombs. There were also anti-aircraft, or flak, craft and more than a hundred LCTs mounted army weapons, ranging from tanks to self-propelled guns. Three LCTs carried 17-pounder anti-tank guns for use against concrete defences. It was from some of these LCTs that Second Army's first shots of D-Day were fired at 6.44am from the SPGs of 9 (Irish) Battery 7th Field Regiment, Royal Artillery on the run-in shoot to Sword–Queen Beach.*

Overhead flew aircraft of the Fleet Air Arm, Royal Air Force, USAAF and other Allied air forces, spotting for the bombarding forces' guns, engaging ground targets or providing protection against possible Luftwaffe attacks. There were few sorties by the Luftwaffe over the beaches, although one of those almost brought to an end the life of a Fleet Air Arm pilot. George Boyd came close to death, not from the guns of a German fighter but from a possible mid-air collision.

> there was 10/10ths cloud at 2,000 feet and we throttled back and turned to coarse pitch just under the cloud base in order to drop our 'jet' tank. Suddenly, out of the cloud, diving flat out, was a Messerschmitt 109 coming at me head-on. He flicked to port and I flicked to port and we missed each other by a few feet.[93]

Although Boyd and his wingman broke to pursue the Messerschmitt, the German fighter had too much of a head start and the Fleet Air Arm men returned to their task of seeking targets for their ships.

As the landing craft approached the British and Canadian beaches the American bombers were completing their raid. The bombing ended ten minutes before H-Hour and helped keep the defenders' heads down. Then came the final feature of the Joint Fire Plan, which had been opened by Bomber Command, taken up by the naval guns, the US bombers and then by guns of the Royal Marines and Royal Artillery as they made for the shore: the release of thousands of 5-inch rockets, some 20,000 being fired in the British sector.[94] The rocket bombardment was unleashed only

* During the run-in shoot, 7th Field Regiment was the central unit and led 74th and 76th Field Regiments by 400 yards.[92]

five minutes before H-Hour. By then the first landing craft were close to the beach as were the first DD tanks.

NOTES

1 Montgomery, *Memoirs*, p. 221.
2 D'Este, *Decision in Normandy*, p. 69.
3 Montgomery, op cit, p. 221.
4 D'Este, op cit, pp. 65–8.
5 Ibid, p. 67.
6 Ibid, p. 512.
7 NA, WO171/376, war diary, Gds Armd Div.
8 NA, WO171/613, war diary, 8 Armd Bde.
9 NA, WO171/838, war diary 4/7 RDG.
10 Frederick, *Lineage Book of British Land Forces, vol i*, p. 7.
11 Ibid, p. 203; NA, WO171/877, war diary, 141 Regt, RAC.
12 NA, WO171/1256, war diary, 2 Armd Bn Ir Gds.
13 NA, WO171/969, war diary, 7 Fd Regt, RA.
14 NA, WO171/1350, war diary, 1 R Norfolk.
15 NA, WO171/1351, war diary, 7 R Norfolk.
16 NA, WO171/1325, war diary, 2 KSLI.
17 Ibid & /1387, war diary, 2 R Warwicks.
18 NA, WO179/2958, war diary, 1 Queen's Own Rifles of Canada.
19 NA, WO171/1288, war diary, 7 DWR.
20 CWGC website: www.cwgc.com .
21 NA, WO171/1256, war diary, 2 Armd Bn Ir Gds.
22 NA, CAB44/242, p. 1.
23 Ibid, p. 49.
24 Bradley, *A Soldier's Story*, p. 249.
25 Mace, *Forrard*, p. 109.
26 Joslen, Orders of Battle, p. 178.
27 NA, WO171/613, op cit.
28 Ellis, op cit, p. 136.
29 Graves, *History of the Royal Ulster Rifles*, vol *iii*, p. 102.
30 Ibid.
31 NA, WO171/864, war diary, Westminster Dgns.
32 NA, WO171/1256, 2 Armd Bn Ir Gds.
33 Devlin, quoted in Dungan, *Distant Drums*, p. 120.
34 McCaughey, quoted in ibid.
35 Montgomery, op cit, p. 236.
36 Bradley, op cit, p. 239.
37 Ibid, p. 239.
38 Ibid, p. 241.
39 Lewin, *Montgomery as Military Commander*, p. 183.
40 NA, WO205/118: Appreciation on possible developments of operations to secure a lodgement area..
41 Montgomery, op cit, p. 223.
42 NA, WO179/2958, war diary, 1 Queen's Own Rifles of Canada.
43 NA, WO171/1288, war diary, 7 DWR.
44 Montgomery, op cit, pp. 223–4.
45 Ibid, p. 225.
46 Ibid, pp. 225–6.
47 NA, CAB44/242, p. 225.

48 Eisenhower, *D-Day to VE Day*, p. 27.
49 NA, CAB44/242, p. 225.
50 Eisenhower, op cit, p. 71.
51 Ibid, p. 73.
52 Brooke, *War Diaries*, p. 554.
53 Ibid, p. 553.
54 Ibid.
55 Butcher diary, 11 July 1944, Quoted in D'Este, op cit, p. 110.
56 Middlebrook & Everett, *The Bomber Command War Diaries*, pp. 522–3.
57 Ellis, op cit, p. 159.
58 Middlebrook & Everett, op cit, p. 523.
59 Ellis, op cit, p. 159.
60 Middlebrook & Everett, op cit, pp. 522–3.
61 Ellis, op cit, p. 167.
62 Bradley, op cit, p. 268.
63 D'Alton, interview with author.
64 Ellis, op cit, pp. 222–3.
65 NA, WO171/425, war diary, 6th A/borne Div.
66 Ibid.
67 Shilleto, *Pegasus Bridge Merville Battery*, p. 46.
68 Neillands, op cit, pp. 29–30.
69 Ellis, op cit, p. 151.
70 Smith, *The History of the Glider Pilot Regiment*, p. 93.
71 Doherty, *Irish Volunteers in the Second World War*, p. 167.
72 Ibid.
73 Ibid.
74 Dungan, *Distant Drums*, p. 124.
75 Doherty, op cit, p. 169.
76 Ibid.
77 Ibid.
78 Hastings, *Overlord*, p. 74.
79 Barber, *The Day the Devils Dropped In. The 9th Parachute Battalion in Normandy – D-Day to D+6*, p. 88.
80 Information from David Truesdale.
81 NA, WO373/49.
82 Doherty, op cit, p. 169.
83 Shannon & Wright, *One Night in June*, pp. 80–1.
84 Ibid.
85 Ellis, op cit, p. 154.
86 Ibid, pp. 153–4.
87 Ibid, p. 169.
88 Barnett, *Engage the Enemy More Closely*, p. 814.
89 Neillands & De Normann, *D-Day 1944. Voices from Normandy*, p. 75.
90 Barnett, op cit, p. 813.
91 Chesneau, *Conway's All the World's Fighting Ships*, p. 5.
92 NA, WO171/969, war diary, 7 Fd Regt, RA. This war diary contains accounts written by the commanding officer and the officers commanding batteries of the regiment. The location of 7th Field Regiment and its batteries on the run-in shoot supports 9 (Irish) Battery's claim to have fired the British Army's first rounds of D-Day..
93 Boyd, *Boyd's War*, p. 50.
94 Ellis, op cit, p. 168.

CHAPTER VII
The first clash

Once more unto the breach

German reaction was strange and provided evidence of the success of the deception operations and Hitler's flawed command system. It also illustrated the degree to which the Allies had obtained air and maritime superiority. German meteorological work had suffered from the loss of Atlantic weather ships and the consequent reliance on short-range forecasting. Such were conditions on 5 June that their commanders considered an attack unlikely for some days, even though minesweepers had been spotted that evening. Rommel had asked to meet Hitler to try to persuade him to adopt a more realistic attitude towards defending the Atlantic Wall and had left for Germany on Sunday 4 June. He was accompanied by Colonel von Tempelhoff, his chief operations officer, and Captain Lang, the ADC responsible for Rommel's personal diary and to whom Rommel had remarked, in April, that the day of the invasion would be, for both Germans and Allies, 'the longest day'. Since the trip to Germany allowed Rommel some home leave, he was at home when he learned that Hitler would see him on the 8th. Lucy's birthday was on the 6th and so Rommel would be able to celebrate with her. On the morning of Lucy's birthday Rommel was arranging her presents in the drawing room when the telephone rang. At the other end was General Hans Speidel*, his chief of staff, with the news that Allied airborne forces had landed in Normandy. Less than three hours later, Rommel rang Speidel for an update. By now it was clear that this was a major Allied operation, an invasion no less. But was it *the* invasion?[1]

Other German commanders had also left their command posts. Sepp Dietrich, 1st SS Panzer Corps, was in Brussels while most of Seventh Army's senior officers were in Rennes attending war games. Feuchtinger, commanding 21st Panzer Division, had, according to Hans von Luck, gone to Special HQ in Paris with his most senior staff[2] although others believed he was having an assignation with a female.[3] Thus many who

* Speidel was to be the first commander of the reformed German army in 1955 and also one of those who helped to create the post-war Rommel legend.

ought to have been at the helm of the immediate response to the Allied landings were away from their posts. For Rommel it must have been like a reprise of El Alamein when he had been home on sick leave, believing that the British attack would not come for another month. Rommel's many skills as a general seemed to have been blighted on these two occasions at least by his not having been in the right place at the right time; as Napoleon might have observed, he would not have been seen as a lucky general.

So it was that German reaction lacked the expected energy and aggression. And Hitler's meddling in command details made a bad situation even worse. Through a combination of factors – including Bradley's refusal to use 'Funnies'* – the American assault on Omaha Beach met many difficulties and a rapid German armoured counter-attack might have caused disaster there; at the very least it would have made the American situation even worse than that at Salerno the previous September. Thanks to Hitler, there was no armour close enough to tip the balance. A panzer division near St Lô could have made all the difference. In vain had Rommel requested permission for such a deployment. Although 21st Panzer was near Caen, this was the only major armoured formation near the beaches. Rommel's plan to defeat the invaders on those beaches was thereby doomed by Hitler's refusal to allow his generals to fight as they wished. Nor would his second option be implemented for the very same reason: since Hitler had forbidden any withdrawal, Rommel's desire to pull back to a river line was ruled out. Furthermore, 21st Panzer was dispersed 'so that a concentration of all its forces in a short time was virtually impossible'.[4] Moreover, in the event of a landing near the Orne, the division was to detach elements to other formations, two infantry battalions going to 716th Division, its twenty-four anti-tank 88s to the same division** and its flak unit to Caen, where it was wiped out by naval gunfire before noon on D-Day.[6]

That no plan survives first contact is an old axiom but a truism nonetheless. So it was with the D-Day assault. Among the first things to go wrong was that the naval bombardment, although subduing enemy long-range guns, did not create the expected damage. The reason was simple: embrasures in the positions overlooking the beaches were placed to cover those beaches rather than the sea and so the seaward sides of

* Part of the reason for this was that the 'Funnies' were based on British tank designs that were not part of the US Army's inventory.

** Of these weapons, twenty-one were ordered west from the high ground upon which Feuchtinger had placed them and they fired not a single shot on D-Day whereas the three 88s that remained in position claimed no fewer than twelve Allied tanks that day.[5]

bunkers, which were pounded by the heavy naval guns, did not have the built-in weakness of an opening. And those bunkers were strong, demonstrating the ability of reinforced concrete, some two metres or more thick, with an earth covering in many cases, to take considerable punishment. Thus assaulting troops would meet more fire than their commanders had expected although the infantry were to land in the wake of tanks that should provide immediate support, and cover. Once again all did not go to plan.

The landing's timing had been arranged to take advantage of a flooding tide, thus reducing danger from underwater obstacles. Such a tide meant that the beach onto which the seaborne force would debouch was narrowing by the minute. The plan called for amphibious tanks to land first, followed by obstacle clearance groups, Flail tanks, assault engineers and infantry in a finely-tuned timetable. Although on some beaches DD tanks did arrive first, this was not true everywhere; on other beaches infantry landed first, or assault engineers, or clearance groups.

And it was at this stage that enemy defences began retaliating more effectively. Although there had been fire on the assault craft as they made for shore, its effectiveness had been diminished by the supporting fire that forced many defenders to stay under cover. As landing craft grounded, that supporting fire switched to the flanks and rear areas and the forward defenders opened up with the artillery, mortars and machine guns that had survived the bombardment. Thus it was that naval clearance parties could be seen working at the water's edge, sometimes submerged by breaking waves, as they tried to clear mined obstacles that were being covered by the tide, but always under fire. Farther up the beach, sappers worked on obstacles that were still fully exposed while Flails beat paths through possible mined areas and AVREs were bridging or pounding obstacles. Infantrymen were often working ahead of the armour and AVREs, to reach cover and overrun positions from which enemy fire was pouring across the shore. Many must have wondered if they had taken a trip to hell itself.

Among the first ashore were men of Hobart's 'Funnies'. Major Sidney Peter Moxham Sutton commanded a Westminster Dragoons' breaching team that landed at H-Hour to clear three lanes for infantry and armour. However, once ashore, it was found that the existing information on enemy dispositions was inaccurate, causing plans to be changed considerably. Against heavy fire, the team, including infantry, Flails 'and a variety of devices' pushed ahead and completed two lanes, one leading inland towards Ver-sur-Mer across an anti-tank obstacle. This was completed by Sutton himself in his command tank, by which time this was the sole Crab of his team still in action. Next day his team was in harbour when the Germans attacked under cover of field artillery at a range of 300 yards. Although wounded in the thigh, Major Sutton continued to command his squadron in a largely dismounted action that 'resulted in the capture of 100 prisoners and six field and anti-tank guns'. Paying little attention to his wound, Sidney Sutton stayed with the squadron for the next six days until he was forced to go into hospital. He was awarded the Military Cross for outstanding and courageous leadership.[7]

Royal Engineers were also early into action with 79th Armoured Division, among them Lieutenant Redmond Christopher Cunningham, who received the Military Cross for 'outstanding qualities of courage, dash and skill'. Lieutenant Cunningham, in an engineers' tank, landed on Queen Red Beach at Ouistreham at 6.00am, commanding No. 1 Troop 79 Assault Squadron of 5th Assault Regiment. His own tank received a direct hit from a heavy gun, both his Flails were knocked out, with all the crew of one Sherman killed, but Cunningham continued making his assault gap. When this was blocked by traffic he immediately began work on a new gap and that afternoon neutralised an enemy anti-tank position, thus allowing a squadron-strength attack on the lock gates at Ouistreham. Cunningham was left in command at those lock gates into the following morning.

From this position he searched the surrounding area thoroughly and uncovered many Germans, several of whom were killed while others were captured. Cunningham also found and removed demolition charges that had been placed to destroy the canal. 'During this period he showed outstanding qualities of leadership and courage which were a constant inspiration to the troop under his command.' He would earn a Bar to his Military Cross at Nijmegen.[8]

All along the beaches there were similar acts of courage and initiative as young men, and some not so young, began the long struggle that would end in Germany itself eleven months later. Many were in action for the first time, others had fought in the desert and in Italy, while some had been in France before, evicted from it by the Germans in 1940 and now returning to liberate Britain's traditional foe, which had become an ally in the past century. Some would not live to get off the beach. At 7.30am Nos 3 and 4 Troops, under Lieutenants Shaw and Burbridge, of B Squadron 22nd Dragoons touched down on Nan sector, with 4 Troop landing in six feet of water. The war diary notes that, apart from some small-arms fire and 'a few shells' there was not much opposition and the tanks reached shore safely to begin sweeping their allocated lanes. Five minutes later A Squadron, with two troops of B Squadron attached, touched down on Queen sector. By 3.30pm the regiment had lost four men dead with another five missing believed killed; six men were wounded. Another five missing men were found to have returned to Britain on a damaged LCT; this vessel had been damaged so badly that it had been forced to quit the beach with a damaged Flail jammed in its door. Several men had died on the LCT, including Lieutenant-Colonel Arthur Cocks, commanding 5th

Assault Regiment, RE. Five tanks had been knocked out and another ten damaged. Two lanes were opened by Flails of No. 4 Troop, C Squadron although the troop suffered many hits; Trooper Leonard Kemp, to whose memory this book is dedicated, was killed when Sergeant Cochran's tank was struck on the turret by an 88 round. By the end of the day, twelve men of 22nd Dragoons had been killed.[9]

On the right flank, 50th (Northumbrian) Division*, supported by 8 Armoured Brigade, was landing on Gold Beach with No. 47 (RM) Commando on its right flank, assigned to capture Port-en-Bessin, between Omaha and Gold Beaches, thereby providing the junction between American and British landings. Spearheading the Northumbrian assault were 231 and 69 Brigades; the latter had been with the Division since July 1940, and had fought at El Alamein, the former had been the Malta Brigade, providing that island's garrison during the siege, and had joined 50th Division in autumn 1943; it had seen further action in Sicily and Italy. In the centre, Juno Beach, the assaulting brigades of 3rd (Canadian) Division were the Canadian 7 and 8 Brigades with 2 Canadian Armoured Brigade supporting. On the Canadian left No. 48 (RM) Commando of 4 Special Service Brigade** was landing while No. 41 (RM) Commando of the same brigade landed on the right of 8 Brigade in 3rd (British) Division's assault on Sword Beach. The commandos were to neutralise coastal defences around Lion-sur-Mer and St Aubin before seizing the radar station at Douvres, which would then be searched by men from No. 30 Commando. That radar station proved an especially tough assignment and did not fall until 17 June. It was

> guarded by two underground fortresses, each furnished with deep and securely concreted living quarters, defended by several anti-tank guns, heavy machine guns and concrete weapon posts, and surrounded by a deep belt of mines and wire. It lay on the top of a crest which commanded an admirable view of the sea, and consequently of the D Day assault.[11]

On Sword Beach, 8 Brigade would be followed by 185 Brigade and then by

* While the term 'Division' is used throughout the text, these formations were normally divisional groups, usually strengthened by an independent armoured brigade; and in the case of 50th Division by a fourth infantry brigade. The brigades were also brigade groups with an armoured regiment under command as well as artillery, engineers and other support.

** The nomenclature Special Service Brigade gave rise to the unfortunate abbreviation of SS Brigade and the use of the term SS troops. On 6 December 1944 the Special Service Group was renamed the Commando Group and the SS Brigades became Commando Brigades, thus ending the embarrassment of a title that called up images of the German SS.[10]

9 Brigade; 27 Armoured Brigade provided 3rd Division's armoured punch. The extreme right of the British sector was the responsibility of 1 SS Brigade, under Lord Lovat, whose No. 4 (Army) Commando* was to be the first commando unit to land, on Queen Red Beach, a mile west of Ouistreham to take the Ouistreham area while the other units of Lovat's brigade would move inland quickly to link up with 6th Airborne Division and provide left flank protection of the beachhead along the Orne's east bank.

Each landing beach was sub-divided into code-named sectors: Sword included Oboe, Peter, Queen and Roger**, each normally a brigade objective, and there were yet more sub-divisions with Queen Beach including Queen Red and Queen White; the latter were normally battalion objectives. Thus the story of D-Day for British and Canadian forces is not simply that of Gold, Juno and Sword but of the smaller stretches of beach being assaulted by brigades, regiments and battalions. As with every story of war, the big picture is made up of a series of smaller pictures, moving right down to the level of the individual infantryman and his comrades in his section, the crewmen of a tank, the gunners of a detachment of Royal Artillery or the sappers of a clearance team.

We have already noted that 50th (Northumbrian) Division was to assault Gold Beach. And it was that formation that achieved the greatest level of success on D-Day, pushing as far as Bayeux, which was in British hands by the morning of the 7th. On Gold Beach the Northumbrians' assaulting brigades – 231 and 69 – were directed on Jig and King beaches respectively. The shore in that sector is low-lying and sandy, fringed by low dunes with soft patches of clay on the foreshore that would present difficulties for heavy vehicles. A lateral road runs near the seafront, behind which stretches wet grassland, patterned with dykes that hinder vehicular and infantry movement. Both beaches were covered by fire from German strongpoints and there were many obstacles, including mines and barbed wire.

Coming ashore on Jig were 1st Hampshire and 1st Dorset Regiments, the former on the right. For 231 Brigade seizure of le Hamel strongpoint was essential. One of several covering Jig Beach, this strongpoint included mines, barbed wire, trenches, an anti-tank ditch and fortified buildings, one of them 'a large and conspicuous sanatorium',[13] as well as

* Two French Troops of No. 10 (Inter Allied) Commando were assigned to No. 4 Commando for the landing.[12]

** An alphabetical sequence was used with the British/Canadian beaches beginning with Item, followed by Jig and King, all in XXX Corps' Gold Beach, then Love, Mike and Nan on Juno. At Omaha the US sub-divisions were Charlie, Dog, Easy and Fox while Utah included Tare and Uncle.

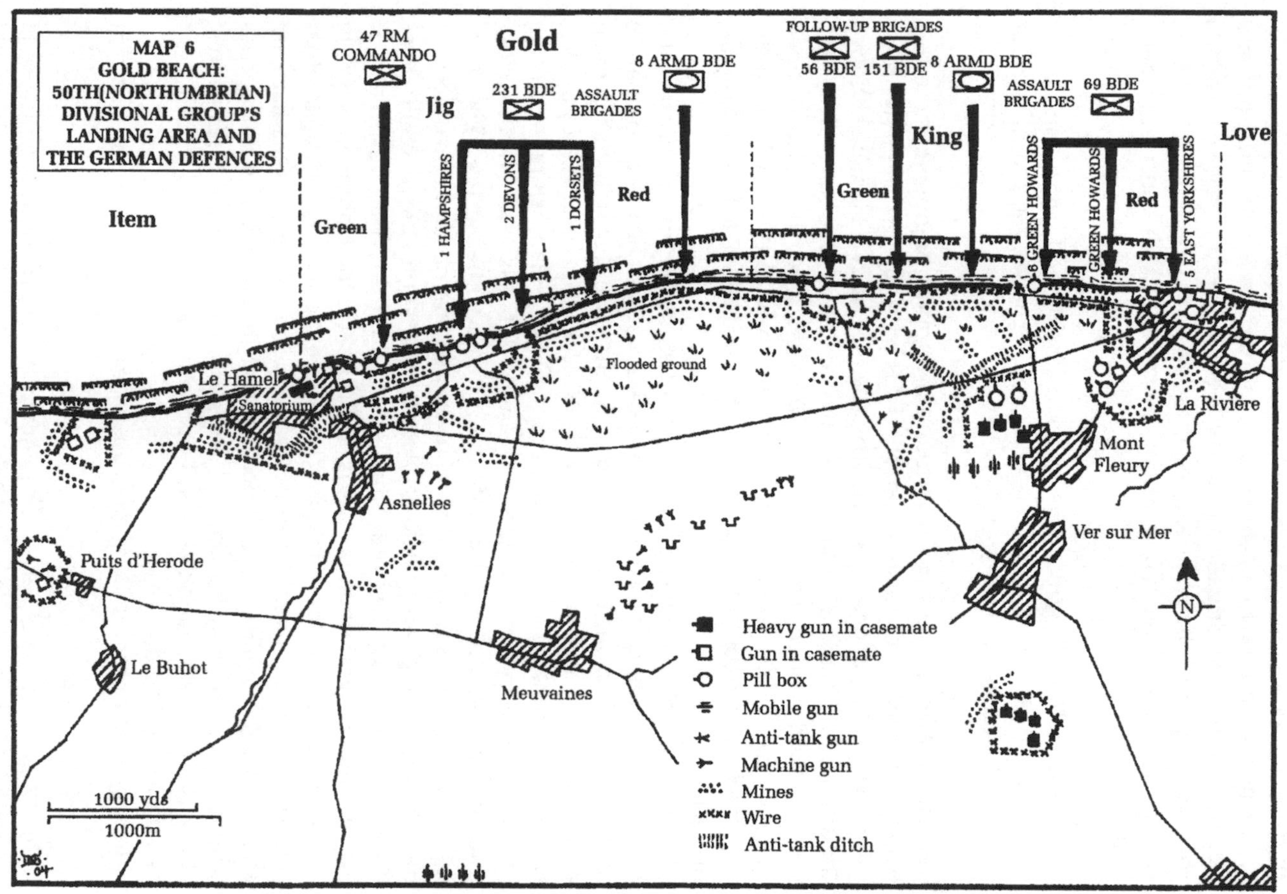
MAP 6
GOLD BEACH:
50TH(NORTHUMBRIAN)
DIVISIONAL GROUP'S
LANDING AREA AND
THE GERMAN DEFENCES
47 RM
COMMANDO
Gold
231 BDE
ASSAULT
BRIGADES
8 ARMD BDE
FOLLOW-UP BRIGADES
56 BDE
151 BDE
8 ARMD BDE
ASSAULT
BRIGADES
69 BDE
Jig
King
Love
Item
Green
1 HAMPSHIRES
2 DEVONS
1 DORSETS
Red
Green
6 GREEN HOWARDS
7 GREEN HOWARDS
Red
5 EAST YORKSHIRES
Le Hamel
Sanatorium
Flooded ground
La Rivière
Mont
Fleury
Asnelles
Ver sur Mer
Puits d'Herode
Le Buhot
Meuvaines
N
Heavy gun in casemate
Gun in casemate
Pill box
Mobile gun
Anti-tank gun
Machine gun
Mines
Wire
Anti-tank ditch
1000 yds
1000m

purpose-built concrete and steel pillboxes. It was held by a force of about company strength, with machine guns, mortars, two anti-tank guns and a field gun. But 231 Brigade's infantry were alone since the sea was too rough to swim the DD tanks ashore; these were to land from their LCTs, which had yet to arrive. Tony Hughes, serving in 24th Lancers, recalled that

> Many swimming tanks were lost and [the others] had to land in the normal way on D and D+1. Our wading tanks landed at various points and times on D and D+1.[14]

Ten tanks of 1st Royal Marine Armoured Support Regiment, mounting 95mm howitzers, were also to join the DDs but only five landed, fifteen minutes late. All but one were struck by shellfire from le Hamel. Although the strongpoint had been attacked by twelve RAF Typhoons with 1,000lb bombs, the defenders were far from subdued. They had also escaped attention from field artillery firing on the run-in to the beach since the earlier loss of two control vessels forced the omission of le Hamel from the fire plan.

In spite of these problems and their inherent augury of disaster, 1st Hampshires suffered relatively light losses as their leading companies landed. Wind and tide carried them some distance east of their intended touchdown area and they landed instead nearly opposite les Roquettes, where stood another German strongpoint. This the Hampshires overcame quickly before moving against le Hamel. But this was an altogether tougher proposition and the infantry ran into intense fire. The commanding officer was wounded as were the forward observation officer for the supporting ships and a field artillery battery commander* while every wireless set was knocked out. Unable to call on fire from destroyers or Royal Artillery units on their way in to the beach, the Hampshires had to await the arrival of the remainder of the battalion. When their other companies arrived, twenty minutes after the initial landings, a flanking attack through Asnelles was planned since a direct attack over the beaches would be suicidal without artillery support. To add to the Hampshires' litany of woe, the battalion's second-in-command was killed shortly after assuming command.

In spite of the fire from le Hamel, obstacle clearance teams were hard at

* Normal British practice was for the commander of a field artillery battery to accompany the battalion that his battery was supporting. In the German and American armies the battery commander was to be found with his battery. The British practice led to much greater trust between infantry and gunners and was one of the reasons that the British artillery arm was the arm of the British Army most feared and respected by the Germans.

work on the beach and cleared one gap on Jig before the rising tide stopped their work. While doing so the teams suffered heavy casualties. At the same time breaching teams were clearing exits to the coast road with their AVREs. On the beach 231 Brigade's build-up continued in steady fashion. Also ashore early were men from 50th Division's reconnaissance unit, 61st Reconnaissance Regiment. A recce regiment's normal job could not be performed in the confines of a beachhead but 61 Recce had two specific tasks: providing contact detachments on the beaches and, from H-hour plus 4, an assault reconnaissance regiment as part of a composite force with 8 Armoured Brigade, an infantry battalion and some RASC. That force was to break out of the beachhead, advance to Tessel Bretteville woods, harbour there for the night and move on next day to seize high ground overlooking Villers-Bocage. However, this plan was to go awry.[15]

The recce Contact Detachments suffered heavily, losing almost half their men killed or wounded with the assaulting infantry. Nonetheless they did 'well by the [Reconnaissance] Corps* badge, time and again beating the normal channels with information of importance'.[16] Some patrols, their wireless sets destroyed, performed sterling service as infantry soldiers. Their major achievement was to set up 50th Division's first signals links on the beachhead.

East of les Roquettes, 1st Dorsets were also landing and were more fortunate than their Hampshire comrades; their Westminster Dragoons' Flails and AVREs landed on schedule and were clearing mines and other obstructions. Although fire from le Hamel was less intense here, there were still casualties among the breaching teams. But the infantry were able to get off the beach, leave a company to form a firm base at les Roquettes and advance inland. At Meuvaines they captured a machine-gun post before bypassing le Hamel to move on Buhot where an enemy strongpoint at Puits d'Herode menaced Arromanches and the neighbouring shoreline.

The third battalion of 231 Brigade, 2nd Devons, landed close to le Hamel at about 8.15. Since the guns of le Hamel had not been silenced and there were still many beach obstacles, the Devons had a dangerous time landing and clearing the beach. Most of the battalion moved around Asnelles and pushed on for Ryes, some two miles south of Arromanches but a company was left to support the Hampshires at le Hamel. Following the Devons were the men of No. 47 (RM) Commando, who were to move inland and then westward behind enemy lines to seize

* The Reconnaissance Corps had been absorbed into the Royal Armoured Corps on 1 January 1944 but it retained its own distinctions. All regiments of the Corps wore a common cap badge, although there were some modifications to the badge in a number of regiments.

Port-en-Bessin. The commandos suffered losses from beach obstacles, many of which had not been cleared due to the rising tide. Three landing craft were damaged and sunk and forty-three men lost their lives; considerable equipment, including wirelesses, was lost. Even so, some 300 men made it ashore, obtained a wireless set from 231 Brigade Headquarters and set off across country to Port-en-Bessin.

On King Beach, some 1,000 yards to the east, 69 Brigade's assault battalions, 6th Green Howards and 5th East Yorkshires, were also ashore. Fewer difficulties had attended their landing since their AVREs and obstacle clearance groups had preceded them. As the Green Howards moved against the strongpoint at Hable de Heurtot, with support from engineer tanks, there occurred an action that resulted in the sole Victoria Cross of D-Day.

> With the help of tanks of 4th/7th Dragoon Guards, however, [the] Yorkshiremen seized their objectives. Prominent in the 6th Battalion was Sergeant-Major Stanley Hollis, who single handed stormed a by-passed pillbox that threatened his company from the rear. It was but the first of the series of heroic exploits that day that won him the only Victoria Cross to be awarded for the D-Day assault.[17]

Appropriately Hollis was a veteran of Dunkirk. He had also served in North Africa and experienced an earlier landing – in Sicily. Stanley Hollis also cleared a nearby trench and went on to take part in a further heroic action that afternoon. In the village of Crepon his company met a German field gun, its crew protected by machine guns. Undeterred, Hollis led the capture of the gun and its crew. 'Wherever the fighting was thickest C.S.M. Hollis appeared and it was largely through his heroism and resource that the objective was gained without any undue casualties.'[18]

Resuming their advance the Green Howards took the battery position near Mont Fleury where the gunners, shocked by the bombardment's intensity, surrendered willingly; the position, hit by bombs and a dozen rounds from HMS *Orion*, seemed not to have opened fire at all. Also near Mont Fleury, the East Yorkshires captured a strongpoint at the lighthouse, with two guns and thirty prisoners, but the earlier part of their day had been much more difficult. Landing near la Rivière, the battalion had been pinned down under the sea wall by heavy fire. Support was called for and destroyers and other support craft closed to engage the enemy positions. Then a Westminster Dragoons' Flail silenced an 88 in its concrete emplacement and the East Yorkshires took the position with forty-five prisoners before moving on to capture the village after several hours at a loss of ninety dead and wounded. Having secured the lighthouse strongpoint near Mont Fleury, the battalion advanced towards Ver-sur-Mer.

At 8.30 the third battalion of 69 Brigade landed. This was 7th Green

Howards who also made for Ver-sur-Mer where they found no enemy at all and so advanced on the battery beyond the village. Once again the effects of bombing and naval bombardment, this time from HMS *Belfast*, left defenders with little spirit. Fifty were made prisoner and four 100mm gun-howitzers were taken; these had fired almost ninety rounds before the position fell.

In 50th Division's area, both assault brigades were moving inland while engineers had cleared two paths through beach obstacles and made two vehicle exits from the beach. A steady build-up of resources of both brigades was taking place: DD tanks from 4th/7th Royal Dragoon Guards and Sherwood Rangers (Nottinghamshire Yeomanry) had landed from LCTs soon after the leading infantry and there were further tanks from 6th Assault Regiment Royal Engineers and the Westminster Dragoons, the latter with Flails. SPGs from three field regiments – 86th, 90th and 147th* – were landing along with anti-tank guns, mortars, machine guns, Bren-gun carriers, jeeps and other vehicles. Progress was good on Gold Beach.

Also landing on Gold–King were eight tanks from 1st Royal Marine Armoured Support Regiment. These were 95mm howitzer-equipped Centaur MkIVs, a variant of a tank developed by Leyland Motors to use a Rolls-Royce Meteor engine but fitted with a Nuffield Liberty engine because of a dearth of Meteors (a converted Merlin aero-engine); when Meteor engines became available the tank was modified to become the Cromwell.[20] The Group had been formed earlier in the year to provide additional fire support for the first assault waves but the Marines' experience had not been good. Scheduled to fire on the run-in, the units were assigned to specially-adapted LCTs fitted with side armour, which made their existing moderate seaworthiness even worse so that, in the poor sea conditions, some had foundered, others had broken down and some came to grief on beach obstacles. Over all five beaches only one in four Centaurs landed within the first fifteen minutes after H-hour and only forty-eight, from a total of eighty, within the first four hours. Even after landing some were disabled by enemy action but the Marines performed good service with the survivors, fighting them as battle tanks once the close-support role became redundant.

Such was the progress of 50th Division that its first reserve brigade – 151, an El Alamein veteran – began landing behind 69 Brigade about an hour before noon. It was followed about noon by 56 Brigade, which landed near Hable de Heurtot, to avoid the fire still sweeping Jig from le Hamel where it had been planned to land. Thus, by early afternoon on D-Day, all four brigades of 50th Division, plus its supporting armour and RM Commando, had landed.

* Respectively 86th (East Anglian) (Herts Yeomanry) Field Regiment, 90th (City of London) and 147th Field Regiment (Essex Yeomanry), all of which were TA regiments.[19]

In the Juno sector, the leading elements of 3rd Canadian Division, 7 and 8 Brigades, landed on Mike and Nan beaches with 7 Brigade tasked to capture Courseulles and Graye, while 8 Brigade's objectives were Bernières-sur-Mer and St Aubin-sur-Mer. Fittingly the naval force carrying and supporting the Canadians was Force J, born of that disastrous experience at Dieppe almost two years before. Tragically, on this morning, Force J lost, or had damaged, ninety landing craft from a total of 306; some became casualties on the way in while others were lost or suffered damage as they withdrew after discharging their loads. Part of the reason for this is the nature of the coast at Juno. Once again it is low-lying with a reef offshore that is exposed at low tides. The only approach free from the danger of striking that reef is through a gap, roughly a mile wide, off the mouth of the Seulles river and opposite the port of Courseulles. Needless to say, the Germans had thickened the beach obstacles thereabouts and strengthened the waterfront. There were the usual mines and barbed wire with concrete pillboxes for machine guns and mortars while houses on the front had been turned into miniature fortresses. Artillery was sited either side of the harbour entrance and could fire east or west along the shore from concrete revetments. Such was the task facing the Canadians at Courseulles. And prospects were no better at Bernières-sur-Mer and St Aubin-sur-Mer where similar defences had been created, while the sole road from the shore had been barricaded with a concrete wall.

Weather conditions forced a change of timings on the Canadian commanders. Originally 7 Brigade had been due to land from 7.35am with 8 Brigade's landing beginning ten minutes later but a ten-minute delay was agreed upon since some landing craft were held up by the rough weather. In spite of this change in timings the schedule still went awry. Most DD tanks, although swum ashore, arrived behind the infantry; only on one sector did DDs precede the infantry as planned. The AVREs suffered delay through their carrying vessels entering the wrong swept channel en route to Normandy and the first infantry wave was also behind schedule. On the final approach the rising tide meant that landing craft had to ground among beach obstacles, since that tide had prevented clearance groups from doing their work and conditions were too rough to work underwater. Thus larger craft had to risk striking obstacles as they came onshore while smaller craft tried to manoeuvre through those obstacles.

> The courage and resolution of their crews matched the occasion and they showed much skill and daring in bringing them in; there was no pause in the landings but the loss and damage to landing craft was severe.[21]

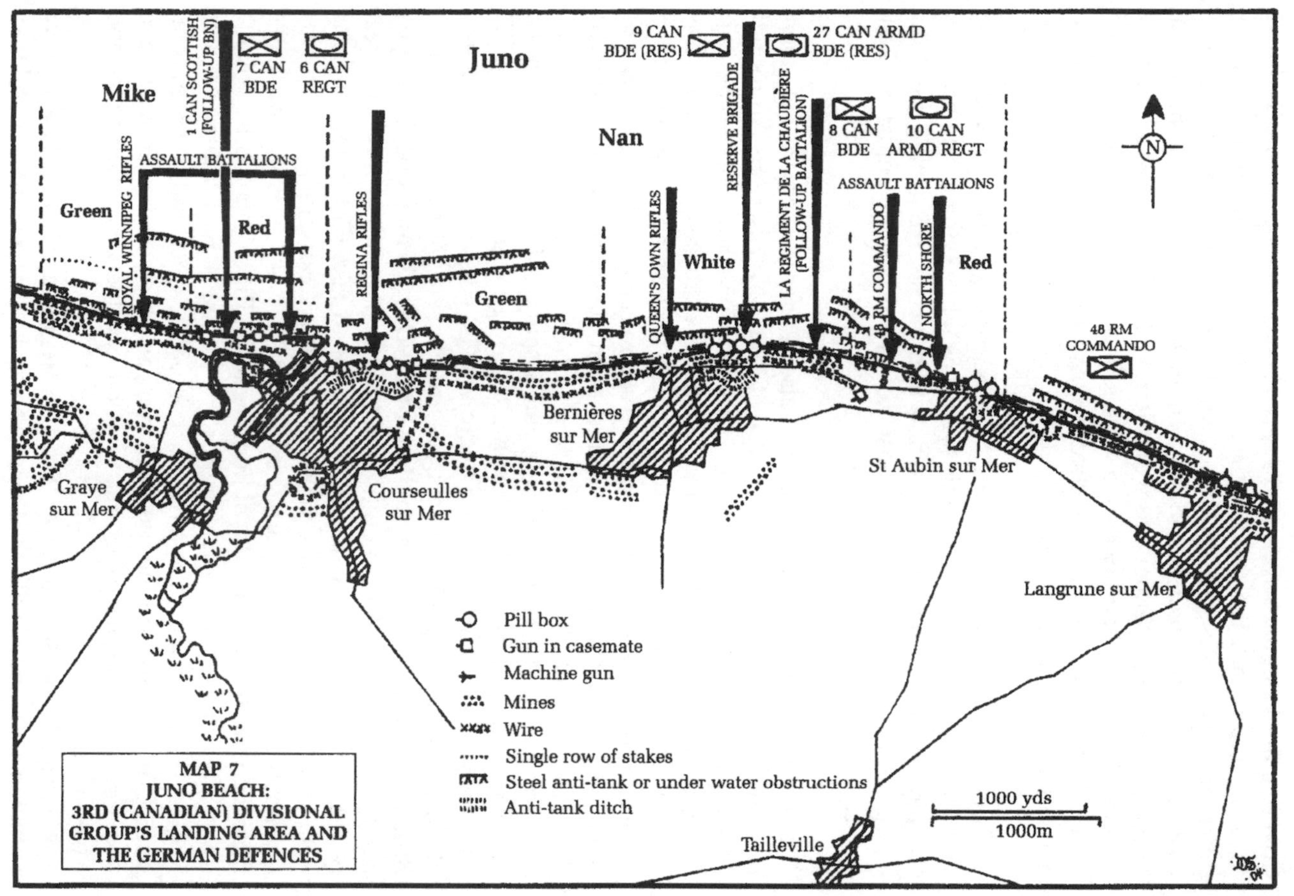
Mike
Juno
Nan
1 CAN SCOTTISH (FOLLOW-UP BN)
7 CAN BDE
6 CAN REGT
9 CAN BDE (RES)
27 CAN ARMD BDE (RES)
8 CAN BDE
10 CAN ARMD REGT
N
ASSAULT BATTALIONS
ROYAL WINNIPEG RIFLES
Green
Red
REGINA RIFLES
Green
QUEEN'S OWN RIFLES
White
RESERVE BRIGADE
LA REGIMENT DE LA CHAUDIÈRE (FOLLOW-UP BATTALION)
ASSAULT BATTALIONS
48 RM COMMANDO
NORTH SHORE
Red
48 RM COMMANDO
Graye sur Mer
Courseulles sur Mer
Bernières sur Mer
St Aubin sur Mer
Langrune sur Mer
Tailleville
Pill box
Gun in casemate
Machine gun
Mines
Wire
Single row of stakes
Steel anti-tank or under water obstructions
Anti-tank ditch
1000 yds
1000m
MAP 7
JUNO BEACH:
3RD (CANADIAN) DIVISIONAL GROUP'S LANDING AREA AND THE GERMAN DEFENCES

Covering fire from destroyers and support craft kept enemy heads down as assault craft made their way to the shore but once on the beach it was a different matter with considerable German fire, especially from mortars. One LCA – 1150 – had its side blown in by a mortar or a mine but fortunately only one soldier was wounded while a mined obstacle blew in the side of LCA 1059 and two men were killed. Of the flotilla of five craft to which these vessels were attached, four were lost but not before they had landed troops.

> despite all difficulties, landing craft bearing infantry . . . landed the soldiers with very few casualties. It was while lying in the breakers among the obstacles or when withdrawing from this perilous position that they suffered most heavily. Mercifully most of their crews were saved.[22]

The Centaurs with the Canadians also suffered because of their unseaworthy craft; of the forty tanks of 2nd Royal Marine Armoured Support Regiment supporting 3rd Canadian Division, only some half dozen were landed on D-Day. Juno Beach had been assigned two groups of small 'Hedgerow' equipped landing craft to clear lanes through beach minefields but, although one group arrived to carry out its task ahead of the infantry at Bernières, only one craft from the second group survived the passage from Britain.

At Courseulles harbour 7 Brigade was assaulting the beaches with the Royal Winnipeg Rifles and the Regina Rifle Regiment, supported by DD tanks of 6th Canadian Armoured Regiment (1st Hussars). Canadians had already earned a reputation for house-to-house fighting in Italy and 7 Brigade's soldiers lived up to that on D-Day. While one Winnipeg company attacked defences on the west of the harbour entrance, the rest of the battalion moving behind the harbour to take Graye sur Mer, the Regina Rifles met the port's main defences in Courseulles, which was defended stubbornly. Supported by Royal Marine Centaurs and tanks from 26 Assault Squadron Royal Engineers, the Rifles eventually took the town after much bitter street fighting; by then it was afternoon. The Reginas were then joined by a reserve company, which had lost men from two LCAs that struck mines on the run-in, and the battalion moved on to take Reviers, some two miles inland at the confluence of the Seulles and Mue rivers.

A company of the Canadian Scottish Regiment, 7 Brigade's reserve battalion, had landed with the Winnipegs and advanced to Vaux and then to Ste Croix where the remainder of the battalion, landing behind the Winnipegs, later joined them. However, the fact that beaches near Courseulles remained under fire while fighting raged in the town delayed the Canadian build-up as the clearing of beach exits fell well behind schedule. This was not aided by the fact that landing craft carrying breaching crews of assault engineers were landing late and irregularly.

On Nan beach 8 Brigade's assaulting battalions – Queen's Own Rifles of Canada and the North Shore (New Brunswick) Regiment, supported by 10th Canadian Armoured Regiment (The Fort Garry Horse), also met strong opposition. The Fort Garry lost one LCT with four tanks aboard to shellfire on the run-in and two of the remaining tanks, which waded in, were knocked out on the shoreline but the regiment still had thirty-four tanks to support the infantry who had preceded them. At Bernières much of the defences had survived the naval bombardment and the Queen's Own Rifles suffered heavy enfilading fire while advancing on the sea wall from the beach. Once at the wall they made a flanking attack and the defenders surrendered quickly. To the east the North Shores had a similar experience at St Aubin-sur-Mer, which was also defended with determination. Assault engineer tanks supported the New Brunswickers but it took some three hours to subdue the garrison and, even when the main position fell, snipers continued harassing the Canadians until nightfall. The North Shore reserve company landed twenty minutes after the initial landing and made immediately for Tailleville to the south.

At 11.30am the third Canadian brigade – 9 Brigade, including the Highland Light Infantry of Canada, the Stormont, Dundas and Glengarry Highlanders and the North Nova Scotia Highlanders – began landing. By then only a narrow strip of very congested beach was available and although some beach exits had been cleared these were blocked from time to time by broken-down vehicles or enemy shellfire. With fighting still underway in Bernières the congestion was aggravated but the situation began to ease when the town was cleared. Even with these setbacks, the main body of 3rd Canadian Division was ashore by 2 o'clock that afternoon. This included the four field artillery regiments – 12th, 13th, 14th and 19th – as well as the third regiment of 2 Armoured Brigade, 27th Canadian Armoured Regiment (The Sherbrooke Fusiliers) and 8 Brigade's third battalion, Le Régiment de la Chaudière.

No. 48 (RM) Commando, with headquarters 4 SS Brigade, landed on the Canadian left flank at about 9 o'clock.

> There was quite heavy fire on the beach and several . . . LCI carrying the Commandos were holed on the beach obstacles. This led, in the state of the sea and owing to the weight carried, to a high proportion of casualties, many of whom were rescued after being 'partially' drowned. They were, however, lost as far as the initial operations were concerned.[23]

There were further losses as the defenders, recovering from the bombardment, manned weapons and opened fire with machine guns as the commandos raced for the sea wall. Of the 400 men of No. 48 Commando, only about half set off on the two-mile march to attack Langrune-sur-Mer, which had also been subjected to heavy fire from the sea. Having reached Langrune, the commandos met a concrete strongpoint accessible only through narrow streets swept by enemy fire. The first assault on the strongpoint failed but it seemed as if success might beckon with the arrival of a Centaur but the tank was disabled by a mine; No. 48's attack went no farther that day.

Similar misfortune befell No. 41 (RM) Commando, which landed with 3rd British Division to the left of No. 48 Commando. The unit lost its second-in-command, Major Barclay, who was killed, and its westward move to link up with No. 48 was thwarted by intense opposition near Luc-sur-Mer.

No. 41 Commando had been attempting to move from Sword Beach to Juno Beach. It was on Sword that 3rd Division, once commanded by Montgomery and chosen by him as an assault division for D-Day, was landing. Sword, between Lion-sur-Mer and Ouistreham, is about two and a half miles in length, flat in nature and with houses along the length of the coast road. Both Lion-sur-Mer and Ouistreham were fortified and another heavily defended and well-protected strongpoint lay midway twixt the pair at la Brèche. West of la Brèche was Queen Beach where 3rd Division was to land on a single brigade front, the assault formation being 8 Brigade, followed by 185 Brigade and then 9 Brigade. The decision to strike on such a narrow front was intended to put the maximum possible weight into the strike to take Caen and link up with 6th Airborne Division.

The first wave of 8 Brigade to hit the beach included companies of 1st South Lancashires and 2nd East Yorkshires who stepped ashore without a single casualty at 7.30. Little enemy reaction was encountered until the troops began landing, another tribute to the support fire's effectiveness. Twenty minutes later the remainder of both battalions were landing. Armoured support for 8 Brigade was provided by DD tanks of 13th/18th Royal Hussars, 27 Armoured Brigade, thirty-four of which were launched at sea. Another six were brought in by landing craft. Of the DD Shermans that set out to swim ashore only two foundered but six were knocked out while beaching. A little later another four tanks were knocked out but the Hussars could still deploy twenty-eight tanks to support the infantry. These could be supplemented by two Centaur troops from 5 Independent Battery, Royal Marines Armoured Support Regiment which arrived within the first fifteen minutes of the landing; another troop landed later. With the leading infantry came breaching teams with assault engineer AVREs and Flails of 22nd Dragoons. The obstacle clearance groups with 8 Brigade had an especially difficult time as the wind was driving in from the sea which was rushing in so rapidly that the groups could make but one clear passage and had to await a receding tide before beginning more; some sappers were washed away as they struggled to make safe mines and bombs attached to the obstacles.*

That fast rising tide meant that the foreshore on Sword was soon restricted to about fifteen yards. Barbed wire separated the shore from the sea front road and there were machine-gun posts at irregular intervals while fire from la Brèche strongpoint swept both shoreline and beach. Fortunately there were few casualties as the infantry crossed the exposed ground to the built-up area that, at least, offered some protection. While a company each of South Lancashires and East Yorkshires advanced to attack the strongpoint, another South Lancs company moved to provide right-flank protection; this was soon joined by the depleted No. 41 (RM) Commando, which was to capture the German position at Lion-sur-Mer. Meanwhile, 2nd East Yorks struck out towards Ouistreham to seize two positions at the south-east of the town. In their wake followed No. 4 Commando with its two attached French troops of No. 10 Commando to take Ouistreham and its battery. As the battle for la Brèche continued, the remainder of 1st South Lancashires advanced on Hermanville-sur-Mer, which was in British hands by 9 o'clock. Just over an hour later la Brèche finally fell with its three guns, three heavy mortars and machine guns, all of which had caused considerable hurt to troops and landing craft on the beach. The South Lancashires had lost their commanding officer killed among 107 dead or wounded. Their East Yorkshire comrades had suffered similar loss. Eight Brigade's third battalion, 1st Suffolk, followed the assault battalions and also experienced a difficult time while landing and moving off the beach. By early afternoon 3rd Division's other brigades – 185, 9 and 1 SS, had landed. To the men of 2nd Royal Ulster Rifles in 9 Brigade the run-in was notable because the shoreline looked so familiar

> until everyone realized that it was the 'wave-top' view that they had spent such a long time memorizing. It was rather a surprise to see so many of the houses still standing, apparently undamaged.[25]

As the Rifles made their run-in, many men were sick because of the very choppy sea but worse followed as they tried to get ashore.

> Many . . . Riflemen being small in size were finding it difficult to get ashore, particularly in view of the fact that over and above their normal kit – heavy enough – they were carrying a bicycle. Company Sergeant Major Walsh of 'A' Company, and Rifleman Ryan, M.M., of 'B' Company did great work by getting a life line ashore from the Landing Crafts Infantry and holding them in such a manner that

* The Royal Engineers lost 121 officers and men killed on D-Day alone.[24]

> others were able to beach themselves with greater ease. Few casualties were experienced on the beach, those there were being from shell and mortar fire.[26]

As on Gold Beach so on Sword a reconnaissance regiment provided Contact Detachments. Here it was 3rd Reconnaissance Regiment (Northumberland Fusiliers), which also formed the Beach Traffic Control Group under Major Gill, who became a casualty in the first hours ashore. While Contact Detachments, of which there were twelve, worked with divisional and brigade headquarters and battalions, the Control Group strove to maintain steady traffic flows through beach exits, in which congestion was building up and space diminishing. In spite of heavy shellfire, the Control Group kept traffic moving and the Beach Exit Officers, Captain Stevens and Lieutenants Brogan, Brough and Farnworth, displayed considerable initiative and were firm in handling traffic. Thus they ensured that vehicles were cleared from the heavily congested beach in the early hours of the invasion. At the planning stage, such traffic control had been identified as a key factor for subsequent success and 'the fact that the flow of traffic forward from the beach exits went relatively smoothly must be largely attributed to Major Gill and his men'.[27]

The 'relatively smoothly' of 3 Recce's historian is a classic example of the understatement so typical of British officers for there was that massive traffic jam caused by the inrushing tide which led to critical delays. With the distance between waterline and the beach exits down to a third of what had been expected, Gill and his men had no easy task. In addition, too many non-essential vehicles were brought ashore in the first hours and it can be seen how difficult was the task of maintaining order in the traffic.

> Even after clearing the beach, vehicles could only move very slowly along a narrow road between minefields; that added to the problems on the beach. The Staffordshire Yeomanry's tanks were static for an hour before the Beach Control Group could get them moving; having cleared the exit the Staffords then entered a nose-to-tail queue that delayed them even more and put plans for the deployment of the regiment well behind schedule.[28]

As with their colleagues of 61 Recce, the Contact Detachments of 3 Recce were often the sole means of communication between units and their headquarters on Sword and, with the Beach Traffic Control Group, must be numbered among the unsung heroes of the assault. In those ranks they stand alongside other undoubted heroes, men such as the obstacle clearance groups, the assault engineers and the crewmen of the landing craft who risked life and limb to bring their charges into shore and then

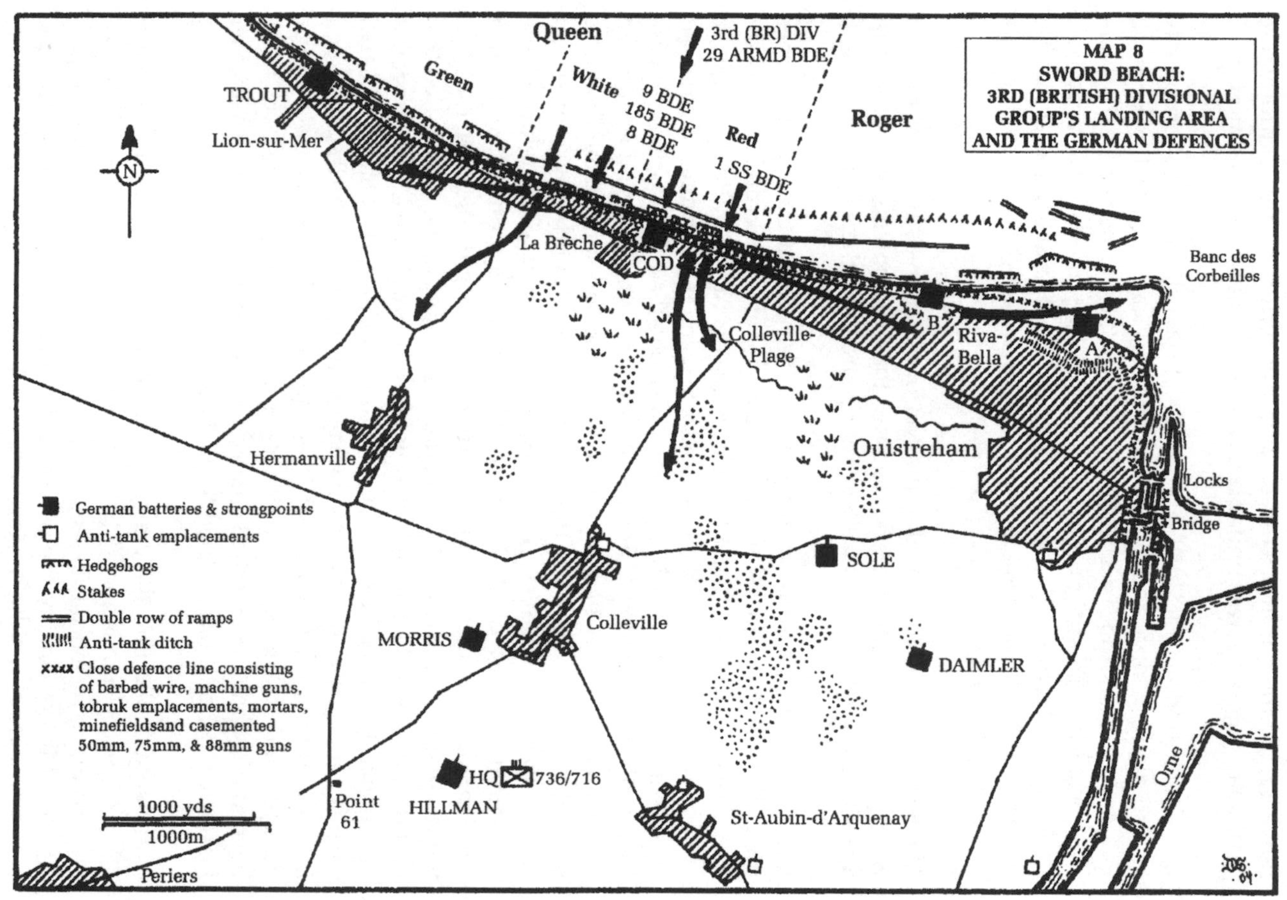
MAP 8
SWORD BEACH:
3RD (BRITISH) DIVISIONAL
GROUP'S LANDING AREA
AND THE GERMAN DEFENCES
Queen
3rd (BR) DIV
29 ARMD BDE
Green
White
9 BDE
185 BDE
8 BDE
Red
1 SS BDE
Roger
TROUT
Lion-sur-Mer
N
La Brèche
COD
Banc des Corbeilles
B
A
Colleville-Plage
Riva-Bella
Hermanville
Ouistreham
Locks
Bridge
SOLE
Colleville
MORRIS
DAIMLER
HQ
736/716
HILLMAN
Point 61
St-Aubin-d'Arquenay
Orne
Periers
1000 yds
1000m
German batteries & strongpoints
Anti-tank emplacements
Hedgehogs
Stakes
Double row of ramps
Anti-tank ditch
Close defence line consisting of barbed wire, machine guns, tobruk emplacements, mortars, minefieldsand casemented 50mm, 75mm, & 88mm guns

move off in their flimsy vessels. But the writer of the Staffordshire Yeomanry war diary was unimpressed with the beach organisation.

> Touched down at 1030 hrs on White beach and had practically speaking a dry landing. A terrible jam on the beach where no organisation appeared to be operating and no marked exits were seen. The majority of our tanks remained stationary for approx. 1 hour . . . Traffic control seemed non [existent] and even after leaving the beach vehicles remained head to tail for long periods on the only available routes.[29]

The text of the war diary held in the National Archives at Kew is marked with pencilled question marks against these comments and it would appear that the diarist's views were not shared by others in the regiment.

Since they were dispersed throughout the British and Canadian beaches the units of 79th Armoured Division have not always received the credit they deserve; but it is difficult to see how the overall operation could have gone as well as it did without their efforts using the 'Funnies' developed in recent years. Anti-tank ditches could be filled by fascine-carrying Churchills or bridged by Churchill AVREs carrying bridging equipment while Sherman Crabs flailed paths for armour and soft-skinned vehicles through the minefields. And then there were the Petard-armed tanks and the Churchill Crocodiles, either of which could deal with enemy strongpoints by use of the Petard's 40lb mortar round that could inflict considerable damage on concrete, or the flame gun of the Crocodile, which created as much fear as it did damage. Many of these men died that first day; this was the fate of the crew of one Churchill of 22nd Dragoons as outlined by the official historian. After a bridging tank and Crabs had cleared a track, with three Crabs damaged, progress was further impeded by an anti-tank ditch, nine feet deep and fifteen wide. A fascine was dropped and an armoured bulldozer set to work filling in the trap. Then, beyond it, a blown culvert had created a water-filled crater which another fascine-carrying Churchill tried to fill. Unfortunately

> the 'tank slid into the crater and gradually disappeared from view except for its fascine.' The crew baled out but were all killed or wounded by mortar fire before they could reach cover. Other sappers freed the fascine by explosives and a bridge 'was dropped from the seaward side on the sunken tank which acted as a pier' but left a gap on the far side; this was filled with logs carried from the shore where the Germans had collected them for the construction of obstacles. 'A causeway was built out and about 0915 hours the first D.D. tank got across behind the assaulting companies' and more followed.[30]

In turn the gunners arrived but their first gun stuck on the bridge and needed three bulldozers and two AVREs to free it. Thereafter the horse and cart of a bemused and 'disinterested farmer' were pressed into service to complete the track, using rubble from damaged houses. At last the way was clear for traffic off the beach.[31]

By 10.30am the British and Canadians had landed fifteen infantry battalions, five Army or Royal Marine commandos, seven armoured regiments plus elements of two Royal Marines' armoured support regiments, nine field artillery regiments, two engineer assault regiments and elements of five beach groups, including detachments from both the Royal Navy and Royal Air Force. And all on a beachhead no more than five miles wide. Small wonder that there was congestion and that some field gunners went into action with waves lapping around them. Such was the narrowness of the beach that at one point it measured but fifteen yards where ten times that width had been expected. On at least two beaches, Gold and Sword, the assaulting divisions had begun moving forward. The Allies had succeeded in gaining a foothold in France, albeit a precarious one. Omar Bradley commented: 'you can always force an invasion, but you can't always make it stick.'[32] And making it stick was what the Allies now had to do.

Eisenhower had already told the world that Allied forces were in France. A press release, or communiqué in the language of the day, had been issued from his headquarters at 9.05am.

> Under the command of General Eisenhower, Allied naval forces supported by strong air forces began landing Allied armies this morning on the northern coast of France.[33]

Credit was given in this statement to all three elements of the Allied forces, each of which played its own vital role in the invasion. Even at this early stage it was clear that the Atlantic Wall had been breached. In fact, the Wall proved to be no more than a skin, lacking the depth that defences need and which Rommel had wanted. Had the Desert Fox had his way, and the time and materials, the Wall would have been five miles in depth with millions of mines and many more other obstacles in the invaders' path. Now, within hours of the first Allied troops setting foot in Normandy, only some strongpoints of the Wall held out.

The initial German reaction had been much slower than expected but this was also a reflection of the degree to which deception plans had succeeded. Although Montgomery had told his commanders that, by the evening of D–1, the Germans would be certain that the Allies were coming in strength to the Bay of the Seine,[34] that was not the case. Even on the morning of the 6th the Germans were still uncertain about what was happening. There are several reasons, in addition to the deception plans, for this. As already noted, German meteorologists were confident that weather conditions precluded an invasion. Because of this the Kriegsmarine had not stationed any patrols in the Channel – and had even failed to notice the concentration of Allied minesweepers operating off the Normandy coast as dusk fell on the 5th. And the Luftwaffe was equally responsible for the failure to note the Allied activity that had begun on the Monday evening. On the morning of D-Day the Luftwaffe was conspicuously absent, that narrowly averted collision between George Boyd and a Bf109 being possibly the morning's only sighting of a German aircraft.

However, Fifteenth Army had intercepted the message to the French Resistance, the Army of the Interior, to begin D-Day operations, although that message, broadcast by the BBC from London, contained no hint of where the invasion might occur. Nor did the Germans regard the resistance as anything other than a nuisance; it was certainly not considered a serious military force, a view shared by SHAEF. Since there had been many false alarms in preceding months, Fifteenth Army was placed on alert and informed von Rundstedt's headquarters which decided that there was no need to place Seventh Army on alert, although a warning was issued of the possibility of widespread terrorist activity.

The absence of so many commanders from their headquarters had an undoubted influence in the state of semi-lethargy that seems to have overtaken the defenders. With Rommel in Germany, Dollman at Rennes, Dietrich in Brussels, Feuchtinger missing and others also absent, there was a definite lack of leadership. Not until 1.35am was Seventh Army finally placed on alert as a result of reports of paratroops landing. But again there was confusion when it was found that many of these 'paratroopers' were dummies: was this all a massive ruse? General Marcks called out his LXXXIV Corps at about 1.00am, but when soldiers of 352nd Division were sent by bicycle to pursue paratroopers about three hours later they found only dummies. As the night wore on, more senior officers became convinced that an invasion had begun. General Max Pemsel, chief of staff of Seventh Army, phoned Rommel's headquarters repeatedly to tell Speidel, Rommel's chief of staff, that this was a major operation and at 3.00am von Rundstedt's headquarters reported to OKW that large-scale airborne operations were underway. Three hours later, von Rundstedt's headquarters told OKW that they considered that an invasion was underway and asked for the release of the armoured reserve, I SS Panzer Corps, stationed near Paris. This is where the baleful influence of Hitler came into play. It was the Führer's firm command that the OKW reserve could be released only on his personal order. Hitler, however, was asleep – and had the habit of sleeping well into the day – and nobody wanted to risk his ire by waking him. The request to release I SS Panzer Corps was denied; it would take another ten hours before the Corps was released on Hitler's order.

After 6 o'clock came news of the Allied naval bombardment and the morning air attacks. Pemsel telephoned Fifteenth Army headquarters forty-five minutes later to tell them that Seventh Army expected to be able to cope without reinforcement whereupon Fifteenth Army's commander took himself to bed. That line of action was also taken by most of Rommel's staff at la Roche Guyon, something it is impossible to imagine happening had Rommel been present. More than an hour after the BBC broadcast the SHAEF communiqué, Rommel left home to drive to la Roche Guyon. Once again he had been caught wrongfooted when Montgomery moved. It took him nearly twelve hours to reach his headquarters.

The inertia that seemed to afflict the German command did not percolate down to the soldiers on the ground whose opposition to the invaders was the typical doughty and scientific defence of the German soldier. This was brought home especially to the Americans trying to land on Omaha Beach: one of the factors that led to the Omaha landings being so bloody was the unexpected presence of an additional German division – 352nd – in the area. Even where second-line garrison divisions, those numbered in the 700 series, were holding the line, stout opposition was often to be found, although many of their soldiers took the first available opportunity to surrender. This was especially true when the soldiers were members of Ost battalions.

Aerial opposition was virtually non-existent as Allied air forces dominated the skies, while that from the Kriegsmarine was but a pinprick in comparison to the Allied naval effort, although that pinprick included the sinking of the Norwegian destroyer, HNMS *Svenner* by German torpedo-boats. A smokescreen laid by Allied aircraft to shield the invading force from heavy guns at le Havre had the side effect of allowing a torpedo-boat flotilla to slip unseen out of that port and attack Allied ships. Although engaged by the latter, the torpedo-boats escaped under cover of the same smoke that had concealed their attack. Two torpedoes passed between the battleships *Ramillies* and *Warspite* while HMS *Largs* avoided another by going full astern; that torpedo passed just a few feet ahead of *Largs*. HNMS *Svenner* was to port of *Largs* and was not so fortunate; a torpedo struck under the boiler room at 5.30am. *Svenner*'s back was broken and she sank quickly but most of the crew were saved. This daring attack was the Kriegsmarine's sole contribution to opposing the invaders that morning.[35] For the rest of the day, German naval activity was summarised by Admiral Krancke who wrote that 'no effective blow could be struck at such a superior enemy force'.[36]

That enemy land forces were much more determined than their air and naval forces did not need to be spelt out for the men landing on the five beaches. Resistance continued to be dogged and movement off the beaches was slow. In Second Army's sector this was most pronounced on 3rd (British) Division's front. The division's assault brigade – 8 Brigade – had made relatively good progress in its early hours. By the middle of the morning Hermanville was in the hands of 1st South Lancashires while 2nd East Yorkshires were clearing the southern outskirts of Ouistreham. The brigade's third battalion, 1st Suffolks, had captured Colleville before moving on to attack two of several enemy strongpoints with codenames that, quaintly, were those of British car manufacturers: Daimler, Hillman, Morris and Rover. There was a further, much smaller, strongpoint known as Sole, close to Daimler; Rover also lacked the heavy guns of Daimler, Hillman and Morris. Morris lay about a half mile before Hillman; the former mounted four 105mm guns while the latter had two weapons of that calibre and a further pair of 75s. Daimler, with four 155mm guns, lay west of Morris on the south-western outskirts of Ouistreham while Sole lay close to Daimler. (See map 8)

The simple statement that Hillman mounted four guns does not begin adequately to explain the position's strength. It was surrounded by barbed-wire belts and girdled by mines, behind which lay an almost perfect example of German military engineering. Sunken bunkers of reinforced concrete protected the defenders while armoured machine-gun cupolas threatened any adversary approaching the complex. And complex it was: Hillman covered an area of 400 by 600 yards – almost fifty acres – and was built so strongly that remnants of it survive today. Morris and Hillman dominated the route south from Colleville and together represented probably the toughest defensive position on the Norman coast. These posts were manned by soldiers from 716th Division, which, although a second-line formation, was quite capable of making best use of the ground that they held; and they had the support of 21st Panzer Division, lying nearby at Caen. Hillman had another advantage: since it was so well camouflaged, Allied intelligence was unaware of its full strength. The soldiers of 1st Suffolks found out just how strong it was on the afternoon of D-Day.

Eight Brigade was to capture both Hillman and Morris and the Suffolks found that Morris posed few difficulties. An artillery bombardment with a further contribution from the Royal Navy convinced the garrison of Morris that holding on was not a good idea; about 1.00pm the defenders surrendered. Hillman was a different story. It had not received the attention from air and sea that other strongpoints had, partly because its true nature and extent had not been recognised; this was illustrated when the first attack upon it by the Suffolks was made by a single company, supported by a breaching platoon and three mine-clearance teams. Furthermore, Hillman was, again unknown to the attackers, the headquarters of 736th Grenadier Regiment and its defenders were determined to resist. A plan to provide supporting fire from a Royal Navy cruiser came to naught because the bombardment liaison officer had been killed and no one else attached to 8 Brigade was trained for this function. And the Staffordshire Yeomanry tanks that should have supported the Suffolk men were delayed by congestion in the beach exits and the roads. Thus that first attack went in unsupported but, although protective wires were breached, the surviving infantry could not close on the objective because of the intense machine-gun fire sweeping the ground before them. Then a tank from the Staffords arrived and was sent forward, with infantrymen sheltering behind it. The Sherman opened fire on the offending cupola but its armour-piercing shells had no effect on the machine-gun post.

A new plan was necessary to neutralise Hillman. By-passing the strongpoint was not an option. When 1st Royal Norfolks of 185 Brigade did just that during the afternoon, the battalion suffered almost 150 casualties from Hillman's fire.* The battle continued well into the evening and tanks of 13th/18th Hussars as well as those of Staffordshire Yeomanry went into action against Hillman. It was a slow, methodical 'crumbling' battle as the attackers had to breach the mine-belt before tackling the concrete emplacements individually. Many defenders proved so obstinate that they fought until the death, usually when an emplacement was blown up. This was a Great War type battle on a smaller scale, but a taste of things to come in Normandy. Fighting continued until 8.00pm.

Next morning Hillman's defenders finally gave up the struggle and left their strongpoint to be made prisoner. Even after the casualties inflicted upon them, 270 officers and men, including a full colonel, went 'into the bag'.[38] Suffolk casualties were surprisingly light with seven dead and twenty-five wounded. This brutal battle had delayed the advance of both 8 Brigade and 185 Brigade, whose 2nd King's Shropshire Light Infantry was to lead the advance towards Caen, supported by the Staffordshire Yeomanry and 7th Field Regiment, with the brigade's other battalions – 2nd Warwicks and 1st Norfolks – to either flank of the KSLI. But two squadrons of tanks were tied up in the battle for Hillman whereas one ought to have been with the Shropshires as they took the road for Caen.

Some historians have criticised the Suffolks' role in this battle, suggesting that the battalion was tardy in its attack. The chief critic has been Chester Wilmot who opined that the Suffolks spent too much time planning their attack. Wilmot termed the critical afternoon planning period as

* The Norfolks believed that they had been fired upon by British troops.[37]

> a luxury which the invaders could not afford . . . The need of the hour was for speed and action, almost regardless of casualties. The way had to be cleared or the initiative . . . lost. And yet the Suffolks spent most of the afternoon organizing their attack and they do not appear to have proceeded with the urgency the situation demanded.[39]

But Wilmot's criticism ignores the fact that the Suffolks had no prior warning that Hillman would be so formidable and were, therefore, not prepared for the form of assault needed to take the strongpoint. Had they, and the divisional command, known the true nature and extent of Hillman a very different type of attack would have been laid on at the beginning. There is no doubting the courage of the Suffolks at Hillman but even that raw courage could not speedily remove the strongpoint. Third Division's advance towards Caen was knocked behind schedule by the need to overcome Hillman.

The delay at Hillman also assisted German operations to counter the Allied advance. In the early hours of the day airborne landings had been the focus of German attention and, in the British sector, detachments from 736th Grenadier Regiment and from the Panzer Grenadier regiments of 21st Panzer Division – 125th and 192nd – had made attack after attack on positions held by elements of 6th Airborne Division on both sides of the Orne but had failed to push the airborne soldiers out. Had 716th Division been a first-rate formation rather than a static garrison division, these efforts might have had more success. With the seaborne landings presenting imminent danger in 716th Division's area, LXXXIV Corps' commander ordered that 21st Panzer Division be pulled out of action east of the Orne to meet 3rd Division's incursion west of the river, although the forward infantry units engaged against 6th Airborne were left to contain the British bridgehead and hold open the Troarn road. By mid-afternoon German commanders had decided that the operations around the Orne presented the greatest danger and required concentrating reserves there. It should be remembered that German intelligence was both scanty and inaccurate for much of that day: Seventh Army did not learn of the Utah assault until 4.40pm, and concentrated efforts against the American airborne troops in the western sector as a result, while LXXXIV Corps believed that the landings on Omaha by the US V Corps had been smashed. Hence the decision to concentrate on the German right flank.

Feuchtinger's division had been well dispersed that morning with a battalion from each Panzer Grenadier regiment forward on either side of the river to oppose both 3rd Division and 6th Airborne, its anti-tank guns forming a gun line along the Périers ridge, supported by a battalion of field artillery south of the ridge, its anti-aircraft guns around Caen and the remainder of the divisional artillery on high ground about fifteen miles south-east of Caen. The division disposed some 16,000 men, 127 Panzer MkIVs, forty assault guns and twenty-four 88mm anti-tank guns with the tanks a few miles north-east of Falaise. On LXXXIV Corps' order, two battlegroups including the tanks, which Feuchtinger had ordered to move against the airborne troops, changed direction to cross the Orne at Caen and Colombelles; one tank company was left to support operations against 6th Airborne. The move was spotted by Allied air reconnaissance and Dempsey asked for air strikes against enemy troop movements into Caen from the south and south-east. This request was made at about 11 o'clock and from then on the battlegroups came under almost continuous air attack, but few casualties were inflicted, the Germans becoming expert at baling out and taking cover under their tanks. By early afternoon 21st Panzer's reconnaissance unit was probing towards 3rd Division's area and it was clear that the division would insert itself between 3rd Division and Caen by that evening. Marcks, LXXXIV Corps' commander, drove to Lebisey, where the start-line for 21st Panzer's counter-attack was situated, to oversee the coming battle. In spite of Allied air interdiction, traffic congestion, changes of orders and other delays imposed by their own command rather than the Allies, 21st Panzer was ready to attack 3rd Division before 5 o'clock. By this stage, Feuchtinger could call upon ninety tanks and two infantry battalions. Another appearance by the Luftwaffe seems to coincide with this counter-attack although the aircraft attacked landing craft at Sword Beach rather than supporting 21st Panzer. Six Junkers Ju88s carried out a low-level raid and scored some hits but lost three or four aircraft shot down.[40]

This counter-attack was to write 'finis' to any British chances of taking Caen on D-Day. Much has been made over the years by many writers and historians about this failure; and it has been used as a cudgel with which to bludgeon Montgomery's reputation. But was the capture of Caen on D-Day ever a realistic aim? Did Montgomery really intend that Second Army, in the form of 3rd Division, should take the city? Or was the possible capture of Caen nothing more than a best-case scenario?

The Caen–Carpiquet area *was* an objective for Second Army. Montgomery said so in his exposition at St Paul's School on 15 May. The airmen were especially keen that the flatter land south and south-east of Caen should be taken for airfield construction while Carpiquet airfield could be put into use by the tactical air forces very quickly. The British official historian supports the view that capturing Caen was a D-Day objective.

> It must also be borne in mind that the D-day task of the assaulting divisions was not only to capture and then link up the beaches along the coast between Port en Bessin and the Orne, but to strike rapidly inland, and by the evening of D-day, to occupy a bridgehead which

> would include Bayeux and Caen and be joined to the ground east of the Orne which the 6th Airborne Division had already seized.[41]

However, that same historian goes on to qualify this statement by outlining the difficulties inherent in such operations.

> It was known that the enemy's nearest armoured division available for prompt counter-attack was stationed immediately east and south of Caen; the quick capture of that key city and the neighbourhood of Carpiquet was the most ambitious, the most difficult and the most important task of Lieut-General J. T. Crocker's I Corps.[42]

Thus the difficulties facing Second Army were anticipated. While capturing Caen on D-Day may have been desirable, it was not essential. Without the presence of German armour, the capture of Caen may have been realistic and Montgomery certainly expressed the intention that the city might be in Allied hands on D-Day; but this can only have been a best-case scenario. No one knew better than Montgomery the tenacity of the German soldier in defence, nor the doughty manner in which the panzer crews would fight; he had learned that lesson at El Alamein and in the pursuit thereafter. The role of Second Army, and First Canadian Army when it formed in Normandy, was to protect the Allied eastern flank, drawing the enemy, and especially his armour, into battle there while allowing US forces to capture Cherbourg and then break out of the bridgehead and swing towards the Seine. Omar Bradley makes this clear:

> Second Army was to seize the road center at Caen on D day and expand its beachhead toward the flat tablelands beyond that city. The American forces would then pivot on the British position like a windlass in the direction of Paris . . . British and Canadian armies were to decoy the enemy and draw them to their front on the extreme eastern edge of the Allied beachhead. Thus while Monty taunted the enemy at Caen, we were to make our break on the long roundabout road towards Paris.[43]

While the average British and Canadian soldier may not have taken kindly to Bradley's suggestion that they were 'taunting' the enemy about Caen, the fact remains that British and Canadian forces were to hold the enemy there, and prevent Fifteenth Army from entering the battle to support Seventh Army. This was a difficult and bloody task that would call for much sacrifice from the young men of both armies but would bring about the result that the Allied commanders wanted.

NOTES

1 Fraser, *Knight's Cross*, p. 485.
2 von Luck, *Panzer Commander*, p. 170.
3 Hastings, *Overlord*, p. 68. Feuchtinger insisted in his subsequent interrogation by Allied intelligence officers that he was at his post when the first invading troops arrived. NA, WO205/1021, Special Interrogation Report, General Edgar Feuchtinger, p. 5 (also numbered p. 6).
4 NA, WO205/1021, p. 5 (also numbered p. 6).
5 Ibid.
6 Ibid.
7 *Volunteers from Eire who have won Distinctions serving with the British Forces.*
8 Ibid.
9 NA, WO171/841, war diary, 22nd Dragoons; Birt, *XXII Dragoons*, pp. 170–1.
10 Messenger, *Commando*, p. 301.
11 Birt, op cit, p. 186.
12 Messenger, op cit, p. 261.
13 Ellis, *Victory in the West*, p. 171.
14 Hughes to author. Ellis notes in *Victory in the West* that 24th Lancers did not come ashore until D+1; in fact, significant elements of the regiment landed on D-Day.
15 Doherty, *Only The Enemy in Front*, pp. 148–9 (no war diary for 1944 has survived for 61 Recce); Willis, *None Had Lances*, pp. 85–6; NA, WO171/613, war diary, 8 Armd Bde.
16 Taylor, *This Band of Brothers*, p. 168.
17 Powell, *The History of The Green Howards*, p. 211.
18 Smyth, *The Story of the Victoria Cross*, pp. 401–2.
19 Frederick, *Lineage Book of British Land Forces*, pp. 522–3.
20 Hogg & Weeks, *The Illustrated Encyclopedia of Military Vehicles*, p. 102.
21 Ellis, op cit, p. 179.
22 Ibid, p. 180.
23 NA, ADM202/99; RM Commandos in Normandy.
24 Army Roll of Honour.
25 Graves, *History of the Royal Ulster Rifles vol iii*, p. 103.
26 Ibid.
27 *History of 3rd Reconnaissance Regiment (NF) in the Invasion and subsequent campaign in North-West Europe 1944–45*, p. 7.
28 Doherty, op cit, p. 141.
29 NA, WO171/863, war diary, Staffordshire Yeomanry.
30 Ellis, op cit, p. 182.
31 Ibid.
32 Bradley, *A Soldier's Story*, p. 256.
33 Quoted in Ellis, op cit, p. 193.
34 Hamilton, *Monty, Master of the Battlefield, 1942–44*, p. 561.
35 Ellis, op cit, pp. 162–3.
36 Ibid, p. 162.
37 NA, WO171/1350, war diary, 1 R Norfolk.
38 D'Este, *Decision in Normandy*, p. 133n.
39 Wilmot, *The Struggle for Europe*, p. 310.
40 Mace, *Forrard*, p. 123.
41 Ellis, op cit, p. 171.
42 Ibid.
43 Bradley, op cit, pp. 239–41.

CHAPTER VIII

The battles around Caen

The foe vaunts in the field

When tanks of 21st Panzer clashed with 3rd Division's spearhead on the Caen road there began not only the battle of that day but another that continues to be waged by historians today. The results of the latter remain elusive but those of the afternoon and early evening of 6 June 1944 are a matter of history. We have already seen that 2nd King's Shropshire LI had moved off alone since the tanks of Staffordshire Yeomanry had been delayed. The other battalions of 185 Brigade, 2nd Warwicks and 1st Norfolks, were also farther back than planned, not having moved off until some hours after the KSLI. When the Norfolks were ordered forward, it was to take high ground to the Shropshires' left; it was at this stage that the battalion suffered heavily while by-passing Hillman when about half their number lost their way in high standing corn and came under fire.[1]

Between Sword Beach and Caen lay country suited to mobile operations. Some regarded it as similar to East Anglia with its rich farmland of open fields beyond the built-up coastal strip. This was neither bocage, nor the little highlands known as the Suisse Normande. Here progress might be expected. En route to Caen, 185 Brigade would cross several ridges, the first a half-mile south of Hermanville, their assembly area. Another two miles south lay the next ridge, topped by the village of Biéville, and, finally, another mile and a half away and but three miles north of Caen, lay the third, crowned by a richly wooded area and Lebisey village. Around the village and wood the Shropshires, supported by the Staffords, and their German foes would clash.

The delays at the beach exits meant that the Staffords could muster less than two squadrons of tanks by noon although the Shropshires were to move off at 12.30pm. After a hurried conference between the brigade commander, Brigadier Pearce Smith, and the Shropshires' commanding officer, Lieutenant-Colonel F J Maurice, both arriving at the meeting outside Hermanville by bicycle, it was decided that the infantry would set off unsupported, allowing the Staffords to catch up along the road.[2]

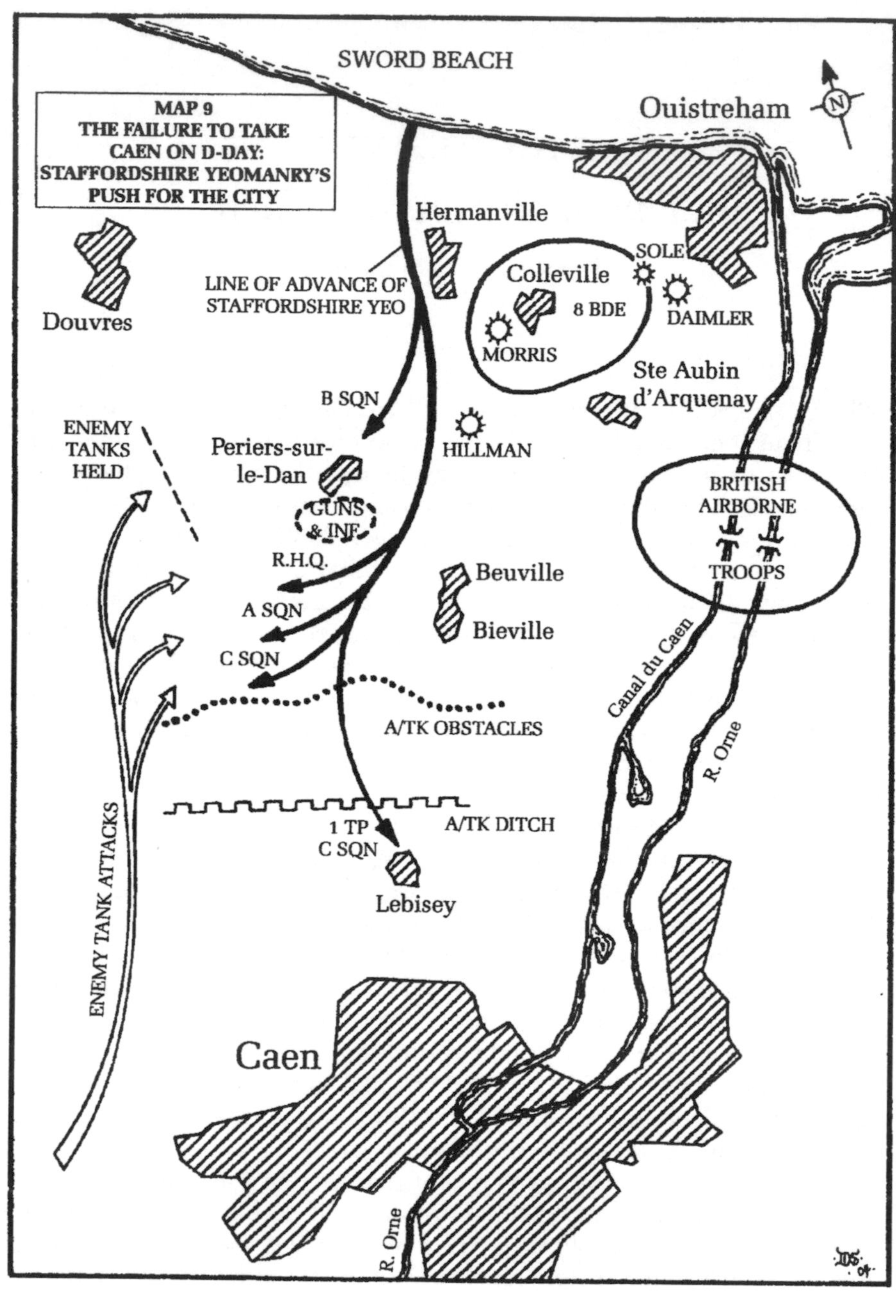
SWORD BEACH
MAP 9
THE FAILURE TO TAKE
CAEN ON D-DAY:
STAFFORDSHIRE YEOMANRY'S
PUSH FOR THE CITY
Ouistreham
N
Hermanville
SOLE
Colleville
8 BDE
DAIMLER
MORRIS
LINE OF ADVANCE OF
STAFFORDSHIRE YEO
Douvres
Ste Aubin
d'Arquenay
B SQN
HILLMAN
ENEMY
TANKS
HELD
Periers-sur-
le-Dan
BRITISH
AIRBORNE
TROOPS
GUNS
& INF.
R.H.Q.
Beuville
A SQN
Bieville
C SQN
Canal du Caen
A/TK OBSTACLES
R. Orne
ENEMY TANK ATTACKS
A/TK DITCH
1 TP
C SQN
Lebisey
Caen
R. Orne

The Shropshires' W Company had a battle at Périers-sur-le-Dan while en route to Caen, meeting strong opposition from an enemy battery, which had not been silenced. By then – about 2.00pm – the leading tanks had caught up, but five Staffordshire tanks and four Westminster Dragoon Flails were disabled by fire from the woods to the right. Z Company went in with the Yeomanry to assault the enemy position but without artillery support. Fortunately, a Polish deserter from the German unit guided the Shropshires through the wire around the battery and the guns were taken and destroyed for the loss of thirty casualties. While this engagement was taking place, the remainder of the battalion and the armour set off for Beuville and Biéville; a Staffords squadron remained to secure high ground, and 185 Brigade's right flank, at Point 61 on Périers ridge. W Company had a brief action around Biéville château where the company commander and two platoon commanders had a narrow escape when a German shell landed nearby while they were planning their next move. Then a group of German tanks forced dispersal. But Biéville was cleared with the help of a Staffords squadron. After that a dash for Caen began.[3]

That dash came to a sudden end at about 4 o'clock when a Staffordshire troop, recce'ing ahead, reported enemy tanks moving up from Caen. The spearhead of 185 Brigade had met 21st Panzer's counter-attack. An urgent order went out to the Staffordshire squadron with the Suffolks at Hillman to move to Biéville. Scarcely had the tanks reached there but some forty German tanks hit them in a fast and furious attack.[4]

Two panzers fell to the Staffords' Shermans and another pair to the Shropshires' anti-tank guns; the remainder veered into the woods, still being engaged by the Shermans and field-gun fire. When the panzers re-appeared they came under fire again, with some losses, and the survivors made for the woods a second time. Joined by other panzers they then made a wide flanking move towards the Périers ridge. But the Staffords' squadron at Point 61 were ready for such a move and engaged their foes, knocking out three German tanks before the remainder withdrew. By now some thirteen panzers had fallen victim to the Staffords or to anti-tank guns; the sole British casualty was a self-propelled anti-tank gun. Other panzers moving to join the battle were strafed by Typhoons, which left two in flames and another four belching smoke.[5]

When this phase of the battle concluded Y Company 2nd Shropshires set off again for Caen. But their dash was ended about a mile short of Lebisey wood by heavy fire from Germans holding the wood and blocking the road. As shells landed in their midst, both leading company commanders were killed. Although two KSLI companies penetrated Lebisey wood, their situation was precarious; both flanks were open and nothing protected their rear while they could hear German tanks beyond the woods in the direction of Caen. As at Hillman, the corn was high, thus reducing visibility and so Lieutenant-Colonel Maurice decided to pull both companies back and consolidate his positions around Biéville and Beuville. By midnight the Shropshires had withdrawn from Lebisey ridge. In the course of that day the battalion had sustained over a hundred casualties. Lieutenant-Colonel Jack Maurice was awarded the Distinguished Service Order for his leadership.[6]

During the night elements of 21st and 12th (SS) Panzer Divisions reinforced Lebisey ridge. They would not be evicted for another six weeks.[7] Once again the true nature of an obstacle had not been recognised; aerial photographs had not revealed how formidable was the ridge with its narrow lanes, heavily covered by trees, and commanding view over the surrounding area.

The other battalion of 185 Brigade, the Warwicks, had found le Port, north of Bénouville bridge, still in enemy hands but, as they prepared to attack – at about 9.00pm – they were distracted by the sight of two large aerial columns as tug aircraft and gliders came in low from the Channel with a fighter escort. One column released its gliders over Colleville to land north of Bénouville bridge while the second flew on towards Ranville where its gliders landed on Zone N. The sight of this great 'balbada' brought cheering from British troops but must surely have caused a sinking feeling in many German stomachs; Seventh Army recorded that 21st Panzer's counter-attack was 'rendered useless by heavily concentrated airborne troops'.[8] The attacking panzers withdrew to positions on a line from Cambes to the Orne canal, between the Shropshires and Caen. The sole German counter-attack of D-Day was over, having penetrated to the coast near Lion, although this involved only a few tanks.[9] Following this interruption, the Warwicks continued their attack, cleared le Port and contacted the airborne at Bénouville before clearing the château south of the bridge. The men of 7th Parachute Battalion were relieved, in more ways than one, by the Warwicks' arrival and were able to join the remainder of the battalion east of the river. Meanwhile the Warwicks continued their advance, finally halting at Blainville, by which time the clock had passed midnight and it was now D+1. By then the Norfolks were stopped for the night between Beuville and Bénouville.[9]

Sixth Airborne Division's position had been much improved by the end of the day. The airborne soldiers had defended their positions with considerable determination and great gallantry, repulsing every attack. They had been assisted by the arrival of Lord Lovat's 1st Special Service Brigade and the skirl of the pipes of Piper Bill Millin, Lovat's personal piper, must have cheered many hearts. Throughout that day the bravery of the airborne troops was tested many times and there were many acts of gallantry, one of which illustrates their determination.

Viewed in the cold light of history many acts of outstanding courage may appear as examples of madness or desperation. That definition might apply to the act that earned the Distinguished Conduct Medal for Private Michael John McGee of 7th Parachute Battalion. McGee, from County Tyrone in Northern Ireland, fought at Bénouville where his company was in action for some twenty-one hours, while cut off from the main body of the battalion and subjected to determined attack from superior numbers of German infantry supported by SPGs and tanks.[10]

On one occasion a German tank* approached the position held by McGee and his comrades. As the tank approached, Michael McGee leapt forward, firing a Bren gun from the hip. While this may have seemed suicidal to his comrades it surprised the tank crew so much that the vehicle stopped, but opened fire on McGee. Other soldiers of McGee's company ran towards the stationary tank and 'put it out of action with a hand bomb'. Michael McGee's courage had saved the day for his company and the subsequent recommendation for the Distinguished Conduct Medal noted that his 'complete disregard for his personal safety was largely responsible for the successful and gallant action fought by his co[mpan]y'.[11]

Michael McGee died from his wounds later that day. He is buried in Bénouville churchyard with some twenty other soldiers, mostly from 6th Airborne, who perished in the area and, therefore, his Distinguished Conduct Medal was a posthumous award. Officially gallantry awards, other than the Victoria Cross and Mention in Despatches, could be not be awarded posthumously and this remained so until 1977; but in this case – as in many others – a Nelsonian eye appears to have been turned to the letter of the law. The recommendation for McGee's DCM went to 5 Airborne Brigade's headquarters where it was approved on 10 June. Next 6th Airborne Division's headquarters gave it immediate approval and forwarded it to corps headquarters on 12 June. It arrived at Second Army headquarters on 16 June and was approved formally on 12 July. The announcement that Private Michael John McGee (since died of wounds) had been awarded the DCM appeared in the *London Gazette* of 22 March 1945. McGee's courage deserved recognition and might even have earned a posthumous Victoria Cross; but those who recommended him probably thought they were more certain of the DCM.[12]

Of course there cannot be medals for everyone and some soldiers are remembered only by headstones in war cemeteries, or French civilian cemeteries, or by names on memorials to the missing. Some receive a little more recognition. One such was a soldier of 22 Independent Parachute Company, Lance-Corporal Edward O'Sullivan. The 22-year-old was

* In the battalion war diary and in the citation for McGee's DCM, the tank is identified as a Panther, although it may have been a Panzer MkIV.

killed on D-Day at Touffreville and buried in the churchyard there. But he will long be remembered in the village since the square in front of the church is named in his memory.[13]

Elsewhere in 3rd Division's area, 8 Brigade was ensconced firmly at Hermanville, Colleville-sur-Orne and Ouistreham, having captured Daimler and most of Hillman, while 9 Brigade was deployed to protect the divisional right flank since elements of 21st Panzer had probed between 185 Brigade and the Canadians. However, 9 Brigade's commander and several brigade staff had been wounded by a mortar bomb and Lieutenant-Colonel Ian 'Tommy' Harris, 2nd Royal Ulster Rifles, had assumed command of the brigade which was disposed on the high ground between Périers-sur-le Dan and St Aubin d'Arquenay, where it remained for the night. Harris was probably unaware that the brigade commander had been told by divisional headquarters, from which he was returning when he was wounded, that 9 Brigade was to concentrate its effort on supporting the airborne bridgehead rather than in advancing to Caen. That evening and night, Royal Engineers and Royal Army Service Corps* bridging troops worked under fire to clear mines, booby traps and other obstacles and build Bailey bridges, capable of taking any tank, over the Orne and the canal. This endeavour confirms that 3rd Division, or elements of it, was to move to support 6th Airborne.[14]

Third Canadian Division had been delayed by the congestion on the beaches and exits but its brigades had pushed forward with vigour over country that was, at first, rolling agricultural land, with high standing fields of corn. South of the Seulles the topography changes, rises are steeper and the valleys of the Seulles and its tributaries create narrow chokepoints. This is especially true of the valley of the Mue river that formed part of the inter-brigade boundary between 7 and 8 Canadian Brigades. The Royal Winnipeg Rifles, with an assault company of 1st Canadian Scottish and tanks of 1st Hussars, led 7 Brigade's advance; the remainder of the Canadian Scottish and the Reginas followed. Although there were many machine guns and artillery pieces covering villages, roads and river crossings en route, no major strongpoints impeded the brigade, which made steady progress. Many Germans surrendered as the Canadians took Banville and Ste Croix-sur-Mer before the Winnipegs advanced towards Tierceville to cross the Seulles while the Canadian Scottish made for Colombiers-sur-Seulles. Reviers was taken by the Reginas thus securing the river crossing there. By 4.00pm most of the brigade group was across the Seulles with 726th Regiment pulling back 'in

* The engineers were from 17 and 71 Field Companies, RE and the bridging troops from 106 Bridging Company, RASC.

some disorder in face of the Canadian advance'.[15] Some half-mile to the Canadians' right, elements of 50th (Northumbrian) Division had taken Creully.[16]

At 4 o'clock the Reginas advanced again, supported by 1st Hussar tanks, and despite heavy shelling near Fontaine-Henri continued south-westwards out of the Mue valley to capture le Fresne-Camilly on the road from Arromanches to Caen via Creully.

Meanwhile 8 Brigade had also been making steady progress, led by Le Régiment de la Chaudière with a squadron of Fort Garry Horse and artillery. Moving off from Bernières at noon, the group took a battery position west of Tailleville and, by 2.30pm, had taken Bény-sur-Mer. Into the bag went fifty prisoners and four 100mm guns of 1716th Artillery Regiment which had been hit by some 200 rounds from HMS *Diadem*'s 5.25-inch guns. Less a company clearing St Aubin on the coast, the North Shores advanced on Tailleville where a battalion headquarters and company of 736th Regiment held out in the ruins. The North Shores had to work through those ruins and Tailleville was not cleared until later that afternoon.

The Chaudière/Fort Garry group moved off from Bény in late afternoon and within an hour had reached Basly. Soon after 5 o'clock they captured Columby-sur-Thaon. To their left, Queen's Own Rifles had taken Anguerny and were closing on Anisy. Skirmishes continued until a late hour. Meanwhile, the company of North Shores at St Aubin had taken the strongpoint, although sniping continued throughout the night, but Royal Marine Centaurs had to be deployed at Langrune, which continued to hold out against No. 48 (RM) Commando. Naval fire was also called for but failed to bring about an enemy submission. Protected by fortified houses, behind minefields and concrete barricades, the Germans defied the efforts of the Commando to knit up Juno and Sword Beaches.[17]

The third Canadian brigade – 9 Brigade – assembled south of Bernières by about 2.30pm and moved off for Carpiquet, some ten miles distant. But their route lay through Bény-sur-Mer from which 8 Brigade was not clear until late afternoon. This delayed 9 Brigade who did not reach Bény until after 7 o'clock. At 6.30pm a group composed of The North Nova Scotia Highlanders mounted on Sherbrooke Fusiliers' tanks set off for Villons les Buissons, capturing en route some mortars and anti-tank guns that had fired on them from the right flank. Villons marked the limit of advance. The Highlanders' battlegroup halted there with soldiers of 3rd British Division only three miles away but with tanks of 21st Panzer between Canadian and British troops. Overnight the group was to create a 'fortress' at the junction of the Anisy–Villons les Buissons and Courseulles–Caen roads while the brigade's main body harboured near Bény.[18]

Perhaps the best progress by any Canadian troops on D-Day came from the tanks of 1st Hussars. Although 7 Brigade was ordered to harbour for the night at Fontaine-Henri, le Fresne-Camilly and on the high ground south of Creully, two Hussar troops had earlier become separated from the infantry – whether by accident or design is not certain – and advanced to the main road and railway between Bayeux and Caen, the day's final objective. Brushing aside light opposition the tanks raced on through Bretteville l'Orgueilleuse and almost to Carpiquet. Then, finding themselves without infantry support, they retraced their tracks to rejoin their squadron. Overall the Canadians could be pleased with their day's progress; their armour had shown considerable initiative, knocking out at least twelve 88s.[19]

On the British–Canadian right, 50th (Northumbrian) Division made best progress of all. With the division complete on shore shortly after noon, it was not long before brigades moved out towards initial objectives while No. 47 (RM) Commando struck westwards to seize Port-en-Bessin and link Gold and Omaha Beaches and the assaulting armies. The divisional right was formed by 231 Brigade whose target was Arromanches and the enemy battery at Longues while, on the left, 69 Brigade was to advance southwards across the Seulles to secure the road between Bayeux and Caen near Ste Croix Grande Tonne. Fiftieth Division had four brigades on D-Day and the two reserve formations – 56 and 151 (Durham) Brigades – were to advance beyond 231 and 69 Brigades; 56 Brigade was to strike through Bayeux to the Drome river while the Durham Brigade was to secure the Caen road and railway between Bayeux and the Seulles.

Arromanches fell to 231 Brigade and was cleared of enemy by about 9.00pm. It had been a long fight with the brigade first taking Ryes and then seizing the Arromanches radar station; at much the same time le Hamel fell. The battery south of Arromanches was abandoned following a bruising bombardment from HMS *Emerald*; the four 105mm guns had not been fired. A destroyer and 147th Field Regiment (Essex Yeomanry) provided a preliminary bombardment of the western half of Arromanches for the infantry assault. With Arromanches in British hands the brigade moved on to occupy la Rosière, where No. 47 Commando had earlier had a brisk engagement, but since Tracy-sur-Mer was occupied by enthusiastic enemy snipers, and night was falling, a halt was called to any further advance until daylight. Meanwhile the commandos were on Point 72, overlooking Port-en-Bessin, ready to attack in the morning.[20]

La Rosière saw many British troops on D-Day, with 56 Brigade also passing through before striking south for Bayeux. A radar station at Pouligny was an intermediate objective but there was no fighting as the Germans abandoned the station, having first set it alight. The brigade's leading battalion, 2nd South Wales Borderers, secured the bridge over the Aure before midnight. Nearby yet another battery had been abandoned after bombing and shelling, the latter from HMS *Argonaut*. A halt was called with the South Wales Borderers at Vaux sur Aure, 2nd Glosters in Magny and 2nd Essex at St Sulpice, having met some light opposition on their advance. Bayeux, the day's objective, remained untaken but was threatened by the brigade.[21]

The Northumbrians' fourth brigade – 151 (Durham) – advanced in two groups, supported by 90th (City of London) Field Regiment. Led by 9th Durham Light Infantry, the right-flank group moved off from Meuvaines on an axis that was more or less the road from Crépon to Bayeux with 6th Durhams and a squadron of 4th/7th Royal Dragoon Guards on the left, moving south from Crépon through Villiers le Sec and thence westwards for Bayeux. Advance elements reached the Bayeux–Caen road by 8.30pm where they halted for the night in the Sommervieu–Esquay sur Seulles area. By that time tanks from 4th/7th Dragoon Guards had moved farther south to report that there was little resistance for almost two miles in the direction of St Leger. Earlier the situation had been markedly different when the Dragoon Guards, having crossed the Seulles, lost four tanks to enemy action at Creully.[22] Some forty German AFVs were spotted by aerial reconnaissance between Rucqueville and Brécy and were engaged by HMS *Orion* about an hour later; three were hit and the others withdrew. Aircraft spotted a trio of large guns shortly afterwards and *Orion*'s guns were again called into action; the guns withdrew to the south. Typhoons also attacked some tanks and other vehicles near St Leger. The value of the forward observer bombardment officers was underlined by this action, as was that of air cover.[23]

A battlegroup from 352nd Division provided tough opposition for 69 Brigade between Crépon and the Seulles. Early that morning 915th Regiment of the division had been ordered westward to deal with an airborne landing between Carentan and the Vire. This was a false alarm and the regiment was instructed to return whence it came. A report that a battalion at Mont Fleury had been overcome brought a change in orders; the regiment was to move eastwards and counter-attack at Crépon. En route, a battalion, with some assault guns, was detached to oppose the Americans at Omaha Beach, leaving I/915th, 352nd Fusilier Battalion and ten guns from 352nd Anti-Tank Battalion to engage 69 Brigade. The clash occurred at about 4 o'clock, at much the same time as 21st Panzer's counter-attack was getting underway, between Villiers le Sec and Bazenville, and ended with the Germans having to withdraw, their commander dead and many of his men falling prisoner to 69 Brigade.[24] A German account noted that only ninety men survived the encounter[25] and were then attached to 726th Regiment, which was to hold a line from Coulombs to Asnelles, an impossible task since 50th Division already held that ground.

The airborne reinforcements that arrived late on D-Day included two battalions from 6 Airlanding Brigade, 6th Airborne Armoured

Reconnaissance Regiment* with light tanks and jeeps, light field artillery, anti-tank guns and medical and supply units. Major-General Gale, 6th Airborne's commander, intended the Reconnaissance Regiment to form the core of a force known as Armoured Recce Group to '(a) carry out deep recce; (b) Impede and delay any enemy movement from the EAST and SE on CAEN'.[27] Sixth Airborne Division's strength was doubled by this insertion; 600 containers of stores and ammunition were also parachuted in. Among the airlanding battalions was 1st Royal Ulster Rifles, whose 2nd Battalion had landed with 9 Brigade, thus giving the Ulsters the distinction of being the sole British regiment to have both regular battalions in action on D-Day.** Both reinforcing battalions –Rifles and 2nd Oxfordshire and Buckinghamshire LI*** – were to attack Hérouvillette and Escoville come the dawn. As the reinforcing air armada flew in, it drew the caustic comment from one weary soldier of 2nd Royal Ulster Rifles: 'I suppose that's what the First Battalion call a f*xxx*ing route march'.[28]

Enemy opposition continued in 6th Airborne's area with attacks at irregular intervals until late evening. At one point the destroyer HMS *Serapis* bombarded German infantry near Longueval. The airlanding troops had remarkably light casualties. Some had expected worse. After a calm and uneventful flight

> until we got over the fleet . . . Well, just as we flew over, [HMS *Arethusa*] let off a broadside and the gliders went about a hundred feet up in the air and then down again, which was very disturbing. Then it got a wee bit rough. There was some ack-ack, and . . . turbulence, and a lot of people were sick, probably a bit of nerves as well as the aircraft.
>
> But the landing was as cushy as we'd ever had a landing. The Germans . . . had spiked [the LZ] with big stakes about nine feet high, which were supposed to impede the gliders. But we landed safely. I think we had only about two casualties in the whole battalion.[29]

* An airborne armoured reconnaissance regiment numbered thirty-two officers and 327 men in a headquarters squadron, a support squadron (with two medium-machine-gun troops – each with four MMGs in carriers – and a mortar troop – with four 4.2-inch mortars in trailers behind jeeps – and an infantry support troop on motorcycles) and two squadrons each with a heavy troop of four light tanks and three troops each of two scout cars and two jeeps. There was only one such regiment in the Reconnaissance Corps' order of battle, 1st Airborne Division deploying only a reconnaissance squadron which was to serve with distinction at Arnhem.[26]

** The Rifles were also the only Irish regiment with TA battalions: 1st and 2nd London Irish Rifles. TA battalions for the Irish infantry regiments were not created until after the war but each regiment raised additional battalions during the war.

*** The brigade's third battalion was 12th Devons.

In fact there was only one casualty; Rifleman Woodburn was injured by mortar fire that set a glider on fire.[30] Landings in exercises had given the battalion more casualties.

> After we cast off it was very quiet, no battle noises . . . apart from what sounded like a sharp rattle of hailstones hitting our wing, I did not associate it with bullets at the time and very soon we touched down to a very good landing . . . we quickly emerged and instead of taking up all round defensive positions around the glider . . . we just stood about having a pee and wondering at the spectacle as hundreds of gliders swooped in to join those already down. Troops were pouring out and busily unloading just like an exercise in England and I was not aware of any enemy fire in my vicinity although later as we moved off, about 10 minutes or so, if that, I heard several mortar bomb bursts.[31]

They had also landed on schedule and the wooden stakes on the landing zones had caused few problems, mostly snapping when struck by a glider or, at worst, tearing a wing off. The Rifles were to concentrate south of Ranville to await orders and Paddy Devlin recalled an amusing episode as they approached Ranville.

> here in the middle of the road was a very drunk elderly Frenchman waving a wine bottle about and shouting 'De Valera, Irlande'. Somebody must have told him we were Irish, he did not appear to realise De Valera was neutral but I found it amusing and nobody said anything to him, we just continued on without stopping . . .[32]

There would not be too many such humorous incidents for the battalion in the days ahead.

As the day ended, the Allies had their foothold in mainland Europe. They had invaded but had now to make the invasion stick. To do so they had to maintain their grip on the beachhead and expand that area of liberated Europe to build up for further operations. That build-up was already underway as the assaulting formations settled down for their first night in France and made ready for whatever the dawn of D+1 might bring. On the beaches a scene of unparalleled energy and effort was unrolling. Throughout that first day, vessels had landed cargo after cargo of men, vehicles, equipment, ammunition and supplies, including anti-aircraft regiments, both light and heavy. Twelve AA brigade headquarters were assigned to 21 Army Group, including seventy regiments, several independent batteries and a Royal Marine AA brigade.[33] The original plan had been for two AA brigade tactical headquarters – 76 and 80 Brigades under XXX and I Corps respectively – to be ashore during D-Day and for elements of each to be in action; first priority was given to light AA guns, some of which landed at H-Hour. By nightfall the brigades should have put ashore twelve 3.7-inch HAA guns, thirty 40mm guns, twelve 20mm guns and six searchlights in XXX Corps' area with thirty-two 3.7s, eighty-four 40mms, sixteen 20mms and twelve searchlights in I Corps' area. Needless to say, these figures were not achieved; although two batteries landed their 40mm and 20mm equipments on Gold Beach in the first ninety minutes, the landing programme then fell behind and, in XXX Corps' sector, only seventeen 40mm and eight 20mm guns were available. These claimed two enemy aircraft destroyed during a raid at dusk. In I Corps' area only two 3.7s were ashore by dusk, with no instruments, but they also claimed two enemy aircraft shot down in that raid. Several troops of LAA guns had also landed, some of which – from 92nd and 4th Canadian LAA Regiments – were to support 6th Airborne Division. No searchlights were landed and there were problems with radios, especially after dark, but AA defences were in place and ready for much more than the Luftwaffe could muster.[34] The RAF had also landed personnel in the beachhead, to liaise with ground forces and provide further defences, including a balloon barrage.

Medical units, signals and military police were among the many who came ashore that day and, of course, the Royal Army Service Corps was represented in large numbers, providing 21 Army Group's logistical backbone. Corps members were decorated for courage in the opening hours of the invasion. Major J R Cuthbertson, commanding 90 Company RASC, with 27 Armoured Brigade, received the Military Cross for his work in maintaining 6th Airborne Division, a task that his company carried out under regular fire from artillery, mortars and small arms. Captain B W M Linden and Staff-Sergeants T Burt and W J Tams of 522 Company received immediate awards of the Military Cross and Military Medal for their efforts in supplying No. 47 Commando in its attack on Port-en-Bessin, all the while under fire from machine guns and tanks. Probably the first General Transport (GT) company to come ashore was 39 GT Company which landed only two hours after the first wave of troops; the company then delivered anti-tank guns to defend the beach maintenance area. This task, performed under constant fire, earned three awards of the Military Medal. Without a port at which to land supplies, the DUKWs of RASC companies were vital on D-Day and subsequently; eleven such companies deployed in Normandy. Two DUKW drivers were awarded the Military Medal on the recommendation of US Army officers.[35]

By nightfall British and Canadians had made remarkable progress, albeit not quite as much as had been hoped. Their initial landings had been

1. C Squadron, 22nd Dragoons. This photograph was probably taken in February 1944 as the Regiment prepared for its part in OVERLORD. Originally intended to fight as an armoured regiment, 22nd Dragoons was re-roled to become one of the specialist units of 79th Armoured Division. One of the soldiers included in this group is Leonard Kemp who was killed on D-Day and to whom this book is dedicated. (Harry Bacon, 22nd Dragoons OCA)

2. 3 Troop, A Squadron, 24th Lancers. Another old regiment re-raised for the war, 24th Lancers served as part of 8 Armoured Brigade, landing on D-Day and fighting throughout the battle for Normandy until the Regiment was disbanded at the end of July when its surviving personnel were posted as reinforcements to other armoured units. When this photo was taken the Regiment was in 29 Armoured Brigade of 11th Armoured Division. (Dr Stephen Pannell, 24th Lancers OCA)

3. Norfolk House, St James's Square, London, headquarters of the Allied Expeditionary Force. (Author's photograph)

4. General Montgomery, dressed as usual according to his own rules, examines a Tetrarch light tank of 6th Armoured Airborne Reconnaissance Regiment as it is driven out of a Hamilcar glider. (Tank Museum, Bovington. 4775/F6)

5. The crew of a Sherman DD tank train in amphibious warfare in Studland Bay, off Dorset. Note the lifejackets worn by the crewmen. (Tank Museum, Bovington. 176/D5)

6. 'Somewhere in England.' The 40mm Bofors portee guns of 6 LAA Battery on parade as they prepare for Normandy. Note that the white star of the Allied Expeditionary Force has been 'doctored' by the insertion of a shamrock to denote the Battery's Irish origin. (Author's collection)

7. Southampton port, 4 June 1944. An overhead shot showing part of the invasion fleet. LCTs are loaded fully and camouflaged. (Frank L Dubervill/National Archives of Canada/PA-137130)

8. En route to France. The view from LCI (L) 306 of 2nd Canadian (262nd RN) Flotilla, showing vessels of Force J heading for Normandy. Note the balloon barrage. On D-Day balloons flying over the Allied beachhead provided German artillery with a reliable aiming reference and had to be cut loose. (Gilbert Alexander Milne/NA of Canada/PA-137014)

9. Let us pray. A chaplain conducts a service on board one of the ships bound for France. (Ken Bell/NA of Canada/PA-132899)

10. A Sherman Firefly of 13th/18th Royal Hussars (Queen Mary's Own) as the invasion force sets sail for France. (IWM, B5105)

11. Landing Craft, Tank (Rocket). These vessels could fire salvoes of rockets from a range of about two miles; LCT (R) (2)s carried almost 800 rockets and LCT (R) (3)s over 1,000. Many rockets failed to hit their targets but did help to force defenders into shelter. (IWM, B5263)

12. Naval vessels, ranging from battleships to destroyers, provided part of the fireplan for the invasion. One of the ships involved was the cruiser HMS *Belfast*, which had been engaged in the sinking of *Scharnhorst* at the Battle of North Cape on 26 December 1943. Today *Belfast*, Europe's last big-gun warship, is a floating museum on the river Thames and is part of the Imperial War Museum. (Author's photo)

13. Soldiers of 9 (Canadian) Brigade go ashore from LCI (L) 125 on Nan White beach on D-Day. (Gilbert Alexander Milne/NA of Canada/PA-137012)

14. A Sherman Firefly goes ashore from an LST. Although this photograph is unlikely to have been taken on D- Day it is a good image of the Firefly and shows off the length of the 17-pounder fitted to this adaptation. One Sherman in every troop was a Firefly and German anti-tank gunners and tankmen tried to destroy the Firefly first as it posed the greatest threat to German tanks. (Tank Museum, Bovington. 4462/E4)

15. Part of the supply chain for the invading troops was provided by amphibious lorries, the ubiquitous DUKW. Here a DUKW of the Royal Army Service Corps loaded with ammunition for tanks and SPGs leaves an LCT and prepares for the run to shore. (IWM, B5014)

16. Canadian soldiers found a German model of the beaches and two of them are seen studying it in this photograph. (Ken Bell/NA of Canada/PA-131438)

17. Only one Victoria Cross was awarded for actions on D-Day. This is an artist's impression of Company Sergeant Major Stanley Hollis, Green Howards, knocking out a German strongpoint. (Green Howards Museum)

18. The Bay of the Seine was necklaced by heavy German gun batteries. This is one emplacement of the Longues battery, which mounted four 150mm guns, and was able to engage targets some ten miles away. (Author's photo)

19. On the night of 5/6 June and the morning of 6 June the German shore batteries were bombed by the RAF and USAAF and then bombarded by ships. This is one of the emplacements of the Longues battery, which was probably struck by a heavy naval shell. (Author's photo)

20. The Longues Battery was captured by soldiers of the Devonshire Regiment on 7 June. Their feat is commemorated by this plaque on one of the emplacements. (Author's photo)

21. German prisoners under guard on Juno Beach as they wait to be taken to England. They do not appear to be concerned about having been captured and may be men from second-line units. Casualties are being taken for treatment in the background and a German strongpoint may also be seen. In the foreground a young Canadian stands guard over the prisoners with a despatch rider by his side. The Don R is wearing the 'Steel helmet, DR Mk1' produced for despatch riders; similar helmets with different liners were worn by airborne and armoured personnel. (Frank L Dubervill/NA of Canada/PA-136280)

22. Ferrying equipment and vehicles from ship to shore on a Rhino ferry. (Ken Bell/ NA of Canada/ PA-171084)

23. During the fighting at Villers Bocage on 13 June, 4th County of London Yeomanry lost several tanks. This is a 4 CLY Cromwell that was destroyed by the German tank 'ace' Michael Wittmann. (Major-General Mike Reynolds)

24. The Germans tried to take the battle of 13 June into the built-up area of Villers Bocage where this Tiger I fell to anti-tank gunners of 1/7th Queen's Regiment. (Major-General Mike Reynolds)

25. Not all anti-tank guns were towed. Many were self-propelled as with this Achilles of 146 Battery, 91st Anti-Tank Regiment, Royal Artillery. Achilles used the British 17-pounder anti-tank gun mounted on the American M-10 chassis. Archer was another British SP anti-tank equipment, with the 17-pounder mounted on a Valentine tank chassis. Royal Artillery units also used the original M-10 with its 3-inch gun. (Major-General Mike Reynolds)

26. Another American equipment in Royal Artillery service; the M-7 howitzer motor carriage, mounting a 105mm gun was known as Priest in British service. This weapon is in action near Lion sur Mer on D-Day although the unit is unknown. (IWM, B5032)

27. One of the many variants of the highly adaptable Churchill tank was this 'bunker buster' used by units of 79th Armoured Division. This 'Funny' was fitted with a mortar, or petard, that could be deployed against reinforced walls or emplacements. The tank shown is at Juno Beach and served with an Assault Engineer unit. (Author's photo)

28. The round for the Churchill 'bunker buster'. (Tank Museum, Bovington. 2245/E3)

29. The toughest opposition came from SS troops and there was much bitter fighting between these hardened soldiers and the Canadians. Here Canadian soldiers have captured a group of SS men on 17 June. (Frank L Dubervill/NA of Canada/PA-163919)

30. Many men died in Normandy, including the crew of this Sherman Crab of 22nd Dragoons. One of the men who lost his life in this tank was Corporal Paddy Addis from Belfast. The Sherman was hit by a German SP which is just visible over the barrel of the gun. This photograph was taken in 1947. (Captain Ian Hammerton, 22nd Dragoons OCA)

31. Gliders were often destroyed on landing, as was the case with this Horsa of 6th Airborne Division on the east bank of the river Orne. (Ken Bell / National Archives of Canada / PA-130172)

32. Casualties could be evacuated by air to England for treatment. The main workhorse of the air transport squadrons was the Douglas C-47 Dakota, two of which are seen in this picture about to depart with casualties. (Ken Bell / NA of Canada / PA-137355)

33. Casualties in Normandy were treated in hospitals run by members of Queen Alexandra's Imperial Military Nursing Service, the QAs. Sisters Paddy O'Loan, of Ballymena, County Antrim, and Ina O'Connell, of Cahirciveen, County Kerry were among the many QAs to serve in Normandy. (IWM, B5854)

34. Among the artillery units deployed in Normandy were heavy regiments equipped with 7.2-inch howitzers. Here a 7.2 pounds German positions at the end of June. (Ken Bell/NA of Canada/PA- 132925)

35. With little threat from the Luftwaffe, British anti-aircraft guns could also be deployed as field, medium and anti-tank artillery. Here the crew of a 3.7-inch heavy AA gun add their support to the battle. This photograph was taken in August near Conde sur Noireau and the gun is firing airburst. (IWM, B9227)

36. Tactical air support was vital during the battle for Normandy. Many veterans recall the support provided by Typhoons of the RAF. A Typhoon MkI is photographed on its airstrip in England. Note the four 20mm cannon that were fitted to the aircraft, which could also carry eight rockets. (NA of Canada/PA-136266)

37. Generals Crocker, I Corps, Dempsey, Second Army, and Bucknall, XXX Corps, after a conference at Dempsey's headquarters. (IWM, B5326)

38. When Caen fell to Allied troops the city had been reduced to rubble. Infantrymen and medics pick their way through some of the debris of the city. (IWM, B6727)

39. Lance-Corporal (later Major) Tony Hughes, 24th Lancers. On his left forearm may be seen the wound stripe that he received after his tank was knocked out at the end of June. Another soldier described him as coming out of the turret like a cork from a bottle. Tony Hughes suffered severe burns to his face and was treated by Sir Archibald McIndoe. (Major Tony Hughes)

40. Somewhere in Normandy. Major Jack Christie, Battery Commander 6 LAA Battery, ponders campaign news. Part of his battery was converted to operate Centaur tanks in an anti-mortar role in July. (Colonel Dan Christie)

41. A French veteran of the Great War greets Allied troops as an ambulance and universal carriers of the South Saskatchewan Regiment drive along the road. (George A Cooper/NA of Canada/PA-131386)

42. Infantry of The Stormont Dundas and Glengarry Highlanders cross a Bailey bridge that has been erected by Royal Canadian Engineers over the river Orne on 18 July. (Ken Bell/NA of Canada/PA-162435)

43. Operation GOODWOOD, the Allied breakthrough into the Normandy Plain against heavy German opposition, 18-19 July 1944. Sherman tanks of 3rd Royal Tank Regiment attacking the Borguebus Ridge. (David Rowlands)

44. A Sherman Crab Flail tank in action. The unit is not known and the photograph may have been taken during training in Britain. Note the bare trees in the background. (Tank Museum, Bovington. 2121/C6)

45. Sappers check for mines near Villers Bocage against the background of an abandoned Panther tank. This was one of the best tanks of the war. The length of its gun can be seen easily; this prompted some British tankmen to talk of German tanks having guns that stretched 'from here to Sunday week'. (IWM, B8573)

46. British pioneers prepare temporary wooden crosses to indicate the resting places of soldiers killed in the battle for Mont Pinçon. The men at work here are Pte Andrew Robertson, of Sunderland, a joiner, and Pte John Nicol, of South Shields, a painter. (IWM, B9032)

47. Polish soldiers of 1st Polish Armoured Division joined 21 Army Group in the latter battles for Normandy. This group of Poles is determined to travel 'On to Warsaw, via Normandy and Berlin' according to the slogan under the jeep's windscreen. The man on the extreme left is a despatch rider whose motorcycle is just visible at the edge of the picture. (Michael M Dean/NA of Canada/PA-129200)

48. Two Canadian generals confer: Major-General Keller, 3rd Canadian Division, and Major-General Foulkes, 2nd Canadian Division, outside the former's headquarters. (Frank L Duberville/NA of Canada/PA-116519

49. Lieutenant-General Brian Horrocks took command of XXX Corps in August. A fast and frightening driver, he is seen here at the wheel of his own car. The XXX Corps flash may be seen on his sleeve. (IWM, B9532)

50. Shermans nose forward slowly in support of Les Fusiliers Mont Royal as the infantry seek out snipers in the ruins of Falaise. (Ken Bell / NA of Canada / PA-132822)

51. Towards the end of the battle for Normandy, Canadian gunners thread their way through the ruins of Falaise en route to providing further support for their comrades. (Ken Bell / NA of Canada / PA-169282)

52. During the final phase of the Battle of Normandy, Major David Currie, Moose Jaw, Saskatchewan, of 29th Canadian Armoured Regiment, earned the Victoria Cross at St Lambert sur Dives. His VC was announced in November when this photograph was taken. (Frank L Dubervill/NA of Canada/PA-131218)

53. The Victoria Cross was also awarded to Lieutenant (later Major) Tasker Watkins of 1/5th Welch Regiment for his part in an action near Balfour on 16 August. (The Welch Regiment Museum)

54. Company Sergeant Major Stan Hollis VC, the only man to be awarded the Victoria Cross for his actions during the fighting on D-Day. (Green Howards Museum)

55. On Juno Beach the French have erected this memorial to those who liberated their land in 1944. (Author's photo)

56. Normandy has many war cemeteries. Foster G Nickerson of 7th Field Artillery Bn, US Army, a Virginian, died on D-Day and is buried at the American cemetery at Colleville sur Mer, overlooking Omaha Beach. This is the cemetery featured in the film 'Saving Private Ryan'. (Author's photo)

57. Two unknown German soldiers rest in this grave along with Willy Triest, who died on 22 June 1944. At first the author thought that at 38 years Willy Triest was too old to be a soldier but he then realised that his own father, then serving with the Royal Artillery in Italy, was seven months older than this unfortunate German. (Author's photo)

58. Mulberry was an important factor in the planning of OVERLORD and much use was made of the British Mulberry Harbour, Port Winston, at Arromanches. Some of Port Winston, which was as large as Dover harbour, survives to this day. In this photograph parts may be seen on the beach and offshore. (Author's photo)

59. With the Germans defeated in Normandy the Allies were able to begin their advance to the Seine. It turned out to be a speedy race that took the Allied armies into Belgium and The Netherlands. En route the specialist tanks of 79th Armoured Division were called on for many tasks, including laying bridges over rivers and other obstacles. A Churchill AVRE displays its bridge-laying capabilities. (Tank Museum, Bovington. 0040/E1)

60. In 1990 the US Government had this plaque erected on Norfolk House to the memory of General Dwight Eisenhower, the Supreme Allied Commander on D-Day. (Author's photo)

relatively successful, especially in comparison to the US landings at Omaha, and as darkness fell, the assault divisions had penetrated some four to six miles over much of a twenty-mile-plus front.[36] But operations had not continued at their initial pace. Some of this has been attributed to a lack of urgency on the part of the commanders but it must be remembered that strong opposition had been encountered, especially from 21st Panzer, which at one point managed to push some tanks almost to the coast. Nor were the attacking soldiers in the peak of condition, having endured a choppy crossing and hazardous landing; many had been violently ill during the run-in. Caen and Bayeux remained to be captured and the beaches had not all been linked. The link-up would soon be complete; Bayeux would fall on the morrow although there would be a further month's hard fighting at heavy cost for Caen.

During the day the Allies had landed over 156,000 men, with 75,215 British and Canadian soldiers alongside 57,500 American troops; another 23,400 had arrived by air, of whom about 7,900 were British or Canadian and the remainder American. The air forces had flown more than 14,000 sorties for the loss of only 127 aircraft and sixty-three machines damaged. Almost 200,000 Allied naval personnel had taken part, of whom about 25,000 were merchant seamen; the Royal Navy's contribution was 112,824 men, with 52,889 US Navy personnel and 4,988 from other Allied navies.[37]

There is no doubting what had been achieved by those who landed on D-Day. The British Official Historian summed up succinctly their achievements.

> the troops had had little time for rest and no relaxation of strain since they left England . . . Their attack had been launched not from a firm base but from unstable waters breaking on an enemy-held coast. Starting under such conditions, to have swept away all but a few isolated fragments of Hitler's Atlantic Wall and to have fought their way inland for an average depth of four to six miles on most of a twenty-four miles front, was surely a notable feat of arms.[38]

The short hours of darkness gave no real opportunity for rest and for many there was the added task of maintaining active patrols or guarding against possible attacks. What little sleep was achieved by anyone was disturbed more than once by the Luftwaffe, which sent a number of aircraft to bomb the anchorages or drop mines; needless to say Allied anti-aircraft gunners responded enthusiastically to these intrusions. But the Luftwaffe's efforts were but a series of very minor pinpricks against what must have been one of the best targets ever presented to German airmen.

By contrast Allied airmen were busy throughout that night. Reconnaissance flights on D-Day had noted significant German troop movements or preparations for movements. In particular, 12th SS Panzer

Division was moving from its base near Rouen while troop trains had been sighted loading near Amiens, Chartres and south of the Loire; these would be moving Panzer Lehr and 2nd SS Panzer as well as 17th SS Panzer Grenadier Divisions.[39] And so Bomber Command was tasked to disrupt their movement by bombing rail and road junctions from Paris to the base of the Cotentin. Aircraft of Second Tactical Air Force also attacked roads leading to the bridgehead and created chokepoints at Falaise, Villers-Bocage and other key points as well as attacking enemy columns.[40]

In the light of the new day that was D+1, the Allies were on the move again. Montgomery met Bradley and Dempsey early to stress the importance of completing the link-up along the beachhead; the Americans needed to join their two bridgeheads, take Isigny and Carentan and thrust across the base of the Cotentin to begin isolating Cherbourg while the British and Canadians had to link up with First US Army at Port-en-Bessin, take Bayeux and Caen and establish their left flank along the Dives. During the day 51st (Highland) Division, which had fought from El Alamein to Sicily, would be landing to strengthen Second Army and might 'cut in behind Caen, moving east of the Orne'.[41]

Much ground activity on D+1, and for several days thereafter, was taken up with consolidating the bridgehead; Allied troops were still thin on the ground and some enemy positions continued to hold out behind the Allied line. Perhaps the most precarious section of bridgehead was the eastern flank, held by 6th Airborne Division. Such were the division's casualties that its parachute battalions were now reduced to some 200 men each* – a total strength for the two parachute brigades of about 1,200 men – while the airlanding brigade was not yet complete; its third battalion – 12th Devons – was to arrive, by sea, on the afternoon of the 7th. Their commando comrades, of 1 SS Brigade, could muster about 400 men per commando. And it was on the eastern flank where now lay the greatest threat; the German armour was on that flank and was expected to concentrate in an effort to wipe out the British bridgehead or prevent Second Army moving closer to Caen.[43]

Sixth Airborne's day was spent fending off counter-attacks, protecting sappers building Bailey bridges and strengthening their defences, especially at the Ranville crossings. They did not always wait for the Germans to come to them; both 3 and 5 Parachute Brigades carried out aggressive patrolling, taking the battle to the enemy wherever possible. At

* The normal strength of a parachute battalion was twenty-nine officers and 584 men in headquarters, headquarters company and three rifle companies. There were 270 fighting riflemen and an anti-tank platoon with ten PIATS. An airlanding battalion was much stronger with thirty-two officers and 817 men; such battalions included a support company and four rifle companies and two anti-tank platoons each with four 6-pounder guns.[42]

the same time, Lovat's commandos were attempting to extend the bridgehead northward, towards Franceville Plage and thence along the coast, as well as recapturing the Merville battery, which had been re-occupied. There was some determined fighting but, in spite of support from HM Ships *Arethusa* and *Mauritius*, the commandos, too weak to achieve their aims, were forced back to le Plein ridge, the holding of which denied the Germans the local advantage of height. Allied forces in the area were still too few in number to hold their gains and extend the bridgehead to the coast.[44]

The airlanding battalions that had arrived the previous night were attempting to enlarge the airborne bridgehead to the south. The Ulster Rifles and Oxfordshire and Buckinghamshire LI took Longueval and Hérouvillette, both of which they held, but valiant efforts to capture another two villages, Ste Honorine and Escoville, were repulsed.[45] Facing the British troops east of the Orne was a battlegroup from 21st Panzer Division, including infantry, tanks and SPGs, two infantry divisions – 346th and 711th – and elements of 716th Division. These were under command of LXXXI Corps which, in turn, was under Fifteenth Army command; the latter had been ordered to destroy the British foothold east of the Orne.[46]

Some relief was en route for the airborne and commando troops as 51st (Highland) Division deployed to the left flank. However, the Highlanders were not sent in full strength initially. The first brigade – 153 – had landed the previous afternoon to await orders. On the morning of the 7th Major-General Bullen-Smith, the divisional commander, came ashore with orders from I Corps for a battalion of 153 Brigade to deploy to Douvres where the German garrison still held out. Thus 5th Black Watch was sent thither. After what almost proved a tragic encounter with Canadian troops in woods near Douvres, the battalion prepared for an attack, during which an 88 knocked out two supporting AVREs. The commanding officer requested additional troops but was told to withdraw and 5th Camerons,* temporarily attached to 153 Brigade, relieved them at Douvres while the brigade's main body was ordered to move via Pegasus Bridge across the canal to reinforce the eastern bridgehead. Although landing on D+1, 152 Brigade did not have the bulk of its transport ashore until two days later when it was ordered from its concentration area near Douvres to the east bank of the Orne to engage the enemy. Finally, 154 Brigade came ashore on D+4 to be held in I Corps reserve; not until 13 June did its first battalion – 7th Argyll and Sutherland Highlanders – go into action, again east of the Orne, with the rest of the brigade following five days later under temporary command of 6th Airborne Division.[47]

Elsewhere on the British–Canadian front, 50th (Northumbrian)

* This battalion was normally part of 152 Brigade.

Division was also consolidating. To their 69 Brigade had fallen the distinction of making the deepest penetration on D-Day, reaching Coulombs and Brécy. On D+1 the brigade advanced yet another few miles to cross high ground and the Bayeux–Caen road at St Leger before linking up with Canadian troops near Bronay and capturing Ducy-Ste Marguerite. Bayeux fell to 56 Brigade, which then established positions on the approaches to the city from St Lô and Caumont to block any counter-attack. In the coastal sector 231 Brigade took the battery at Longues and some 120 prisoners; after firing 115 rounds, the battery's guns had been silenced on D-Day by HMS *Ajax*, of River Plate fame. Looking west along the coast No. 47 (RM) Commando was fighting for Port-en-Bessin, a battle that continued throughout the day with much street fighting while RAF Typhoons and HMS *Emerald* supported the suppression of strongpoints overlooking the town. The Marines made ground throughout the day, scaled the eastern heights at dusk to take a position on the clifftop and continued the struggle until 4.00am on the 8th. Into the bag went the garrison commander and 300 men. Although Marine casualties were heavy the little port would prove invaluable. In fact, almost before the battle ended, Royal Naval personnel were surveying the harbour facilities. The first contact with Americans on the right would be made on D+2 by men of 231 Brigade which captured a strong position on the Drome river near Port-en-Bessin. But the Germans still held most of the Drome's west bank between Port-en-Bessin and Seully and were trying to prevent the knitting together of the British and American bridgeheads.[48]

A battlegroup from 8 Armoured Brigade, led by 61st Reconnaissance Regiment,* was being assembled to break out of the beachhead on the evening of D+1, advance ten miles to Tessel Bretteville, harbour for the night, and then strike out at daybreak to seize the high ground near Villers-Bocage. That high ground commanded the country for miles around; the battlegroup was to hold on there for three or four days until relieved by stronger forces.[50] Behind this plan lay the memory of the failure to exploit initial success in Operation SHINGLE at Anzio earlier in the year and a resolution that such failure would not be repeated in Normandy. But the weather knocked out the timetable for this plan. Rough seas caused several Rhino** ferries that were to transport 61 Recce

* The group included 61 Recce, less a squadron, 147th Field Regiment, although it was noted that only one battery might be available on D-Day, 288 Anti-tank Battery, less a 6-pounder troop, a detachment of 505 Field Company with two bulldozers, a company of 1st Dorsets on bicycles, with the entire battalion to join later, A Company 2nd Cheshire Regiment, less a platoon, with their MMGs and 186th Light Field Ambulance.[49]

** Rhino ferries were constructed from a number of pontoons linked together and motorised; their size could vary according to the number of pontoons used in the construction. They were very susceptible to poor sea conditions.

from LSTs to the shore to break away and just over half the regiment landed on D-Day. The second-in-command, Major Philip Brownrigg, was still aboard an LST on the morning of the 7th. He contacted his commanding officer, Lieutenant-Colonel Mount, by radio to be given

> a new rendezvous for the rest of the Regiment; then he ordered A Squadron to move there. As the rendezvous was well within the bridgehead, I was slightly disturbed a few minutes later to hear the Squadron Leader report that he was held up by heavy machine-gun fire. This penetrated the armour of several . . . carriers, but Corporal Billingham, although wounded, drove on into the middle of the enemy position, throwing grenades, until he collapsed with a wound in the head. Soon afterwards I called up the Commanding Officer again, but he cut me short: 'Get off the air; I'm shooting Boches'.[51]

Many of the 'Boches' Mount was shooting were Russian and not especially enthusiastic about the war; they generally preferred surrendering to fighting. During the day most of 61 Recce landed and the regiment spent an 'uneasy night' while awaiting orders.[52]

During D+1 the Canadians were attacked in strength by 12th SS Panzer Division, which had begun moving to the battle zone the previous day. Led by Sherbrooke Fusilier tanks and North Nova Scotia Highlanders, 9 Canadian Brigade advanced southwards along a minor road through Villons-les-Buissons, Buron and Authie to Carpiquet. Having cleared both les Buissons and Buron, taking two 88s and a multi-barrelled mortar – the first seen in Normandy – the brigade pushed on towards Authie where heavy shelling struck them. Enemy guns were engaging them from St Contest but the Canadians' own field artillery was either out of range or moving and calls for naval support did not get through. The decision was taken to pull back north of Authie and hold a position there. While this move was being executed tanks of 12th SS Panzer crashed into the Canadians and overran some positions. There followed a tank battle between panzers and Sherbrooke Shermans in which each side suffered many casualties as the Canadians fell back on Buron. The panzers continued attacking up to the edge of the village before a Canadian counter-attack forced their withdrawal. Under cover of darkness the Canadians withdrew to higher ground at les Buissons, leaving Buron in a limbo between the protagonists.[53]

The Canadians had had their first taste of battle with Panzer Meyer's soldiers with both sides taking heavy losses; eighty-four Nova Scotia Highlanders were killed and 128 captured, the Sherbrookes had twenty-six men killed, twenty-one tanks destroyed and another seven damaged. Although the Canadians claimed thirty-one enemy tanks destroyed, German losses were only nine Mark IVs. But it was a day that left a cruel legacy; the Canadians had been 'introduced to the savage and desperate methods accorded to prisoners by this notorious 12th SS Panzer Division'. In the battle and its immediate aftermath at least twenty-seven Canadians were believed to have been 'murdered in cold blood' by the SS; this 'was to remain an unsavoury characteristic throughout the campaign'.[54] Although the Germans fought with courage and outstanding battle discipline, their anti-tank guns firing only forty rounds, their escutcheon had been blotted by the treatment meted out to Canadian prisoners.

West of the Mue, 7 Brigade had advanced southwards for about four miles to occupy Putot-en-Bessin and Bretteville l'Orgueilleuse. Outposts were established at la Villeneuve and at Norrey-en-Bessin, astride the railway and south of the Bayeux–Caen road.[55] Seven Brigade was also to be hit by 12th SS Panzer on the 8th.

Third British Division were still engaged with 21st Panzer on the 7th with 185 Brigade making an unsuccessful attempt to take Lebisey ridge. Not even the firepower of three field regiments – seventy-two 25-pounders – and a Royal Navy cruiser could eject the Germans. Although the Warwicks, later reinforced by the Norfolks, made some inroads into the woods, even reaching the edge of Lebisey village, the Germans held on, their machine guns dominating the ground. When darkness descended the attacking infantry were withdrawn, having suffered heavy casualties. They would spend the next two days re-organising. The overall task of 3rd Division on D+1 was to seize the high ground north of Caen, close the gap on the divisional right flank where 21st Panzer had pushed through and link up with the Canadians. That unsuccessful attack by 185 Brigade was part of this plan, as was an attack by 9 Brigade at Cambes which was also unsuccessful, although the brigade occupied Périers sur le Dan and linked up with the Canadians.[56] However, I Corps had foreseen the possibility of the attempt to take Caen on D-Day being repulsed and had a contingency plan: to mask Caen for three or four days until 51st (Highland) Division and 4 Armoured Brigade became available to take part in a much stronger attack, Operation SMOCK.[57] But Caen was to remain out of grasp for another month.

At the end of this second day the Germans

> had halted the British and Canadian advances towards Carpiquet and Caen; it would take another month for the Allies to recapture the ground won by the HJ on this fateful day – a day which ended with the Canadians still having 115 combat-ready tanks, the vast majority of which had not fired a shot.[58]

Similar fighting occurred over the next few days but Cambes, one of the strongest German positions, fell to 9 Brigade on the 9th after an attack by 2nd Royal Ulster Rifles and East Riding Yeomanry. The Rifles and

Yeomanry tanks crossed over 1,000 yards of open country under shell, mortar and machine-gun fire, taking almost 200 casualties and losing four tanks but capturing their objective on which they were joined by 1st King's Own Scottish Borderers, who helped secure the sector. In this action men of the Ulsters earned three Military Crosses*, a Distinguished Conduct Medal and three Military Medals.[59]

On the morning of the 8th, German patrols probed the Canadian front at Bretteville l'Orgueilleuse and a counter-attack developed quickly. At Villeneuve the Canadian outpost was withdrawn and tanks from 12th SS Panzer were driven off. Further armoured attacks were made on Putot and Bretteville where fighting continued into the night. And it was under the cover of the gloaming that tanks from a second battlegroup of 12th SS Panzer penetrated Bretteville. Battle raged around battalion headquarters and A Company Regina Rifles throughout the night, with some twenty-two Panthers circling the Canadians. Although the Germans believed resistance to have ended on several occasions, the Canadians fought doggedly on, although battalion headquarters lost contact with all but D Company. The Rifles remained in their positions until relieved several days later.[60]

The Winnipegs had also come under attack on the morning of 8 June with infantry and tanks from a battlegroup of 26th Panzer Grenadier Regiment, a battalion of Panthers and several SPGs trying to cross the railway line. The first attack was driven off but the enemy returned. Again pressure on the Canadians was considerable, with the attackers receiving increasing support from mortars and artillery, but, although the Germans penetrated between company positions, the Winnipegs remained defiant. By early afternoon all three forward companies had been surrounded, some positions had been overrun and ammunition was low. The forward companies were pulled back on to the reserve company between Putot and the Caen road and the village was shelled heavily. A counter-attack was launched with 1st Canadian Scottish and a tank squadron supported by two field regiments and some 4.2-inch mortars and, in spite of many casualties, the village and nearby railway crossing were back in Canadian hands by nightfall.[61]

The two panzer divisions in action on D+1 were under command of I SS Panzer Corps which had been ordered to drive the British into the sea.[62] The Germans had been unable to concentrate in sufficient force to achieve that aim, having had to react to British and Canadian operations in order to slow the Allied advance. Rommel's plan to destroy the Allies on the beaches had been made redundant by events. On 8 June Panzer Group West was given responsibility for the intended mass counter-attack but, on the ground, little changed.[63]

* Many accounts only note two MCs but a third was awarded to the RSM.

German movement was becoming increasingly difficult, as Rommel had predicted, due to Allied air superiority. Luftflotte III had a nominal strength of 891 aircraft when the invasion began[64] although under 500 machines were serviceable. Losses, according to the Luftwaffe, in the first four days totalled 208 aircraft, with another 105 damaged. Reinforcements began arriving after a few days and Luftwaffe records indicate an average of 400–500 sorties per day over the first thirty days of the Normandy battle.[65] However, these were flown mostly in defensive roles well outside the main battle area to prevent Allied strikes on road and rail communications. Most of these would not have been seen by German soldiers on the ground in the front line, leaving them with the same attitude to their airmen as British soldiers during the days of the Dunkirk evacuation.

By contrast Allied air power was clear to all. The most obvious element was the interdiction of enemy transport with rocket-firing Typhoons, fighter-bombers and light bombers striking every target that showed itself. Even pilots on other duties joined in attacking German ground targets. But these were risky affairs; low-flying aircraft were usually met with intense fire from small arms as well as light AA weapons and many Allied aircraft failed to return. Among those who joined in this seeming 'free for all' were Fleet Air Arm pilots whose principal task was target spotting but, after a number of FAA aircraft had been lost, orders were issued to desist from this practice.

> We lost several aircraft through ground strafing, which we weren't supposed to do. In fact, after D plus two we were forbidden to ground strafe, because that was when you were vulnerable, when you were low.[66]

The risks were already high. George Boyd's squadron lost several aircraft over Normandy: two were shot down by flak, another was believed to have been hit 'by a 16-inch shell from HMS *Nelson* while spotting at low level in bad visibility'.[67] Yet others fell victim to Allied aircraft, the clipped-wing Seafires being mistaken for Messerschmitts in the heat of combat despite the prominent black-and-white stripes, or invasion markings, painted on Allied tactical aircraft to assist identification.[68]

While tactical aircraft carried out interdiction strikes, strategic bombers supported the ground forces. Bomber Command was making night attacks on transport targets; on 7 June about 337 heavy bombers struck from low level at key railway targets with the loss of twenty-eight machines and crews. At American request another 112 Bomber Command aircraft struck at the Fôret de Cerisy, south-west of Bayeux, at what was believed to be a concentration of enemy armour. Railways were attacked at many other places over the following nights and Lancasters hit the Saumur railway tunnel on the Loire with 12,000lb 'Tallboy' bombs, the first time these had been used. Eighth US Air Force continued the operations by daylight. Attacks by heavies on railways and airfields continued over the following days and included a raid by 671 Halifaxes, Lancasters and Mosquitoes on communications targets on the night of 12–13 June. Targets included railway facilities at Amiens/St Roch, Amiens/Longeau, Arras, Caen, Cambrai and Poitiers, all of which had either been the sites of battles or, in the case of Caen, about to become one.[69] Over Cambrai a Canadian airman, Pilot-Officer Andrew Charles Mynarski, from Winnipeg, earned a posthumous Victoria Cross when his Lancaster was set on fire by a night fighter. The crew were ordered to abandon the plane but when Mynarski was about to jump he realised the tail gunner was trapped in his turret. Andrew Mynarski fought his way through flames to reach the stricken gunner and attempted to release him but the turret could not be freed. Eventually the gunner waved Mynarski away but by the time the young officer left the Lancaster his clothing was on fire, as was his parachute. He died in the care of French civilians.[70] The gunner survived and his testimony led to the award of Mynarski's posthumous Victoria Cross.*

Rommel had resumed command of Army Group B late on D-Day but it was D+1 before he was at the front. Neither then, nor on the following day, did he make his presence felt strongly; the Rommel of the desert, of France in 1940 was not in evidence in those early days in Normandy. Thus his plan to throw the Allies into the sea was a non-starter. Nor was von Rundstedt's preferred option any more of a starter: as Rommel had predicted, Allied air power made movement very difficult. Concentration of sufficient armour to counter-attack and break the Allies was impossible given the attention Allied aircraft were paying to roads, railways and everything that moved upon them in daylight. Seventh Army, taking the brunt of the invasion, was reacting indecisively and Rommel was not helping matters. Instead of acting as a commander, he was looking at tactical pictures, dashing from one location to another to discuss local situations with local commanders. No firm plan was handed down to Army Group B or Seventh Army. One of Rommel's biographers has described this period thus:

> he allowed himself to be distracted from concentration upon the stated aim of his pre-invasion strategy – the immediate counterattack on enemy penetrations. As so often in the past, he failed to detect the central strategic issue, and became immersed in tactics. From the outset, he became committed to roping-off the enemy lodgements, and was transfixed by each local threat.[71]

* Andrew Mynarski is buried in the cemetery at Meharicourt, east of Amiens.

The Army Group commander seemed more concerned with matters that lay in the purlieu of local commanders rather than those of his own level. Part of this was certainly due to Rommel's long-held belief that local commanders would not always exploit each situation to its fullest potential and that they should always have to reckon with their commander-in-chief appearing to take personal control.[72] But part must also be due to Rommel's lack of intelligence on Allied intentions. In the days immediately after the invasion he was more concerned with the Cotentin where he deployed most of his reserves. He had no idea of British and Canadian intentions but documents found on the bodies of dead American officers had alerted the Germans to the intentions of the American corps: capturing Cherbourg and St Lô. This had the effect of running counter to the Allied strategic intention that the bulk of enemy forces would be concentrated against the British eastern flank of the bridgehead. In the meantime, von Rundstedt ordered more formations to the battle area, including three armoured divisions – 2nd Panzer and 1st and 2nd SS Panzer Divisions – while instructing two infantry divisions to prepare to relieve the armoured formations already engaged, allowing them to reform for counter-attack. He also asked OKW for further reinforcements and drew additional artillery units from three artillery schools.[73]

All Seventh Army formations between the Orne and Vire – I SS Panzer Corps, 352nd and 716th Divisions – were placed under General Geyr von Schweppenburg, commanding Panzer Group West. Von Schweppenburg's headquarters had been allocated an operational role on D-Day, transferred to Army Group B and placed under Seventh Army. But its move from Paris was tortuous with constant attacks from Allied aircraft, resulting in the loss of three-quarters of its radio equipment, and it did not become fully operational until 9 June. Even then, there was no massed armoured attack. Although von Schweppenburg persuaded Rommel of the need for such an operation, the three available divisions, none at greater than half strength, could not be concentrated effectively until the 10th. On that evening von Schweppenburg was wounded and his operations staff wiped out when Allied planes bombed his headquarters. Central control of the group was destroyed and renewed Allied attacks made it necessary to switch formations to defensive tasks, which they were to perform with deadly effectiveness.[74]

While Rommel dithered, the Allies brought more divisions ashore. Second Army was strengthened by the arrival of the Desert Rats, 7th Armoured Division, the first elements of which landed in XXX Corps' area on D-Day. The division, under Major-General G W E J Erskine, was almost complete by the 10th although much of its transport and its infantry had yet to be landed. By then it had seen its first action in Europe when A Squadron 5th

Royal Tanks supported 56 Brigade and B Squadron the commandos in their endeavours on 50th Division's flank. A few days later 49th (West Riding) Division, a veteran formation under Major-General E H Barker, began disembarking and was followed, on 13 June, by 11th Armoured Division, although an advance party came ashore on D+3, in the Canadian sector. It was to be some days before 11th Armoured went into action. Although the division was unblooded, it was led by one of the best armoured commanders of the war, Major-General G P B 'Pip' Roberts, who had fought in the desert and brought a wealth of experience to 11th Armoured, which had had as its first commander that outstanding prophet of armoured warfare Percy Hobart. A day after 11th Armoured's arrival, 15th (Scottish) Division, an infantry formation, also arrived. Commanded by Major-General G H A MacMillan, this division had seen no service thus far in the war but its soldiers were keen to show that they were as good as the veterans of 51st (Highland) Division. It was another ten days before another British infantry division arrived: 43rd (Wessex) under Major-General G I Thomas, soon to be known as 'Butcher' to his soldiers. The Wyverns had a sad beginning to their campaign when many soldiers of their Reconnaissance Regiment lost their lives while still aboard ship. Two more infantry divisions joined Second Army's order of battle on 27 June: 53rd (Welsh) under Major-General R K Ross and 59th (Staffordshire) under Major-General L O Lyne. The Staffordshire Division was to be broken up to reinforce other formations of Second Army soon after the Normandy campaign. Finally, the Normandy order of battle of Second Army was completed with the arrival, on 28 June, of Guards Armoured Division, under Major-General Allan Adair. Of all the contradictions that make up the British Army this had to be one of the most unusual: an armoured – i.e., cavalry – division made up of foot soldiers, but foot soldiers who considered themselves the best in the world and capable of any role.[75]

Those troop movements kept Britain's ports busy; and also the men who manned the vessels maintaining a regular cross-Channel ferry service. Sub-Lieutenant Michael d'Alton, first officer on LCT-796, recalled that his vessel operated between Weymouth and Normandy over the week immediately following D-Day, irregularly during the first two days but then settling into a routine. LCT796 made about eleven or twelve round trips during that period. As on the first voyage, vessels would assemble south at 'Piccadilly Circus' before sailing to Normandy. LCTs often struggled to maintain their course during these voyages, their unwieldy shapes and low speed making matters difficult. To keep within the swept channel the LCTs would travel crabwise, at a sharp angle off-course, and, on one occasion, LCT796 was having great difficulty in maintaining course, as the compasses seemed to have gone completely awry. The vessel was carrying three or four US Army pantechnicons and the captain finally called to the bridge the American NCO in charge to ask what the lorries were carrying in case that might be affecting the compasses. The pantechnicons turned out to be mobile laundries whose generators were causing the compass problems, which could have been averted had the LCT's crew known beforehand what the cargo was.[76]

As well as follow-up formations, much of the paraphernalia of an army group headquarters was assembling in Normandy. Montgomery had remained in Britain on D-Day but sailed at 9.30 that evening for Normandy on board the destroyer HMS *Faulknor* which arrived off the beaches early on D+1. Montgomery visited Bradley on board USS *Augusta* as well as Dempsey and Admiral Vian on board HM Ships *Scylla* and *Bululo*, which were alongside each other. Then Eisenhower and Ramsay arrived in Ramsay's flagship and a further meeting was held before returning to *Augusta* where news from Omaha was positive. Montgomery disembarked on D+2, making himself unpopular with the Navy since he insisted on being brought so close to shore that *Faulknor* grounded on a sandbank. He then established his Tactical Headquarters in the grounds of Creuilly château.[77]

By 10 June, Montgomery noted, the assault beaches had become a continuous lodgement area, which was

> sixty miles long and varied in depth from eight to twelve miles;* it was firmly held and all anxiety had passed. There had been considerable cause for alarm on OMAHA beach in the early stages; but that situation was put right by the gallantry of the American soldiers, by good supporting naval fire, and by brave work by fighter-bomber aircraft.[78]

Although some German troops held out within the Allied lodgement area, these presented no real threat to the beachhead.

The vessels that chugged across the Channel included tugs hauling elements of the Mulberry harbours to Normandy and ships that would be sunk to provide breakwaters for those harbours, the British facility at Arromanches, soon named Port Winston, and the American on Omaha Beach. Almost midway between these artificial harbours, Port-en-Bessin was coming into use as the terminal for fuel being pumped ashore from tankers in the bay. Meanwhile, much material for the invading forces was still being discharged across the beaches.

In those early days on the beaches, and as the invaders began pushing

* In *Normandy to the Baltic*, published in 1947, Montgomery had described the length of the beachhead as being 'over fifty miles'.

inland, doctors played an essential part. One RAMC doctor, Captain Gordon Sheill, received the Military Cross for his work in charge of a Regimental Aid Post at Haute Longueville between 8 and 10 June. Since the Germans were inflicting considerable casualties on the invaders, his RAP was very busy, with many units passing their wounded there for attention while German casualties were also being brought in. Sheill treated both Allied and enemy casualties against a constant backdrop of aerial bombardment, and with artillery and mortar rounds landing all around.

> [Captain Sheill's] quiet efficiency and skill were without doubt instrumental in the saving of many lives, and his unflagging energy and cheerfulness throughout these difficult operations were an inspiration to officers and men alike.[79]

Casualties were also being treated in hospital ships anchored offshore while a speedy evacuation procedure, which soon included air evacuation, had been arranged for cases needing treatment in Britain. Hospital ships were manned by the Royal Army Medical Corps and Queen Alexandra's Imperial Military Nursing Service, the QAs. Even when one hospital ship, *Amsterdam*, was torpedoed, QAs continued to care for their patients and did all they could to ensure their rescue. Several were decorated, including Sisters Ellen Hourigan and Lily McNicholas, both of whom gave up places in water ambulances to assist patients in evacuating the ship. Sister Hourigan did not escape until *Amsterdam* capsized when she slid down the starboard side, by now almost horizontal, shortly before the ship slipped below the waves.[80]

In his *Memoirs* Montgomery noted that he did not consider the early capture of Caen as vital, although senior airmen were anxious that Second Army should take the high ground between the city and Falaise, an area suitable for constructing airfields. Although conceding that this was his original intention, Montgomery commented that acquiring ground to the east was not as important as 'by hard fighting to make the enemy commit his reserves' in that sector, thereby drawing pressure from the Americans and assisting their operations, which would lead to the breakout. In this strategy, opined Montgomery, the Allies were assisted by the fact that Caen was a vital road and rail centre through which all the main routes from east and south-east to the Allied lodgement area passed. And since the bulk of German reserves were based north of the Seine, these would have to converge on Caen as they moved to oppose the Allies.[81]

The strong armoured opposition to any direct advance on Caen made Montgomery decide on an outflanking move to encircle the city. Second Army was to execute this operation with I Corps pushing 51st (Highland)

Division into the bridgehead east of the Orne, thence to strike south towards Cagny, some six miles south-east of Caen. To the west, XXX Corps would strike southwards with 7th Armoured Division towards Villers-Bocage and Noyers and then across the Odon to the high ground overlooking Evrecy. Once the Desert Rats had established themselves on that high ground 1st Airborne Division would fly in to seal the gap between Cagny and Evrecy. This, the final phase of the operation, would begin on 10 June. Air Marshal Leigh-Mallory argued against the use of 1st Airborne, claiming that the division could not be landed in strength sufficiently concentrated to achieve Montgomery's aims. The division was not called upon as neither prong of the attack reached its objective.[82]

From 6th Airborne's bridgehead, east of the Orne, 51st (Highland) Division and 4 Armoured Brigade were to attack southwards but neither had completed assembly by the morning of 10 June and so the operation was delayed, with 153 Brigade now scheduled to cross the Orne that evening for a new operation planned for the 12th. Fighting continued around the airborne bridgehead with renewed enemy attacks on the morning of the 10th. German troops struck at the commandos in the Bréville area but, despite some limited penetrations, the situation had stabilised by early afternoon. Other attacks against the paratroopers' positions culminated in an assault by an infantry battalion supported by SPGs, but fire from HMS *Arethusa* helped smash this attack and the rout was completed by a bayonet charge by the paras. One wounded German prisoner, commanding a unit of 346th Division, told his captors that his battalion had been all but wiped out in the previous twelve hours.[83] At Ranville another attack was routed and the attackers mauled so severely that a further German battalion was close to destruction. When 153 Highland Brigade crossed the Orne that evening it was held near Ranville with only 5th Black Watch placed under command of 3 Parachute Brigade for an attack on Bréville on the morrow. That evening a detachment of paras occupied the château de St Côme as a jumping-off point for the attack on Bréville. However, the attack was beaten off by heavy fire, the Germans even bringing anti-aircraft guns into action against 5th Black Watch who withdrew to the château, having suffered some 200 casualties in their first battle in Normandy.[84]

On XXX Corps' front, 7th Armoured Division was to attack on the morning of 10 June to seize high ground near Hottot, jumping off between the Seulles and the Aure on 50th Division's front. With Hottot taken, 8 Armoured Brigade, then in the salient east of the Seulles, would pass from 50th (Northumbrian) to the command of 7th Armoured Division to join the latter on their advance southwards. Although this would double the armoured strength of the Desert Rats it would add only a single infantry battalion; and it was in infantry that the division lacked strength. By the

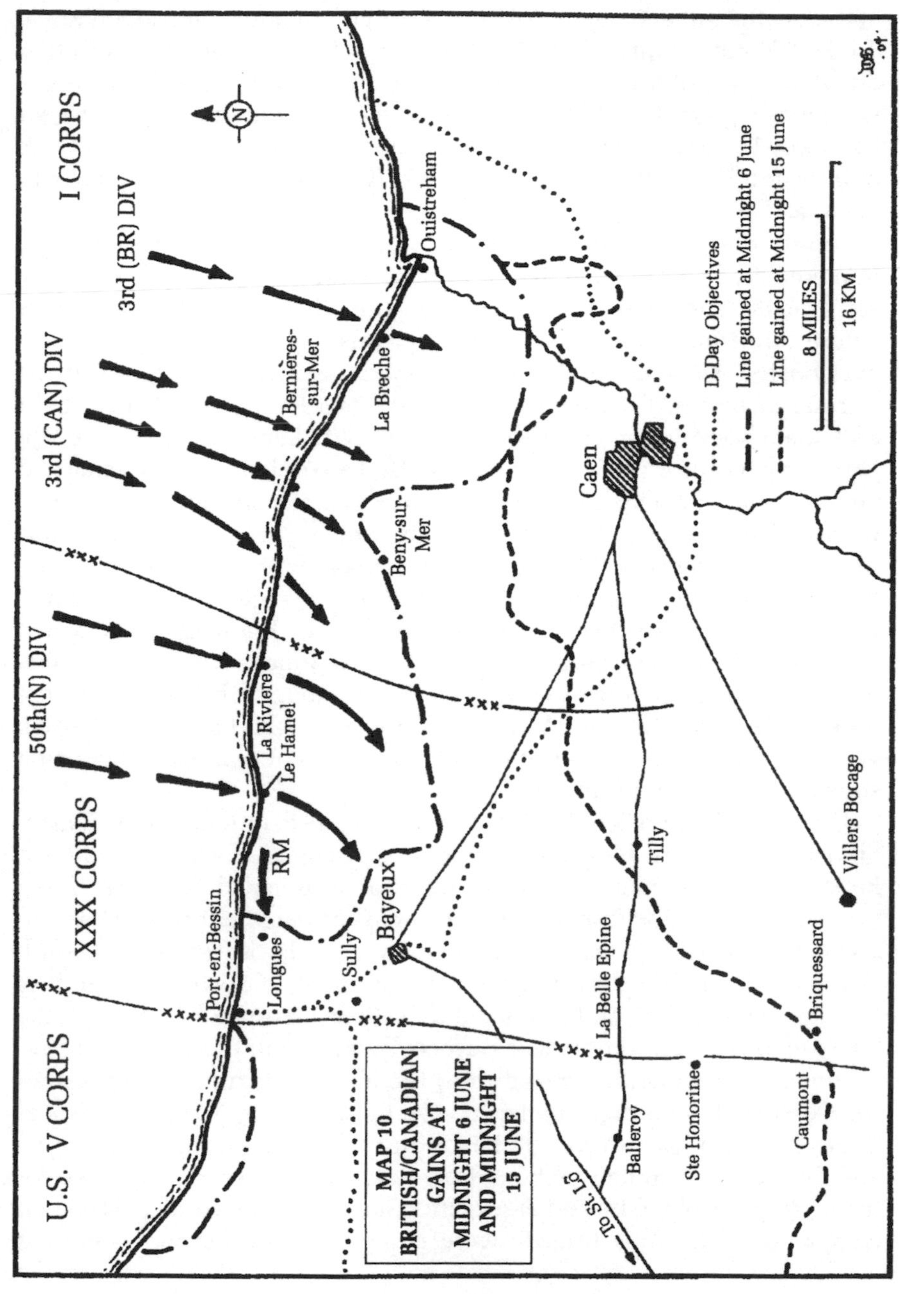
U.S. V CORPS
XXX CORPS
50th(N) DIV
3rd (CAN) DIV
3rd (BR) DIV
I CORPS
Port-en-Bessin
Longues
RM
Le Hamel
La Riviere
Bernières-sur-Mer
La Breche
Ouistreham
Sully
Bayeux
Beny-sur-Mer
Caen
La Belle Epine
Tilly
Villers Bocage
Briquessard
Caumont
Ste Honorine
Balleroy
To St. Lô
MAP 10
BRITISH/CANADIAN GAINS AT MIDNIGHT 6 JUNE AND MIDNIGHT 15 JUNE
D-Day Objectives
Line gained at Midnight 6 June
Line gained at Midnight 15 June
8 MILES
16 KM

10th only the three regiments of 22 Armoured Brigade – 1st and 5th Royal Tanks and 4th County of London Yeomanry (Sharpshooters) – as well as 5th RHA, part of 8th King's Royal Irish Hussars, the divisional reconnaissance regiment, and two companies of 22 Armoured Brigade's motor battalion, 1st Rifle Brigade, were ashore and there was a 'general shortage of transport'[85]; the three battalions* of 131 (Queen's) Infantry Brigade had yet to arrive.

For its part, 8 Armoured Brigade had been in action in the days immediately before it was due to link up with 7th Armoured Division, assisting the Canadians at Putot-en-Bessin and then outflanking Loucelles before capturing Audrieu on 9 June and pushing south to high ground overlooking Tilly-sur-Seulles at Point 103; this area was critical to the German defences. The brigade's Shermans met Panthers of Panzer Lehr and there were bitter engagements with 24th Lancers supporting 8th Durhams in capturing St Pierre on the 9th. Panzer Lehr counter-attacked next morning, knocking out twelve Lancers' tanks and forcing a British withdrawal before a counter-attack in which Lancers and Durhams recaptured St Pierre and forced the Germans to withdraw towards Tilly. In the course of fighting since D-Day 8 Armoured Brigade's regiments had suffered many casualties, among them Captain Keith Douglas, killed while on an unauthorised foot patrol on 9 June[86] and one of three Sherwood Rangers officers killed that day.** Douglas had served in the desert, was already a well-known poet and writer – his book *From Alamein to Zem Zem* is a classic – and, at twenty-four years of age, one of the rising stars of English literature.

The Sharpshooters led 7th Armoured's advance, moving off at 5.45am on 10 June. Before long the regiment was engaged with the enemy, knocking out a German tank in the village of Jerusalem, but also receiving unwelcome attention from small parties of German infantry who kept up an aggressive defence that demanded a sweep of Jerusalem by 2nd South Wales Borderers. The Welshmen took a mixed bag of prisoners, including two Japanese, a Turk and a Russian as well as Germans.[87] Although the Sharpshooters went on to clear Bucéels by nightfall, the village was reoccupied by German infantry during the night, which only emphasised the Desert Rats' shortage of infantry. On the Yeomanry's right, 5th Royal Tanks had also had several clashes with the enemy, losing sixteen men and five tanks. Eventually A Squadron reached Verrières and stopped for the night to be joined by 2nd Essex; 2nd Glosters held Jerusalem. The two companies of 1st Rifle Brigade were deployed with the two armoured

* These were 1/5th, 1/6th and 1/7th Queen's Royal Regiment (West Surrey).

** Keith Douglas was commissioned into The Derbyshire Yeomanry and is shown on the Army Roll of Honour as belonging to that regiment. He is buried in Tilly-sur-Seulles war cemetery.

regiments but there were nowhere near enough infantry for the tasks demanded of them.[88]

When fighting resumed next morning the Essex and Glosters made successful attacks supported by the armoured regiments but the advance was stopped by a line of dense woodland. There was a limited resumption on the 12th when 131 Brigade arrived,* supported by 1st Royal Tanks but, again, topography militated against any breakthrough by armour and Bucknall decided to halt 7th Armoured's operation and move the division round the right flank since 1st US Division, advancing on Caumont, reported only slight opposition. Thus the link with 8 Armoured Brigade never occurred.

Seventh Armoured's new thrust was to take it along the boundary with First US Army, from St Paul du Vernay, through Livry and Briquessard towards Villers-Bocage with 22 Armoured Brigade in the van; 1st Royal Tanks were not included in the brigade order of battle but 1/7th Queen's were present with 5th RHA; elements of the Irish Hussars reconnoitred to front and flanks. The other battalions of 131 Brigade, and 1st Royal Tanks, were still engaged with the enemy but would follow as soon as possible.[90]

That move met opposition at Livry where the Hussars lost a tank and infantry had to be called to clear the village, the advance grounding to a standstill in the meantime. At 8.00pm Livry was clear and the division was ordered to harbour for the night; the column's tail did not reach the harbour area until midnight. It was also dark when 131 Brigade disengaged to join the division; by dawn the column was passing through St Paul du Vernay. Meanwhile the Americans had reached Caumont, which they occupied on the morning of the 13th.[91]

As the Americans were occupying Caumont, 7th Armoured was back on the road for Villers-Bocage with 22 Armoured Brigade leading; the Queen's Brigade, with an Irish Hussars' squadron under command, was to occupy an area around Livry. The advance began at 5.30am with the Sharpshooters aiming to take and hold high ground about a mile north-east of Villers-Bocage, 1/7th Queen's the town itself, 5th Royal Tanks high ground a mile to the south and a battery of Norfolk Yeomanry, the divisional anti-tank regiment, covering between the two armoured regiments. Although recce patrols met some small enemy parties there was no other contact for over three hours and A Squadron Sharpshooters with A Company 1st Rifle Brigade motored into Villers-Bocage to be met by a joyous citizenry cheering them to the echo. The little group had made good progress and carried on to the high ground beyond Villers-Bocage where the tanks left the road at Point 213, which they were to hold. Sharpshooter and Green Jacket officers held an O Group, which was

* According to Field Marshal Lord Carver, then commanding 1st Royal Tanks, 1/5th Queens was still in the process of landing.[89]

attended by Viscount Cranley, commanding the Sharpshooters, who came up in his scout car.[92] This provided an opportunity for the soldiers to indulge in the perennial habit of British soldiers: a brew-up. Then a scene of relative calm suddenly became one of brutish action.

Without warning several enemy tanks, identified as Tigers, appeared to the south of the Caen road and fired on the British vehicles, setting two tanks and all the riflemen's lorries ablaze. A Rifle Brigade 6-pounder, commanded by Sergeant Bray, came into action and hit three enemy tanks before being destroyed by a direct hit. For the leading group of 7th Armoured Division a very dangerous situation had developed in no more than two or three minutes: the group was cut off from the main body, the dismounted Green Jackets were separated from their officers and German shells and machine-gun bullets filled the air.

> Then all hell seemed to break out in the east side of the little town – German spandaus opened fire from the upper windows of the houses, the streets became filled with smoke and there was the crash of breaking glass and falling slates. A Tiger that appeared through the smoke was impervious to the 75-mm shot that Major Carr, the second-in-command of the C.L.Y., pumped into it.[93]

Carr's tank was hit almost immediately and burst into flames with most of the crew killed and Carr wounded seriously. There followed a protracted and bitter battle in which the enemy tanks generally proved superior to the Sharpshooters' Cromwells. Both sides were surprised at the other's appearance but the Germans reacted more quickly and most of the Sharpshooters and 1st Rifle Brigade were cut off with many taken prisoner. The Official History suggests that opposing 7th Armoured was 2nd Panzer Division,[94] recently arrived from Amiens, which had been en route to the Caumont sector. In fact, as Michael Reynolds demonstrates in his book *Steel Inferno*, the damage was done by a handful of Tigers, commanded by a young SS tank officer, Michael Wittmann, Germany's leading tank 'ace'. Of 2nd Panzer Division's tanks there were none; only small elements of the division had reached Villers-Bocage by the time of this encounter.[95]

In Villers-Bocage, where fighting continued until dark, Lieutenant Cotton and Sergeant Brammall of the Sharpshooters, supported by anti-tank guns of 1/7th Queen's, carried out some successful actions, claiming hits on six Tigers. Michael Reynolds notes that at least one Tiger and a Mark IV were knocked out by PIATs and by sticky bombs hurled from first-floor windows while German sources confirmed that three tanks of one company were lost to 'close range weapons' and six Tigers and two Mark IVs were found in Villers-Bocage after the battle; the two Tiger companies involved suffered ten dead and twelve wounded.[96] During the battle occurred an episode that must have appeared surreal to both British and German soldiers: the local fire brigade turned out to try to extinguish the flames from blazing German tanks.[97] It would seem that the sense of vocation of the local *sapeurs pompiers* transcended the bitter realities of global conflict. Prisoners taken included men from Panzer Lehr* and 2nd Panzer Divisions; the presence of the first had been expected but the second was not, although ULTRA decrypts had indicated that it was en route to Normandy. German attempts to penetrate 7th Armoured's front were held off with little difficulty. Excellent artillery support was available and, in addition to 5th RHA, the division could call on 3rd RHA and an AGRA** (Army Group Royal Artillery), plus 1st US Division's artillery.

When the commander of 131 Brigade was cut off near Amaye the divisional commander told Lieutenant-Colonel Michael Carver of 1st Royal Tanks to take over the brigade. Carver's command 'consisted only of Michael Forrester's 1st/6th Queens and ourselves, with supporting anti-tank and field artillery and a squadron of 11th Hussars'***[99] but, with orders to secure Briquessard and two crossroads north of the village, he deployed to cover both points and sent the recce troop of 1st Royal Tanks to contact US troops to the right. By evening 131 Brigade was well established and Carver received orders for the following day: open the road to 22 Brigade at first light and keep it open.[100]

As the day came to an end Villers-Bocage was evacuated and a new perimeter established. In 22 Armoured Brigade losses had been heavy: the Sharpshooters had lost regimental headquarters, including their commanding officer, and A Squadron with most of their personnel dead, wounded or missing; Rifle Brigade casualties included almost all A Company dead, wounded or missing with only a few men escaping. Twenty-seven tanks had been destroyed as well as the soft-skinned vehicles that had gone forward. Only slight enemy shelling and minimal patrolling activity disturbed the night. With daylight 5th Royal Tanks moved out towards their positions of the 13th on Tracy Bocage ridge while the remainder of the brigade held a box east of Amaye. The latter was found to be clear of enemy and was occupied; infantry patrols found enemy troops in Tracy Bocage village. Without strong infantry support it

* The title Panzer Lehr indicates an armoured training formation and Allied intelligence at first believed the division to be made up of raw troops, hence 'training'. It came as a considerable shock to discover the quality of the division, which was made up of men who had been instructors in armoured warfare and had, therefore, much experience in battle, often on the Russian front. Panzer Lehr was also well equipped.[98]

** This AGRA included 53rd Heavy Regiment and 7th and 64th Medium Regiments.

*** This was, in fact, a squadron of 8th King's Royal Irish Hussars.

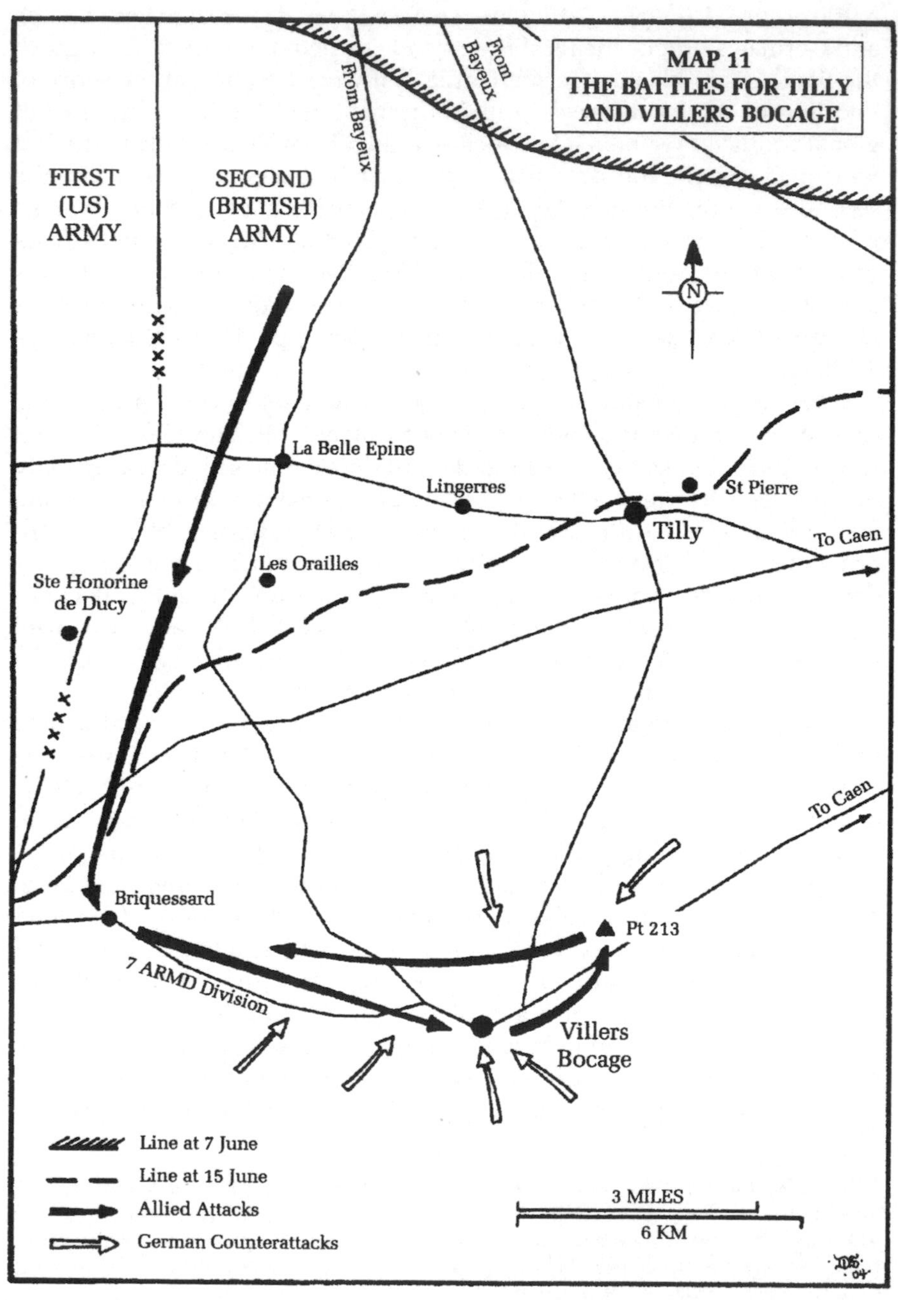
MAP 11
THE BATTLES FOR TILLY
AND VILLERS BOCAGE
From Bayeux
From Bayeux
FIRST
(US)
ARMY
SECOND
(BRITISH)
ARMY
N
La Belle Epine
Lingerres
St Pierre
Tilly
To Caen
Les Oreilles
Ste Honorine
de Ducy
To Caen
Briquessard
Pt 213
7 ARMD Division
Villers
Bocage
Line at 7 June
Line at 15 June
Allied Attacks
German Counterattacks
3 MILES
6 KM

was considered that the ridge could not be held and 50th Division, who were expected to provide that support, had run against Panzer Lehr and could not get forward in the direction of Tilly. Bucknall therefore ordered 7th Armoured to adjust its line to keep the right flank in 'the closest possible touch with the Americans',[101] which meant pulling back from the Villers-Bocage sector. This was to be done that night.

> It was a sad disappointment that the brilliant thrust conceived by General Bucknall which had carried the Division to Villers-Bocage, far behind the enemy's lines to a deeper penetration than was to be made for many weeks to come, could not be supported. It was a remarkable gain at a time when expansion of the beach-head was badly needed, but there were just not the additional infantry available to give the Division the backing required in close country of this type – nor was there that element of good fortune which might have made just the difference.[102]

Michael Reynolds suggests that the argument of insufficient infantry does not tally with the fact that most of 1st Rifle Brigade and two Queen's battalions

> remained uncommitted on the critical day and that one complete infantry brigade (151) was in Corps reserve; in fact two infantry brigades of the 49th Infantry Division were also unemployed – they were released to the 50th Division on the night of 13th June. Any of these three infantry brigades could have been allotted to Erskine before his Division set off on its epic task, and the blame for this failure to concentrate sufficient forces at the right place at the right time must be laid at the door of Bucknall, the commander of XXX Corps.[103]

Michael Carver's force secured the road to 22 Armoured on the 14th and had some successful actions against the opposition, destroying in one engagement two Panthers, a Tiger and several Mark IVs, as well as driving the enemy back. Although it was a frenetic day, Carver was disappointed to learn of the withdrawal plan as he 'thought that we had seen off the enemy'.[104] The withdrawal was to take place under cover of darkness and with RAF heavy bombers striking at Villers-Bocage, both to distract the Germans and cover the sounds of withdrawal. Before that could happen, at 7.00pm, the enemy launched a determined attack with two infantry battalions and some thirty tanks. In this action the difficulties of the bocage were demonstrated fully and the Desert Rats' historian noted that the country 'was so thick that it was possible to see only to the next hedge'.[105] But Allied artillery bombarded the attackers and their forming-up positions, thereby shattering the attack. The British perimeter was ringed by blazing German tanks; it was believed that a dozen tanks had been hit with anti-tank gunners claiming eight. German infantry losses were heavy. There were no further attacks that evening and quiet had descended over the battlefield by 9.00pm.

Such was the degree to which the enemy had been hit that the withdrawal took place without interference and the Desert Rats took up new positions from the junction with 1st US Division, east of Caumont, through Briquessard and Torteval. A three-mile gap, between the divisional left and 50th Division's right, was covered by 8th Hussars until the Northumbrian Division could advance to close it. On 17 June a German attack at Briquessard was met by 1/6th Queen's supported by C Squadron Irish Hussars; the latter lost eight killed and had five tanks destroyed in this action. Thereafter it was decided to relocate the line behind Briquessard ridge. In those positions 7th Armoured remained for the rest of June, although the armour was held back from the front. The main burden fell on the infantry, of whom there were still not enough, and there was little opportunity for rest during the short hours of darkness; morning Stand-to was at 4.15am and evening Stand-to at 10.15pm. Soldiers lived in slit trenches while patrols in the difficult countryside were tiring and dangerous and the enemy was always aggressive so that there were many casualties, especially from shell and mortar fire. It was with relief that 7th Armoured handed over to 2nd US Armored Division before moving back close to Jerusalem to rest and refit. Their three weeks of action had cost 1,149 casualties, a high price to pay but typical of the battle for Normandy.[106]

NOTES

1 NA, WO171/1350, war diary, 1 R Norfolk.
2 NA, WO171/1325, war diary, 2 KSLI.
3 Ellis, *Victory in the West*, p. 203.
4 Ibid, p. 204 .
5 Ibid.
6 NA, WO171/1325, war diary, 2 KSLI.
7 Ellis, op cit, pp. 228–9.
8 Ibid, p. 204.
9 Ibid, pp. 204–5.
10 NA, WO171/1239, war diary, 7 Para Bn.
11 NA, WO373/52.
12 *London Gazette*, 22 Mar 1945.
13 Shillito, *Pegasus Bridge Merville Battery*, p. 179.
14 NA, WO171/410, war diary, 3rd Br Division, Jun–Aug, 1944; WO171/616–617, war diary, 9 Bde, May–Jun & Jul–Aug 1944.
15 Ellis, op cit, p. 207.
16 Ibid.
17 Ibid, p. 208; NA, ADM202/99; RM Commandos in Normandy.

18 Ellis, op cit, p. 208.
19 Ibid, p. 209; NA, WO179/3005, war diary, 1st Hussars.
20 NA, ADM202/99; RM Commandos in Normandy.
21 Ellis, op cit, p. 210.
22 NA, WO171/838, war diary, 4/7 RDG.
23 Ellis, op cit, pp. 211–12.
24 Quoted in ibid, pp. 210–11.
25 Ibid.
26 NA, CAB44/247, p. 227.
27 NA, WO171/425, war diary, 6 A/b Division.
28 The polite version of this comment is quoted in Graves, *History of the Royal Ulster Rifles*, p. 104.
29 Lieut (later Maj) J Chapman MC, 1 RUR, i/v with author.
30 The name of the casualty was provided by David Truesdale.
31 Devlin, *Reminiscences of a Rifleman in Normandy*, p. 59.
32 Ibid.
33 Routledge, *Anti-Aircraft Artillery, 1914–55. History of the Royal Regiment of Artillery*, p. 301.
34 Ibid.
35 Sutton, *Wait for the Waggon*, pp. 181–2.
36 Estimated from war diaries, official accounts and Ellis, op cit, passim.
37 Ellis, op cit, pp. 222–3.
38 Ibid, p. 213.
39 Ibid, p. 236.
40 Middlebrook & Everitt, *The Bomber Command War Diaries*, op cit, p. 523–4; Ellis, op cit, p. 234.
41 Ellis, op cit, p. 226.
42 NA, CAB44/247, p. 227.
43 Ibid; NA, ADM202/99; RM Commandos in Normandy.
44 NA, WO171/425, war diary, 6 A/b Division; Ellis, op cit, p. 205.
45 NA, WO171/425, war diary, 6 A/b Division; Ellis, op cit, p. 227.
46 Ellis, op cit, p. 227.
47 Salmond, *The History of the 51st Highland Division*, op cit, pp. 139–42.
48 Ellis, op cit, p. 232; NA, ADM202/99; RM Commandos in Normandy.
49 NA, CAB44/246, pp. 73–4.
50 NA, WO171/613, war diary, 8 Armd Bde.
51 Doherty, *Only the Enemy in Front*, pp. 148–9.
52 Ibid.
53 Ellis, op cit, p. 229; NA, WO179/2893–2894, war diary, 9 Cdn Bde, May–Jun & Jul–Aug 1944; WO179/3010, war diary, 27 Cdn Armd Regt,; WO179/2960–2961, war diary, Regina Rifle Regt, Jan–Jun & Jul–Dec 1944.
54 NA, CAB44/247, p. 192.
55 Ellis, op cit, p. 229.
56 Ibid, p. 228; NA, WO171/410, war diary, 3rd Br Division.
57 NA, WO171/258, war diary I Corps HQ; CAB44/247, p. 180.
58 Reynolds, *Steel Inferno*, p. 70.
59 NA, CAB44/247, para. 86.
60 Ellis, op cit, p. 229.
61 Ibid, pp. 229–30.
62 Reynolds, op cit, p. 63.
63 Ibid, p. 76.
64 Ellis, op cit, p. 233.

65 Ibid.
66 Boyd, i/v with author.
67 Boyd, *Boyd's War*, p. 51.
68 Ibid.
69 Middlebrook & Everitt, op cit, p. 526; Ellis, op cit, pp. 235–6.
70 Middlebrook & Everitt, op cit, p. 527; Military Historical Society, Lummis Files.
71 Macksey, *Rommel, Battles & Campaigns*, p. 208.
72 Liddell Hart, *The Rommel Papers*, passim, but see especially pp. 516–19 on 'Modern Military Leadership'.
73 Ellis, op cit, pp. 237–8; Fraser, *Knight's Cross*, p. 461.
74 Ellis, op cit, p. 238.
75 Keegan, *Six Armies in Normandy*, p. 335.
76 D'Alton, interview with author.
77 Montgomery, *Memoirs*, pp. 252–3.
78 Ibid, p. 252.
79 Doherty, *Irish Men and Women in the Second World War*, p. 173.
80 *Kiltimagh Life and Times 1945*, per P Sobolewski.
81 Montgomery, op cit, p..
82 Ellis, op cit, p. 247.
83 Ibid, p. 248.
84 Ibid, pp. 247–8; Salmond, *The History of the 51st Highland Division*, pp. 142–3.
85 Verney, *The Desert Rats*, p. 191.
86 Hills, *By Tank Into Normandy*, p. 87.
87 Verney, op cit, p. 191.
88 Ibid, p. 192; Ellis, op cit, p. 252.
89 Carver, *Out of Step*, p. 183.
90 Verney, op cit, pp. 192–3.
91 Ibid.
92 Ellis, op cit, p. 254; Verney, op cit, p. 192; Carver, op cit, p. 183.
93 Verney, op cit, pp. 193–4.
94 Ellis, op cit, p. 255.
95 Reynolds, op cit, pp. 102–5.
96 Ibid, p. 106.
97 Verney, op cit, pp. 194–5.
98 Jarymowycz, *Tank Tactics from Normandy to Lorraine*, p. 100.
99 Carver, op cit, p. 183.
100 Ibid.
101 Verney, op cit, p. 197.
102 Ibid.
103 Reynolds, op cit, p. 108.
104 Carver, op cit, p. 185.
105 Verney, op cit, p. 198.
106 Ibid, p. 200.

CHAPTER IX
Caen holds out

Bend up every spirit

While the Desert Rats held their new positions three British infantry divisions were engaged elsewhere. The newly arrived 49th (West Riding), and 50th (Northumbrian), pushed south and south-west against Hottot and Tilly on 15 June. Fighting raged for several days, especially around Tilly, which fell on the 19th. On 13 June 51st (Highland) attacked Ste Honorine as part of the pincer move on Caen. Airborne troops had suffered heavy casualties in unsuccessful attacks on Ste Honorine. Jack Chapman's platoon of 1st Royal Ulster Rifles was to secure the start-line for an attack by a battalion from 51st (Highland) Division.

> We cleared the start-line without any bother, they took over and we got back. I got hit on the way back and most of my platoon was wiped out. And they [5th Cameron Highlanders] got about halfway across a large open space and got massacred themselves.[1]

In fact the Camerons took Ste Honorine but were forced to withdraw when counter-attacked by panzer grenadiers and SPGs. As the Germans followed up this withdrawal Chapman's platoon was mortared heavily; he and several of his men were wounded.*

As 5th Camerons were attacking Ste Honorine, 2nd Seaforth moved against Demouville but the Camerons' failure to hold the former, and heavy German artillery fire, made the Seaforth task impossible; the battalion was withdrawn to defensive positions on high ground north of Ste Honorine; 5th Seaforth filled the line between their 2nd Battalion and the Camerons at Longueval. Nine days later the Camerons, with detachments from 2nd Seaforth and armour from 13th/18th Royal Hussars, but no preceding or accompanying artillery fire, attacked Ste Honorine again and took the village after determined fighting. They fought off several fierce counter-attacks before handing Ste Honorine over

* Although seven men of the Rifles are recorded as having been killed that day it is not possible to ascertain which platoons they were serving with.

to 2nd Seaforth who were relieved later by 5th Seaforth 'in that village of evil memory'.[2]

Capturing Ste Honorine was some small help to the British troops on the left flank since it eased the pressure in the salient east of the Orne. It also helped morale in 51st (Highland) Division whose historian admits that 'the normal very high morale of the Division fell temporarily to a low ebb'.[3] This he ascribes to several factors, including the fact that this was the first time in two years' fighting that the division had assumed a defensive role. Then there was a 'kind of claustrophobia [that] affected the troops' from fighting in thick woods under constant shelling and mortaring.[4] The mortaring would intensify when 7 Werfer Brigade arrived, bringing multi-barrelled Nebelwerfers into action against the Highlanders.[5] And, of course, the division was being broken up with battalions 'sent here and there and everywhere under all sorts of command' rather than fighting as a division. Nor, as we shall see, would this state of affairs end for some time. For the time being the north-eastern pincer move on Caen had been stopped by determined resistance and, as Montgomery later wrote, any further attempts to enlarge the Orne bridgehead met similar spirited and 'very determined enemy reaction'.[6]

With efforts by 7th Armoured and 50th (Northumbrian) Divisions to thrust to Caen on the right flank also blunted, the former were ordered to hold firm while 49th and 50th Divisions continued the offensive. But, as we have already seen, this was also unsuccessful; only some small villages, including Tilly, were taken. I Corps was forced to consolidate against persistent attacks by armour from 12th SS Panzer and 21st Panzer Divisions. Any forward movement was difficult and costly. Although, from 15 June, a new corps – VIII – was arriving to reinforce Second Army, its leading formation – 11th Armoured Division – was two days behind schedule and this slowing of the build-up would affect future operations. The problem would also be exacerbated by the weather.

Between D-Day and 16 June the Allies had landed more than 500,000 men* with some 81,000 vehicles, 46,000 of them British and the remainder American, and over 183,000 tons of stores. Second Army held seven days' rations and both British corps carried sufficient fuel for 150 miles with an adequate reserve behind them.[7] Nor was there a shortage of ammunition, although that commodity had been rationed. Impressive as these figures are, the build-up programme was running two days late, although, arguably, it had been too optimistic; this had already influenced operations. Had 7th Armoured Division's infantry brigade, 33 Armoured Brigade and 49th Division landed as scheduled then they could have

* This figure includes 278,000 American and 279,000 British and Canadian troops.

played a significant part at Villers-Bocage and the high ground beyond might well have been in Allied hands before 2nd Panzer Division arrived in strength sufficient to turn the battle. The British Official Historian believed that had the build-up progressed as planned then Caen might have fallen. But the city still held out with Rommel investing much effort in its defence, for, should Caen fall, British armour would have a clear run to the Seine and Paris and the Germans could write off France. Rommel had also deployed the 88s of III Flak Corps south and east of Caen where they could take heavy toll of Allied armour.[8] Those who suggest that the 88's effect was exaggerated have never sat in a tank facing a line of these magnificent and potent weapons; they were among the war's most effective tank killers.

Montgomery's hope to take Caen had come to naught but he had drawn the bulk of the German armour to its defence. By 18 June, the anniversary of the Battle of Waterloo, four panzer divisions were deployed between Caumont and Caen, with 2nd Panzer astride the boundary of the two Allied armies. Nor had the enemy been able to pull his armour back to regroup for a major armoured counter-attack. On the western flank, 17th SS Panzer Grenadier Division had been committed around Carentan while fresh infantry divisions including 3rd Fallschirmjäger and 353rd Infantry, were deployed near St Lô, or in the Cotentin.[9] Rommel was also trying to protect Cherbourg. By now, however, the advantage lay with the Allies; and Rommel recognised this.

On 18 June Montgomery drafted fresh orders which would be finalised next day: First Army was to capture Cherbourg, clear the Cotentin and develop operations against la Haye du Puits and Coutances as soon as possible. From the 24th, XV US Corps was to come ashore through Omaha Beach. Its three infantry divisions would allow Bradley to strike out southward, towards Granville, Avranches and Vire; Bradley's left was to maintain close contact with Second Army, thereby protecting Dempsey's right. For its part, Second Army was to take Caen and provide a strong eastern flank for 21 Army Group by drawing enemy reserves there. Operations against Caen would continue as a pincer movement, the eastern arm thrusting from the Orne bridgehead north of Caen and the western striking across the Odon and Orne.[10]

However, Montgomery's plans had to be delayed since, because of poor weather, additional time was needed to land essential units and ammunition stores; the new operation was postponed until 22 June. But the weather worsened and a gale 'of unprecedented violence' blew up between 19 and 22 June, delaying matters even further. Described as the worst storm in living memory, or the worst Channel storm for many years, this gale, 'the great storm' in many accounts, may not have been as bad as suggested. Max Hastings notes that winds never exceeded force six, 'a moderate blow by nautical standards'.[11] The Official Historian writes of a wind of over thirty knots raising 'waves of six to eight feet' that increased 'at times to gale force'.[12] However, thirty knots is force seven on the Beaufort scale and a moderate gale; even a fresh gale – force eight – indicates winds of up to forty knots. Ellis further states that 'no such June storm had been known in the Channel for over forty years'.[13] Whatever the wind strength – and it did not reach storm force – it knocked the build-up programme even further behind. But matters could have been much worse. Had Eisenhower not gone ahead on 6 June, this would have been the alternative date for D-Day. Postponement would have been necessary yet again, pushing the invasion into July and leaving very little time for operations in favourable weather and for sufficient build-up to sustain the Allies through the winter. Perhaps those who described this gale as the 'great storm' had that thought in mind: that a postponement from 6 June might have meant no invasion at all in 1944. Some perspective is placed on the severity, or otherwise, of the gale by Brooke's not mentioning it in his diaries, although he notes, for 19 June, that 'News from France is good, the Cherbourg peninsula has been cut off by the Americans'.[14]

Montgomery was coming under pressure about his alleged tardiness in Normandy and his failure to capture Caen. In his *Memoirs* he states that the criticisms were based on the misconception that Caen had to be taken to enable a breakout towards the Seine and provide airfields on the eastern flank. Montgomery asserts that he never intended to break out in the eastern sector and nor was he fighting to capture airfields; he aimed to defeat Rommel. That achieved, he argued, all else would follow, including airfields. But the original COSSAC plan had envisaged a breakout in the Caen–Falaise area and Morgan, who had drawn up that plan, was now Eisenhower's deputy chief of staff and no lover of Montgomery, who had denied Morgan credit for his good work. It would seem that Morgan was leading a campaign against Montgomery in which the airmen participated enthusiastically. Monty had worked closely with 'Maori' Coningham in the desert – their headquarters were usually side by side – but such was not happening in Normandy. Coningham, now commanding Second Tactical Air Force, wanted airfields around Caen but Montgomery was not providing them. Monty felt that the New Zealander was aggrieved because they were no longer equal partners as in the desert and that this created a difficulty in the command structure.[15] In his inimitable fashion Montgomery was adding even more enemies to those he already had; Air Marshal Tedder was to be one of his most severe critics in the campaign and in post-war years.

The effects of the 'storm' were felt most severely at the Mulberry harbours. On D+1 the first elements of these great, prefabricated facilities began crossing the Channel; the American harbour was constructed off Port St Laurent and the British at Arromanches. Although the former was a little more sheltered than the British, being closer to the lee of the Cotentin, it sustained worse damage through a combination of tidal factors and the pattern in which the blockships and Phoenix caissons had been arranged. As a result the American harbour was abandoned. While Port Winston suffered considerable damage to some outer breakwaters, piers and pierheads the main breakwaters held; the harbour sheltered about 500 landing craft and other vessels, some of which discharged cargoes during the gale. On Juno Beach, eighteen LSTs unloaded during the 'storm', thanks to the shelter of the Gooseberry breakwater that survived the elements.[16]

For some days afterwards much effort was expended on clearing wreckage and there was an inevitable reduction in troop numbers and the amount of equipment landed. In the four days immediately before the weather intervened a daily average of 15,774 men, 2,965 vehicles and 10,666 tons of stores had arrived in the British sector; American figures were 18,938 men, 2,929 vehicles and 14,308 tons. In the four days – 19–22 June – of severe weather this dropped to 3,982 men, 1,375 vehicles and 4,286 tons in the British sector and 5,865 men, 1,052 vehicles and 3,064 tons in the American sector. Second Army had been two brigades behind schedule in its landing timetable before the gale; afterwards the shortfall was three divisions.[17]

Montgomery had to postpone his new operation with the limited attack east of the Orne now scheduled for 23 June and the major attack, on the right flank, two days later. But the weather had allowed Rommel to bolster his defences and additional troops had been moved in, with reduced pressure from Allied air forces because of weather conditions. Those reinforcements included the completion of 2nd Panzer Division, now deployed with both armour and infantry west of Villers-Bocage, 353rd Division, which moved into the Cotentin to face the Americans, and a battlegroup from 266th Division, which deployed west of the Vire. In addition, the remaining troops of 3rd Fallschirmjäger Division arrived, as did a heavy anti-tank battalion which deployed west of the Vire while Headquarters LXXXVI Corps completed its move east of the Orne; a medium battery and three troops of heavy artillery also arrived in the corps area.[18]

We have already seen (p. 169) how 51st (Highland) Division took Ste Honorine in Montgomery's renewed offensive on 23 June and held it against counter-attack. Two days later the emphasis switched to Second Army's western flank where XXX and the newly arrived VIII Corps were to launch Operation EPSOM. Since VIII Corps, commanded by Sir Richard O'Connor, had not completed landing, it was to be reinforced by 4

Armoured and 31 Tank Brigades,* thereby bringing its tank strength up to some 600; the corps included 11th Armoured, 15th (Scottish) and 43rd (Wessex) Divisions. The latter was less its reconnaissance regiment following a Luftwaffe attack on the Bay of the Seine. One of Hitler's new 'secret' weapons was the 'oyster' mine, unsweepable by any contemporary system, and detonated by the pressure of a ship passing overhead. Some were dropped in night raids and in one week – 22–29 June – sank eight ships and damaged another seven. Among those sunk was *Derry Cunihy* on which men of 43 Recce awaited disembarkation on the morning of 24 June. Early that morning

> before reveille . . . a landing craft came alongside with orders . . . to steam to another and safer beach to unload. Nearly all were still asleep, the men in the holds or on deck and the officers either in the cabins beneath the bridge or on the boat deck. The ship's engines started up and . . . there was a violent explosion which split the ship in two . . . The stern half began to sink rapidly, and in a matter of seconds, number five hold was under water . . . The men of A Squadron and HQ Squadron in number five hold had very little chance of escape. The fortunate were thrown clear, although few . . . understand how they escaped.[19]

In all, 180 men were lost and another 150 injured, a tragedy that cost more than a squadron in casualties and left the regiment ineffective. Disembarking from *Derry Cunihy* had been delayed due to sea conditions; had the ship's passengers disembarked on time the men of 43 Recce would never have been victims of that mine. Following the disaster 43 Recce was held at Pouligny during July to re-form and re-equip while its division went into action. To restore the regiment to fighting strength a squadron from 161 (Green Howards) Recce** was deployed to France to become the new A Squadron.[20]

The Wessex Division's introduction to Normandy had not been good but it would achieve a reputation as a tough fighting formation with the

* The presence of 'armoured' and 'tank' brigades was due to the British policy of having tanks to fight tanks and tanks to support infantry. Until the advent of the American Grant and Sherman tanks, the former were usually known as 'cruisers' and were speedy but not well armed while the latter were known as Infantry, or I-tanks and included machines such as the Churchill, which was adapted for a number of roles in this and other campaigns. The Cromwell, with which 7th Armoured Division was equipped, came from the 'cruiser' line.

** Although 161 (Green Howards) Recce was a Yorkshire regiment and 43 Recce had formed from a TA battalion of the Glosters, the new squadron fitted in well with the West Country men and the marriage was a successful one, inspiring to this day loyalty to the Glosters from Yorkshiremen.

divisional commander, Thomas, gaining Montgomery's trust as a man who could be relied upon to achieve results. However, in the initial stages of EPSOM it was given a consolidation role, taking over ground won by 15th (Scottish) Division. For EPSOM, VIII Corps was to deploy its own artillery with XXX Corps and I Corps, on the right and left flanks respectively, supporting them, providing over 700 guns. In addition, three cruisers and the monitor *Roberts* were to co-operate with the bombardment programme while air support would come from fighters and bombers, the latter striking enemy flank and rear positions. Prior to EPSOM, XXX Corps was to launch Operation DAUNTLESS to secure the Noyers area and cover VIII Corps' right flank; this would involve capturing Rauray, situated on a spur of high ground overlooking the area through which VIII Corps was to thrust southwards. DAUNTLESS was to take place on 25 June with EPSOM following next day.[21]

On the morning of 25 June 49th (West Riding) Division moved off with 146 Brigade on the right and 147 on the left; the division's third brigade, 70, was held back alongside 8 Armoured Brigade. Artillery support came from the division's own field regiments, an additional field regiment and a battery of self-propelled anti-tank guns, while five regiments of VIII Corps and part of two AA brigades, deployed in a ground role, were also on call. Against the attackers were ranged Panzer Lehr and part of 12th SS Panzer with up to eighty 88s of III Flak Corps. The weather promised both to help and hinder the attackers, with thick ground mist persisting for some hours in the early phase. By 9.15am, 4th Lincolns, 146 Brigade, supported by a squadron of 24th Lancers, had taken Bas de Fontenay and the brigade's two attacking battalions – the other was 1/4th King's Own Yorkshire LI – moved on to the edge of woodlands on the spur of high ground north of Vendes. At Fontenay 147 Brigade faced much tougher opposition with the Hallamshires, the sole attacking battalion, unable to get beyond the village's northern edge. Not until 9.00pm did 147 Brigade deploy a second battalion and, following fierce fighting, the enemy was forced out of Fontenay; skirmishes continued throughout the night. Although Army Group B's situation report for that night noted that the British attack had opened a gap five kilometres wide and two deep (about three miles by one and a quarter), the Rauray spur on VIII Corps' flank was still in German hands when O'Connor's attack began on the morning of the 26th.[22]

Once again weather intervened with air support suffering since much of it was to come from English-based aircraft. With poor conditions grounding most of those machines, EPSOM was supported only by the Normandy-based No. 83 Group. This was the first day since D-Day that air support from Britain was not available to Second Army. Overnight it had rained heavily in Normandy and the new day was misty when 15th (Scottish) Division left its start-line at 7.30am to seize the bridges over the

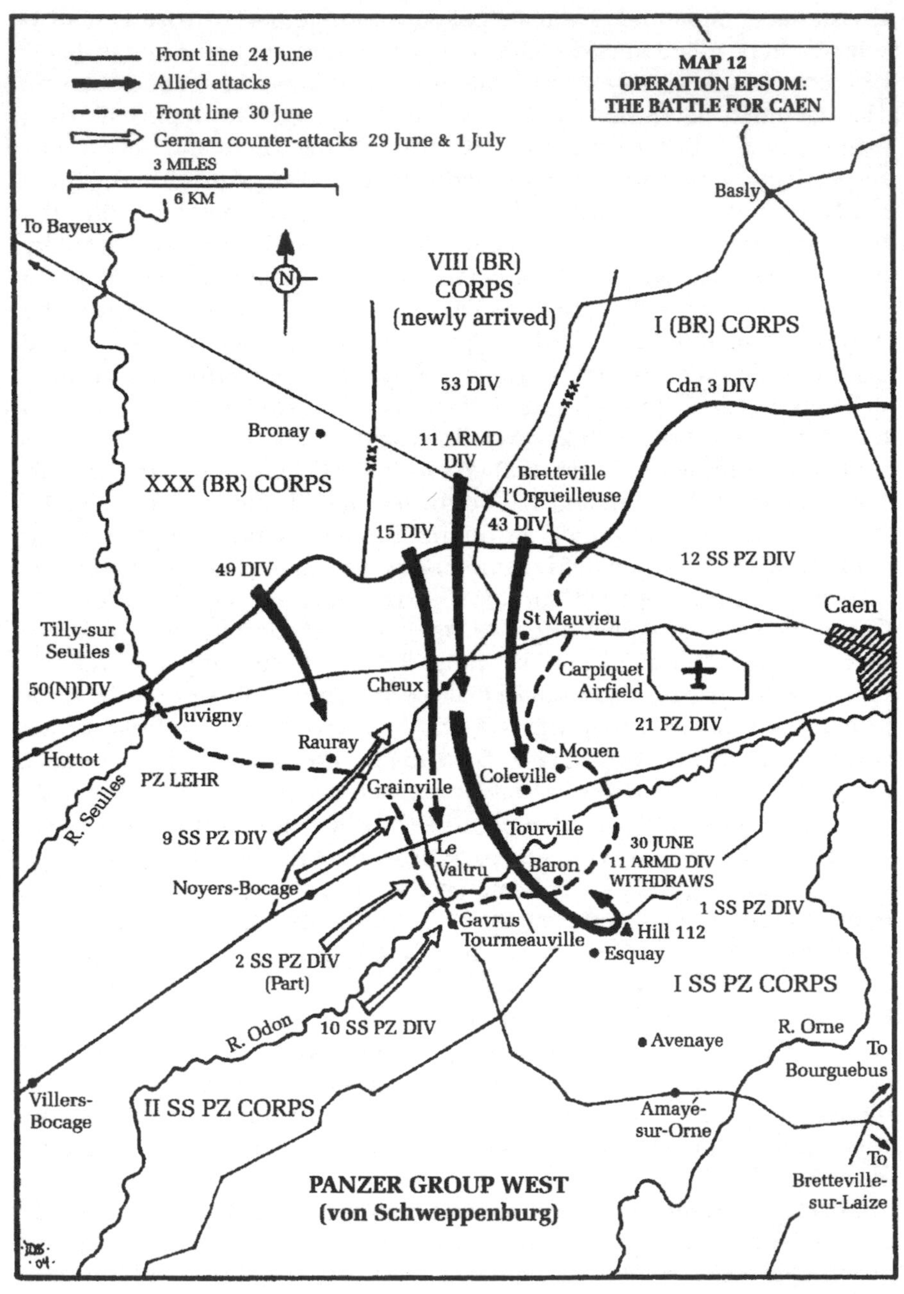
Front line 24 June
Allied attacks
Front line 30 June
German counter-attacks 29 June & 1 July
3 MILES
6 KM
MAP 12
OPERATION EPSOM:
THE BATTLE FOR CAEN
To Bayeux
Basly
VIII (BR)
CORPS
(newly arrived)
I (BR) CORPS
53 DIV
Cdn 3 DIV
Bronay
11 ARMD
DIV
XXX (BR) CORPS
Bretteville
l'Orgueilleuse
15 DIV
43 DIV
49 DIV
12 SS PZ DIV
Caen
Tilly-sur
Seulles
St Mauvieu
Carpiquet
Airfield
50(N)DIV
Cheux
Juvigny
21 PZ DIV
Hottot
Rauray
Mouen
PZ LEHR
Grainville
Coleville
R. Seulles
Tourville
9 SS PZ DIV
30 JUNE
11 ARMD DIV
WITHDRAWS
Le
Valtru
Baron
Noyers-Bocage
1 SS PZ DIV
Gavrus
Hill 112
Tourmeauville
Esquay
2 SS PZ DIV
(Part)
I SS PZ CORPS
R. Odon
10 SS PZ DIV
R. Orne
Avenaye
To
Bourguebus
Villers-
Bocage
II SS PZ CORPS
Amayé-
sur-Orne
To
Bretteville-
sur-Laize
PANZER GROUP WEST
(von Schweppenburg)

Odon, some five miles distant, after which 11th Armoured would pass through to carry out a similar coup de main on the Orne, thereby clearing the way to the high ground south of Caen.

The leading brigades were 46 (Highland), on the right, and 44 (Lowland) whose soldiers, supported by tanks of 31 Tank Brigade, marched forward over soft ground through dripping crops, and under an umbrella of artillery. Initially, progress was good but, as the Scots advanced, they found that some enemy posts had survived the bombardment and dealing with their determined defenders meant that the infantry lost their artillery protection. In the subsequent stiff fighting, both brigades sustained heavy losses, especially as they attacked the villages in their path where opposition was even tougher since the Germans had done all they could to strengthen the defences. The first village taken was la Gaule for which there was a sharp battle but the next to be taken, St Mauvieu, Cheux and le Haut de Bosq, all required hand-to-hand fighting through streets and ruined buildings. It was a bloody series of fights, made all the more so by the German tactic of rapid counter-attack, which was demonstrated most effectively in St Mauvieu. Here the Germans counter-attacked not just once but twice, each assault being launched by infantry and tanks from 12th SS Panzer Division, supported by some tanks from 21st Panzer. Both attacks were pushed back, for which much credit went to the supporting gunners who showered the attackers with shellfire. Even when 46 Brigade was consolidating its gains the enemy did not desist; 1st Glasgow Highlanders, who took over Cheux, were hammered by shells and mortar bombs from higher ground south of the village. Cheux was reduced to rubble and blocked by the detritus of battle. The Glaswegians suffered heavily: over 200 casualties in their first day in battle. At le Haut de Bosq, a 'long straggling village', the enemy held on in the southern end and to either side as well as on rising ground south of the village. From these positions, they continued to fire on the Scots with mortars, machine guns and tanks.[23]

While the Scots had been advancing, 11th Armoured Division had followed up and, shortly after noon, was ordered to push through the Scots towards Tourmauville, Gavrus and the bridges over the Odon. But 29 Armoured Brigade found such doughty opposition beyond Cheux that it was unable to initiate a dash for the bridges. Instead the brigade became involved in several hours of bloody fighting that achieved no gains. Once more the Scottish infantry were ordered forward, beginning a further advance at about 6.00pm with 227 Brigade now in the van. But, again, progress was slow. The roads to be used by the division passed through the ruins of Cheux, now a bottleneck, under constant bombardment from higher ground. Even torrential rain was not affecting the enemy's accuracy; with Cheux registered by his weapons most rounds found their mark. Once clear of Cheux the Scots' problems were not over. Only two roads led to the Odon bridges at Gavrus and Tourmauville. On the eastern route the leading troops reached Colleville but the main force was pinned at the Salbey stream, only a mile from Cheux. There they stayed for the night. Matters were no better on the western route where the advancing force was stalled just outside Cheux; fighting continued there and round le Haut de Bosq until darkness brought the advance to an end. In the fading light, exacerbated by heavy rain, there was no possibility of evicting the Germans from their positions that night. To the west XXX Corps had also been stalled, having taken only the northern sector of the Rauray spur. As the rain intensified Allied aircraft had been grounded, making it a battle between ground troops. The first day of EPSOM had ended with the Germans still on the high ground south of Cheux and the Rauray heights and claiming the destruction of fifty British tanks.[24]

Also in action were the units of 8 Armoured Brigade and the experiences of one member of 24th Lancers exemplify those of tank crews in Normandy. Lance-Corporal Tony Hughes was the wireless operator to the troop leader of No. 5 Troop in A Squadron.

> Orders for 26th June were for A Sqn to exploit towards the villages of Le Manoir and Tessel Bretteville in support of the Motor Battalion [12th King's Royal Rifle Corps], 5 Troop leading. At first light snipers were discovered in the hedges round our position and the first hour was spent flushing them out. At approx. 9am we advanced down the road which ran down the East side of Tessel wood. As was our practice the Troop Leader's tank was leading.[25]

There followed an engagement in which two German tanks were engaged; the first was hit twice and knocked out but the second fired two rounds at Tony Hughes' tank, which was hit twice in rapid succession. At the time the enemy tanks were identified as Tigers but it was later discovered that they were Panthers.

> A tank behind us radioed that there was a tank in the hedge on our right. I looked through my periscope and saw a puff of smoke from the hedge about 40 to 50 yards away. The gunner yelled that we had been hit. Next thing I knew was the whole turret was ablaze – there was a flash of blinding white. I remember struggling through the hatch and think I succeeded in getting the whole of my body out when the tank blew up and I found myself on the other side of the hedge with a shower of flaming objects all around and I crawled as fast as I could away from the tank . . . into a slit trench.[26]

The commander of the following tank, Lance-Corporal Lilley, later described Tony Hughes' exit from his Sherman 'as like a cork out of a bottle'.[27] Tony Hughes was burned badly about the face and became a patient of Archibald McIndoe at East Grinstead. His burns might have been worse had he not decided that morning to wear his leather jerkin, leather gauntlets and scarf, since the early morning had been quite chilly. His Sherman was carrying extra ammunition on the turret floor and this had exploded. The tank commander, Lance-Sergeant Fred Bartlett was awarded the Military Medal; neither the driver nor the co-driver, Troopers William Heath and Geoffrey Dean, survived. Peter Hancock, the gunner, did survive but with very serious burns.[28]

German sources describe the day as 'a complete defensive success' but one achieved only at the cost of I SS Panzer Corps deploying its last reserves, while both 21st and 12th SS Panzer had been 'taxed to the utmost'.[29] To continue fighting against this British penetration, 1st SS Panzer Division and II SS Panzer Corps* were ordered to attack northwards on the 27th, their right flank on the Orne, with 2nd Panzer Division's tank battalion and 8 Werfer Brigade under command. The Germans continued to suffer the attentions of the Allied airmen; both SS armoured formations had been delayed en route to the front by air attacks. Once again, ULTRA had played its part with 21 Army Group Headquarters learning, on 20 June, that 1st SS Panzer Division had begun moving from Belgium on the 17th. As a result air strikes were ordered against the railways being used while there were further attacks on key targets by strategic bombers. The end result was that 1st SS Panzer Division was not available for action on 27 June; some of its infantry went into battle on the 28th but the division's main body did not arrive until 9 July.[31] Even in such depleted form, 1st SS Panzer was a formidable opponent.

With the new day the British advance resumed; 43rd (Wessex) Division took over the ground gained by 15th (Scottish) so that the latter could move forward again, which they began to do at 5.00am. Poor weather precluded aircraft from bases in England offering support. Perhaps because of this the Luftwaffe made an appearance but found that fighters from No. 83 Group in Normandy were more than a match for them. While the Scots pushed forward, the Wessexmen came under attack from enemy armour in the St Mauvieu–Cheux area. A number of probing attacks were fought off, the worst of which penetrated Cheux, and the Germans lost six tanks.[32]

Although 15th (Scottish) Division was stalled on the road to Grainville, with fighting throughout the day around le Haut du Bosq, the eastern prong of the divisional thrust took Colleville, Tourville and Mondrainville

* The corps included 9th SS Panzer Division Hohenstaufen and 10th SS Panzer Division Frundsberg.[30]

before 2nd Argylls of 227 Brigade captured intact the bridge over the Odon at Tourmauville to establish a small lodgement on the south bank. Into that lodgement rolled tanks of 23rd Hussars, from 11th Armoured Division, which then advanced to expand the bridgehead. The Hussars were followed by 159 Brigade, 11th Armoured's infantry, and by the other regiments of 29 Armoured Brigade. Eleventh Armoured Division's objective was a hill south-east of the bridge, where the ground rises steeply to a wide and flat-topped crest, Hill 112, which was to be the scene of much bitter fighting. An attempt was made by 15th (Scottish) Division to take Grainville from the east but, although the outskirts were reached before nightfall, it was held strongly and thus an assault was delayed until daylight. On VIII Corps' eastern flank both 4 Armoured and 31 Tank Brigades had been supporting the infantry and, by nightfall, were deployed to meet attacks from either flank. Meanwhile XXX Corps had taken Rauray but the Germans clung tenaciously to the high ground to the south. The second day of EPSOM was over and, although British formations had made some progress, the Germans, in spite of all the pressure, continued resisting with determination.[33]

With improved flying conditions during the afternoon the tactical air forces had been able to provide much more support and, after dark, light bombers struck at enemy formations behind the battle area and along the roads, while Bomber Command put up over 1,000 aircraft, of which some 200 attacked rail centres through which German reinforcements were moving to Normandy. Fighter-bombers had also caused considerable damage at Carpiquet where tanks were reported to be assembling. And so, on the morning of the 28th, Second Army was expanding the Odon bridgehead with 159 Brigade creating a defensive perimeter while 29 Armoured Brigade passed through the wooded area near Baron to continue the attack on Hill 112. Opposition was fierce and well organised with tanks, anti-tank guns, mortars and machine guns skilfully camouflaged in the surrounding countryside. As British troops advanced they met fire from their front, from both flanks, and from the rear, the latter from the woods north-east of Baron. Real progress was not possible and so 11th Armoured Division was told to remain in its bridgehead position until the area between Cheux and the Odon had been cleared, a task assigned to 15th (Scottish) and 43rd (Wessex) Divisions.[34]

The battle intensified as the enemy ratcheted up pressure on both flanks of VIII Corps, while feeding additional troops into the fray. In a change from previous days the Germans risked troop movement in daylight, under weak air cover from the Luftwaffe, although strong anti-aircraft artillery defences were provided around Villers-Bocage, whence the troops were moving. More Allied soldiers were joining the battle with 32 Guards Brigade, Guards Armoured Division, coming under the Wessex Division's command to strengthen the left shoulder of Second Army's salient.[35] The village of Mouen changed hands twice during the day, being taken by British troops before falling again to 21st Panzer. Two battalions from 15th (Scottish) Division, supported by tanks, moved to clear the area between the road to Grainville and the Rauray spur but were stopped by strong opposition; by then Grainville was in British hands and a counter-attack that penetrated the town was driven off. Much bitter fighting took place as infantry and armour strove to clear the country between Colleville and Grainville; this led to the capture of le Valtru. But the Germans still controlled the close country south of le Valtru although 2nd Argylls had captured Gavrus and the nearby bridge. The Argylls, who appeared to be making a habit of seizing bridges, had moved westward through woods on the south side of the river from Tourmauville, where 11th Armoured Division had assumed responsibility for the bridge, to Gavrus. Since the road between Gavrus and le Valtru was still in German hands, the Argylls were isolated, but undaunted.[36]

Elsewhere 29 Armoured Brigade continued its stiff fight around Baron; 3rd Royal Tanks, having relieved 23rd Hussars, with men of 8th Rifle Brigade held the northern part of Hill 112 against a determined counter-attack by tanks supported by a heavy mortar bombardment. The Tanks and Green Jackets not only beat off the attack but also improved their own positions. Day three of EPSOM was ending with VIII Corps much better disposed to meet the expected counter-attack. Although no additional advance had been made, many enemy positions threatening the rear and flanks of the corps had been eliminated. Prisoners included soldiers from 2nd Panzer Division and 1st and 2nd SS Panzer Divisions. The two SS formations had just begun arriving in the battle area, 1st from near Bruges and 2nd, Das Reich, from Toulouse in southern France; Das Reich had been delayed en route by Allied aircraft and was understrength due to shortage of transport.* Although placed in army group reserve near St Lô, a battlegroup from Das Reich hastened to the front against the British after the opening of EPSOM and entered battle against 49th (West Riding) Division.[37]

Knowing that a massive counter-attack was imminent, General O'Connor was keen to secure his position north of the Odon. Although VIII Corps' salient bit into the enemy front by over five miles, it was less than two miles in width and it appeared that all enemy armoured formations in Normandy were readying themselves around it for an assault. Not until his flanks were broadened and made safe could O'Connor risk further advance; to do otherwise would risk the possible destruction of his corps. On VIII Corps' right, XXX Corps was on the Rauray spur but had been forced out of Bretteville; the Germans still

* En route elements of the Division had also massacred civilians in the village of Oradour-sur-Glane.

controlled the south-western approaches to the salient. I Corps had delayed its planned attack on Carpiquet. Later, Montgomery would assert that all was working according to plan; that the Germans were massing their armour against Second Army on the left flank and that his probes towards Caen had been intended to achieve this end. But what were the Germans now planning?

On the enemy side a peculiar command situation had developed with Seventh Army's commander, Dollmann, becoming the most senior German officer in Normandy. Hitler had called both von Rundstedt and Rommel back to Germany, leaving Dollmann with the full burden of command. The unfortunate Dollmann had panicked on learning that the British had captured the Odon bridge. The timing could hardly have been worse, since the Americans had taken Cherbourg the day before – the 26th. In the usual chain of command, responsibility for reaction, and for explaining to Hitler, would have rested with von Rundstedt and Rommel rather than Dollmann. With both out of the theatre Dollmann felt an unbearable burden. On the morning of 28 June he ordered II SS Panzer Corps' commander, SS General Paul Hausser, to counter-attack immediately to clear the breach south of Cheux.[38] This order conflicted with Hitler's preferred plan, which the Führer had approved on 17 June, that the major counter-attack should strike towards Bayeux at the junction of the Allied armies. But this is almost beside the point since Hausser informed Dollmann that II SS Panzer Corps could not be ready until the 29th. Faced with the prospect of explaining all this to Hitler, Dollmann decided that only one course of action was open to him: suicide. Thus, von Rundstedt's headquarters, Rommel's headquarters and Seventh Army's headquarters were all without commanders at a critical time. But German staff officers never lacked initiative and the chiefs of staff at all three headquarters took up the slack. Hausser himself told Seventh Army that he would prefer to organise his corps before attacking the salient but that he could launch a counter-attack, if necessary, on the 29th. Two hours later, at 3.00pm on 28 June, Army Group B headquarters informed Seventh Army that Hitler had appointed Hausser as supreme commander in Normandy until von Rundstedt and Rommel returned to their respective headquarters. Thus Hausser became the first Waffen-SS officer to command an army.[39]

On the morning of the 29th, Second Army's soldiers awaited the counter-attack but the morning passed without any being launched. Second Tactical Air Force was busy harassing enemy troop movements towards the front; the Gunners also played their part in this harassment programme. Subsequent study of Seventh Army's telephone log, and interrogation of Hausser, confirmed that the action by Gunners and airmen had prevented the planned counter-attack taking place. On XXX Corps' front some minor attacks were driven off and, on VIII Corps' eastern flank,

43rd (Wessex) Division recaptured Mouen and the nearby Bas de Mouen to add to Marcelet, which had been taken the day before. Thomas's division was now able to clear the close country southwards as well as pushing one battalion over the river. These gains helped strengthen the salient, as did others by 15th (Scottish) on the right, although these were less significant, the division being forced back on reaching the railway near Grainville. But there was one very significant gain in the form of a German officer captured during the afternoon on whose person were found the plans for an enemy counter-attack; the officer had been reconnoitring for the attack. At 6.00pm that attack was launched with infantry and armour, of about brigade strength, advancing along the axis of the Noyers–Cheux road. In the subsequent battle some tanks broke through the Scottish line and reached Cheux, to be knocked out there, while the balance of the attacking force was driven off, the artillery playing a major part in defeating the German effort. Before nightfall, one of 4 Armoured Brigade's regiments swept the ground between Grainville and the Noyers road to clear up pockets of enemy troops.[40]

The attack on 15th (Scottish) Division was not the sum total of Hausser's effort; some time earlier enemy troops had thrust towards le Valtru but, just as the Scots were being hit, this attack was repelled and the situation restored. South of the Odon another thrust was made towards Baron that forced a Rifle Brigade company to withdraw from advanced positions on Hill 112. However, the Argylls still held the bridge at Gavrus, defying heavy shell and mortar fire. A fourth prong to the attack had been planned but some forty tanks due to take part in this were attacked by Typhoons as they drove from Caen to Carpiquet; this put an end to the attack. Luftwaffe aircraft had also appeared but were seen off by Allied fighters. As the fourth day of EPSOM faded into darkness, Second Army had much cause to be grateful to the Gunners whose skill had been so vital in breaking up German attacks, along with the tactical air forces, which had flown some 1,000 sorties.[41] Added to these two critical weapons were the guns of naval vessels in the Channel. A German report described their gunfire as 'murderous' and that of the artillery as 'terrible'.[42] That report went on to admit that much of the attacking force had been destroyed in its assembly area, thus ending any hopes of immediate major counter-attack.

That the threat was all but over for the time being was not obvious to either Dempsey or O'Connor. Both felt that the attacks on the 29th were only preparatory thrusts for a major armoured onslaught that might occur next day. And so Dempsey ordered the bridgehead south of the Odon to be reinforced by a brigade from 43rd (Wessex) Division with 159 Brigade coming under command of 15th (Scottish) Division; 11th Armoured was to withdraw from its advanced positions near Baron and on Hill 112 to bolster the salient against attack. The men of 29 Armoured Brigade were surprised – and disappointed – to be ordered to abandon Hill 112 for which they had fought so hard.[43] That evening the weather added its own contribution to the frustrations of the British soldiers when a five-hour torrential downpour began, turning the ground into a soft, treacherous and misery-inducing mess.[44]

During the night Bomber Command's heavies bombed enemy armour believed to be massing for the coming attack; over 200 aircraft dropped about 1,000 tons of bombs around Villers-Bocage.[45] Since elements of both 9th and 10th SS Panzer Divisions had been identified in action during the 29th, Second Army believed that the German build-up was continuing with their main effort yet to come. Intelligence from ULTRA would only have strengthened that belief, since this included information about the moves of the armoured divisions to the salient but would not have been so up-to-date as to reflect the fact that the German main effort had been seen off. This misconception of enemy intentions in the upper echelons of Second Army brought an end to Operation EPSOM as the army prepared to meet a counter-attack.

But there was no German move on 30 June. British commanders continued to believe that the enemy was still preparing his counter-attack and were strengthened in this belief by reports of much activity behind German lines on the night of 30 June–1 July. When, early in the morning of 1 July, the Germans launched a heavy mortar bombardment on the Gavrus sector, followed by an infantry attack, belief in an imminent major counter-attack increased. But that attack at Gavrus was beaten off with the Gunners again playing a major role; twelve regiments of artillery hit the attackers who broke off their advance before reaching Gavrus. Two attempts to renew the attack, including a broadening of it to the Baron sector, were also smashed by intense artillery fire. North of the Odon another attack had slightly more success, some tanks breaking through British forward positions. Eventually the enemy was driven off with heavy losses in men and tanks. Further attempts were also defeated, with British artillery punishing the attackers heavily. The final attack that day was beaten before it even started as German infantry, forming up with their tanks in full view of the British troops near Queudeville, were fired on with every available weapon.[46]

The Official Historian noted that the day had cost the enemy some twenty-two tanks and that, although British casualties had been considerable, 'our position was unshaken'. He goes on to comment that the Germans had suffered 'a sharp defeat' but retained the potential to counter-attack, asserting that this was the sector of the front where the German 'potential for offensive was strongest' and that EPSOM had

> forestalled and spoiled the last German effort to break the Allied front that could be made while there were still some fresh armoured

> divisions with which to attempt it; from then on much armoured strength was gradually frittered away as it had to be used to plug holes in their own defences.[47]

But while the German armour had suffered, Second Army had surrendered the initiative, especially with the withdrawal from Hill 112. Although Montgomery congratulated 15th (Scottish) Division on their efforts, there was no real reason for satisfaction with what had been achieved. As Michael Reynolds notes

> much had gone wrong on the British side and, despite what may have been said and written later about drawing as much German armour as possible on to the British sector, there can be no doubt that EPSOM had been a major effort to break through the German defences to the west of Caen, and it had failed . . . Dempsey's decision to go on the defensive at a critical stage in his offensive is just as incomprehensible as Bucknall's over Villers-Bocage – perhaps even more so in view of his overwhelming superiority in firepower: witness being able to call, at very short notice, for 100 heavy bombers* to obliterate Villers-Bocage on 30th June in order to interrupt 9th SS Panzer's part in the counter-attack. It is clear that if the Germans had their problems as a result of EPSOM, the British did too.[49]

British commanders were aware that much had gone wrong. In 11th Armoured Division, 'Pip' Roberts relieved 159 Brigade's commander, while two battalion commanders were also replaced. As one squadron leader of 3rd Royal Tanks commented, this was

> after only twenty-four hours of battle. It only goes to show that exercises on the Yorkshire moors are no substitute for actual battle and there is no telling how men will behave under fire.[50]

Michael Carver had been promoted to command 4 Armoured Brigade and, after 'a period of not too extensive action' under 11th Armoured Division, sacked his brigade major, having 'quickly realised that . . . [he] was not up to the job'.[51] He also had his second-in-command transferred, considering that he 'served no useful purpose'. Carver felt that the commanding officer of 2nd King's Royal Rifle Corps, 4 Armoured's infantry battalion, Lieutenant-Colonel William Heathcote-Amory, who

* Bomber Command sent 266 aircraft to bomb Villers-Bocage. These planes dropped 1,100 tons of bombs 'with great accuracy' from a height of 4,000 feet. Two machines, a Lancaster and a Halifax, were lost.[48]

had distinguished himself in North Africa, 'had lost his grip' and asked for his relief, which was approved.[52]

British commanders were not alone in losing their jobs. On 1 July Geyr von Schweppenburg was sacked by Hitler, to be replaced by General Hans Eberbach at the head of Panzer Group West while, the following day, von Rundstedt resigned, having been told that his health was suspect.[53] Both von Schweppenburg and von Rundstedt had committed the cardinal error of not seeing matters from Hitler's viewpoint. While the Führer had urged the defence of Cherbourg to the last round, von Rundstedt had accepted its loss when Carentan fell to the Americans; Rommel had even managed to withdraw some of 77th Division from the Cotentin before US forces sealed off the peninsula. But when Rommel returned from Berlin to Normandy after the battle of the Odon, he found that Schweppenburg had persuaded Speidel, Rommel's chief of staff, that German forces should be evacuated from the Caen bridgehead so that they might be out of range of Allied ships in the Bay of the Seine. Von Rundstedt had agreed with Schweppenburg's assessment and forwarded it to Berlin, noting his own approval of the plan. Neither could remain in post, given Hitler's obsession with holding ground. Rommel countermanded Schweppenburg's order on I July; the ground around Caen was to be held.[54]

Von Rundstedt's replacement was Field Marshal Gunther von Kluge, a soldier from the Prussian tradition and veteran of the Eastern front. No admirer of Rommel, he tried to assert his own authority over that of the commander of Army Group B. Von Kluge also wanted to create confidence in his command that Normandy could be held but, in spite of the V1s that gave Rommel some optimism, it was not long before he had to accept reality: the Germans were fighting a losing battle and would have to retreat.[55]

With Second Army stalled at the end of June, this is an appropriate point to look at the greater picture, not only in Normandy but also on the Eastern Front. Cherbourg had fallen and the Americans had entered the city on 26 June; resistance ended next day. On 1 July American troops secured Cap de la Hague on the north-west corner of the Cotentin and within a week had taken la Haye-du-Puits across the neck of the peninsula from Carentan. The peninsula was almost completely in Allied hands and the Americans would soon be able to begin their breakout while possession of the Cotentin would allow laying of the PLUTO pipeline to begin. Admiral Vian, the British Task Force Commander, returned to England on 30 June, to be followed by Admiral Kirk, his US counterpart, three days later. With Vian's withdrawal, Operation NEPTUNE came officially to a close, although the navies still had much to do to support 21 Army Group. Headquarters were established ashore for both British and

American sectors, with the former designated Flag Officer British Assault Area and the latter Flag Officer West.* At the end of NEPTUNE the Allies had landed 850,279 personnel, 148,803 vehicles of all descriptions and 570,505 tons of stores. By then, also, an equally impressive operation was underway far to the east.[57]

On 22 June the Red Army had launched its summer offensive against Germany's Army Group Centre, attacking with 146 infantry divisions and forty-three armoured brigades along a line stretching some 350 miles from Velikie Luki in the north to south of the Pripet Marshes. Army Group Centre, under General Busch, disposed three infantry armies and a panzer army with more than a million men, 1,000 tanks and 1,400 aircraft. The Soviet intention was to break through Army Group Centre and push the invaders – Finns and Germans to the north, Hungarians, Romanians and Germans to the south – out of Mother Russia. Once underway the momentum of the Soviets – their infantry and armour reinforced by more than sixty per cent – had taken the three main bastions of German defence – Vitebsk, Mogilev and Bobruisk – within a week; by early-July most German forces had been pushed back over the pre-war border between the USSR and Poland with thousands of Axis soldiers dead or captured.[58]

German cities were having some relief from the night raids of Bomber Command as Harris's aircraft continued striking targets crucial to the Normandy campaign. But they had other and urgent targets to add to those they had been pounding relentlessly: launch sites for V1 flying-bombs. The first of these Fieseler Fi103 pilotless aircraft, the first cruise missiles, had been launched at Britain on 13 June – D+7; Swanscombe, near Gravesend was the first site of a flying-bomb strike.[59] Attacking V1 launch sites was not a new experience for the bombers; they had struck so successfully at the original sites that the Germans had been forced to build much simpler ski-ramp launchers. These were more difficult to detect and had proliferated greatly. Since the V1 flew at a speed that made interception by fighters difficult and at a height too great for light AA guns but low for heavy guns, it would take time for an effective home defence to be created and the destruction of launch sites became a priority, especially after a V1 landed on the Guards' Chapel in Wellington Barracks, close to Buckingham Palace and 10 Downing Street, during a service on the morning of 18 June. The night before the first major operation against flying-bomb sites had taken place when 114 aircraft bombed one at Oisemont, near Abbeville. No aircraft were lost but no results were observed.[60] From then on, increasing numbers of bombers struck at launch sites throughout the Battle of Normandy in Operation CROSSBOW.

* The posts were held by Rear-Admiral J W Rivett-Carnac RN and Rear-Admiral J Wilkes, USN.[56]

Although V1s were not launched against the beachhead,* nor against the ships, there were other threats to the latter. The U-boat fleet had been deterred almost completely from menacing shipping by the strong anti-submarine screen created on the western seaward flank. Although some submarines penetrated the screen their effect was negligible, only two frigates falling victim to them during June, as was that of the surviving E-boats along the Channel coast. But, in the early hours of 6 July, a new menace appeared when a 'strange object' was seen moving through the Trout line, the Allied eastern sea flank. This object was engaged by fire from the support squadron, at which point it launched a torpedo and made its escape. Other similar intruders followed in quick succession, although well dispersed. Each was fired upon in turn. It was subsequently discovered that nine had been sunk. The intruders were the German equivalent of Italian and British human torpedoes, although much more primitive than either. Known as a 'Marder', or marten, the German weapon was improvised from two torpedoes, one above the other with a pilot astride the uppermost torpedo behind a perspex hood. The explosive had been removed from the upper torpedo and the pilot fired the lower weapon when he had identified his target; the torpedo raced towards the target at some 20 knots, almost ten times as fast as the 2.5 knots of the Marder. Having released his torpedo the pilot then attempted to escape, if he could. The Marder was not submersible and depended on its low lines to avoid detection.

On this first expedition the torpedoes struck two small minesweepers and fifteen of the flotilla of twenty-six made it back to base. As well as the nine that were sunk, two others broke down before reaching the attack area. A further attack was made two nights later when twenty-one Mardern left le Havre. On this occasion none returned, as all had been sunk and only a few pilots were rescued. Their toll was one minesweeper sunk and the Polish destroyer *Dragon* damaged badly. *Dragon* continued to contribute to the campaign as the ship was scuttled to extend the Gooseberry breakwater off Sword Beach.[62]

The Luftwaffe had suffered heavily during June, with some 808 aircraft of Luftflotte III destroyed while the Reich Luftflotte lost 185 machines in action against Allied bombers striking at targets in Germany. Luftflotte III made 13,829 sorties in Normandy during June, less than one-tenth of those flown by the Allied air forces; even considering only those Allied sorties that were in direct support of ground forces in Normandy – over 130,000 – the ratio is still about one to ten.[63] Nonetheless, the Luftwaffe had done some damage: witness the destruction of *Derry Cunihy* by a mine, while

* Some did land in the assault area in the last two weeks of June but these had apparently gone astray; no damage was caused to shipping.[61]

German aircraft sank a destroyer and a frigate as well as three merchant vessels; another three warships and four merchant vessels were damaged.[64] But Allied superiority in the air and on the sea is demonstrated by a study of shipping losses during Operation NEPTUNE. Of the huge armada that sailed to Normandy, much of which plied back and forth between Britain and Normandy, only twenty-four warships and thirty-five merchantmen were lost with a further fifty-nine and sixty-one respectively damaged.[65] While these figures do not include landing craft and other small craft, they indicate that German reaction on the waves and in the air was little more than a nuisance.

In fact, German artillery on the British east flank was a greater menace to Allied ships in the Bay of the Seine than either the Kriegsmarine or the Luftwaffe. Montgomery had earlier intended to extend the British sector to the Dives river but this plan had been cancelled, leaving the ground between the Orne and Dives in German hands. Here was much wooded land in which to conceal artillery batteries while, east of the Dives, were two heavy coastal batteries at Bénerville and Houlgate. The latter installations continued firing at shipping in the bay and on Sword Beach. Although battleships and cruisers bombarded the locations, firing more than 1,000 heavy and medium shells, the guns were not silenced. Some were destroyed and the batteries fell silent from time to time but then returned to action. Likewise with the artillery batteries camouflaged in the woodlands: neither ship- nor land-based fire could silence these because the batteries moved as soon as their positions were registered. The net effect of this enemy fire was to damage a number of landing ships, as well as the small headquarters ship, *Locust*, some ferries and a corvette; an ammunition coaster was set alight when hit by German fire. As a result the landing of personnel was transferred to Juno Beach and, from 25 June, landing ships and coasters were also transferred. At the end of the month the Allies decommissioned Sword Beach.[66] This may be seen as some small success for the defenders and as a failing of Montgomery's overall plan; it certainly may not be described as something that happened according to his 'master plan'.

When Operation NEPTUNE ended numbers of British and American troops in Normandy were virtually equal, with both armies deploying the equivalent of fifteen or sixteen divisions, although in the case of Second Army one division was Canadian, and due to transfer to First Canadian Army when that formation was established in France. Lieutenant-General H D G Crerar, commanding First Canadian Army, arrived in Normandy on 18 June but Montgomery decided that there was insufficient room to accommodate another army headquarters and so Crerar's headquarters remained in England; it would not become operational until 23 July. Battle casualties until 30 June totalled 61,732, of whom 8,469 had been killed, 42,353 wounded and the remainder were missing. Of the dead, 3,356 were

British or Canadian and 5,113 American; 15,815 British and Canadians had been wounded and 26,538 Americans; of the missing 5,527 were British or Canadian and 5,383 American.[67] To replace these battle casualties, 79,000 replacements had been posted to France, of whom 38,000 were British or Canadian and the remainder American. In England nine US divisions were ready to sail for France while, across the Atlantic, further formations were preparing to sail; those moves would eventually increase the US element of the Allied Expeditionary Force to sixty-one divisions. By contrast 21 Army Group, which would become the British and Canadian group when 12 US Army Group formed, would never exceed twenty divisions and, at this stage, only the equivalent of some six British and Canadian divisions waited in England for the call to France. British manpower was being stretched to the limit. As early as February, General Alexander had been told that there would be no further reinforcements from the UK for Eighth Army in Italy; losses there would have to be made good by retraining redundant anti-aircraft gunners, Royal Navy and RAF personnel while, during the winter of 1944–45, infantry battalions in Italy would be forced to reduce from four to three rifle companies. That manpower shortage would also affect 21 Army Group, as we shall see in due course.

Among British units to land in early-July was 27th Light AA Regiment, whose 6 LAA Battery landed at le Hamel on 4 July.* Deployed along the St Martin-les-Entrées–St Leger road, they were amazed to be told not to fire at any aircraft unless it committed 'a hostile act'.[69] The originator of this order was none other than Dempsey who was being flown by Air Vice Marshal Harry Broadhurst in the latter's light aircraft when RAF Regiment LAA guns fired on the plane, a captured German Fieseler Storch bearing British markings. This close shave prompted Dempsey to issue the order restricting the actions of all anti-aircraft guns under his command.

Such enforced idleness was anathema to Major Jack Christie, commanding 6 LAA Battery, and when his battery had a visit from Brigadier Rawlins, XXX Corps' Commander Royal Artillery, Christie expressed the view that 'we are not earning our pay' and asked for an alternative task for his Gunners. Rawlins obliged by ordering two troops of 6 LAA Battery to convert to manning self-propelled artillery. Told that he should have his troops ready for this role within three days, Christie asked for, and was given, an extra day. And so A and C Troops were assigned to manning four Centaurs previously manned by Royal Marines; drivers were provided by the Royal Armoured Corps.[70] The Centaurs

* The regiment's other two batteries were 113 and 149.[68]

were described as being 'clapped out' but, nonetheless, the gunners would go into action with them in a counter-mortar role from mid-July until the end of the month.

As July began most German armour remain ranged against Second Army's front with elements from eight panzer divisions identified in that sector. By contrast First US Army appeared almost untroubled by significant panzer forces. Omar Bradley's forces had now secured the Cotentin and First Army was re-organising to break out on the western flank.

> We were to sweep south of the Cotentin past Avranches and there cut off the Brittany peninsula at its neck. After pausing only long enough to secure Brittany and its choice selection of deepwater ports, the American forces were to turn east and, with the right flank on the dry, sandy banks of the Loire, close to the Seine–Orléans gap south of Paris.[71]

As the Americans wheeled into their advance, the remainder of 21 Army Group's line was to pivot with them and move forward to the Seine between the coast and Paris. It was expected that there would be an enemy regrouping and that the Seine crossing would be contested strongly.[72] Bradley met with Montgomery on 27 June and told the latter that he intended First Army to attack down the road to Coutances. On 30 June Montgomery issued that plan as part of a 21 Army Group directive which emphasised that First Army would strike the main blow in the breakout operations while Second Army kept the German armour locked up around Caen. Bradley's operations began at 5.30am on 3 July when Major-General Troy Middleton's VIII Corps moved off to secure the start line for the breakout. Unfortunately, there was to be no quick success for First Army.[73]

As Middleton's corps prepared for its advance, Second Army was readying itself to hammer at Caen yet again. On 1 July orders were issued for the capture of Carpiquet, Operation WINDSOR, which was to be achieved by the 4th, followed by a major assault on Caen, Operation CHARNWOOD, about four days later. By then, an additional formation, 59th (Staffordshire), would be available to fight alongside both 3rd British and 3rd Canadian Divisions.

NOTES

1 Lieut (later Maj) J Chapman MC, i/v with author.
2 Salmond, *The History of the 51st Highland Division*, p. 143.
3 Ibid, p. 144.
4 Ibid, p. 145.
5 Ellis, *Victory in the West*, p. 265.
6 Montgomery, *Normandy to the Baltic*, p. 222.
7 Ellis, op cit, pp. 264–5.
8 Ibid, p. 265.
9 Ibid, p. 274.
10 Montgomery, *Memoirs*, p. 271.
11 Hastings, *Overlord*, p. 197.
12 Ellis, op cit, p. 272.
13 Ibid.
14 Brooke, *War Diaries*, p. 560.
15 Montgomery, *Memoirs*, pp. 256–7.
16 Ellis, op cit, pp. 272–3.
17 Ibid, p. 274.
18 Ibid.
19 Doherty, *Only The Enemy*, p. 162.
20 Ibid.
21 Ellis, op cit, pp. 275–6.
22 Ibid, pp. 276–7; NA, WO171/286–287, war diary, VIII Corps HQ, Jun–Jul & Aug–Sep 1944; WO171/337–338, war diary, XXX Corps HQ, Jul 1944; WO171/499–500, war diary, 49th Division, Jun & Jul 1944.
23 Ellis, op cit, pp. 277–8; Reynolds, *Steel Inferno*, pp. 124–6; NA, WO171/646, war diary, 44 Bde; WO171/648, war diary, 46 Bde.
24 Reynolds, *Sons of the Reich*, p. 20.
25 Maj Tony Hughes to author; Willis, *None Had Lances*, pp. 158–9.
26 Willis, op cit, pp. 158–9.
27 Hughes to author.
28 Willis, op cit, p. 159; Hughes to author; Army Roll of Honour.
29 Quoted in Ellis, op cit, p. 279.
30 Reynolds, *Sons of the Reich*, p. 1.
31 Reynolds, *Steel Inferno*, p. 129.
32 Ellis, op cit, p. 280.
33 Ibid.
34 Ibid, p. 281; see, however, the account by Maj-Gen 'Pip' Roberts, commanding 11th Armd Division in *From the Desert to the Baltic*, p. 166.
35 Ellis, op cit, p. 281.
36 Ibid, p. 282.
37 Reynolds, *Steel Inferno*, p. 129.
38 Ibid, p. 132.
39 Ibid.
40 Ellis, op cit, p. 283.
41 Ibid, p. 284.
42 Ibid.
43 Close, *View from the Turret*, p. 112; Ellis, op cit, p. 285.
44 Reynolds, *Steel Inferno*, p. 139.
45 Middlebrook & Everitt, *The Bomber Command War Diaries*, p. 536.
46 Ellis, op cit, p. 286.

47 Ibid.
48 Middlebrook & Everitt, op cit, p. 536.
49 Reynolds, *Steel Inferno*, pp. 140–1.
50 Close, op cit, p. 113.
51 Carver, *Out of Step*, p. 192.
52 Ibid.
53 Ellis, op cit, pp. 321–2.
54 Fraser, *Knight's Cross*, p.505.
55 Hastings, *Overlord*, p. 175.
56 Ellis, op cit, pp. 293–4.
57 Ibid, p. 294.
58 Pitt, *Military History of World War II*, pp. 244–6.
59 Haining, *The Flying Bomb War*, p. 37.
60 Middlebrook & Everitt, op cit, p. 531.
61 Ellis, op cit, p. 307.
62 Ibid, pp. 300–1.
63 Ibid, pp. 306–7.
64 Ibid, p. 295.
65 Ibid.
66 Ibid, p. 293.
67 Ibid, p. 307.
68 Frederick, *Lineage Book of British Land Forces*, p. 824.
69 Doherty, *Wall of Steel*, p. 193.
70 Ibid.
71 Bradley, *A Soldier's Story*, p. 317.
72 Ibid.
73 Ibid, p. 319.

CHAPTER X
The struggle continues

Steed threatens steed

Carpiquet airfield, a Luftwaffe base since 1940 with all the defences of a wartime airfield, was Second Army's first objective. There was much 'concrete and wire, many pill-boxes and anti-aircraft guns', making Carpiquet an important strongpoint in Caen's defences. At the beginning of July the garrison included 26th Panzer Grenadier Regiment and tanks from 12th SS Panzer Division, all in well-camouflaged fortifications.[1]

Before Montgomery's assaults could begin, SS Major-General Willi Bittrich, commanding II SS Panzer Corps, ordered his divisions to renew their attacks on 1 July; Bittrich was unaware that EPSOM had fizzled out and that the British bridgehead south of the Odon had all but ceased to exist. At 3.30am on 1 July a heavy artillery and mortar bombardment opened II SS Panzer Corps' offensive. At 4.00am 10th SS Panzer Division Frundsberg attacked the British positions. By 5.00am the SS men were on the retreat with over 300 dead.[2]

Bittrich's other division, 9th Hohenstaufen, which attacked at 6.00am, had greater initial success. This attack, led by Otto Meyer's 9th SS Panzer Regiment with Hohenstaufen and Der Führer Panzer Grenadiers, under smokescreen cover, was towards le Haut du Bosq, through the sector including Rauray and Château Grainville. The attackers reached Rauray, having passed through some forward British positions, but were stopped outside the village.[3] In bitter fighting both sides suffered severe casualties; on the British side 1st Tyneside Scottish – a Black Watch TA battalion – had 132 casualties, according to its commanding officer, Lieutenant-Colonel Warhurst,[4] but another officer, Major John Samson, later wrote that just over 200 men were left at the end of the day; the battalion's official history notes that it needed to replace about 400 men.[5] The Tyneside Scots fought hard and took a heavy toll of their aggressors, claiming ten panzers knocked out by the anti-tank platoon alone; 24th Lancers claimed another nine tanks and two SPGs, 217 Anti-tank Battery a further six, and medium guns five in one engagement with estimated totals ranging between ten and fifteen. Warhurst believed that the 'total . . . German AFVs put out of operation by British forces on the Rauray front must have been substantial, but conservative estimates put the figure at around 35'.[6] British tank losses included three Shermans of 24th Lancers and two from Sherwood Rangers, 8 Armoured Brigade having played a major part in defeating this attack.*

As ever, the British artillery was a vital element of the defence with ten field and two medium regiments involved. That evening, a British counter-attack, including 24th Lancers and Crocodile flamethrowers, regained the ground taken by Hohenstaufen. German losses were heavy; one regiment lost 328 men, of whom fifty-one had been killed while Kampfgruppe Weidinger's casualties totalled 642, including 108 dead. The latter's commander later complained that the most advanced elements of his group had to withdraw in daylight, thereby suffering heavier casualties.[7]

These bloody engagements mark the absolute end of the EPSOM battles but, strangely, merit no mention in the British Official History. Nonetheless, they indicate the German ability to mount well-executed operations even in the most adverse conditions and Michael Reynolds is surely right when he suggests that, without Montgomery's EPSOM offensive, 'Hitler's strategy of driving a wedge between the Americans and the British with his Panzer Corps, and then pushing each Army into the sea, might well have succeeded.'[8] Certainly Hitler seemed pleased with this battle since it proved that, even with air superiority, massive firepower and greater mobility, the Allied armies might yet be locked up in Normandy. But any chance of pushing the Allies into the Channel had vanished. The build-up of VIII Corps during EPSOM is proof enough of that: even with its many casualties, the corps' ration strength was 22,735 more on 30 June than at the beginning of EPSOM.[9]

Operation WINDSOR opened late on 3 July when HMS *Rodney*'s 16-inch guns fired on buildings around Carpiquet. *Rodney* loosed fifteen aircraft-directed rounds from 26,200 yards. That night 214 Brigade of 43rd (Wessex) Division deployed around Verson to protect the right flank of 8 Canadian Brigade** who were to advance from Marcelet, held by 32 Guards Brigade – still under Wessex command. Then, at 5.00am on the 4th, Second Army's artillery loosed their opening bombardment and,

* An excellent account of the Battle of Rauray may be found in Kevin Baverstock's *Breaking the Panzers: The Bloody Battle for Rauray, Normandy, 1 July 1944*, published in 2002. Baverstock's father served in 1st Tyneside Scottish and this book is a classic example of the best type of unit history.

** For this operation 8 Canadian Brigade was reinforced with an additional infantry battalion, from 7 Brigade, and had under command, or at its call, a regiment of SPGs, three squadrons of 'Funnies' from 79th Armoured Division, a machine-gun battalion, twenty-one artillery regiments and two squadrons of rocket-firing Typhoons, as well as the 16-inch guns of HMS *Rodney*.

fifteen minutes later, the leading soldiers from two battalions, Chaudière and North Shore, advanced either side of the Carpiquet road, supported by Fort Garry tanks. Unfortunately for the Canadians, the Germans knew their plans, having the key to the Canadian command's codes. Prior to WINDSOR German wireless intelligence had noted a large increase in traffic between armoured units opposing them while an increase in Allied patrol activity on 3 July led to the conclusion that an attack was in the offing, although there was no clear indication of its objective. Hubert Meyer, senior staff officer of 12th SS Panzer, realised that a 'breakthrough on our south wing would threaten the whole front north of Caen from the rear and make the city impossible to hold'.[10]

Armed with the knowledge of an imminent Allied attack, with armour concentrating east of Norrey and St Mauvieu, Meyer moved up some tanks and a single 88, the latter borrowed from Caen's anti-aircraft defences, and arranged defensive fire from artillery and mortars, the latter restricted by ammunition shortages. One Canadian regimental history suggested that Carpiquet airfield was the last bastion of Caen and 'the strongest and best we had so far encountered'.[11] The Chaudières' historian comments that the battalion would be facing the 'cream of the German Army'.[12] While the quality of their opposition is undoubted, the numbers involved tell a different story. Wilhelm Mohnke's 26th SS Panzer Grenadier Regiment, from Hitlerjugend, held Carpiquet. Mohnke's regiment, already understrength, disposed only about a company against two Canadian battalions and two tank squadrons. The odds appeared to be against the Germans but German soldiers, especially SS, had a very different concept of the possible outcome of such a situation – it did not involve their being overrun.

One German account, from Hitlerjugend's commander, describes his soldiers' tactics. The company commander in Carpiquet was to make a fighting withdrawal to the village's eastern edge, thereby drawing the attackers into Carpiquet whereupon German artillery and mortars, including 88s to the east of Carpiquet, would fire on previously registered targets. At the same time, tanks waited to hammer the outskirts of Carpiquet once the Canadians appeared.[13] The Chaudières took Carpiquet, which then became an inferno, while the 88s of 2nd SS Flak Company stopped Canadian tanks or infantry from making any further movement, either southward or eastward. It seems likely that the German garrison of Carpiquet village was no more than fifty men.

As the Chaudières advanced on the village, the Royal Winnipeg Rifles were attacking the airfield, having moved off from Marcelet across completely open ground. The Winnipegs were hit by fire from Nebelwerfers on leaving their start-line and then met the fire of most of 1st SS Panzer Grenadier Battalion and some Mark IVs deployed in hangars on the airfield. It took until 9 o'clock for the Canadians to reach the first hangars where they were brought to a standstill. Their supporting tanks had been assisting with fire from static positions and did not move up until some four hours later, together with some Crocodiles. The Fort Garry tanks clashed with the Mark IVs and some Panthers (Mark Vs) of 4th SS Panzer Company but could not break through. After this battle SS Senior Sergeant Rudolf received the Knight's Cross; with his Panther Rudolf was credited with destroying six Shermans. Unsurprisingly, the Canadians had to withdraw, the Winnipegs and Fort Garry pulling back some half mile to a small wood west of the hangars; this occurred at about 3.40pm. A further Winnipeg attack was repulsed when Panthers moved onto the ridge south of the airfield just before 6 o'clock. There was now no possibility of the next phase taking place (The Queen's Own Rifles were to capture the eastern end of the airfield). At 9.00pm 8 Brigade's commander, Brigadier K G Blackader, ordered an end to the attack; thirty minutes later Fort Garry and Winnipeg survivors were back at Marcelet.[14]

Although they had taken Carpiquet and part of the airfield, the Canadians had failed in their overall objective since the enemy still held the control tower and southern hangars. Casualties had been heavy: both Winnipegs and North Shores lost 132 men each, from overall Canadian losses of 377 killed, wounded or missing.[15] The defenders' losses were 155 men, including the company commander at Carpiquet, Captain Eggert, but no German tanks were lost, in spite of attacks by rocket-firing Typhoons. (Poor weather had kept the fighters on the ground until late afternoon.) It seems incredible that an understrength battalion, supported by less than a company of tanks and six 88s, could defy and defeat four infantry battalions and the equivalent of two armoured regiments, all with the support of over 700 guns, including those of a battleship, and tactical aircraft. But that is what happened on 4 July at Carpiquet. Nor was the fighting over; the Germans decided that the Canadian hold on the village threatened Caen itself and that a night attack should be launched to retake Carpiquet.

That attack was made under cover of darkness with 2nd SS Panzer Grenadier Battalion relieving the airfield's defenders and 3rd SS Panzer Grenadier Battalion attacking from a start-line on Route Nationale 13 towards Carpiquet. Although one company suffered casualties when hit by its own artillery, the battalion made good progress and by daylight had overrun a Chaudière company to reach the railway. But that was their limit, British and Canadian gunners proving every bit as effective in defensive fire as their German counterparts the previous day; and both North Shores and Chaudières put up a spirited defence. The German divisional commander ordered a withdrawal to a defensive line along RN13.[16]

Such was the effectiveness of Hitlerjugend's defence of Carpiquet airfield that Dempsey became convinced that Operation CHARNWOOD might not take Caen quickly and with the least possible casualties. He resolved to call in Bomber Command.[17] His concern may be understood when one examines the defences of Caen as outlined in the Official History; these had been strengthened greatly since D-Day, with anti-tank ditches and weapon pits extended and supplemented by minefields and other obstacles. Natural topography had been used to best advantage and villages* around the city had been turned into almost tank-proof mutually supporting strongpoints.

> Behind this belt, round the fringe of the city, were other artillery and mortar positions; on the west were the unsubdued positions at Carpiquet airfield. The front from Hérouville on the Caen canal, through Lebisey to the railway near Cambes was held by . . . 16th Luftwaffe Field Division of LXXXVI Corps, with some tanks of the 21st Panzer Division in support . . . From there, through Gruchy to Carpiquet airfield and the Odon near Verson, the front was held by I SS Panzer Corps with the 12th SS Panzer Division, the 7th Werfer Brigade and detachments of the 1st SS Panzer Division. In reserve near the Orne about five or six miles south of Caen lay the rest of the 1st SS Panzer Division which was only now completing its move, and distributed in the corps area were the dual-purpose 88mm guns of at least one regiment of III Flak Corps. West of Verson stood II SS Panzer Corps facing the British VIII Corps salient.[18]

Added to Dempsey's concerns was a damning report from Crocker, I Corps' commander, about the Canadian performance at Carpiquet. Crocker attributed the Canadians' failure to 'a lack of control and leadership from the top', blaming Keller, commanding 3rd Canadian Division, for the rebuff. Since the Canadians would play a major role in CHARNWOOD, Dempsey could not but be concerned about this report from the commander of the corps that would assault Caen. Both Crocker and Dempsey recommended Keller's removal, a proposal with which Montgomery agreed, passing on his comments to Lieutenant-General Crerar of First Canadian Army.** Keller was not removed, although he was wounded later in the campaign.[19]

The request for heavy bombers for CHARNWOOD was made by Montgomery, supported by Eisenhower, who, on 7 July, had sent the former a letter that suggested, tactfully, that 'he get a move on'.[20] There is another suggestion, in the unpublished papers of Air Commodore Kingston-

* Lebisey, la Bijude, Galmanche, Gruchy, Franqueville, Cussy and Couvre-Chef.

** Even when under British operational command, Commonwealth commanders could be sacked only by their own command; army commanders could be sacked only by their governments.

McCloughry, that Churchill threatened Montgomery with dismissal unless Caen was taken 'by Monday.'[21] In response to that ultimatum Montgomery is said to have told Churchill that he could take Caen 'by tomorrow' if Churchill would give him what he needed: heavy bombers.

I Corps' preparations moved into their final phase with three divisions – 3rd Canadian, 59th (Staffordshire) and 3rd British – poised to attack, supported by 2 Canadian and 27 Armoured Brigades as well as 'Funnies' from 79th Armoured Division. The corps had been reinforced to a strength of 115,000 men and would have artillery support from the guns of the attacking divisions, those of Guards Armoured and 51st (Highland) Divisions and 3rd and 5th Army Groups Royal Artillery (AGRAs). Once again the Royal Navy would lend support, employing the battleship *Rodney*, the monitor *Roberts* and the cruisers *Belfast* and *Emerald*. *Rodney* fired the first shots, twenty-nine rounds from its 16-inch guns striking a hill north of Caen, Point 64, where the roads from Lebisey and Epron merge en route to Caen. This important junction was shelled in the late afternoon of 7 July, some hours before the heavy bombers appeared. As I Corps attacked, VIII Corps went on twenty-four hours' notice to assault from the west with 43rd (Wessex) Division towards St André on the Orne; this operation would include seizing Hill 112.

Bombers from Nos 1, 4, 6 and 8 Groups were assigned to attack the Caen defences and 467 Lancasters, Halifaxes and Mosquitoes took part; 2,276 tons of bombs were dropped in 'a very accurate raid'.[22] The intention had been for the bombers to hit the fortified villages north of Caen but concern that this might cause heavy casualties among nearby Allied troops caused a change of plan. In the revised plan the target area was moved closer to the city to include its northern outskirts and a stretch of open country. As a bombing operation it was completely successful with very few losses: only one Lancaster was shot down by AA fire, although three other machines crashed behind Allied lines. As an aid to the attacking troops the raid's value was doubtful. The bombing line had been set at 6,000 yards forward of the nearest Allied troops, leaving German forward defences unscathed as the assault went in. Normally, this would have been no great problem since the German system of defence in depth usually allowed forward defences to be held lightly with the defenders pulling back into the intermediate and rear areas to the strongest defences but Caen's forward defences were held in some strength. Moreover, the fact that the advancing troops would have to move almost four miles before reaching the bombed area meant that defenders in those areas would have time in plenty for recovery and preparation. Since most bombs dropped were fused to detonate six hours later there were few German casualties in the raid, although those closest to the bombing were badly shaken. But the northern edge of the city became a nightmare for infantry and an impassable obstacle for tanks. Caen was destroyed, with most of its buildings demolished, although it appeared as if divine intervention spared the Cathedral, Abbaye-aux-Hommes and the Bon Saveur hospital, where many civilians were sheltering.

The bombing raid began at 9.50pm as VIII Corps artillery fired on anti-aircraft positions around the city. Less than an hour later the raid was over and, at 11 o'clock, the guns of I and VIII Corps, with those of the Royal Navy, began counter-battery fire on enemy artillery positions, at the same time hitting the village strongpoints. Overhead light bombers began harassing attacks behind enemy lines; their targets included twenty-six trains. At 4.20am on the 8th all the artillery opened fire in front of 3rd British and 59th (Staffordshire) Divisions. Both formations advanced rapidly with 3rd Division's leading brigade at Hérouville and Lebisey within an hour, while the Staffordshire Division's two leading brigades were in the outskirts of la Bijude and Galmanche at much the same time.[23]

Second Tactical Air Force and Ninth Air Force joined in at daylight; the fighters of the former struck just ahead of the attacking troops while the US medium bombers carried out interdiction raids on targets including bridges, enemy gun areas and forming-up positions. The large-calibre guns of ships in the Bay of the Seine also came into play with devastating effect, their fire being directed by slow-flying Royal Artillery spotter planes. At 7.30am the attack's second phase began with fresh troops of 59th Division advancing towards Epron and St Contest while 3rd Canadian Division joined in with a brigade striking towards Authie via Buron and Gruchy. As the infantry moved forward in this new phase the main weight of supporting artillery was again to their front.

In the Lebisey sector, on the extreme left, the advance went well but, in the centre, at la Bijude and Galmanche, 12th SS Panzer Division again demonstrated its stubborn determination to hold on. A similar story was developing at Epron and St Contest while a trench system, just west of la Bijude, was holding up progress. To deal with this problem, Crocker ordered 3rd British Division to deploy some armour on to the high ground at Point 64, north of Caen and, subsequently, placed his reserve armour – 33 Armoured Brigade – under 3rd Division's command. Although the Canadians were in Buron by 8.30am, Hitlerjugend soldiers were ready to fight to the death in the rubble of the village; it took most of that day to overcome them. During the battle for Buron, Hitlerjugend made several attempts to evict their attackers with tanks but these came to naught and the Canadian armour, supported by a battery of 17-pounder anti-tank guns, eventually wore down their opponents, the 17-pounders being credited with destroying thirteen tanks.[24] Casualties were heavy on both sides; the assaulting Canadian North Shore battalion lost 262 personnel dead or wounded while its supporting tank squadron was reduced to four runners from fifteen. There was another stiff fight at Gruchy although nowhere near as bloody as at Buron. Novel tactics may have helped:

sixteen Bren-gun carriers from the divisional recce regiment made an old-style cavalry charge, all guns blazing, into the enemy positions.[25] This seems to have knocked the defenders off balance since it was a departure from the normal stolid pace of British and Canadian operations.

At 2.30pm Canadian troops moved against Authie and St Louet, both of which fell within an hour, followed by Franqueville, from which enemy troops were seen withdrawing. The next phase began at 6.30pm and, within two hours, the Canadians had taken Cussy and knocked out six counter-attacking tanks. They also menaced Ardenne from which the Germans withdrew that night, allowing the Canadians to take possession next morning.

Third British Division had also made sound progress, clearing the area around Lebisey and advancing with 33 Armoured Brigade support to take Point 64 and the surrounding high ground. From there they could look down on Caen from 'the position they had hoped to gain on D-day'.[26] Their advance had been relatively smooth, impeded only by some heavy shelling and mortaring from east of the Orne and a brief foray by enemy tanks at Hérouville. At day's end they were sending patrols into the outskirts of Caen but as darkness was falling and the city was a mass of rubble no units moved in. Meanwhile, 59th (Staffordshire) Division had been slugging all day to take St Contest and the ruins of la Bijude although they had not secured their other objectives. That the division was taking part in its first major battle may have had something to do with its relative lack of progress against determined German opposition but the courage of its troops could not be doubted.

Nor could one doubt the defenders' courage. The right flank of Hitlerjugend was threatened when 16th Luftwaffe Field Division* collapsed. Reports came in that la Bijude had to be abandoned and Epron was threatened, that 3rd SS Panzer Grenadier Battalion was surrounded in Buron, that Carpiquet airfield had fallen, together with Gruchy, Authie and Franqueville. Counter-attacks were being beaten off and only artillery and mortar fire, combined with a counter-attack by Panthers and Panzer Grenadiers prevented the Reginas from taking Ardenne Abbey. Meyer asked for permission to withdraw but Dietrich, commanding I SS Panzer Corps refused, stating that Hitler had ordered Caen to be defended at all costs. Eventually Dietrich's headquarters conceded that being forced to the Orne's south bank could not be considered 'a withdrawal contrary to

* Luftwaffe field divisions were composed of men who no longer had ground roles with the air force. Instead of assigning them to infantry training units for retraining, Hermann Göring, head of the Luftwaffe, wanted to maintain his own control over these men and keep them as part of the Luftwaffe. Their training as infantry was of a much lower standard than that to be found in the army or the Waffen-SS.

orders' and Meyer issued the order for withdrawal. At the end of this day, Hitlerjugend had lost over 600 casualties, ten Panthers and twenty-two Mark IVs.[27]

That evening Rommel approved the withdrawal from the Caen bridgehead of all heavy weapons from LXXXVI, I SS and II SS Corps for a regrouping south of the Orne. Strong infantry and engineer forces were to maintain a perimeter around Caen, withdrawing only under attack from superior forces, in which case they would take up a new line along the Orne's east bank and across to Venoix and Bretteville, north of the Odon. Allied operations closed down for the night and helped the Germans execute their retreat. Hitlerjugend's commander later wrote that had the Allies attacked through the night his division could not have survived.[28] Night-time British activity was limited to reconnaissance patrols along the enemy front and intruder aircraft of Second Tactical Air Force. It soon became clear that no general German withdrawal was underway.[29]

Caen finally fell the following day. Both British and Canadian forces were advancing from early morning with 3rd British Division sending tank patrols forward before entering Caen. Although 2nd Royal Ulster Rifles claimed to have been the first British troops into Caen this was disputed by 3rd Reconnaissance Regiment (NF), detachments of which, under Lieutenants Darrell and Lewis, preceded the Irish battalion into the city.[30] The Ulsters were probably the first to enter in battalion strength and perhaps both can claim the distinction with some justification. Those who entered Caen found rubble blocking the streets to be more troublesome than the snipers who remained under cover or the mortar bombs still landing in the city. Lieutenant James Campbell, D Company 2nd Royal Ulster Rifles, compared scrambling across the rubble to trying to walk on the Giant's Causeway of his native Northern Ireland.[31] And so the soldiers of 3rd Division pushed into the city that had eluded Second Army since D-Day. Meanwhile 59th (Staffordshire) Division had taken all its objectives by noon while the Canadians cleared Carpiquet and seized Bretteville sur Odon. In the early afternoon Canadian armour met 3rd British Division and by 6.00pm I Corps was up to the Orne at Caen and to the Odon above the confluence of those rivers. Some bridges were still intact* but had either been blocked with rubble or were defended by German troops on the other bank of the river while 1st SS Panzer Division Leibstandarte Adolf Hitler had moved closer to Caen to delay any further Allied advance.

Caen cost I Corps heavily. Some 3,500 men became casualties, with the most severe blows falling on the Canadians and Staffords, each division

* The Germans allowed bridges to survive so that they might be used in counter-attacks.

losing over a thousand men. In the armour some eighty tanks had been destroyed or damaged. But the cost had also been high for the Germans whose war diaries show that 16th Luftwaffe Field Division lost three-quarters of its strength while every battalion commander west of the Orne was either dead or wounded. SS formations had not suffered so heavily, principally because they had been trained to a much higher standard and were, therefore, better soldiers; Michael Reynolds points out that 12th SS Panzer had suffered fewer casualties to this point in the campaign than had 3rd Canadian Division and its supporting 2 Armoured Brigade with 4,138, even though the Canadians had done less fighting.[32] Bombing Caen had had no effect other than to bolster Allied morale; few, if any, Germans had been killed and, in spite of the assertion of Major-General David Belchem,[33] then Montgomery's chief operations officer, that bombing caused extensive damage to many enemy defensive installations and headquarters, no material damage had been suffered by the defenders.

But the capture of Caen had not been an objective for the sake of the city. Possession of Caen would yield no benefit to the Allies other than opening the way to the excellent tank country beyond. So it was that capturing Caen allowed Montgomery to turn his mind to further operations that would, hopefully, assist the breakout from Normandy. To the west the Americans were nearing St Lô, which allowed the prospect of a truly strategic offensive, with both First and Second Armies landing blows that would finally break the Germans in Normandy and begin the race to the Seine. While preparations were being made for such operations, Second Army was to expand its bridgehead south of the Odon by recapturing Hill 112 and taking Eterville and Maltot. This task was assigned to 43rd (Wessex) Division, reinforced by 46 (Highland) Brigade, from 15th (Scottish) Division, and two brigades of armour, 4 Armoured and 31 Tank. Two AGRAs (3rd and 8th) as well as the divisional artillery of 11th Armoured and 15th (Scottish) Divisions would also contribute to Operation JUPITER, planned to begin on 10 July at 5.00am with a start-line in the Orne bridgehead that now stretched from Verson to Baron, 214 Brigade having moved in alongside 129 Brigade on the night before Caen fell.

Hill 112 is unlikely to merit a glance from the tourist motoring through Normandy. Perhaps a cycling tourist might give it a second thought. Neither is likely to think that this unremarkable feature, which 'rises gently from the valley of the Odon river, which is itself little more than a stream'[34] was once a place of blood and death, of pitched battle and human misery. Yet it was, and General Eberbach of Panzer Group West told II SS Panzer Corps' commander that it was 'the pivotal point of the whole position . . . in no circumstances may it be surrendered'.[35] And thus more British and German troops were doomed to die over this glorified mound of earth and the valley in its shadow in a battle that did much to earn General Thomas of 43rd (Wessex) Division the soubriquet of 'Butcher'.

Thomas's optimistic plan called for two infantry brigades, supported by Churchills from 31 Tank Brigade, to seize Maltot and Hill 112 in seventy-five minutes, after which 4 Armoured Brigade, commanded by Michael Carver, with Thomas's third brigade would pass through to advance the six miles to the Orne; 46 (Highland) Brigade would secure the left flank. Carver was concerned that a wood on the reverse slope of Hill 112 should be firmly in British hands before his leading regiment passed over the hill.

> If it were not, my tanks would be shot up from the rear as they went forward. After further heated argument and objections from the infantry, it was agreed. My plan was for The Greys to lead, as they had had the easiest time in the previous operation.[36]

Carver had already argued with Thomas over artillery support and won the argument with 'assurances of ample artillery support (Thomas having tried to fob me off with smoke screens)'.[37] Obviously, relations between armour and infantry were not ideal.

The slopes of Hills 112 and 113 offered little cover, the wood to which Carver referred being one of the few areas of cover. Good use was made of that wood, dubbed 'das Wäldchen der halben Bäume' (the wood of the half trees) by the Germans and the 'Crown of Thorns' by the British,* which concealed a pioneer company, part of the very strong defences that included a platoon of Mark IVs with twenty-five Tigers also in the vicinity. Those defences inflicted horrendous casualties on the attacking British infantry, 5th Wiltshires, 4th Somerset LI and 4th Wiltshires, and on the Churchills of 7th Royal Tanks. By 9.00am the attackers had reached the Eterville road, along the crest of the ridge on which sit Hills 112 and 113, but had already suffered heavily as the ridgetop seemed to disappear in 'the fumes, smoke and dust of battle'.[38] The plateau, about a mile square, had yet to be cleared, and the Germans were fully alert. Although some defensive positions had been overrun, many defenders had survived and brought fire to bear on the Somersets from the rear as well as engaging the follow-up troops; 4th Somerset LI lost three of its four company commanders, while one company lost all its officers and was commanded by a sergeant. German reinforcements were racing up and, although British follow-up battalions were preparing for the next phase, Hill 112 was still in enemy hands. The Tigers that had arrived that morning in St Martin were advancing to join the fray and the slopes seemed to be littered with brewed-up Churchills.

* The Tiger crews of 102nd SS Tank Battalion called the wood 'das Kästenwäldchen' (the little box-shaped wood) while to The Duke of Cornwall's Light Infantry it was 'Cornwall Wood' and to 53rd (Welsh) Division it was 'Diamond Wood'.

The battle continued with the British unable to clear the crest or advance and the Germans unable to shift the surviving British from the slopes where they were now entrenched. Attacks on British positions cost the Germans seventy men, three Tigers and several Mark IVs.[39] As we have seen, Michael Carver refused to send his tanks over the crest until the wood had been cleared, and he now contacted Thomas's headquarters to re-affirm that arrangement. Thomas then came on the radio to tell Carver that all

> forward objectives had been secured, and that therefore I must start my forward thrust. I said I was on the spot, as his infantry brigadiers were not, and that, if he did not believe me, he could come and see for himself. This, not surprisingly, did not please him. He insisted that I should order my tanks to advance over the crest. I said that, if I did, I expected that the leading regiment would suffer at least 75 per cent casualties, as a result of which they would not be able to reach their objective. He asked me which regiment I proposed to send. I told him it was The Greys. 'Couldn't you send a less well-known regiment?' he replied, at which I blew up. Finally he accepted my arguments, but relations between us, poor to start with, were permanently soured.[40]

That evening a further attack was launched with 5th Duke of Cornwall's LI supported by Churchills of 7th Royal Tanks. Some progress was made but the Germans were as stubborn as ever and, although the Wessex Division had all four brigades and much armour on the ridge and the slopes behind at the end of the day, the enemy was still determined not to yield. During the night SS troops counter-attacked several times and confusion soon prevailed around Hill 112. Tiger tanks accompanying the attacking infantry later withdrew and fighting continued into daylight and throughout the following day, during which Carver sent a squadron of Greys to support the infantry in the wood. But German artillery fire forced an infantry withdrawal and the tanks also pulled back. The Cornwalls lost all their anti-tank guns and suffered some 240 casualties, after which they withdrew to the Eterville road. Over two days of fighting the Wessex Division and its supporting armour lost about 2,000 men, with little to show for it.* The Official History tries to put a gloss on this by stating that the Germans lost half of Hill 112;[41] but that ignores the fact that Thomas's attack had failed. If there was any element of success at all, it was that their efforts had held two SS panzer divisions – 9th and 10th – away from the American front for a few days that might prove vital to the breakout from the Cotentin; and they had also drawn elements of 1st SS and 12th SS Panzer Divisions eastward and away from Bradley's army.

* One of the best accounts of the JUPITER battle is from Major J J How in his book *Hill 112: Cornerstone of the Normandy Campaign.*

Hills 112 and 113 had lost none of their importance and would continue as focal points in fighting between the Orne and Odon. Both protagonists had suffered heavily with, as ever, the greatest blows falling on the infantry. Dempsey recorded that he and Montgomery had been warned that the infantry casualty rate was such that it would soon 'be impossible to replace them',[42] making it necessary to break up some divisions to keep others in existence. Before long, the truth of this would come home to Second Army with 59th (Staffordshire) Division the first to suffer disbandment. Strangely, Montgomery makes no mention of this looming manpower crisis in either his *Memoirs* or in his account of the campaign, *Normandy to the Baltic*. In the latter he draws attention to the new corps coming into Second Army's order of battle: II Canadian Corps, with 2nd Canadian Division joining 3rd Canadian Division; and XII Corps, which took over VIII Corps' sector. He also refers to the 'considerable regrouping' within Second Army on 12 and 13 July; the Canadian Corps deployed between XII and I Corps.

This regrouping preceded another series of battles, the aim of which Montgomery explained to Eisenhower in a telegram on 13 July as working up 'to a big attack next week'.[43] In this phase, XII and XXX Corps were to launch sustained operations on the left flank to pin the German armour there. Four new German infantry divisions had arrived in Normandy and it was essential that these not be permitted to relieve the panzers for operations against the Americans who were expected shortly to begin the breakout from Normandy, their previous efforts having failed. The attacks by XII and XXX Corps – Operation GREENLINE – would precede Second Army's major armoured offensive, Operation GOODWOOD; this would begin on the 18th, a day later than originally planned, and the day before Bradley's First Army began 'a heavy attack with six divisions about five miles west of St Lô'[44], as a prelude to Operation COBRA. Of his own plans for GOODWOOD, Montgomery wrote to Brooke on the 14th that three armoured divisions would lead the attack since casualties had already affected the fighting efficiency of the infantry divisions and the terrain in which they were fighting was ideal for defence.

> we do the attacking and the Boche is pretty thick on the ground. I would say we lose three men to his one in the infantry divisions.
>
> But the Second Army has three armoured divisions, 7, 11 and Gds. These are quite fresh and have been practically untouched. A fourth armoured division will be complete . . . by 27 July, i.e. the Canadian Armd Div.
>
> Having got Caen, my left flank is now firm; my whole lodgement area is very secure and is held by infantry divisions. And available to work with the infantry I have eight independent armoured Bdes . . . with a tank strength of over 1000 tanks.

> And so I have decided that the time has come to have a real 'show down' on the Eastern flank, and to loose a corps of three armoured divisions in to the open country about the Caen–Falaise road.[45]

In a post-war interview, Dempsey confirmed that infantry casualties and the number of tanks available 'vitally affected the conduct' of GOODWOOD. Before the operation, he learned from his deputy adjutant-general 'that the personnel situation was serious' with infantry casualties 'at a rate beyond replacement' should they continue as before. He determined, therefore, 'to have as few personnel casualties as possible'. On the other hand, the 'number of available tanks was high and if necessary the Army Commander was prepared to accept heavy losses in them, providing the losses in men were low'.[46] Dempsey appears to have taken much the same view as Montgomery had at El Alamein: using tanks would save infantrymen's lives; both seemed to believe that tanks could be lost without significant personnel losses.

But before Montgomery's 'show down' could take place, the preliminary operations of GREENLINE began under artificial moonlight – searchlights directed on the base of the clouds – on the night of 15 July with attacks across the front from west of Caen to Tilly sur Seulles. Striking out from the Odon bridgehead, XII Corps was to secure a firm base on the road southwest from Bougy through Evrecy in preparation for a further advance, should circumstances permit, towards Aunay sur Odon or Thury-Harcourt. At the same time XXX Corps would secure the area around Noyers in readiness for exploitation to high ground north-east of Villers-Bocage. The fighting of the next few days gained little ground but served a useful purpose by keeping 1st SS Panzer, 10th SS Panzer and 2nd Panzer Divisions in battle while 9th SS Panzer was brought forward from reserve to assist counter-attacks. British divisions involved in GREENLINE included 49th (West Riding) which captured Vendes in two days of heavy fighting, and with many casualties, from 276th Infantry Division, one of the new German arrivals in Normandy. Hottot fell to 50th (Northumbrian) Division, bringing to an end a series of scraps that had lasted for a month. During the battle for Hottot, A Squadron 4th/7th Royal Dragoon Guards

> had a wonderful day and KO'd 5 Panthers, one anti-tank gun and one half-track and captured intact one 'People's Car' and one half-track which were brought back for use in the Regiment. Sergeant Harris* was responsible for 4 Panthers and Captain Stirling for 1.[48]

The Welshmen of 53rd (Welsh) Division took Cahier and held it against

* Sergeant Harris was subsequently awarded the Distinguished Conduct Medal.[47]

determined counter-attacks while 59th (Staffordshire) took Haut des Forges but failed to wrest Noyers from 277th Infantry Division, another new arrival. Bougy and Gavrus were taken by 15th (Scottish), which also entered Esquay but could not overcome sustained enemy pressure; the Germans held the village eventually with the Scots suffering almost 1,000 casualties. Although gains in ground were of little significance, the fact that Second Army was so heavily engaged convinced the Germans that the British intended to break out from the Caen bridgehead 'forward across the Orne in the direction of Paris'.[49] The strategic deception plan was still working: Hitler warned that a second invasion could yet occur in Fifteenth Army's area and thus that formation remained locked there. But whether all this was worth the overall cost in casualties – 3,500 – is debatable. It certainly appears a profligate use of that very limited resource, the infantry soldier.

The armoured corps leading GOODWOOD was to be VIII Corps, under Sir Richard O'Connor. At the same time, II Canadian Corps was to undertake Operation ATLANTIC, capturing the southern part of Caen from Colombelles to Faubourg de Vaucelles, bridge the Orne and be ready to advance to the line Cormelles–Fleury sur Orne and across the river to Eterville. In Montgomery's view this was 'vital'; only when this had been achieved could VIII Corps carry out its task. I Corps was to secure the left flank in the Orne bridgehead against attack from east and south-east; to achieve this 3rd British Division was to establish itself in the area Bures–Troarn–St Pair–Emiéville–Touffreville.[50]

O'Connor's corps deployed about 750 tanks in its three divisions[51] and, to gain maximum surprise, these would stay well west of the Orne before moving eastward under cover to attack from an unexpected quarter. This was 'the shallow and congested bridgehead east of the Orne' – hence the need for 3rd Division to secure the left flank there; another 350 tanks were available to support I Corps. But the plan for deploying VIII Corps created its own problems: all three divisions would have to use roads that were under regular German shellfire, crossing the Orne river and canal between Ranville and the sea over three double bridges. It was obvious that they could not sally forth to battle as a solid corps but must follow each other across the bridges and into action; this led to the armoured brigades preceding the infantry brigades into battle. O'Connor suggested that the infantry might be made more mobile, and better protected, by improvising armoured personnel carriers from SPGs but he was over-ruled by Dempsey and the offensive suffered as a result.[52] (One wonders if O'Connor was inspired by the Canadian use of Bren-gun carriers to create a highly mobile infantry force at Gruchy just over a week earlier.) Artillery support also suffered since most guns had to be kept west of the Orne until the tanks' advance had begun and, as the armour moved forward, the guns' effectiveness would be reduced until they, in turn, could cross the Orne. Needless to say, heavy bombers were to be called into action again. Finally,

> the attack was to be made not where the enemy was weak but where he had prepared his strongest defence, in country which gave him almost everywhere the advantage of ground observation and fields of fire.[53]

The area into which VIII Corps was to attack was held by three infantry divisions, 346th, 16th Luftwaffe and 272nd, plus 21st Panzer and 1st SS Panzer Divisions. However, 16th Luftwaffe Division was but a shadow of its former self, having been mauled badly in earlier fighting while 1st SS Panzer Division Leibstandarte Adolf Hitler had four battalions* in corps reserve west of the Orne. To the Germans' advantage was the fact that British intelligence was unaware of Leibstandarte's presence between Ifs and Cintheaux. Dietrich's other formation of I SS Panzer Corps, Hitlerjugend, was re-organising with elements at Lisieux and north-west of Falaise. Some sources suggest that this deployment was due to von Kluge seeking to block a breakout from east of Caen towards Paris but it seems that the true reason was Hitler's continuing fear that the Allies were planning a further landing between the Seine and the Orne.[55]

German defences, the work of Eberbach of Panzer Group West, were disposed in considerable depth – to almost eight miles – another fact not appreciated by British intelligence. German armour included a company with Germany's newest tank, the King Tiger or Tiger II,** from 503rd Heavy Tank Battalion. With three-dozen Tigers in total, the battalion was positioned to support Kampfgruppe von Luck and act as divisional reserve to 21st Panzer.[56] The company of Tiger IIs had fourteen tanks, the only examples of this monster to fight in Normandy.[57] Total German tank strength was estimated at about 230 tanks.[58] Reynolds has shown that actual German tank strength was much greater, with some 377 tanks, StuGs and SPGs available.[59] No German anti-tank minefields had been laid, which allowed their armour much freedom of movement. By contrast, British armour would have to negotiate a belt of British minefields. This could not be gapped until the advance was underway since it was under German observation, especially from the Colombelles factories, the stacks of which overlooked the entire Orne bridgehead.

Nor were these the sole flaws in this plan, drawn up by Dempsey and approved by Montgomery. We have already noted that the bridgehead

* These were 2nd SS Panzer, 1st SS StuG, 3rd SS (SPW) Panzer Grenadier and 1st SS (SP) Artillery Battalions.[54]

** Also known as the Tiger Royal or Royal Tiger.

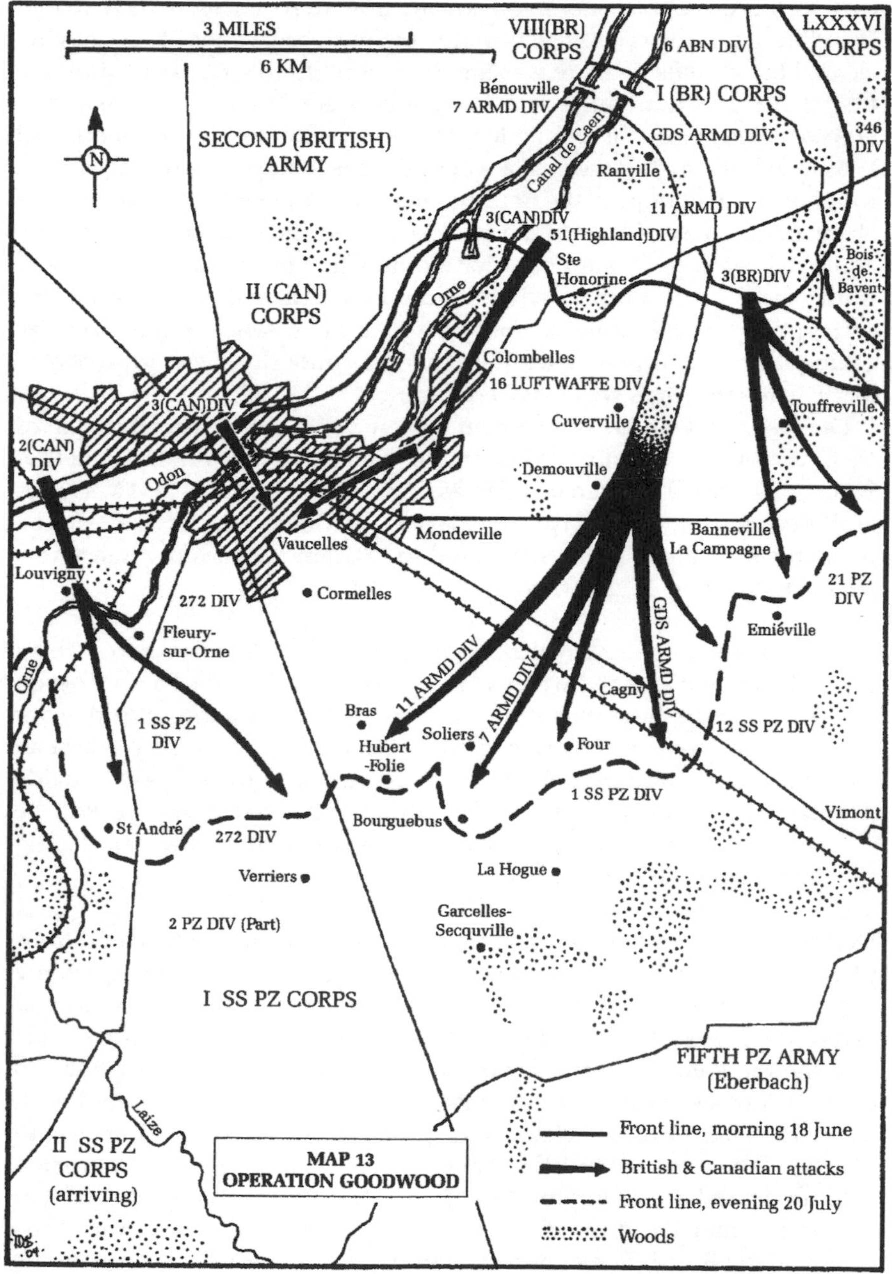

MAP 13
OPERATION GOODWOOD

east of the Orne was too small for an armoured corps, which would therefore have to travel in file under enemy observation. Even having cleared the minefields there was insufficient room to spread out since the first stretch of the advance was along a corridor less than a mile-and-a-quarter wide on its three-mile length, being restricted by the industrial suburb of Caen to the west and a wooded ridge to the left. After five miles, roughly at the bottom of the Bourguébus ridge, the tanks would also run ahead of the cover of most of the artillery and would have only some SPG-equipped batteries for support. Montgomery had presided over a scene of traffic chaos at El Alamein when he devised a plan superimposing one corps upon another; now he was repeating the essence of that error by asking a corps with some 8,000 vehicles to undertake the approach to battle that VIII Corps was required to do.

Dempsey had issued an order on 17 July setting definite objectives for each armoured division: Vimont for Guards Armoured; Garcelles-Secqueville and St Aignan de Cramesnil for the Desert Rats and Verrières and Rocquancourt for 11th Armoured. In doing so, he had placed restrictions on the objectives outlined to O'Connor by Montgomery in a personal note two days earlier.

> To engage the German armour in battle and write it down to such an extent that it is of no further value . . . as the basis of the battle. To gain a good bridgehead over the Orne through Caen and thus improve our positions on the eastern flank. Generally to destroy German equipment and personnel, as a preliminary to a possible wide exploitation of success. . . . The three armoured divisions will be required to dominate the area Bourguébus–Vimont–Bretteville, and to fight and destroy the enemy.[60]

Dempsey's revised objectives have about them the air of a less ambitious plan, in which taking ground was as important as destroying enemy armour. Montgomery, for all his failure to grasp what armour could and could not do, realised that the enemy's armour had to be destroyed. He also showed some strategic vision in his suggestion that there might be an exploitation of success: his notes state that the 'armoured cars should push far to the south towards Falaise, and spread alarm and despondency, and discover "the form".'[61] In 1951 Dempsey was arguing that the 'campaign was conducted according to a previously laid down strategic plan' that demanded that the bulk of enemy strength, especially his armour, be drawn to the British flank, thereby allowing US forces to break out on the western flank.[62]

The ground over which VIII Corps was to advance, although more open than the bocage, favoured the defender as it rose gently to the Bourguébus ridge, which VIII Corps' historian describes as affording

> complete observation over almost the entire area . . . whilst the defenders had the benefit of long fields of fire and facilities for concealed movement in the woods and villages, of which they did not fail to take advantage. Whilst therefore the country generally was by no means as enclosed as that fought over in 'Epsom', it still gave the enemy plenty of cover, particularly in the vicinity of the villages, enabling him to site his anti-tank weapons in cleverly hidden positions from which full use could be made of their superior range. The numerous villages, too, provide a series of mutually supporting strong points not more than 1,500 yards apart, which if garrisoned with resolute troops make a perfect natural defence line. The enemy therefore was not slow to adapt these as the backbone of his second defence zone.[63]

Naturally the ridge, overlooking the southern exits from Caen, was the main objective while the villages of Bras, Hubert-Folie, Bourguébus and la Hogue, on the northern and north-eastern ends of the ridge, dominated the lower flat and open ground to the north and east. Norman houses, with strong walls around houses, gardens and orchards, were ideal for defence. Another critical factor, dictated not by natural but by industrial topography, was the railway embankment from Caen's north-eastern environs to the mines and quarries south of Grainville. This embankment, some two-and-a-half miles long, presented a serious obstacle even to tanks which had to negotiate it where bridges carried the railway over roads or tracks; the embankment also cut off any view to its west from le Mesnil-Frémentel and Grentheville, thereby creating two discrete elements to the battleground. The eastern element was dominated by Bourguébus and la Hogue and the western by Bras and Hubert-Folie.

As already noted heavy bombers deployed in the opening phase of VIII Corps' operation 'to counter-balance the strength of the enemy's position in the opening attack'. Both British and American aircraft were involved. Bomber Command struck first at German positions on the flanks of the corridor along which the armour was to pass, bombing an area of some 1,000 acres on the left flank, including Touffreville, Sannerville, Banneville, Guillerville and Manneville, all of which were to be taken by 3rd British Division, and another area of similar acreage on the right, encompassing Colombelles steelworks. In both areas British heavies were to drop 500- and 1,000lb bombs to create severe cratering. A third area would also receive the attention of Bomber Command: some 340 acres, including the fortified village of Cagny, in the line of advance was to be bombed using instantaneous fuses to reduce cratering. American heavies were to strike on the extreme left, covering Troarn, and to the south of the armoured advance, including the enemy gun lines about Soliers, Hubert-

Folie and Bourguébus and the area between Bourguébus and Frénouville. Medium bombers from Ninth Air Force would also engage forward German positions, including Cuverville, Giberville and Démouville. Fighter-bombers of Nos 83 and 84 Groups, RAF, were to attack pinpoint targets, including bridges, gun positions, troop and tank concentrations, and provide close support for attacking formations, while fighters from the Air Defence of Great Britain* would provide cover against any possible Luftwaffe interference.[64]

The bombers opened proceedings, with over 1,000 RAF machines dropping more than 5,500 tons of bombs. To the tankmen it was a most impressive and

> terrifying sight . . . One imagined really [that] the battle's over. You know, how could anyone survive all this? All we've got to do now is skirt our way round these great bomb craters. We finally got across the bridge at about two o'clock.[65]

As with so many of his fellow Irish Guardsmen, Lieutenant John Gorman, whose thoughts these were, was about to go into action for the first time. Such was the congestion in the bridgehead that schedules had slipped and thus the recollection that Gorman's unit, 2nd (Armoured) Battalion Irish Guards did not cross the Orne until two o'clock. Although 11th Armoured moved off on schedule, the other two divisions were delayed; 7th Armoured noted that the 'Division [was] badly congested by Gds Armoured Div who came too far WEST and blocked our exit against 11th Armoured. 22 Armd Bde eventually deployed 1600 hrs'.[66] Thus British tanks moved forward in divisional groupings, one behind the other; the entire purpose of putting together an armoured corps had been lost.

So it was that 11th Armoured Division was first to take the field, with armoured cars from The Inns of Court Regiment** reconnoitring ahead. The division advanced under cover of a bombardment by some 200 guns, with a similar number firing concentrations on selected targets; naval fire – from HM Ships *Enterprise*, *Mauritius* and *Roberts* – supplemented the artillery. Eleventh Armoured's two brigades, 29 Armoured and 159 Infantry, advanced on separate axes, with 29 on the eastern flank and 159 on the western, the latter supported by tanks of 2nd Northamptonshire Yeomanry, the divisional reconnaissance regiment, which Roberts was using as an additional armoured regiment. Objectives for the attacking

* Or ADGB, the name by which the former Fighter Command was now known.
** The Inns of Court Regiment was under command of 11th Armoured Division, on loan from Headquarters I Corps.

brigades were the le Mesnil-Frémentel area for 29 Armoured, followed by the higher ground around Verrières and Rocquancourt, some five miles beyond there, and Cuverville and Démouville for 159 Brigade, which would then join the armoured brigade to advance to the final objectives. At first all seemed well; initial encouraging reports from The Inns of Court appeared to be borne out by an apparently demoralised enemy, many of whom surrendered to advancing tanks.[67] Although co-ordination between artillery and tanks was not perfect, and the guns were asked to delay resuming their fireplan by twenty minutes to allow the tanks to cross the railway line, the advance continued and more Germans gave themselves up. But, soon after 9 o'clock, the tanks had moved out of artillery range; the guns then had to cross the river to come within range of the battleground. Thirty minutes later, 8th Rifle Brigade, 29 Armoured Brigade's motor battalion, was left to clear up le Mesnil-Frémentel while 23rd Hussars masked Cagny on the left flank and 3rd Royal Tanks and 2nd Fife and Forfar Yeomanry advanced towards the final objective. By 10 o'clock, 159 Brigade had cleared Cuverville and was moving on Démouville.[68] However, the good fortune that had appeared to smile on the British was about to change.

> The flow of traffic over the bridges and southwards towards the battle front was getting behind schedule and the enemy was recovering from the bombardment and offering stiffer resistance. Much of the more heavily bombed area had been passed and, although Cagny was reduced to ruins, the '88' guns which defended it and Tiger tanks in the Cagny woods had escaped destruction, as had the defences of Emiéville and other gun areas to the south.[69]

Behind 29 Armoured Brigade's tail, the foremost units of Adair's Guards Armoured Division had been brought to a stop shortly before 10 o'clock, while 7th Armoured Division's leading tanks, crossing by another bridge, were being held up by the rear Canadian brigade, now fighting a most determined opponent at Colombelles. When the Desert Rats' tanks did move, they became mixed up with those of the Guards. This was probably the cause of the complaint in the former's war diary that Guards Armoured had come too far west and blocked the Desert Rats' exit.

O'Connor, already well aware of the congestion, ordered Adair to get his armoured brigade 'down to Vimont as fast as you can'[70], an order with which Adair endeavoured to comply but in the execution of which he was baulked by stiffening resistance. The leading units of Guards Armoured – 2nd (Armoured) Grenadiers and 1st (Armoured) Coldstream – had no sooner crossed the first railway than they were engaged from the flank by enemy armour and anti-tank guns deployed between Emiéville and

Cagny. This forced a change of plan for 5 Guards Armoured Brigade* that saw the Grenadiers attack Cagny while the Coldstream continued towards Vimont, but sidestepped right to avoid Cagny and advance on the line of the railway; 2nd (Armoured Reconnaissance) Welsh Guards were to find a way through the enemy near Emiéville. Needless to say, this change added to the congestion since the Coldstream move meant detouring around le Mesnil-Frémentel and putting their tanks across the Desert Rats' axis of advance. All this confusion meant that it was thirty minutes past noon before 23rd Hussars could leave their positions near Cagny to rejoin 3rd Royal Tanks and the Fife and Forfars who were now engaged on the slopes of Bourguébus ridge.

By this time a counter-attack had been underway for almost three hours with 21st Panzer and 1st SS Panzer striking out from the south-east and south respectively. Since Cagny was a vital element of their defensive plan, the Germans were determined to hold the village, fearing that its loss would allow the British to split LXXXVI and I SS Panzer Corps. But it had taken the Germans some time to get underway as many of 21st Panzer's tanks had been damaged or destroyed in Bomber Command's assault; not until midday were the surviving tanks fit for action. The fighting strength of the division, with 503rd Heavy Tank Battalion under command, was about 100 tanks. I SS Panzer Corps had been disposed overnight south of the bombed area and was able quickly to deploy forty-six tanks, and some SPGs, in two battlegroups.[71] These advanced against Guards and 11th Armoured Divisions but without having achieved the concentration that might have allowed them to regain the Caen–Troarn road, their task in this attack. Once again, Allied air superiority proved a major disruptive factor for German armour.

Meanwhile Guards Armoured had been plugging away at Cagny and the surrounding area, while the Welsh Guards were trying, vainly, to fight through the Emiéville woods. By 6.00pm the Grenadiers, with infantry from 32 Guards Brigade, had infiltrated Cagny, which was in their hands some ninety minutes later. As this battle was raging, 2nd Irish Guards had by-passed Cagny to secure a footing on the ridge to the east. This was achieved against stern opposition from 21st Panzer that included much close fighting – and the first encounter with the latest German tank, the Tiger II. That encounter resulted in a Tiger II being knocked out, in unconventional fashion, by a Sherman of the 'Micks'.

* This brigade included 2nd (Armoured) Grenadier Guards, 1st (Armoured) Coldstream Guards, 2nd (Armoured) Irish Guards and 1st (Motor) Grenadier Guards. The infantry brigade of Guards Armoured Division – 32 Guards Brigade – included 5th Coldstream Guards, 3rd Irish Guards and 1st Welsh Guards. The Division later re-organised into 'family' groupings, marrying armoured and infantry battalions of the same regiment to form Grenadier, Coldstream and Irish Groups.

There was a certain amount of serendipity in the encounter, arising from Lieutenant John Gorman's Sherman *Ballyragget* bogging in a patch of marshy greensward while on the approach. Ordering two of the other tanks of his troop, No. 4 Troop in No. 2 Squadron, to carry on, Gorman held the fourth tank back to effect a rescue and in about thirty minutes *Ballyragget* was moving again. By this stage the rest of No. 4 Troop was far ahead and, in his haste to rejoin, John Gorman mistook the gesticulations of a wounded fellow officer as an exhortation to advance at best speed. As a result

> we charged up a cornfield, towards a hedge at the top of the rise, and turned the corner into a lane which ran along the hedge. When we swung round into the lane it was horror personified. There 300 yards ahead was a Tiger Royal; behind it and to my right were three other Tigers in support.[72]

Faced with this predicament – and Gorman's tank was not a Firefly – the young officer recalled a discussion with his driver about dealing with just such an occurrence. Rather light-heartedly they had concluded that their only viable tactic was the naval one of ramming. This he now decided to do and gave the order. The Sherman charged forward at the metal monster, its crew as yet unaware of the presence of *Ballyragget*; in fact the Tiger II's main armament – the 88mm gun in its L/71 version – was trained on the main body of No. 2 Squadron at the bottom of the rise where Gorman had seen his fellow officer. This placed the turret gun at a 90-degree angle to the Sherman; the other German tanks were also deployed to fire on the Shermans below. Although the gunner reported a stoppage in *Ballyragget*'s main armament, he managed to clear this and

> as Corporal Baron was accelerating towards the Tiger Royal, Guardsman Scholes from 50 yards was able to put a high-explosive shell onto the Tiger's turret. The effect of such an explosion on a crew confined in a small space is quite devastating and as we raced towards it, the Commander's head emerged from the turret.[73]

John Gorman had gained the precious advantage of surprise over his opponent while the HE shell that smashed into the Tiger II's turret must have added to the Irishman's advantage. The huge turret could traverse but slowly and before it had turned sufficiently to engage the Sherman *Ballyragget* had crashed into the Tiger. After the collision the Tiger's 88 was protruding some two feet beyond the Sherman. Aware that the other Germans would be eager to engage his now disabled Sherman, Gorman ordered his crew to abandon *Ballyragget*, at much the same time as the Tiger's crew abandoned their vehicle. At this point the Sherman that had towed *Ballyragget* out of the boggy ground appeared and was fired on by the other German tanks. Three rounds struck the Sherman which burst into flames; two crew members died immediately while the commander, Sergeant Harbinson, although rescued by one of the other two men, was burned so badly that he died ten days later.[74]

Anxious that the temporarily disabled Tiger II should remain out of action, John Gorman decided that he would seek out his Firefly, commanded by Lance-Sergeant Workman, and 'brew up' the Tiger. It was then that he discovered what the Tiger and its cohorts had been engaged in when *Ballyragget* interrupted their activities.

> The Tiger Royal had fired at Workman and the shot had been high and had taken his head off. So he was lying in the tank over the gun with no head and the turret was absolutely full of blood. The gunner was covered in blood, his sights were covered in blood . . . the loader [was] in the same position. They, just, really were pretty shaken. We got the poor body out of the tank and we cleaned up the sights. We at least got the sights going. The tank was okay.[75]

Taking command of the Firefly, and with another Sherman covering him, Gorman returned to the scene of his encounter with the Tiger II, avoiding the lane on which the Micks' other tanks had been ambushed. Then he gave the gunner the order to fire on the German behemoth.

> Five shots went high and wide, rocketing up into the sky. The gunner's hand was shaking and the sights were smeared with blood, but five misses in succession was too much. 'Take it easy, boy, and have a go at the old Tiger.' The gunner was years older than he, but Lieutenant Gorman had the paternal manner of a policeman, for he had been reared in, and was going back to, the Royal Ulster Constabulary. The gunner took a deep breath and tried again. 'Well done! Two hits on the turret; now put one into the new Tiger.' Three seconds later both the disabled Tiger and the Sherman were burning brightly.[76]

Although 2nd Irish Guards' war diary identifies all the German tanks as Panthers[77], the tank that John Gorman engaged was later identified positively as a Tiger II, the first example of this apotheosis of German tank design seen in Normandy. Although he considered his actions as foolhardy and his survival as a matter of luck, there was no doubt that Gorman's leadership, courage and coolness in a desperate situation had saved several lives and destroyed the enemy tank. This was recognised when he was subsequently awarded the Military Cross for this, his first, action.

Meanwhile German anti-tank guns in le Poirier and Frénouville had stopped the Coldstream while 7th Armoured Division had had 'a frustrating time'.[78] Not until noon did the Desert Rats' first unit, 5th Royal Tanks, clear the bridges over the Orne and, in spite of all efforts, only one armoured regiment – again 5th Royal Tanks – was in action south of the Caen–Vimont railway before darkness. At Grentheville 5th Royal Tanks skirmished with enemy infantry before being counter-attacked by armour; the latter were driven off with the loss of two tanks on each side.[79] But Britain's most famous armoured formation had been unable to play any significant part in this first day of GOODWOOD.

For the crews of VIII Corps' tanks there was little rest that night. The routine of an armoured regiment demanded that tanks be serviced after laagering for the night and this, with other administrative duties, left little time for eating and sleeping. One veteran of 3rd Royal Tanks recalled that

> We leaguered down by a quarry near the embankment. During the night there was some shelling and one or two enemy bombers ranged the area. This made for a disturbed few hours with little chance of sleep. Some replacement tanks and crews came up during the night; most of the crewmen had baled out during that first day.[80]

The second day began early with tank crews ready to move just before 5.00am. There was a little good news: some medium artillery units had moved up during the night to support the renewed advance. But the Germans had also been able to replenish and when the British advance resumed it was against much stronger opposition. Progress was slow. Even so, the company of 1st Rifle Brigade with 5th Royal Tanks captured Soliers, although Major Apsey, commanding the Green Jacket company, was wounded. From there 5th Royal Tanks moved against Bourguébus, knocking out two Tigers and a Panther en route; the village was reached at about 6.00pm. With a direct attack ruled out by the ferocity of the resistance the squadrons began working around both flanks. The nearby village of Four fell to 1st Royal Tanks*, supported by C Company 1st Rifle Brigade less than three hours later. Seventh Armoured Division had made their mark on this second day of GOODWOOD, although Bourguébus remained in enemy hands. Elsewhere, Guards Armoured had occupied Cagny and 11th Armoured took Bras and Hubert-Folie against equally stiff opposition. Rocket-firing Typhoons played an important part in the latter battles; Bras fell to 2nd Northamptonshire Yeomanry and 3rd Royal Tanks, supported by H and F Companies 8th Rifle Brigade while a

* The battalion was now commanded by Lieutenant-Colonel E H Gibbon following the promotion of Michael Carver to the command of 4 Armoured Brigade, which had lost its previous commander, the redoubtable John Currie DSO** MC, who had been killed on 26 June.

squadron of 2nd Fife and Forfar Yeomanry, with G Company 8th Rifle Brigade, took Hubert-Folie. Although many prisoners were taken and much enemy equipment destroyed or captured, this had been achieved at a high cost. Major Bill Close of 3rd Royal Tanks recorded what it meant to his squadron and battalion.

> It had been a hard battle with two days of heavy fighting. The battalion had lost well over sixty tanks with heavy personnel losses. In my own squadron I had lost seventeen tanks out of my complement of nineteen, over half being completely destroyed. All my officers were casualties, except Johnny Langdon, and only one troop sergeant, Buck Kite, was with me at the end. Practically every man in the squadron had baled out at least once.[81]

Close had baled out himself when his tank took a direct hit from an 88 shell that came through the front of his Sherman, killing outright both driver and co-driver.

Bourguébus finally fell next morning to 5th Royal Tanks. Near Bras, the Caen–Falaise road was cut by 4th County of London Yeomanry who took 100 prisoners, captured several guns and knocked out some tanks, including a Tiger. The Canadians, who had cleared Cormelles and Vaucelles the previous day, were beaten back from Verrières; but Guards Armoured took Frénouville. At this point the weather, so often unfavourable since D-Day, took a hand; the skies opened and a violent thunderstorm swept the countryside. Soon slit trenches were flooded and tracks inundated to such an extent that wheeled vehicle movement was impossible; in 7th Armoured Division's area, some tanks bogged down and had, temporarily, to be abandoned. Because of the conditions, a halt was called to Operation GOODWOOD that afternoon.[82]

That evening the armoured brigades were pulled back and infantry relieved them in the line. II Canadian Corps began taking over the right sector of VIII Corps' area while I Corps began relieving Guards Armoured. Even when the armour moved back they continued to receive the enemy's attention; the Desert Rats' historian notes that 22 Armoured Brigade's 5th Royal Tanks 'were heavily shelled' in their laager at Démouville. Next day – 21 July – Montgomery drafted a fresh directive stressing that

> we must improve and retain firmly our present good position on the eastern flank and be ready to take quick action on that flank ... the enemy must be led to believe that we contemplate a major advance towards Falaise and Argentan, and he must be induced to build up his main strength to the east of the river Orne, so that our affairs on the western flank can proceed with greater speed.[83]

At least some of the 'present good position' was due to the efforts of the Canadians and 3rd British Division, whose role in GOODWOOD should not be overlooked. On the final day of battle – the 20th – 2nd Canadian Division, last in action at Dieppe, was charged with capturing the Verrières ridge but, before moving forward, had to await 7th Armoured Division's withdrawal. This gave the Germans time to prepare for a fresh attack on the ridge, which was held by men of 272nd Division supported by 1st SS Panzer Division, with some seventy tanks, while a battlegroup from 2nd Panzer Division was also present, having been moved from the Noyers–Caumont sector. About a hundred tanks awaited the renewed Allied attack while artillery from II SS Panzer Corps was available to help the defenders.[84]

Early in the afternoon four battalions from 4 and 6 Canadian Brigades* and two squadrons of tanks moved forward against the ridge supported by the corps artillery and with Typhoons on call for air support. Although the advancing Canadians reached the Hubert-Folie–St André road, occupying two farms, the troops moving towards Verrières were counter-attacked from the left by enemy armour and infantry. The spearhead troops were cut off, and the remainder withdrew to the road, which was held with difficulty. Meanwhile the units advancing on the right reached their objective on the ridge and were bringing their anti-tank guns up when they, too, were counter-attacked before the guns could be deployed. After some confused fighting they were also driven back to the line of the road. St André sur Orne and St Martin de Fontenay fell to Canadians who held on to both villages against repeated counter-attacks and heavy shellfire from across the Orne; all II SS Panzer Corps' artillery was brought to bear on St André.[85] And then the thunderstorm hit, turning the battlefield into a quagmire, grounding the Typhoons, interfering with radio communications and generally making life miserable, especially for the infantryman.

The battle between Canadians and Germans, Operation ATLANTIC to the former, continued into the next day with 2 Canadian Armoured Brigade** coming under command of 2nd Canadian Division and giving their attackers a bloody nose. Although one counter-attack broke through the Canadians at Point 72, allowing German infantry and tanks to probe almost to Ifs, the situation was restored when a fresh Canadian battalion entered the fray, pushed the enemy back with the support of a creeping

* These were The Essex Scottish, from 4 Brigade, Les Fusiliers Mont Royal, The Queen's Own Cameron Highlanders of Canada and The South Saskatchewan Regiment, from 6 Brigade.

** The brigade included 6th Armoured Regiment (1st Hussars), 10th Armoured Regiment (The Fort Garry Horse) and 27th Armoured Regiment (The Sherbrooke Fusiliers Regiment).

bombardment and sealed the line. Further attacks at dusk were also repulsed. By now, of course, Montgomery had decided to hold his 'present good position'.

For their part 3rd British Division had failed to take Troarn and Emiéville on the 19th but had secured Banneville la Campagne and the Manneville–Guillerville area. With Troarn masked by the division, the ground between there and Emiéville was fairly secure.

The British Official History suggests that GOODWOOD was a success since 'it had greatly improved our position on the eastern flank and had kept the enemy's armoured divisions fighting there'[86] but that it had not achieved all that had been intended. Montgomery makes little mention of GOODWOOD in his *Memoirs* but in *Normandy to the Baltic* states that 'We had, however, largely attained our purpose.'[87] This he details as an advance of 10,000 yards by VIII Corps, clearing Caen's eastern suburbs, more than doubling the size of the Orne bridgehead and mounting a threat to Falaise that caused the enemy to commit reserves to prevent a British breakthrough. In addition, many casualties were inflicted upon the enemy, significant numbers of tanks having been destroyed and some 2,000 prisoners taken.[88] Dempsey, whose plan this operation was, considered GOODWOOD 'highly successful', arguing that VIII Corps'

> plans were efficient and well carried out by formations with the possible exception of 7 Armd Division which he regarded as lacking in drive on this occasion, and in large measure responsible for the fact that the geographical objectives were not entirely gained.[89]

He also stated that

> as soon as the armoured onrush had come to a halt and it was plain that only hard fighting by infantry would enable the advance to continue, the C-in-C and he decided to wind it up as rapidly as possible. In fact this decision was reached by the end of the first day and thereafter his attention was already centred on planning 'Bluecoat'. There were some minor changes of dispositions and some further small engagements before Corps were informed that further major operations were to be called off but these were purely for local tactical reasons.[90]

Dempsey's explanations, made in 1951, have about them a defensive air. It is difficult to accept that the 'plans were efficient' when one considers the congestion and confusion in the bridgehead, the ample warning that the Germans had of the British moves – this was no surprise attack – and the problems with artillery support as the armour advanced. Dempsey's suggestion that 7th Armoured Division lacked drive 'on this occasion' is hardly borne out by the facts, which tend to support the argument that the Desert Rats suffered from congestion in the bridgehead, especially since they were the last armoured division to move out. The late Field Marshal Lord Carver once told this author that he did not consider this criticism of 7th Armoured to be valid. And objective examination of the facts would seem to support Carver rather than Dempsey.[91]

Dempsey cannot be held entirely responsible for GOODWOOD's problems. His plans were approved by Montgomery, whose experience of massive congestion in Operation LIGHTFOOT, the El Alamein offensive in October 1942, should have made him wary of the problems inherent in pushing an armoured corps through such a restricted area as the Orne bridgehead. But Montgomery never seemed to have any real understanding of the limitations of armour – and this from a man whose brother-in-law was the armoured guru Hobart – and demonstrated that lack of understanding to soldiers of 2nd (Armoured) Irish Guards whom, accompanied by the Secretary of State for War, he visited towards the end of the Normandy campaign. Monty chose to make one of his morale-boosting speeches in which he claimed that

> Even though the Germans might escape through the Falaise gap, he hoped to destroy them west of the River Seine. After that, he said, they would 'roll up the Buzz Bomb bases and see the cliffs of Dover from the coast of Calais. In the fighting to date we have defeated the Germans in battle; we have had no difficulty in dealing with the German armour, once we had grasped the problems. . . . We have nothing to fear from the Tiger and the Panther tanks; they are unreliable mechanically, and the Panther is very vulnerable from the flanks. Our 17-[pounder] will go right through them. Provided our tactics are good, we can defeat them without difficulty.'[92]

This speech was made to some very cynical soldiers, many of whom wondered if Montgomery was talking about the same armoured warfare in which they had been engaged. On arriving in France the 'Micks' had seen much evidence of the superiority of German armour, including many burnt-out Shermans; Monty even made this speech against the backdrop of 'dead' Shermans. They also saw some examples of German tanks and wondered at Tigers and Panthers with their gun barrels that seemed to stretch 'from here to Sunday week'.[93] By August, when they listened to Monty's speech, the Irish Guards were aware of what their regimental historian described as 'a basic and ineluctable problem': that all German tanks could destroy the Sherman but that only one Sherman in four – the 17-pounder-equipped Firefly – could put a round through the armour of most German tanks. Further experience in Normandy, and in subsequent fighting, would only strengthen the average British tankman's view that he fought in a tank with 'the softest armour known to man' that would burn when hit to such an extent that he called the Sherman the 'Ronson'* while his foes dubbed it the 'Tommy Cooker'.

Was GOODWOOD any more than an effort to draw German forces off the Americans, now preparing to break out of the bridgehead? Montgomery insisted that this was all that was intended and Dempsey argued that this was the limit of his intentions. And yet, in the afternoon of the first day of GOODWOOD, Montgomery sent a highly optimistic signal to Brooke claiming that the morning's operations had been completely successful and issued a press communiqué suggesting that Second Army had broken through. Even the following day, when Brooke visited Montgomery at his headquarters, the CIGS found 21 Army Group's commander 'in grand form and delighted with his success east of Caen'.[94] But that press statement had done much to harm Montgomery's reputation, especially with the Americans, and has led to considerable argument over the objectives of GOODWOOD since. Dempsey denied that there was a strategic objective in the form of a planned breakout, maintaining that the aim was to pin down the enemy on the eastern flank. When told that the original Second Army instruction, issued on 13 July, 'specified that one armoured division was eventually to be positioned in Falaise' and that this instruction had been copied to Eisenhower's headquarters but that no cancellation of it was made generally, Dempsey insisted that he 'had never before heard of this instruction and, expressing surprise, asked to see a copy'; this was forwarded for his inspection at the War Office on 13 March 1951. No doubt, this was the document that led to the misunderstanding between Eisenhower and Montgomery and has caused the spilling of so much ink and the expending of so much energy in argument over the past sixty years.

Dempsey concluded that

> The Press interpreted the battle as a deliberate attempt to break-out, and one that had failed. *Their misappreciation followed the view taken in various higher quarters, R. A. F. and American.* Maurice Chilton, my Chief of Staff, was very upset about it and urged me to take steps to check such a 'slander'. I told him: 'Don't worry – it will aid our purpose and act as the best possible cover-plan'. For I could see that such criticism would tend to convince the enemy that we were trying to break-out in the Caen area, and would help to keep him fixed there while Bradley was mounting his fresh break-out attack.[95]

* From the advertising slogan of the eponymous cigarette-lighter manufacturer that their product lit first time, every time.

Whatever the true intention, GOODWOOD had ground to a standstill with heavy losses to both sides. Allied infantry casualties were high – in spite of the avowed intention to minimise them by using the largest possible armoured force. Losses totalled 5,537 in all arms. The greatest toll – 1,818 killed, wounded or missing – fell on VIII Corps with I Corps suffering 1,656 casualties, II Canadian Corps slightly less at 1,614 and XII Corps 449; XXX Corps, with no direct part in GOODWOOD, had 631 casualties for the same period of 18–22 July.[96] Since D-Day Second Army had lost 45,795 casualties; those for GOODWOOD account for almost fourteen per cent of all British casualties since the campaign opened. Small wonder that, in his classic account of the battle for Caen, Alexander McKee describes GOODWOOD as the 'death ride of the armoured divisions'.* Both Dempsey and Montgomery considered that the armour was less precious than the infantry: Dempsey wrote that

> our strength in tanks was increasing all the time – tank reinforcements were pouring into Normandy faster than the rate of tank casualties. So we could well afford, and it was desirable, to plan an operation in which we could utilise that surplus of tanks, and economise infantry.[98]

Such an attitude – and it reflects Montgomery's when planning Operation SUPERCHARGE at El Alamein, when he was prepared to accept 100 per cent casualties in the armour – indicates a lack of understanding of armour's capabilities and even its basic role; it certainly shows no sign of an understanding of the necessity for armour and infantry to work in close harmony. And it almost suggests that both men felt that tanks could be knocked out without losing their crews. The degree of callousness inherent in that attitude can also be perceived in Dempsey's refusal to allow O'Connor to use improvised APCs for his infantry; although that may equally have been a result of Dempsey's lack of vision.

The plain fact remained that GOODWOOD had come to a standstill and Second Army would have to re-organise for another attack. This time 21 Army Group would punch with both fists: Bradley's First Army had taken St Lô and was preparing to break out of Normandy. If Montgomery had intended to push Second Army through the crust of the enemy defences before the Americans it was now too late.

While Montgomery, Bradley and Dempsey planned their new offensive the list of *dramatis personae* on the German side had lost one principal

* This is the title given by McKee to the chapter of his book, *Caen: Anvil of Victory*, dealing with GOODWOOD.[97]

character. On 17 July, the day before GOODWOOD, Field Marshal Erwin Rommel was travelling towards the little Norman town of Vimoutiers, unaware that his foes in 21 Army Group were about to approve a plan for the SAS to raid his headquarters at la Roche Guyon and kill him, when fate, in the form of Allied fighter aircraft, intervened. The air sentry in the back of Rommel's car spotted planes and shouted a warning. Rommel's driver attempted to reach a spot where it might have been possible to take cover but the leading fighter hit them before this could happen and the car swerved and crashed off the road. Rommel had already been wounded before the second plane strafed the car and its occupants again. The Desert Fox was treated in a nearby French monastic hospital before being moved to a military hospital at Bernay, some twenty-five miles away. His driver, Daniel, died of his injuries while Rommel suffered a fractured skull and facial injuries. The Desert Fox's part in the Normandy battle was over.

Three days later, Rommel's life entered its final phase when a bomb exploded in a hut at Hitler's headquarters at Rastenburg in East Prussia. Although several men were killed or mortally wounded, Hitler survived. In the aftermath of this failed plot to assassinate the Führer, Rommel was implicated in its planning, if only by association with some of the planners, and was subsequently forced to commit suicide to protect his wife and son – and the carefully nurtured image of a German hero. That image even crossed to the opposing side with Winston Churchill making favourable comment on this great general in the House of Commons. For Rommel was admired in the British forces and had become a legend within those forces during the North African campaign. He would live long in the memories of men who had fought against him.

NOTES

1 Ellis, *Victory in the West*, p. 309.
2 Reynolds, *Sons of the Reich*, p. 30.
3 Ibid.
4 NA, CAB106/963.
5 Quoted in Baverstock, *Breaking the Panzers. The Bloody Battle for Rauray, Normandy, 1 July 1944*, p. 155.
6 Baverstock, p. 154.
7 Reynolds, *Sons of the Reich*, pp. 30–1.
8 Ibid, p. 31.
9 Quoted in ibid, p. 31.
10 Quoted in McKee, *Caen: Anvil of Victory*, p. 195.
11 Le Geste du Régiment de la Chaudière, quoted in McKee, op cit, p. 194. As befits a French-Canadian regiment, the regimental war diary was also written in French.
12 Ibid.
13 Meyer, quoted in Reynolds, *Steel Inferno*, p. 146.
14 Ibid, pp. 146–7.

15 Stacey, *The Victory Campaign*, p. 155.
16 Reynolds, *Steel Inferno*, p. 148.
17 Ibid, p. 149.
18 Ellis, op cit, p. 311.
19 Reynolds, *Steel Inferno*, p. 149.
20 Quoted in D'Este, *Decision in Normandy*, p. 309.
21 Ibid, p. 311.
22 Middlebrook & Everitt, *The Bomber Command War Diaries*, p. 539.
23 Ellis, op cit, op cit, p. 314.
24 Ibid.
25 Ibid, p. 316.
26 Ibid, p. 315.
27 Reynolds, *Steel Inferno*, op cit, p. 155.
28 Ibid.
29 Ellis, op cit, p. 315.
30 Doherty, *Only The Enemy*, p. 144.
31 Information from David Truesdale.
32 Reynolds, *Steel Inferno*, p. 156.
33 Belchem, *Victory in Normandy*, p. 150.
34 How, *Hill 112*, p. 146.
35 Quoted in Ellis, op cit, p. 318.
36 Carver, *Out of Step*, p. 193.
37 Ibid.
38 How, op cit, p. 160.
39 Reynolds, *Sons of the Reich*, p. 39.
40 Carver, op cit, p. 194.
41 Ellis, op cit, p. 318.
42 NA, WO285/10.
43 Ellis, op cit, p. 328.
44 Ibid.
45 Ibid, p. 329.
46 NA, CAB106/1061.
47 NA, WO171/838, war diary, 4/7 RDG.
48 Ibid.
49 Quoted in Ellis, op cit, pp. 333–4.
50 Ellis, op cit, p. 336.
51 NA, CAB106/1061.
52 Baynes, *The Forgotten Victor*, pp. 204–5.
53 Ellis, op cit, p. 335.
54 Reynolds, *Steel Inferno*, p. 171.
55 Ibid.
56 Ibid.
57 Jarymowycz, *Tank Tactics from Normandy to Lorraine*, p. 100.
58 Ellis, op cit, p. 336.
59 Reynolds, *Steel Inferno*, p. 172.
60 Stacey, *The Victory Campaign*, p. 168.
61 Quoted in Baynes, op cit, p. 199.
62 NA, CAB106/1061.
63 VIII Corps History, p. 78.
64 Ellis, op cit, pp. 337– 8.
65 Lieut (now Sir) John Gorman MC, 2 Ir Gds.
66 NA, WO171/439 war diary, 7th Armd Division.
67 Ellis, op cit, p. 340.

68 Ibid.
69 Ibid.
70 NA, WO171/287, war diary, VIII Corps HQ.
71 Ellis, op cit, p. 342.
72 Gorman, *Times of my Life*, p. 38.
73 Ibid, pp. 38–9.
74 Doherty, *Irish Volunteers in the Second World War*, p. 238.
75 Ibid.
76 Fitzgerald, *History of the Irish Guards in the Second World War*, pp. 382–3.
77 NA, WO171/1256, war diary, 2 Ir Gds.
78 Ellis, op cit, p. 343.
79 Verney, *The Desert Rats*, p. 205.
80 Close, *A View from the Turret*, p. 124.
81 Ibid, p. 130.
82 Verney, op cit, p. 207.
83 Quoted in Ellis, op cit, pp. 350–1.
84 Ibid, p. 349.
85 Ibid, p. 350.
86 Ibid, p. 351.
87 Montgomery, *From Normandy to the Baltic*, p. 250.
88 Ibid.
89 NA, CAB106/1061.
90 Ibid.
91 Carver to author.
92 Fitzgerald, op cit, p. 247.
93 Ibid, p. 366.
94 Brooke, *War Diaries*, p. 571.
95 NA, CAB106/1061.
96 NA, WO171/139 war diary, 21 Army Gp, A Br.
97 McKee, *Caen*: *Anvil of Victory*, pp. 263–82.
98 NA, CAB106/1061.

CHAPTER XI

The final battles

Show us here the mettle of your pasture

Dempsey was already planning Second Army's next offensive as GOODWOOD bogged down in the mire of the thunderstorm. To the right Bradley had secured the start line he had long wanted for his breakout. Both armies had learned many valuable lessons thus far, with the Americans introducing a device enabling the Sherman to burst through the bocage's high banks; this was the Culin cutter, devised by Sergeant Curtis G Culin Jr from New York,*[1] but inspired by another soldier's off-the-cuff comment, a set of prongs made from metal salvaged from beach obstacles. British tanks were also fitted with these prongs but, generally, too late for use in Normandy.

The value of close co-operation between armour and infantry had been brought home forcefully to the British – yet again – with measures introduced to create more harmonious liaison. Possibly the principal measure was the creation of battlegroups in which infantry and armour worked together. So quickly was this innovation implemented that Guards Armoured Division, which had probably the best organisation to establish really harmonious, integrated battlegroups, forced some strange marriages. Instead of marrying like with like, the division established battlegroups that married Irish and Coldstream battalions, 2nd (Armoured) Irish with 5th (Motor) Coldstream and 1st (Armoured) Coldstream with 3rd (Motor) Irish, although Grenadiers did 'marry' Grenadiers. This arrangement was simply a matter of happenstance; the Irish Guards' historian notes that armoured Irish and motor Coldstream battalions were camped in neighbouring fields when the organisation was created. In September, the marriages would be 'modified' to match Irish armour with Irish infantry and Coldstream armour with Coldstream infantry; both brigade headquarters remained in being. Across the divisions of Second Army similar marriages were performed.[2]

* Culin was awarded the Legion of Merit for his invention. Although he tried to have the soldier who gave him the idea acknowledged formally this never happened. Culin was invalided home after losing a leg in the battle for the Hürtgen forest.

From now on Second Army would send infantry into battle mounted on tanks from their affiliated armoured units. And O'Connor's idea of armoured personnel carriers would become reality when First Canadian Army put APCs into the field in Operation TOTALIZE in early August.[3] Had such tactics been used in GOODWOOD the operation might well have led to a British breakout. As it was, Rommel, *in absentia*, had won his last battle against his adversary of El Alamein. For this was the only occasion in Normandy when the Germans fought a battle in which they enjoyed tactical advantage, as well as the strategic advantage of knowing when and where the attack was to be launched.

On the other side of the hill Field Marshal Gunther von Kluge, in addition to his responsibilities as C-in-C West, had assumed command of Army Group B following Rommel's wounding. Von Kluge had been sceptical of reports to OKW from his predecessors but, although his forces had held against GOODWOOD and ATLANTIC, he now realised that neither von Rundstedt nor Rommel had exaggerated: there was no hope of Germany obtaining a victory over the Allies in Normandy; and certainly no possibility of the invaders being pushed back into the sea. Carlo D'Este sums up von Kluge's situation thus:

> GOODWOOD shattered the false optimism . . . implanted in von Kluge by OKW and Hitler, and even he was forced to accept that the fighting ability of his forces had been sapped to the point of desperation. Strategically, the new positions he was forced to defend with Panzer Group West were hopeless. There was little left with which to reinforce Eberbach, and if this line cracked the entire flank would collapse. Had Rommel been permitted to build a new defensive network weeks before when his panzer divisions still retained most of their strength, it might have been a different matter. Now, however, the only unanswered question in von Kluge's mind was how much longer Army Group B could continue to hold out.[4]

To date, the contest in Normandy had been like a match between top soccer teams with the visiting side enjoying many advantages although the home team had greater experience and better training. But the match conditions tired the experienced team to the point of exhaustion and, despite their legendary determination, grittiness and innovative skills, their opponents, although also tired, had greater weight and more resources. As the match approached its conclusion the visitors were also beginning to use those advantages to much better purpose. But it was the men in the officials' dugouts who would stamp their marks indelibly on the contest. Von Kluge, experienced and confident of his men's ability, was suffering doubts for the first time and knew that the end was not far off. Opposing him were two managers, or three, if one includes Eisenhower, with Montgomery the most experienced but lacking confidence in his team, as he had done in North Africa, and Bradley lacking experience, but learning rapidly, and with confidence in his protégés; Eisenhower was happy to call encouragement from the directors' box. Von Kluge had now come to agree with Rommel; the struggle could be won only by the Allies. He wrote to Hitler saying that 'there is no way of finding a battle technique which will neutralise the positively annihilating effects of their air attacks short of giving up the battle area', going on to point out that the moment was fast approaching 'when this front already so severely strained will break'. Once that happened the Allies would be in relatively open country where the Germans' lack of mobility would be a deadly disadvantage.[5] This letter did not reach Hitler until 23 July, or even later, which was not the most propitious time to give such news to the Nazi dictator, although, according to the British Official History, there is evidence that Hitler had begun to consider withdrawal from Normandy and that OKW was making plans for alternative defensive lines along the Seine, the Somme and in the Vosges mountains.[6]

By the time that Hitler received von Kluge's despairing missive, further changes were occurring in 21 Army Group. Crerar's First Canadian Army became operational on 23 July with I British Corps under command and responsibility for the Allied eastern flank. II Canadian Corps remained under Second Army with Dempsey extending his right flank westwards to Caumont, relieving the US division there. At the same time US forces were re-organising to create 12 US Army Group*, including First Army and Third Army; this grouping would become operational on 1 August with Bradley commanding.[7] Although Montgomery would command all ground forces until Eisenhower decided to take direct command and bring SHAEF headquarters to France, the Americans were paying less and less attention to Montgomery, whose star was on the wane in their eyes. (Bradley commented that he and Montgomery were on equal footing as army group commanders from the moment 12 US Army Group became operational but acknowledges that Montgomery maintained *temporary* overall command as Eisenhower's deputy.[8])

The American seizure of St Lô on 19 July allowed First Army to make ready for a major offensive from there. This was to be Operation COBRA, due to be launched on 24 July; with the British Operation BLUECOAT, to be launched six days later, this marked the first truly strategic offensive by 21 Army Group and the beginning of the German armies' death agonies. The

* This title was chosen to continue the illusion that there was still a First US Army Group in south-east England, making ready to move to the mainland.

American offensive from St Lô was to lead to the breakout from Normandy and thus has become the subject of many claims, including the inevitable American claims that it was planned as a breakout, which begs the question: what were American forces trying to do beforehand? They also include the inevitable Montgomery claim of credit for the concept of the operation[9], reiterated by Montgomery's biographer Nigel Hamilton, who points out that COBRA simply fulfilled a strategy defined by Montgomery on several occasions since D-Day.[10] Indeed it could be argued that had COBRA been co-ordinated with GOODWOOD – it had originally been intended to begin on 19 July – the Allied breakout might have occurred sooner. However, COBRA was delayed by First Army's difficulties before St Lô, followed by adverse weather that prevented the heavy bomber strikes Bradley wanted before launching his ground forces. In the period between the end of GOODWOOD and the opening of COBRA, Montgomery ordered pressure to be maintained on the eastern flank to strengthen further the 'German belief that we contemplated a major advance towards Falaise and Argentan, and encourage the Germans to keep on building up strength in the east rather than against the Americans'.[11] To achieve this, II Canadian Corps was to make a limited attack down the Falaise road on the 25th. Planned to begin at dawn, this was scheduled originally to follow COBRA, but poor weather kept the bombers on the ground and COBRA did not get underway until the 25th.

Preparations for II Canadian Corps' attack, reinforced by Guards and 7th Armoured Divisions, were observed by the Germans, convincing Eberbach that a renewal of the GOODWOOD offensive would coincide with better weather that would allow the air forces to support ground troops. Assuming that the British aimed to break through to Mézidon and Falaise, Eberbach used the lull in operations to bolster his eastern flank; 9th SS Panzer Division deployed to the woods west of Bretteville sur Laize, which would allow it to hit the flank of any British southward thrust. After relief by 326th Infantry Division near Caumont, 2nd Panzer Division crossed the Orne to be close to 9th SS Panzer while 116th Panzer Division, just arrived from Fifteenth Army, concentrated near St Sylvain. Although 10th SS Panzer Division was still in action, Eberbach also intended to move it to Bretteville as soon as possible.[12]

Before dawn on 25 July, II Canadian Corps advanced along the axis of the Caen–Falaise road. East of that road, 3rd Canadian Division, supported by 2 Canadian Armoured Brigade, struck out from Bourguébus towards Tilly la Campagne, which was held by 1st SS Panzer Division, which was also deployed in the neighbouring area with reinforcements in the woods behind la Hogue. Before the sky had lightened the Germans had counter-attacked, starting a day-long battle. By nightfall, the leading Canadian brigade had suffered heavy losses with its supporting tank squadron all but wiped out. The attack had come to naught and the survivors retired to Bourguébus. Meanwhile, 2nd Canadian Division had also moved off in the early hours, advancing west of the Falaise road with two brigades abreast. On the right flank the attack was soon halted. St Martin and St André sur Orne were entered but neither was freed from enemy troops and while Canadian soldiers twice entered May sur Orne before noon they were forced to withdraw on both occasions. At Fontenay le Marmion the attacking battalion lost over 300 casualties and could not wrest the village from its defenders. There was slightly more success on the left flank where Verrières was captured and held but efforts to advance to Rocquancourt were stopped by intense anti-tank fire on the rise beyond Verrières. Throughout the day over 1,700 sorties were flown by the air forces in support of II Canadian Corps, with rocket-firing Typhoons flying over fifty missions in direct response to requests for help from ground troops.[13]

This was the limit of the Canadian operation. Although the armour waited to advance down the Falaise road, there was no gap to exploit since enemy defences had stopped the infantry. Tanks of the Desert Rats and 2 Canadian Armoured Brigade deployed to blunt counter-attacks and, in brisk fighting with elements of 1st and 9th SS Panzer Divisions, inflicted heavy losses on the enemy but lost fifty-six tanks themselves, the equivalent of an armoured regiment. Guards Armoured Division was not called forward to battle. With Canadian casualties at some 1,500 men in this cruel day's fighting,[14] Dempsey decided to call off the offensive that, at least, had helped the Americans in the west; the latter had met much weaker opposition and was making headway despite heavy casualties when American aircraft bombed soldiers of 9th and 30th Divisions.* Among the dead was Lieutenant-General Lesley J McNair, the new titular commander of First US Army Group and the highest-ranking US Army officer to die in combat in Europe. McNair was buried in secrecy with news of his death suppressed until a new commander could be announced for his fictional command, which was still in England.[16]

Bradley was disappointed with the first day's advance in COBRA which saw his troops move only two miles. But the following day things began to improve, although VIII Corps met stout resistance while VII Corps was able to gain ground; but a 'daring gamble by General Collins to deepen his penetration in the target area by committing two . . . mobile armoured columns before the time was ripe for an exploitation'[17] made the difference and the Americans suddenly found the enemy crumbling. Bradley then placed VIII Corps under General George Patton, who was waiting for his Third Army headquarters to become operational on 1 August; Middleton continued as corps commander. Suddenly there was a war of movement.

* Over 600 men were killed or wounded in the two divisions; Carlo D'Este places the figures at 111 dead and 490 wounded.[15]

Within days US armour was forging ahead with four armoured divisions beginning to move south of Coutances by the 29th. Next day VIII Corps' leading formation, 4th Armored Division, entered Avranches, gateway to Brittany and southern Normandy. From Avranches, Combat Command A of 4th Armored took Pontaubault, four miles south, and the still intact bridge over the Sélune river, which ensured that the channel to the west and south could be consolidated. Crossings of the Sée and Sienne rivers were also taken.[18]

Von Kluge told his chief of staff, Blumentritt, that the Americans would be able to do what they wanted once they got through at Avranches. Describing the scene as 'a madhouse' he accepted that, without reinforcement in infantry and anti-tank weapons, his left wing was doomed and although two armoured divisions had been moved from the British sector these were mauled so badly that they could not provide the necessary strength. And now George Patton 'the Allied general the Germans most feared'[19] was about to be let loose. On 1 August 12 US Army Group became operational under Bradley who handed command of First Army to Courtney Hodges while Patton's Third Army became operational with Troy Middleton's VIII Corps and Wade Haislip's XV Corps under command. Third Army was about to begin its famous race into Brittany but Bradley was to ensure that the bulk of Third Army would move in a different direction – eastwards to the Seine through the Orléans gap; this decision was taken on 3 August and Montgomery agreed immediately. As he had done at El Alamein, Monty was now to seize an opportunity offered by circumstances and later declare it to be the natural outworking of his master plan. In doing so, he demeaned the American initiative – it is difficult to conceive of any British general, except O'Connor, taking the gamble taken by 'Lightning Joe' Collins – and his own ability to change strategy and tactics to match conditions.

Realising that First US Army had now delivered the 'main blow of the whole Allied plan' and 'was making excellent progress' Montgomery resolved to do whatever possible to further American operations.[20] With all six enemy armoured divisions facing Second British and First Canadian Armies now deployed east of Noyers, he decided that Second Army should attack west of Noyers to 'deal a very heavy blow . . . where there was no armour at all'.[21] Dempsey was to regroup for a fresh offensive with at least six divisions from the Caumont area; this operation would begin as soon as possible. Eisenhower asked Montgomery to speed up Second Army's attack in the Caumont area:

> I feel very strongly that a three-division attack now on Second Army's right flank will be worth more than six-division attack in five days' time . . . now as never before opportunity is staring us in the

> face. Let us go all out on the lines you have laid down . . . and let us not waste an hour in getting the whole affair started.[22]

Second Army was about to launch Operation BLUECOAT which would lead to some of the toughest fighting seen in Normandy. Beforehand, there was a re-organisation throughout the British and Canadian sector with both armies shifting their weight towards the Allied centre, requiring virtually every formation in both armies adjusting position. In VIII Corps, some formations did not receive movement orders until almost noon on 28 July and then

> had to pull out from the other side of the Orne and drive forty or fifty miles along roundabout and crowded routes through the back areas, always mindful of the need for secrecy. Thanks to good staff work, good march discipline and, above all things, air superiority, all needed for opening the attack on the 30th were able to cross their start lines (hastily briefed and a little breathless, perhaps) on time.[23]

Second Army was to attack with XXX and VIII Corps south from Caumont into the country between the Orne and Vire and prevent the Germans from using the hills about Mont Pinçon on which to pivot a staged withdrawal from the American assault. At the same time, pressure was to be maintained all along the British and Canadian front. Although from Caumont it was difficult to distinguish specific features on the wooded ridges to the south, two hills were prominent: Point 361 at the western end of Mont Pinçon ridge and Point 309, two miles to the west. The former is about 1,200 feet above sea level and topped by woods; it was to be the first day's objective for 43rd (Wessex) Division of XXX Corps while 50th (Northumbrian) was to secure Amaye sur Seulles near Villers-Bocage on the Wessexmen's left. Point 309, distinguishable by quarry workings just below the summit, was assigned to 15th (Scottish) Division of VIII Corps on the first day. To the Scots' right, 11th Armoured was to secure the area around St Martin des Besaces. Each corps would have an armoured division in reserve, ready to exploit progress; these were 7th Armoured in XXX Corps and Guards in VIII Corps.

The country into which Second Army was to attack was difficult, being the densest form of bocage with many tree-covered hills and valleys. Of metalled roads there were few and only one capable of carrying two-way traffic led south from Caumont; others were narrow by-roads or farm tracks lined with high hedges and banks while many small streams cut through the landscape in every direction. Picturesque these may be in peacetime but they presented a nuisance to advancing fighting units, especially since the bridges could support neither tanks nor other heavy vehicles, while the banks were marshy. Two large rivers, the Vire, on the west flank of the advance, and the Souleuvre, crossing the front some ten miles south of Caumont, had cut deep valleys into the countryside and were major obstacles, especially for armour.

The haste with which BLUECOAT was planned reduced the potential artillery and air support and, to preserve secrecy and obtain maximum surprise, there would be no preparatory counter-battery or air bombardments. Once the attack had begun, the Gunners would fire concentrations on known German forward defence positions and against entrenched positions in the bocage; some seventy-five per cent of the 25-pounder shells were fused for air burst.* Subsequently advancing troops would be supported, as required, by bombardments or concentrations of fire. About an hour after the attack began, Bomber Command was to attack four areas some three miles ahead of XXX Corps and Ninth Air Force was to bomb three areas ahead of VIII Corps. During the afternoon a further bombing attack would be made on 15th (Scottish) Division's final objective. As ever, close support would be on call from the tactical air forces. But the weather that had so often hindered air operations since D-Day intervened yet again; 30 July dawned grey and sultry with thick, low clouds that permitted no fighter or fighter-bomber attacks until the afternoon. The heavies were also affected; more than half the 700 Bomber Command aircraft assigned to XXX Corps' front were recalled since their targets were not visible; the remainder bombed Amaye sur Seulles and Cahagnes from low level – less than 2,000 feet – while American mediums struck at les Loges and Dampierre, in front of VIII Corps, through dense cloud.[24] The preliminaries did not augur well for Second Army.

Both corps began their advances on three-brigade fronts with XXX Corps leading off on the left at about 6.00am with two Northumbrian brigades – 56 and 231 – and one Wessex – 130. Thirty minutes later, VIII Corps moved off, led by 227 Brigade of 15th (Scottish) Division and 29 Armoured and 159 Brigades from 11th Armoured. Intense fire met them but their biggest problem in the early phase came from extensive minefields along the front. Although Sappers had spent the night clearing and marking routes to the start lines and 79th Armoured Division's Flails accompanied the leading brigades to beat paths through the minefields, those obstructions were a greater hindrance than expected. The Germans had had plenty of time to sow these 'Devil's Gardens' since, around Caumont, the front had changed hardly at all since mid-June. For some six weeks, until only a few days before BLUECOAT was launched, 2nd Panzer Division had held this front and appeared to have had mines in plenty

* An airburst shell, as its name implies, exploded above the ground and discharged shrapnel on anyone beneath the burst. Airburst shells were especially effective against infantry, even those who were dug in with no overhead protection.

which they had scattered all over their forward area and about emergency reserve positions. For their part, the Allied divisions opposing them had also been liberal in the use of mines, especially on possible enemy routes of advance.[25]

The Northumbrian brigades, each supported by a squadron of tanks from 8 Armoured Brigade, began crossing the main Caen–Caumont road at about 6.00am and thrust towards the seam line of 276th and 326th Infantry Divisions. On the left 231 Brigade fought through wooded ground between Orbois and St Germain d'Ectot, making steady progress and repulsing a counter-attack from elements of 276th Division. When night fell the brigade held a shallow bridgehead across a stream some 2,000 yards from its start line. Their fellow north-countrymen of 56 Brigade were less successful; having cleared the forward slope of St Germain d'Ectot ridge soon after crossing the start line, they were unable to advance down the reverse slope due to the attentions of the Germans deployed in strength on the next ridge, less than a mile away.

The third attacking formation on the XXX Corps front was 130 Brigade of 43rd (Wessex) Division, which attacked at 8.00am. For this assault, 130 Brigade was strengthened by an additional battalion and supported by an armoured regiment; the group's task was to take Briquessard and the area around Cahagnes, some two miles to the south. Briquessard was bombed by a single RAF heavy; the attack was particularly successful, shaking the garrison so much that the village was in British hands soon after midday. Thereafter a crossing was made of the stream behind the village. However, a mile to the right, the advance ran into fields full of anti-personnel mines, which hampered progress while, on one short stretch of lateral road, Sappers uncovered forty-nine anti-tank mines laid by the Americans during their time holding this front. Eventually, at 7.00pm, a fresh attack was made against Cahagnes, this time from the north-west. By nightfall leading elements of 130 Brigade had cleared la Londe and the high ground just before Cahagnes was reached by midnight. As the Official Historian comments 'It had been an unrewarding and rather baffling day for XXX Corps'.[26]

In contrast, VIII Corps made much better progress and day's end saw its leading elements up to six miles south of Caumont. O'Connor led with the Jocks of 15th (Scottish) Division on the left flank and 11th Armoured on the right; 6 Guards Tank Brigade supported the Scottish infantry while 11th Armoured had been re-organised into two balanced battlegroups.[27] The lessons of GOODWOOD had been taken to heart; and not before time for this battle was being fought in tight bocage where the advantage lay with the defending infantryman with his Panzerfaust, the anti-tank gunners with their skilfully concealed weapons, or the machine gunners with their devastating weapons. And thus 11th Armoured Division advanced in two columns with 29 Armoured Brigade commanding the left column, of two armoured regiments, the motor battalion and an infantry battalion, while 159 Brigade commanded the right column with an armoured regiment and two infantry battalions; 2nd Northamptonshire Yeomanry, the divisional reconnaissance regiment, followed up under divisional command. The division's tasks included right flank protection for 15th (Scottish) Division, capturing St Martin des Besaces and the ridge west of the village, and exploiting south-westwards beyond the Forêt l'Evêque.

The left column of 11th Armoured advanced steadily during the morning and skirted the fighting around Sept Vents. About the wooded ground near Cussy some sharp skirmishes occurred which continued throughout the afternoon. When darkness fell the leading troops of the right column were past Dampierre, by which time their fellows on the left had taken St Jean des Essartiers, about two miles short of St Martin. At several points along the front the division was in contact with the enemy while farther west their neighbours in the American sector – of V US Corps – had been impeded beyond the Caumont–St Lô road. There would be no halt for the night; 11th Armoured was to continue its advance while the corps armoured car regiment went forward ready to exploit the situation at dawn on 31 July.[28]

Meanwhile 15th (Scottish) Division had also had a brisk day's fighting, having moved off on a single-brigade front; this was 227 Brigade, reinforced by a fourth battalion and accompanied by A and B Squadrons 15th (Scottish) Reconnaissance Regiment. The infantry soon met opposition: on reaching the forward slopes of Caumont ridge they were struck by heavy defensive fire while seven Churchills from 3rd (Tank) Battalion Scots Guards, of 6 Tank Brigade, and two Flails were knocked out by mines. Following this inauspicious start paths through the minefields were cleared for the tanks that soon came up to the infantry. Both recce squadrons 'mopped up pockets of German resistance along the way but it was a difficult advance with hedges, woods and the inevitable mines to hamper movement'.[29] However, by 10 o'clock the first objectives had fallen although there remained the dangerous task of winkling out snipers and Panzerfaust parties. This delayed the infantry who would carry out the next phase of the attack but the tanks surged ahead under artillery cover. As they advanced the Churchills poured machine-gun fire into hedges and orchards and shelled every building. Early afternoon saw the tanks at Point 226, near les Loges; the Hervieux carrefour was but a mile to the west and some tanks were soon at that crossroads. The latter were then ordered to seize the hill at Point 309, without waiting for infantry, while other tanks carried an infantry battalion forward to lend support. This move was made because 15th (Scottish) Division's left flank was exposed to the enemy, 43rd (Wessex) having been held up across the corps boundary. Executing this move the Churchills found that la Morichesse les Mares was held by enemy tanks and infantry and thus wheeled left to race straight for the hill. Some tanks bogged or overturned but the others carried on and by 7.00pm the leading squadron was atop the hill to find that the Germans had retreated hastily. Although there was some sniping from nearby undergrowth, the hill was held until the infantry arrived as dusk was falling.

Around les Loges, which 6 Guards Tank Brigade had been ordered 'to hold at all costs',[30] the Churchill squadron and infantry company deployed about Point 226 were buffeted severely by shell and mortar fire, which began at about 6.00pm. In a matter of minutes, eight Churchills had been knocked out. Then a trio of Jagdpanthers* appeared over the hill to knock out several more Churchills. But the German tank destroyers were engaged by the other Guards tanks and driven off; two were later found abandoned nearby, their tracks shot off. Unusually, the Germans did not follow up this attack – a sure sign that they were being worn down – and, with infantry reinforcements arriving, the area around Point 226 was re-organised. Infantry continued mopping-up operations in the 15th (Scottish) area until after midnight by which time 46 Brigade held Point 309 in strength, its anti-tank guns having been manhandled up the hill. Other brigades deployed in echelon to protect the open left flank while the Guards' tanks overnighted with the infantry in their forward areas. For the Churchill crews this had been their first day in action but they had lived and trained with the infantry for more than a year and trust had grown up between them. It had been a successful first day.

Although 15th (Scottish) Division's flank was open there was much more disruption and disorganisation in the enemy ranks. Second Army's advance had exposed the flank of II Parachute Corps, which was facing the Americans in the neighbouring sector; the paratroopers had lost all contact with 326th Division on their right. The latter's headquarters had been knocked out by a bombing attack while two of its regimental headquarters were surrounded by British tanks. Such was II Parachute Corps' predicament that von Kluge authorised a withdrawal after nightfall to fresh positions running westward from St Martin. This was not von Kluge's only move; he also ordered 21st Panzer to join LXXIV Corps near Caumont. The division began moving from east of the Orne, where it had been in reserve, late in the day, while it was still light and, harried by Allied aircraft, its leading tanks took some five hours to cover twenty miles. Those tanks were about three miles short of Cahagnes by 10.00pm.[31]

There was no let up in Second Army and, thanks to the Sappers' endeavours, the minefields that had delayed XXX Corps had been cleared

* The Jagdpanther, or hunter-panther, was a Pz Mk V, or Panther, tank chassis on which was mounted an 88mm anti-tank gun, which was capable of destroying any Allied tank.

or breached by the morning of the 31st, allowing 43rd (Wessex) to begin a right hook against Cahagnes by dawn. As the Wessexmen drew within striking distance of the village they were met by a sharp enemy riposte that developed into a bitter close-quarter battle. Eventually the Germans were driven off with severe losses and Cahagnes fell into British hands that afternoon. Thereafter ground south of the Briquessard stream was cleared and St Pierre du Fresne was liberated. But the first dawn of August saw yet another German counter-attack with infantry supported by armour. Once this assault had been beaten off, the Wessex Division's advance continued towards Point 361, the hill at the Bois du Homme's eastern corner. German resilience was demonstrated as the first British troops reached Point 361 to be attacked by three heavy tanks; but two of the beasts bogged and the third fell victim to an anti-tank gun.[32]

The Desert Rats had been ordered to move forward through the Wessex Division's area to take Aunay sur Audon from the west, 50th (Northumbrian) Division having been delayed in its advance towards Amaye sur Seulles. For the men of 7th Armoured, what followed must have created a feeling of déjà vu as they met traffic congestion en route. With a lack of roads running south on XXX Corps' front and the bocage restricting movement to roads, the division was forced to move through the outskirts of Caumont. There they ran into elements of other divisions, including the tail of 43rd (Wessex), all trying to negotiate the town. The Desert Rats could but crawl forward. By nightfall their leading tanks were only at Breuil, still five miles short of Aunay. Of enemy opposition there had been little; the real delays had been caused by 'appalling congestion'.[33] Thus XXX Corps had had another disappointing day although it was now better poised to strike south-eastwards across the Odon and over Mont Pinçon.

On the other side 21st Panzer had attempted on several occasions throughout the 31st to assemble for counter-attack but each time Typhoons of No. 83 Group rocketed or bombed the assembly areas about the Bois du Homme, frustrating every move. Even so, the German tankmen persevered but it was 1 August before they launched their main effort, with some Tigers, against the positions of 15th (Scottish) Division. These attacks were beaten off by combined fire from Scottish infantry, tanks of 6 Guards Tank Brigade, mortars and artillery. In spite of the punishment dealt out to them, the Germans made more probing attacks before finally withdrawing towards evening to be followed up by British infantry and tanks. As darkness descended on that first night in August, 15th (Scottish) held Point 309 firmly and had cleared la Ferrière and Galet.[34]

Those days on the cusp of July and August also saw the two armoured divisions on the right of the Scots achieve significant success. The leading troops of 11th Armoured worked their way round St Martin des Besaces on the night of 30–31 July to launch a two-pronged attack in the morning. By 11.00am tanks had broken through the anti-tank screen to clear the village while reconnaissance troops probed southwards. At 10.35am a squadron of Household Cavalry armoured cars, which had probed through l'Evêque forest, reported that a bridge over the Souleuvre river, five miles behind the enemy front line, was intact and clear of enemy. Another troop of armoured cars was despatched, with some tanks, to secure the bridge; the cars were destroyed in an ambush en route but the tanks reached and secured the bridge. As a result, 11th Armoured was able to send troops across the river that night to the hills west of le Bény-Bocage to establish a bridgehead and occupy the slopes of Point 205. Contact was also made with American troops and arrangements agreed to defend the right flank.[35]

That afternoon, having learned of the capture of the Souleuvre bridge, O'Connor ordered Guards Armoured to move up on the left of 11th Armoured to secure additional routes over the river near le Tourneur. The Guards' advance met stiff opposition from 21st Panzer in the hills south-east of St Martin and it was the morning of 1 August before a successful attack was put in that left Points 192 and 238 in the hands of 5 Guards Brigade. Such had been the opposition from 21st Panzer, and the known strength of the division on the way ahead, that 32 Guards Brigade was passed through to take the final objective. Although brigade titles were still in use the formations executing these advances were now mixed battlegroups. The renewed attack saw the bridge at le Tourneur secured by the Guards shortly after dark. On this day, also, le Bény-Bocage fell to 11th Armoured Division and armoured cars probed southwards to within two miles of Vire. But the enemy was building up strong resistance in the area and no attack was launched; Vire was now an American responsibility and Second Army was to wheel to its left. This would take XXX Corps to the Orne and VIII Corps towards Condé sur Noireau and Flers. It also left Vire to the Germans, no one in Montgomery's headquarters seeming to realise that the town was there for the British to take.[36]

In the face of Second Army's aggression 21st Panzer abandoned attempts to take Point 309 and the German armour was pinned to the British front. Thus 84th Infantry Division, en route to the Canadian sector from east of the Seine, was diverted to Seventh Army while 89th Infantry Division, from Fifteenth Army, was to prepare to join Panzer Group West. Eberbach, the Panzer Group commander, told Army Group B headquarters that LXXIV Corps' front on the Caumont sector was now the critical area and asked if 9th SS or 12th SS Panzer Divisions could be moved immediately to that area. Von Kluge did not make an immediate decision but, having considered all factors, decided to move II SS Panzer Corps with 9th SS and 10th SS Panzer Divisions plus 8 Werfer Brigade,

668th Anti-tank Battalion, when it arrived, and corps troops to the threatened area where the corps would take 21st Panzer under command.[37] And so it was that Second Army's offensive was now drawing two additional German armoured divisions to its front, formations that might otherwise have been deployed against the Americans. The orders to the newly-arriving formations were straightforward: 10th SS Panzer was to stop the British advance on Aunay; 9th SS Panzer was to gain the line from le Tourneur to Point 205 at le Bény-Bocage and form a junction with II Parachute Corps at Carville. Even with this healthy reinforcement, Eberbach was not confident, telling Speidel that the armoured corps might check the British but would not stop them; his view was that withdrawal to the Seine was the most sensible move. This view was passed to von Kluge. By coincidence, at much the same time, the question of withdrawal was being discussed at Hitler's headquarters, planning for such a contingency having already begun at OKW. Although he realised that withdrawal in the west might soon be necessary, Hitler was determined not to give any ground – and especially not to lose the U-boat bases in western France – and von Kluge was ordered to stand and fight. Thus the final phase of the battle for Normandy was dictated by a Führer who had never visited the ground he was now demanding his soldiers should struggle to hold.

Second Army continued its pressure with VIII Corps launching 11th Armoured Division towards Tinchebray and Guards Armoured towards Estry and Vassy on 2 August. In the initial stages of these attacks progress was good and opposition, generally from groups of infantry and tanks, was overcome at several locations. As the day wore on, opposition stiffened but did not prevent 11th Armoured occupying Etouvy on the right flank by day's end. The division's leading elements were now atop the Périers ridge from which they had a commanding view of the Vire–Vassy road. For their part, Guards Armoured had its reconnaissance battalion, 2nd Welsh Guards, on the high ground above Estry, having by-passed elements of 21st Panzer Division at Arclais, Montcharivel and Montchamp; the clearing of these locations was left to the following infantry.

Both British armoured divisions had made deep penetrations, something that many commentators consider that British armour could not do, leaving much ground to be cleared of enemy troops. Thus there was considerable fighting as mopping-up continued until that ground and flanks were secured. By now the first elements of 9th SS Panzer Division were arriving and taking the field in desperate efforts to recapture the Périers ridge east of Vire and the Souleuvre bridge at le Tourneur.[38] Neither effort met with success, the attackers being rebuffed with considerable loss.

Vire had become critical to the Germans. Seven major roads met in the town, which had suffered heavily from Allied bombing, and it was the junction between Eberbach's Panzer Group West and Hausser's Seventh Army. The former lay east of Vire while Seventh Army was to the west with its flank threatened by the Americans; in fact its loose left flank had been swung back to prevent the Americans enlarging their breakthrough. In those early days of August the inter-army boundary was almost porous and Eberbach was ordered to close the gap to ensure that the Allies did not invest Seventh Army; it was to carry out this order that II SS Panzer Corps was moving up on the left of LXXIV Corps.[39]

Not only did a German inter-army boundary lie close to Vire but so too did an Allied boundary, with the agreed demarcation between British and American armies east of the town. British patrols had already pushed forward to Vire but, with the town in the American sector, no effort was made to seize it, although it was lightly held. However, as VIII Corps held its ground on the Estry and Périers ridges, fighting off efforts to dislodge them, and infantry moved up to support the armour, clear the ground that had been taken and firm up the outer flanks of the British salient, the Germans strengthened Vire's defences. The new British dispositions saw 3rd Division move into the salient from Caen, to be joined by 15th (Scottish). This would allow VIII Corps' advance to continue on a four-division front but, to begin with, 185 Brigade from 3rd Division took post on the right flank of the salient with the Scottish 44 Brigade on the left.[40]

On Second Army's left, XXX Corps had not made such good progress although 43rd (Wessex) Division's initial progress had been promising. The Wessexmen had moved off from Bois du Homme in the early hours of 2 August and, shrugging off several attacks by small enemy battlegroups, advanced three miles through some very difficult country. In doing so, they drove elements of 21st Panzer out of Jurques and captured Hill 301, about two miles south. Resistance stiffened next day as troops of 10th SS Panzer were encountered. On the left of 43rd (Wessex) the Desert Rats were unable to reach Aunay and, in spite of both armoured and infantry attacks on the 2nd and 3rd, were forced back almost to Breuil by counter-attacks from 10th SS Panzer.[41] This put the division back almost where it had started nearly forty-eight hours before and precipitated the relief of its commander, Major-General Erskine, by Major-General G L Verney, formerly commanding 6 Guards Tank Brigade.[42] That relief, on 4 August, coincided with a change in corps commanders with Lieutenant-General Brian Horrocks arriving from England to succeed Bucknall at the helm of XXX Corps.[43] But the corps had not been entirely unsuccessful since 50th (Northumbrian) Division had seized the high ground of Amaye sur Seulles, to the west of Villers-Bocage, along with a regimental headquarters from 326th Infantry Division, complete with regimental commander.

The push forward by 43rd Division seemed to offer the first true opportunity for 43rd Reconnaissance Regiment to operate in its intended role and the regiment concentrated near la Londe on the morning of 3 August.

> A violent battle had been fought over the fields in which we harboured and the ground was littered with dead – British and German. Arriving in darkness, with a German air raid in progress near by, several of the men settled down for the night by their vehicles to discover in the morning that they had been lying near corpses. One corporal mistook a body for a sleeping comrade whom he needed for a job and made some attempt to rouse him.[44]

The orders issued to 43 Recce called for two squadrons to pass through the infantry and advance on two axes: Jurques–Ondefontaine and Jurques–le Mesnil-Auzouf–la Tautainerie. B Squadron, operating on the latter axis, was delayed in moving off by Tiger tanks on high ground overlooking the road from Jurques to le Mesnil. Typhoons were called upon to attack the Tigers but, in spite of a rocket attack, the Tigers were still there when a subsequent recce patrol probed forward. Needless to say, B Squadron did not move off. Following an unsuccessful infantry and armour attack next morning the squadron returned to harbour. During the night of 4–5 August, 5th Duke of Cornwall's LI cleared the hilltop, finally allowing B Squadron to move off. As it did so, it came under attack from the air. But the attackers were not from the Luftwaffe; they were RAF Typhoons. Fortunately the fighters failed to hit the Assault Troop's half-tracks and there were no casualties.[45]

In the meantime strategic bombers continued operations against communications and supply targets as well as flying-bomb sites. One such raid on 4 August had two targets, V1 storage sites at Trossy-St-Maxim and Bois de Cassan. Over Trossy, two Lancasters were shot down, one of them piloted by Squadron-Leader Ian Willoughby Bazalgette of No. 635 Squadron. Bazalgette, a Canadian by birth,* carried on to release his markers and bombs even after his machine had been hit by anti-aircraft fire. After leaving the target the Lancaster went into a steep dive but Bazalgette regained control, enabling four crewmen to bale out. With his bomb-aimer wounded and mid-upper gunner overcome by smoke or fumes, Bazalgette stayed at the controls in an effort to make a good crash-landing and thereby save his comrades. Although he brought the Lancaster in on an apparently good crash-landing, the aircraft exploded and all three were killed.** Bazalgette was subsequently awarded the Victoria Cross.[46]

Since von Kluge was now conducting a tactical withdrawal under orders from Hitler, this is an appropriate point to look at the broader picture in

* His father was English and his mother was Irish.

** Bazalgette and his fellow crew members are buried in the village of Senantes.

Normandy. Operation FORTITUDE had kept Fifteenth Army deployed in anticipation of a further invasion and thus no reinforcements had been released previously to Seventh Army. That situation was changing as Fifteenth Army formations began moving to the Normandy front where four Allied armies were now pushing their full weight against the exhausted soldiers of Seventh Army and Panzer Group West, now renamed Fifth Panzer Army. Patton's Third US Army had entered the fray on 1 August and was striking into Brittany while First Army continued pushing from St Lô and threatening to outflank Seventh Army. Dempsey's Second Army was advancing in the Caumont sector while Crerar's First Canadian Army was engaged on the left flank. At long last, Montgomery's forecast of the way in which OVERLORD would develop was coming to pass. Ellis, the British Official Historian, notes that 'apart from Brittany the Allied position on August the 1st closely approximated to the position in the forecast from which a wheel eastwards would begin'.[47] He does not note how far behind schedule this was.

For von Kluge the most critical sector in those first days of August was around Caumont where the British advance threatened to break his line near Vire, at the hinge of Panzer Group West and Seventh Army. For that reason he was now deploying II SS Panzer Corps westwards to counter the British threat, even though he also needed to ensure that the British and Canadians did not break through on the eastern flank to thrust towards Falaise. With reinforcing infantry divisions from Fifteenth Army he hoped to stabilise his front by deploying armour where that front was most threatened. However, as German generals had experienced so often before, his plans were superseded by fresh orders from Hitler. At about 1.00am on 3 August, von Kluge received the following order from his Führer.

> The front between the Orne and the Vire will mainly be held by infantry divisions. To this end the infantry divisions which are approaching will be wheeled to the north and, if necessary, the front line will be taken back, so that a new main defence line will be formed and held on the general line: Thury-Harcourt–Vire–Fontenermont.
>
> The armoured formations which have up to now been employed on that front must be released and moved complete to the left wing. The enemy's armoured forces which have pressed forward to the east, south-east and south will be annihilated by an attack which these armoured formations – numbering at least four – will make, and contact will be restored with the west coast of the Cotentin at Avranches – or north of that – without regard to the enemy penetrations in Brittany.[48]

Von Kluge was not a man to query or contest an order from Hitler, irrespective of his personal views on the wisdom of that order, and so he issued instructions for the redeployment. Seventh Army was to use the newly-arrived 84th and 363rd Infantry Divisions to release battlegroups of 2nd SS Panzer and 17th SS Panzer Grenadier Divisions while Panzer Group West would assemble 1st SS Panzer Division north of Falaise with another armoured division. This panzer group was then to attack on both sides of Sourdeval 'so that the enemy between Mortain and Avranches will be annihilated by a thrust from east to west'.[49] That counter-attack, which would again seal the Cotentin front, was to be commanded by General von Funck of XLVII Panzer Corps and would include von Funck's corps alongside LXXXI Corps with 2nd, 9th and 116th Panzer Divisions, as well as battlegroups from 2nd SS Panzer and 17th SS Panzer Grenadier Divisions. Neither von Funck's headquarters nor 9th Panzer Division was yet available; the former was en route from Rouen and the latter from Avignon. (In addition, 708th Infantry Division was moving up from Royan, on the Garonne estuary, to come under command of LXXXI Corps alongside 9th Panzer.) While regrouping took place the planned attack had to wait; it could not begin until the night of 6–7 August at the earliest.

Montgomery, still commanding all Allied ground forces as Eisenhower's deputy, was issuing orders to the Allied armies for an eastward advance at much the same time as von Kluge was issuing his for what would become known as the Mortain counter-attack. In contrast to von Kluge, Montgomery planned an advance by four armies rather than four divisions. The first element of Montgomery's plan required the Allied right flank to swing towards Paris, thereby forcing Army Group B against the Seine; all crossings of the river between Paris and the coast had now been destroyed. Second Army was to continue thrusting to the south and south-east while First Canadian Army was to launch a strong attack towards Falaise, which was to start, if possible, on the 7th; this was Operation TOTALIZE. Montgomery modified his plan slightly two days later. Although the general plan remained a swing of the right flank pivoted on the left, he now extended the inter-army group boundary as far as the Seine; this extension would run through Tinchebray, Argentan and Dreux to Mantes-Gassicourt. Having secured Falaise the Canadians were to hand that town to Second Army before advancing eastwards towards Lisieux and Rouen while Second Army would make for Argentan and Laigle and thence for the Seine below Mantes-Gassicourt where it was to be ready to force a crossing between there and les Andelys. At the same time Bradley's American army group would advance on a broad front, its right flank swinging quickly eastwards and then north-eastwards towards Paris. 'Plans were under preparation for the use of airborne forces* in advance of the American columns in order to hasten the closure of the Orléans gap.'[51]

* These were to include two British divisions in an operation intended to secure Chartres thereby preventing an enemy escape between Orléans and Paris.[50]

Panzer Group West began withdrawing on the night of 3 August, falling back on the line Thury-Harcourt–Vire. Second Army followed up closely, led by 53rd (Welsh) and 59th (Staffordshire) Divisions of XII Corps. Although there was little opposition, the British divisions were hindered by a profusion of mines and booby-traps on all possible routes. Having endured constant mortaring in the front line near le Bon Repos, 53rd (Welsh) Reconnaissance Regiment was pleasantly surprised to learn that the enemy had pulled back from the crossroads there during the night of 3–4 August. A patrol from B Squadron, under Sergeant Robbie Robinson, had gone forward to check if a Mark IV was still dug in near the crossroads and ascertained 'that the forward and secondary line of the German foxholes were not manned and were quite empty'.[52]

Following that report a mobile patrol was sent out to 'draw fire or capture prisoners for information'.[53] Among the very first British troops to set off in pursuit of the retreating enemy, this patrol soon found evidence of enemy minefields and booby-traps.

> But at this time the Squadron suffered some casualties. The Assault Troop had come up to clear a passage for us through the mines when one man trod on one and was rather badly wounded. However I felt a lot better now and we continued again through the now harmless minefield and past the barrier into the shell-torn village of Esquay. I wirelessed back that we had reached the first objective and we moved on keeping a constant watch on the ruins for snipers.[54]

And so the advance continued. By nightfall on 4 August XII Corps' right flank had linked with troops of XXX Corps among the shattered buildings of Villers-Bocage of unhappy memory. In the centre O'Connor's corps had reached Evrecy and the left was at the Orne near Amaye with the Welsh Division clearing the river's east bank as far as Grimbosq. The Staffordshire Division, with 34 Tank Brigade and 56 Brigade under command, had also reached the Orne farther upstream. Second Army's line now stretched from the loop of the Orne close to Thury-Harcourt back to the shadow of Mont Pinçon, still in enemy hands; the line, therefore, bent back on itself and the obstacle that was Mont Pinçon would have to be cleared. This would be achieved after some desperate fighting and much courage on both sides.

Before that 59th (Staffordshire) Division's infantry had begun wading the Orne near Brieux and by daybreak on 6 August three battalions* had crossed to establish a footing that allowed engineers to start bridging. In spite of mortar fire the Sappers had a bridge in place by 7.30am that could

* These were 7th Royal Norfolk, 6th North Staffordshire and 7th South Staffordshire.

carry vehicles up to nine tons, while a tank squadron had forded the river to join 176 Brigade's infantry. The tanks were a welcome sight as counter-attacks had already begun. But the fighting died down, allowing the division to consolidate and expand its bridgehead. Fighting flared up again on the evening of the 7th when a battlegroup of 12th SS Panzer Division – Kampfgruppe Wünsche – struck at the British positions.[55] By now a second squadron of 107th Regiment RAC was supporting 176 Brigade in the bridgehead.

Although the SS battlegroup was attacked by fifty-four Mitchell bombers there were few German casualties since their anti-aircraft fire was so effective that three dozen Mitchells were hit, some so badly that they could not return to their bases in Britain. At 6.30pm on 7 August the Germans attacked under a curtain of shellfire. Before long German tanks had reached Grimbosq and, less than two hours after beginning the assault, Tigers had closed to the Orne and were reported to be within a quarter mile of the bridge at le Bas. In this fighting 107 RAC lost some twenty-eight tanks while most of 7th South Staffords were forced back across the Orne. However, British artillery FOOs had an excellent view of the battleground and surrounding area and produced superb artillery support for the beleaguered brigade in the bridgehead; seven artillery regiments provided firepower at a rate of 1,000 rounds per gun per day.[56] RAF Typhoons also struck the attackers with 500lb bombs. Under cover of darkness another battalion, 1/7th Royal Warwicks, crossed to reinforce 176 Brigade and the enemy tanks pulled back. During the 8th the surviving tanks of 107 RAC were relieved by 147 RAC. The German battlegroup had prevented the British from expanding their bridgehead but, in spite of their determined attacks, had been unable to destroy it; further attacks also failed to achieve this aim. Having made seven attacks, Wünsche was ordered to withdraw and move as quickly as possible to the Potigny area, north of Falaise, where a further crisis was underway. His battlegroup had lost nine Panthers and 122 men but although several Tigers were damaged, none were lost. British casualties had been heavy: 7th Royal Norfolks lost forty-two killed, 111 wounded and seventy-three missing while 6th North Staffords suffered seventy-six casualties.[57]

The courage demonstrated on both sides was exemplified by subsequent gallantry awards; on the British side these included a Victoria Cross as well as several Military Crosses. That Victoria Cross was awarded to Captain David Jamieson of 7th Norfolks who

> throughout 36 hours of bitter and close fighting . . . showed superb qualities of leadership and great personal bravery. There were times when the situation appeared hopeless but on each occasion it was restored by his coolness and determination. He personally was

> largely responsible for holding the bridgehead over the river and although wounded twice he refused to be evacuated.[58]

Jamieson's was the second of four Victoria Crosses in the hard ground fighting of those early August days; three went to Second Army and the fourth to First Canadian Army. The first was earned by another Royal Norfolk soldier, Corporal Sidney Bates, on 6 August when 1st Norfolks came under attack from 12th SS Panzer some five miles north-north-east of Vire at Sourdeval.* An accurate heavy artillery and mortar programme hit the Norfolk positions, which the enemy had pinpointed, as the attack started. When the main attack developed some thirty minutes later, heavy machine-gun and mortar fire was concentrated on the junction of the Norfolks' two forward companies.

Sidney Bates commanded a section in one of those companies; his section suffered casualties as mortar bombs fell around them. Assessing the situation, Bates decided to move his section to another position where he believed he could counter the enemy thrust more effectively. By now the Germans had pushed a wedge into the area occupied by the forward companies and some fifty to sixty enemy troops, supported by machine guns and mortars, threatened Bates's section. With the situation becoming increasingly desperate, Sidney Bates grabbed a Bren gun and

> charged the enemy, moving forward through a hail of bullets and splinters and firing the gun from his hip. He was almost immediately wounded by machine-gun fire and fell to the ground, but recovered himself quickly, got up and continued advancing towards the enemy spraying bullets from his gun as he went. His action by now was having an effect on the enemy riflemen and machine-gunners, but mortar bombs continued to fall all around him.
>
> He was then hit for the second time and much more seriously and painfully wounded. Undaunted, he staggered once more to his feet and continued towards the enemy, who were now seemingly highly surprised by their inability to check him. His constant firing continued until the enemy started to withdraw before him.[59]

At this point, Bates was hit a third time by mortar-bomb splinters that would prove fatal. Although he fell, he continued firing his Bren until his strength failed him completely. By then the Germans had withdrawn and the situation in the battalion's forward area had been restored. Two days later Sidney Bates, who had just turned 23 on 14 June 1944, died of his wounds. The *London Gazette* carried the announcement of his posthumous Victoria Cross on 2 November, noting that 'by his supreme gallantry and

* Spelt Sourdevalle in 1944. This is the spelling used in the *London Gazette*.

self-sacrifice he had personally retrieved what had been a critical situation'. His Cross was presented to his father, a Camberwell rag-and-bone man, by King George VI at Buckingham Palace in March 1945.[60]

Ten days after Bates's gallant action the third Victoria Cross of this fighting was won by Major Tasker Watkins of the Welch Regiment in an action that we shall consider shortly. In the meantime much fighting took place on the British and Canadian fronts while the counter-attack ordered by Hitler was launched at the Americans around Mortain on 7 August, the day on which the Canadians initiated Operation TOTALIZE towards Falaise. The long struggle for Normandy was coming to an end; but it was an end every bit as bloody and horrific as the earlier fighting in the ancient duchy.

The Mortain attack, Operation LÜTTICH, was aimed at Avranches from a start line between Vire and Mortain; it was intended to cut off the Americans south of the axis of advance before swinging north-east to the Channel coast to drive the Allies into the sea. It was not von Kluge's plan but Adolf Hitler's and was made in Berlin without advice from generals on the ground.

> Hitler was also insisting that the attack should not be made until 'every tank, gun and plane was assembled'. Every detail was specified including the exact roads and villages through which the assaulting troops were to advance. General Blumentritt, Chief of Staff CinC West, complained after the war to Milton Shulman, 'All this planning had been done in Berlin with large-scale maps and the advice of generals in France was not asked for, nor was it encouraged.'[61]

Hitler's intentions became known to Allied commanders through ULTRA intercepts but not before Montgomery issued his orders on 4 August. The Allies became aware of the German dictator's orders in time to 'take steps to counter it and to make Hitler's order the agent of his own army's destruction'.[62] As Ralph Bennett comments:

> Foreknowledge at this juncture and on this scale made Ultra security more vital than ever. The Allied command had always planned to make the eastward advance to the Seine from about the line it had now reached; here was Hitler proposing, by a large-scale attack in the opposite direction, to double its effect and to run his head into a noose of his own devising. Hotter news there could hardly be, yet no unwise use of the information was made, and the secret was safely kept.[63]

The Mortain attack was stopped by the stubborn courage of American soldiers with support from Allied aircraft. On the ground much credit was due to 30th Infantry Division, which was almost destroyed in the battle, and 823rd Tank Destroyer Battalion without whom, Michael Reynolds suggests, 'elements of von Funck's forces might well have reached the vicinity of Avranches before the arrival of the Typhoons'.[64] Attacks by those Typhoons also helped ensure that no breakthrough occurred, although RAF pilots did make some attacks on their own troops, such was the confusion of the fighting; other 'friendly fire' incidents involved Allied artillery and infantrymen firing on their fellows. Some of the fighting in this counter-attack fell on British troops; the incident in which Sidney Bates earned his posthumous Victoria Cross was but one example of British involvement.

As the Germans strove to reach Avranches in Operation LÜTTICH, First Canadian Army was opening its first major offensive. Operation TOTALIZE aimed to break the German defences astride the Caen–Falaise road before exploiting to Falaise. First Canadian Army was ready to move on the night of 7–8 August and much planning and thought had gone into this operation; General Crerar had told Lieutenant-General Guy Simonds, commanding II Canadian Corps, to plan such an operation 'several days before Monty issued his Directive'[65] although Montgomery does not attribute the plans to either Canadian. The extra days that Crerar's initiative provided for preparation allowed Simonds to build up his striking force and implement some new ideas. One of the latter was a concept turned down by Dempsey when O'Connor had wanted to try it out in Operation GOODWOOD: the conversion of Priest SPGs to armoured personnel carriers. No reference was made to Dempsey on this occasion, since this was a Canadian operation, and seventy-six Priests were 'defrocked', their 105mm guns removed, to create improvised APCs dubbed 'Kangaroos'.

For Operation TOTALIZE II Canadian Corps was to include Simonds' own 2nd and 3rd Canadian Divisions, as well as 4th Canadian Armoured Division,* which had arrived in Normandy in the previous week, to which were added 51st (Highland) Division, the British 33 Tank Brigade** and

* The division included 4 Armoured Brigade (21st Armoured Regiment (The Governor-General's Foot Guards), 22nd Armoured Regiment (The Canadian Grenadier Guards), 28th Armoured Regiment (The British Columbia Regiment) and The Lake Superior Regiment as motorised infantry) and 10 Infantry Brigade (The Lincoln and Welland Regiment, The Algonquin Regiment and The Argyll and Sutherland Highlanders of Canada (Princess Louise's)); 29th Reconnaissance Regiment (The South Alberta Regiment) was included in the divisional troops.
** Including 1st Northamptonshire Yeomanry, 144th and 148th Regiments RAC; the latter was replaced by 1st East Riding Yeomanry from 16 August 1944.

another newly-arrived armoured formation, 1st Polish Armoured Division.* The latter would compensate for inexperience with an enthusiasm for getting to grips with the enemy that was the product of wishing to avenge their country's sufferings over the previous five years. And the Poles would play a major, albeit short, part in the battle for Normandy.

Ronald Lewin has described Simonds' plans as something that

> Patton might well have studied . . . for in daring and ingenuity they surpassed anything so far attempted by the British army – or the Americans. Simonds' difficulty was this: he had to thrust down the Caen–Falaise road amid open country which, as several preliminary probes had revealed, gave ample scope to the 88s, the mortars and the machine-guns in the strong enemy line. This hard crust he had to crack with his armour: but until his armour had reached the crust he must keep the heads of the enemy down without providing the conventional warning of an artillery preparation. He therefore adopted the wholly unconventional plan of using heavy bombers, *in a tactical role at night*, to carpet the flanks of his line of advance; meanwhile his assault troops moved in the centre, the forward infantry being transported in armoured troop carriers . . . Ingenious devices were also evolved for the maintenance of direction in this unprecedented attack: radio-directional beams for the tanks, target-indicator shells with coloured bursts, tracer from Bofors firing on fixed lines, and searchlights to illuminate the sky as the moon failed.[66]

Nor did Simonds' innovative thinking end there: the attacking force was to deploy in separate columns, each on a four-tank front, with vehicles 'packed nose to tail',[67] and 'Funnies' preceding each column to clear minefields and provide engineer support. More than 1,000 bombers would support the attack while, as the assaulting formations moved forward, some 360 guns were to fire a bombardment in their path.[68]

The Canadian plan deserved to be successful but its success was only partial. At 11.30pm on the 7th Operation TOTALIZE opened with the leading formations crossing their start line between Soliers and St André sur Orne; east of the Falaise road the attack was led by 51st (Highland) Division and 33 Armoured Brigade while to the west of the road 2nd Canadian Division was supported by 2 Canadian Armoured Brigade. Tasks assigned to these formations included capturing la Hogue on the

* The division included 10 Armoured Brigade (1st and 2nd Polish Armoured Regiments and 24th Polish Armoured (Lancer) Regiment) and 3 Infantry Brigade (1st Polish (Highland) Battalion, 8th and 9th Polish Battalions) with 10th Polish Mounted Rifle Regiment among the divisional troops.

left, St Aignan de Cramesnil and Gaumesnil in the centre and Caillouet, close to the Laize river, on the right. Thereafter 1st Polish and 4th Canadian Armoured Divisions would pass through to assault the next defence line. This phase was to begin at 2.00pm on the 8th with the Poles taking the high ground east of the Potigny–Falaise road while the Canadians gave their attention to the heights between Potigny and the Laize valley. As Polish and Canadian armour went forward, 3rd Canadian Division was to occupy the ground between the infantry and armoured divisions. While these operations were taking place I Corps, on the left, was to maintain its front against possible counter-attack but, as the Canadian operation progressed and Simonds' corps broadened its penetration, it was to be ready to take over part of the Canadian front.[69]

TOTALIZE was being launched against a front held by I SS Panzer Corps with 89th Infantry Division under command; this recently formed* division had taken over Leibstandarte's sector four days earlier and an SS battlegroup was deployed behind it. The latter – Kampfgruppe Meyer – moved to the area south-east of Bretteville-sur-Laize on 7 August with forty-seven tanks, including eight Tigers of Michael Wittmann's 101st Heavy Tank Battalion, and twenty-seven Jagdpanzer IVs.[70] There was considerable artillery, including about a hundred 88mm and 75mm anti-tank guns. Von Kluge also ordered the move of most of Hitlerjugend to prevent a possible British breakthrough between Vire and Thury-Harcourt and, although Dietrich protested this order, von Kluge had his way; Kampfgruppe Wünsche, still engaged against the British at Grimbosq, was to follow next day. However, it proved impossible to implement these moves.

An hour before midnight on 7 August Bomber Command began its part in the operation; 1,019 aircraft** deployed for the bombing mission with five aiming points in front of the Allied ground forces. The attacks were controlled carefully to prevent casualties to Allied soldiers, as a result of which only 660 machines bombed; the targets could not be seen clearly by the others. Ten Lancasters were lost, seven to German fighters, two to anti-aircraft fire and one to an unknown cause.[72] Bombs were dropped on Fontenay le Marmion and May sur Orne on the right flank and from la Hogue to Marc de Magne on the left; the Canadian official history notes that not a single bomb fell on Allied troops. Thirty minutes after the first bombers struck, the assault columns crossed their start line, led by Flails and AVREs of 79th Armoured Division. The vehicles of II Canadian Corps added their own cloud to the dust storm already raised by bombs. This huge cloud was the reason the bombers were called off after two-thirds of them had dropped their loads. Needless to say, such poor visibility led to

* It had been formed in Norway in the spring of 1944.

** This force included 614 Lancasters, 392 Halifaxes and thirteen Mosquitoes.[71]

crashes and collisions amongst the advancing vehicles but the columns continued their charge and, although the defenders began to recover from the shock of the bombing and to increase their defensive fire, the Jocks of 51st (Highland) Division's 154 Brigade had de-bussed from their APCs before daylight to capture Garcelles-Secqueville, Cramesnil, St Aignan and 140 prisoners. By 7.00am the Canadians had taken Point 122, on the main road near Cramesnil, and the westward-running ridge; they went on to reach Caillouet later in the morning.

There was much tough fighting for the follow-up infantry but other objectives were eventually taken; May sur Orne and Fontenay le Marmion had escaped the worst of the RAF's attentions which helped delay their capture as did nearby minefields; Tilly la Campagne continued to hold out. As the morning wore on both the natural mist of the harvest season and the unnatural mist of the night's bombing started clearing and the Germans made strenuous efforts to regain lost ground; several counter-attacks were made against St Aignan and Point 122. In these battles there were many casualties on both sides; in one clash the Canadians lost twenty tanks and the Germans eleven. British and Canadian troops resisted all the enemy pressure and the morning's gains were held. Once again the tactical air arm provided vital direct support while other Allied aircraft strafed German tanks, and transport attempting to reach the battlefront.[73]

The Polish and Canadian armoured divisions were now closing up on the fighting, ready to pass through and force a way to the German second line between St Sylvain and Bretteville sur Laize and thence to the high ground before Falaise. Originally this phase was to have had the support of a second RAF bombing attack but weather conditions intervened to prevent many aircraft from the previous mission landing at their own bases and, therefore, not having time to refuel and take on a new bomb load. It was decided to deploy B17 Flying Fortresses of the US Eighth Air Force, the first of which began bombing just after 12.30pm, at St Sylvain and Bretteville. They were followed by further waves making for Cauvricourt and Gouvix. However, the formations lost some cohesion due to anti-aircraft fire and many were unable to distinguish their targets in spite of coloured markers put down by the artillery. Of the 678 bombers in the mission, fewer than 500 bombed but, tragically, many were wide of the mark and more than 300 casualties were suffered by British, Canadian and Polish troops; some bombs even fell in Second Army's area west of the Orne.[74] Ten bombers were lost to AA fire.

The progress of the armoured divisions was not as good as that of the first wave. Both were unblooded and had some difficulty making their way forward, thereby losing much of the advantage of the bombing and renewed artillery bombardments. Near St Aignan the Poles met their first German counter-attack, from tanks and infantry trying to recapture the village and, although they fought on to Robertmesnil, about a mile ahead, they were engaged by Tigers as they emerged from the woods there; the enemy tanks had been concealed on the edge of St Sylvain. This engagement, in which the Poles claimed six enemy tanks, brought an end to 1st Polish Armoured Division's progress for the day.

The determination of Hitlerjugend soldiers brought the Allied advance almost to a standstill. Kurt Meyer, known as Panzermeyer, commanding 25th SS Panzer Grenadier Regiment of Hitlerjugend, had recognised the heavy bomber attack and the outburst of Allied artillery as the prelude to a major attack and reacted accordingly.

> He immediately moved forward to Urville, where he met Wilhelm Mohnke, who had been seriously deafened by the bombing. Early reports indicated that the 89th Division's forward positions had been overrun and that organised defence had, to all intents and purposes, collapsed. In reality, many of the forward 89th Division troops in places like Tilly and Fontenay-le-Marmion fought on stubbornly well into the afternoon.[75]

Although by-passed, pockets of 89th Division continued to fight well into the afternoon, thereby assisting Meyer's plan to form a new defensive position on the next suitable line, the high ground about Potigny and the valley of the Laison. No more than a stream, this watercourse was less than six feet wide and three in depth but lay in a wooded shallow valley that, Meyer realised, offered an excellent tank obstacle and the opportunity to slow Allied progress, allowing 85th Infantry Division, now moving up to reinforce the line, to deploy to the south-east. Moving on to Cintheaux, not much more than half a mile from the Canadians in Gaumesnil, he found an SS anti-tank platoon covering the Caen–Falaise road. But he also found soldiers from 89th Division streaming to the rear in confusion and disorder. This was a rare enough sight for Meyer to record it in his memoirs.

> I am seeing German soldiers running away for the first time during these long, gruesome, murderous years. They are unresponsive. They have been through hell-fire and stumble past us with fear filled eyes. I look at the leaderless groups in fascination. My uniform sticks to my body, the fear of responsibility making me break out in a sweat . . . I jump out of the car and stand alone in the middle of the road, talking to my fleeing comrades. They are startled and stop. They look at me incredulously, wondering how I can stand on the road armed with only a carbine . . . They recognise me, turn round, and wave to their comrades to come and organise the defence on the line of Cintheaux.[76]

Meyer's effect on the frightened infantrymen may be a reflection of fear of the SS but is equally likely to reflect the standard of German training. Leaving Cintheaux, Meyer then returned to Urville where he met Eberbach. The commander of Fifth Panzer Army was no more than three miles from the leading enemy soldiers and his presence could only have been inspiring to his soldiers. This was yet another comment on the quality of German training and leadership. Eberbach gave Meyer permission to implement his plan for a counter-attack by Kampfgruppe Waldmüller, with thirty-nine Mark IVs from 2nd SS Panzer Battalion and eight Tigers under Wittmann. Waldmüller was to attack and seize the ground around St Aignan, held by 1st Black Watch and tanks of 1st Northamptonshire Yeomanry, before moving on to secure the woods south-east of Garcelles.

Meyer had his force assembled as American bombers appeared for the second phase of TOTALIZE and, typically, ordered the attack to begin as soon as he realised the bombers' intentions. Closing with the advancing enemy offered a better chance of keeping his men away from American bombs. In the subsequent fighting the Poles suffered heavily, losing over two dozen tanks from one regiment. They were not alone: 1st Northamptonshire Yeomanry lost twenty tanks and sixty-three men with their commanding officer among the wounded. German losses were 178 men and, perhaps, eleven tanks, including five Tigers. Among the Tigers lost that day was that of Michael Wittmann. Michael Reynolds notes that

> The loss of the Tigers was almost inevitable, for their axis of advance was parallel to the main Caen–Falaise road, over completely open ground and with open flanks. It seems that on this fatal occasion the Tiger's reputation as a virtually invulnerable tank caused even Wittmann to throw caution to the wind. It is hardly surprising that he and his crew were amongst those listed as 'missing'![77]

In fact, Wittmann was dead, killed either when his Tiger was knocked out by a Sherman Firefly of 1st Northamptonshire Yeomanry, or when he baled out of his stricken tank. The tank ace's mount had fallen victim to a gunner of a British yeomanry regiment; Trooper Joe Ekins not only destroyed Wittmann's tank but two other Tigers as well. 'No German gunner could have fired more accurately than Firefly Joe Ekins . . . at St Aignan, with three Tigers destroyed by three shots.'[78] Wittmann's fatal error was not to recognise that

> the classic Normandy situation had been reversed. 1st Northamptonshire Yeomanry at St Aignan and 144 RAC at Cramesnil, both with . . . about a dozen Firefly Shermans on call, had sidled up to the side of the main road and were hidden, awaiting just such an attack, the powerful Fireflys now defending.

> The Tigers came down alongside the road, their guns bristling towards the west, where firing had been heard. They passed in front of the lone 1 NY Firefly guarding farthest forward supported by two 75mm Shermans. Capt Tom Boardman commanded Firefly gunner, Joe Ekins, to fire his 17pdr. Within minutes the Wittmann troop was wiped out by that one gun. Wittmann was proved not to have been immortal.[79]

But Meyer's counter-attack had written *finis* to Simonds' attack. Against less determined opposition it might have succeeded but, although the operation was well executed and showed much better cooperation between infantry and armour, there were still lessons to be absorbed. Meyer's analysis is apposite: 'We have unbelievable luck as the enemy fails to execute a single co-ordinated assault.' He also assessed the Allied effort, with a tank attack divided into phases, as being akin to 'a cavalry charge with meal breaks'.[80]

Fighting would continue for several days but the thrust for Falaise had been stopped short. However, the Canadians were making ready to start afresh with a renewed assault codenamed Operation TRACTABLE. Elsewhere Mont Pinçon, the dominating feature of the area known as the Suisse Normande and which rises to about 1,200 feet, had come under attack from 43rd (Wessex) Division who had secured Ondefontaine on the 5th before moving out southward to link up with 15th (Scottish) Division. For the Mont Pinçon attack a brigade group of 129 Brigade and 13th/18th Royal Hussars deployed to le Mesnil-Auzouf to spearhead the advance. The plan called for a broad-front approach, via Duval on the left flank and by wheeling through St Jean de Blanc on the right. Strong opposition was encountered a mile short of Mont Pinçon. Here a steam crossed the front of the advance and the Germans had chosen to make it a key defensive feature by doing their utmost to prevent Allied troops from crossing. This was Fifth Panzer Army's new defence line along which, according to Eberbach, eight battalions from two divisions – 276th and 326th Infantry – were deployed. Around St Jean and between Duval and la Varinière, fierce fighting took place and General Thomas decided to abandon the attack from this direction and concentrate instead on the western face of the height. This fresh attack would be reinforced with another brigade – 130 – brought across from Ondefontaine to strike against the north face.[81]

The assault on Mont Pinçon was no easy undertaking. A natural strongpoint, the feature was difficult to approach from the west where attackers would have to overcome rough, steep slopes covered by mortars, machine guns and artillery. Needless to say, the other approaches could also be swept by very intense fire. At 2.30pm on 6 August, under a blazing sun, the attack began and the leading troops of 5th Wiltshires came under heavy fire as they approached the stream; the

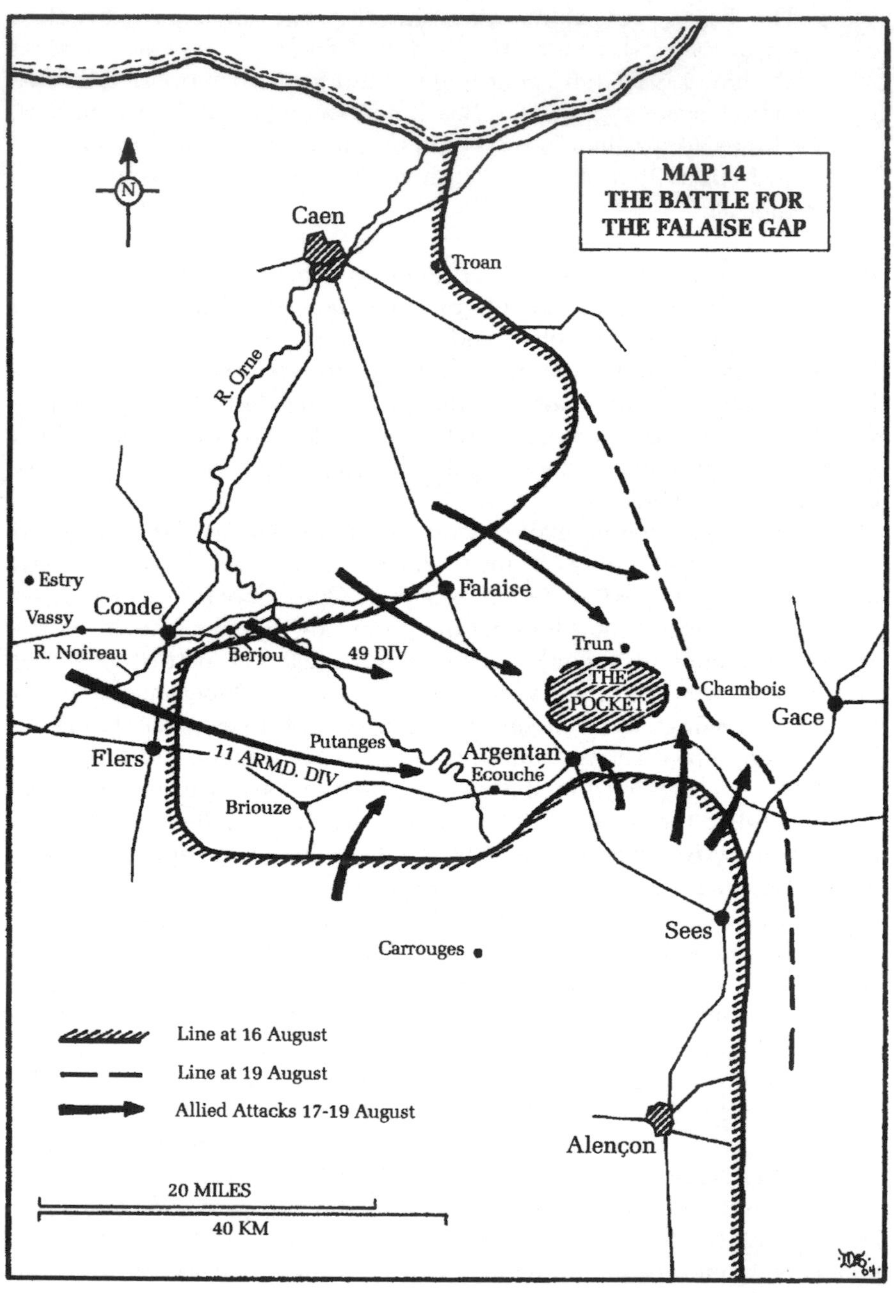
MAP 14
THE BATTLE FOR
THE FALAISE GAP
N
Caen
Troan
R. Orne
Estry
Conde
Vassy
R. Noireau
Berjou
49 DIV
Falaise
Trun
THE
POCKET
Chambois
Gace
Flers
11 ARMD. DIV
Putanges
Argentan
Ecouché
Briouze
Sees
Carrouges
Line at 16 August
Line at 19 August
Allied Attacks 17-19 August
Alençon
20 MILES
40 KM

battalion had already been reduced to two companies in the previous day's fighting and was soon reduced to an effective strength of sixty men. Nonetheless, inspired by the courage of their commanding officer, Lieutenant-Colonel John 'Pop' Pearson DSO*, the survivors went forward. Shortly afterwards, Pearson was killed by a bullet through the heart.[82] But 13th/18th Hussars had two troops of Shermans across the stream to surge forward for the crest. Although one overturned into a quarry and another lost a track, seven Shermans reached the crest and were followed by the remainder of the squadron by about 8.00pm. Then thick fog descended and assisted two battalions of 129 Brigade to reach the plateau where they dug in close to the Germans. When dawn came and the fog lifted those defenders were brought to battle and defeated; some 200 prisoners were taken. The assaulting battalions – 4th Somerset and 4th Wiltshire – were then relieved by 7th Somerset and 1st Worcester.[83]

On 10 August the Canadians broke off TOTALIZE but preparations were already underway for TRACTABLE, due to open on the 14th, the day before Allied forces began landing in southern France in Operation DRAGOON, previously ANVIL. Between those dates – on 12 August – XV US Corps of Patton's Third Army under Major-General Wade Haislip took Alençon, another significant step in developing the Allied strategy for victory in Normandy. Alençon lies south-south-east of Falaise and its fall threatened von Kluge's armies with containment. The thrust towards Alençon had entailed considerable risk for Third Army. Patton's command had been pushing eastwards towards le Mans, which was captured on the 8th, when Bradley sensed the possibility of cutting off sizeable German forces. With 21 Army Group pushing down from the north through Falaise and 12 Army Group containing the Germans around Mortain and swinging up from the south, the opportunity had been created 'to cut off the enemy west of that north–south line and destroy his Seventh Army'[84] and thus Montgomery now became responsible for 'coordinating the maneuvers of all four Allied armies'.[85] Eisenhower, who was with Bradley at the time that XV Corps began its attack towards Alençon, assured the latter that, if necessary, Third Army's leading troops could be supplied by air. XV Corps' thrust was a risk but one of those calculated risks that commanders must take.

The fresh Canadian effort became necessary when further reinforcements from Fifteenth Army strengthened the German screen before Falaise. Although 3rd Canadian Division made a spirited double attack on the enemy redoubt in Quesnay woods on the evening of the 10th, regrouping was obviously necessary for a full-scale attack on Falaise.

* Pearson's own regiment was The South Lancashire Regiment (Prince of Wales's Volunteers).

Some regrouping had occurred on the 10th when the boundary between I Corps and II Canadian Corps had been modified and 51st (Highland) Division and 33 Armoured Brigade returned to the command of the former. Highlanders had reached Poussy la Campagne while 49th (West Riding) Division had relieved the Poles and began advancing towards Vimont on the northern flank. Dempsey's Second Army, meanwhile, had maintained pressure between the Orne and Vire; on the left XII Corps had all but cleared the Grimbosq forest after some difficult fighting and patrols were in contact with the Canadians near the Laize. Thury-Harcourt, on the Orne, had been entered by reconnaissance troops who had found the town to be held strongly. XXX Corps was pushing forward from Mont Pinçon towards Condé sur Noireau but, facing doughty opposition, was still five miles short of the town, while VIII Corps, to their right, was approaching Tinchebray; Estry was still a German strongpoint.[86]

By now the German field commanders had lost that most important aspect of command – freedom to re-organise as they saw fit. Von Kluge and his army commanders should have been able to concentrate on realigning their defences against the new dangers imposed by the Allied encircling movements. Instead they were receiving daily orders from Hitler to renew the westward attack with details of how they were so to do; but the forces that the Führer demanded be used in this attack were needed desperately for defence. Only on 11 August did Hitler accept finally that the American advance had to be defeated first; on von Kluge's recommendation, he ordered an attack in the Alençon–le Mans area. But even nature seemed to be conspiring against the Germans. Eberbach wrote that, because of the phase of the moon, there were only six hours each day when attack was possible; these were between 3.00am and 9.00am, and then only if ground mist persisted after daylight. Otherwise attacks could not take place in daytime, 'owing to the enemy's supremacy in the air'.[87] And that air supremacy also restricted resupply to night hours, further reducing the time available for attacking.

Allied pressure was now telling on the Germans. As dusk fell on 11 August St Barthélémy and Mortain were under attack; both would be in American hands next morning. The rest of the German salient had been lost and communications were under threat from the Canadian offensive towards Falaise and the American attack towards Alençon. East of Mortain the German front swung behind Barenton and both Fifth Panzer and Seventh Armies were in real danger of encirclement. Only a narrowing gap to the east remained open for escape. This would become known as the Falaise Gap.

On 8 August Montgomery had agreed verbally with Bradley that the Americans should thrust northwards from le Mans; he confirmed this on the 11th. His general intention – to destroy enemy forces between the

Loire, Paris and the sea – had been set out in a directive on 6 August and remained unchanged but he now saw the possibility of sealing up the bulk of von Kluge's forces, which were west of the line Caen–le Mans. Since the gap through which German supplies were coming was being constricted more and more, Montgomery decided to concentrate on closing it. To this end, 21 Army Group 'would thrust southwards and eastwards to secure Falaise and Argentan' while 12 Army Group would 'swing its right wing northwards from le Mans up to Alençon and then on to the general line from Carrouges to Sées', about a dozen miles south of Argentan. Trapped enemy forces would be destroyed in the pocket thus created but both army groups were to be ready, if it seemed that the enemy might escape, to execute operations up to the Seine.[88]

And so the final phase of the battle for Normandy saw First Canadian Army's II Corps and Second Army's XII Corps fight their way southwards between the Orne and Laize with O'Connor's corps clearing the Cinglais forest on the 12th and making contact with the Canadians to their left. Thury-Harcourt was cleared next day and XII Corps was on the road leading to Falaise. Second Canadian Division captured Barbéry and Moulines on the 12th, took Tournebu the following day and then crossed the Laize to create a bridgehead near Clair Tizon. That bridgehead was expanded on the 14th and the Canadians were now less than six miles from Falaise; XII Corps' leading elements were about seven miles from the town. Elsewhere XV US Corps was under twenty miles away with two armoured divisions leading. These included the French 2nd Armoured Division, under General Leclerc who had fought with Eighth Army in North Africa; this was the first French division to fight under Allied command in the liberation of France.* Alongside Leclerc's Frenchmen were the soldiers of 5th US Armored Division. Another American corps, 'Lightning Joe' Collins' VII Corps, began advancing north-east from Mayenne on the 13th, First Army having concluded mopping-up operations around Mortain. Collins felt that he could take Falaise and Argentan, close the gap and finish off the Germans before 21 Army Group's forces began moving. But Bradley demurred, stating that he felt that it was no longer so important to close the gap since most German forces had already escaped. Neither tactical air reconnaissance nor ULTRA supported Bradley's interpretation of events. The American armies were now to turn their attention to the drive for the Seine. What prompted this change of mind on Bradley's part, for hitherto he had been keen to envelop enemy forces in Normandy and had proposed moves to this end to Montgomery on 8 August? Max Hastings comments that:

* Leclerc had expressed a wish to fight under British command in France as a result of his experience with Eighth Army.

> It was almost as if Bradley had lost all interest in the 'short envelopment' which he himself had proposed to Montgomery . . . He now seemed determined instead to concentrate upon trapping the Germans against the Seine, the rejected 'long envelopment'. In these days an uncharacteristic uncertainty of purpose, a lack of the instinct to deliver the killing stroke against von Kluge's armies, seemed to overtake Bradley. General Gerow of V Corps, sent to take charge of the situation at Argentan after Haislip's departure, found the command there almost completely ignorant of the whereabouts of the Germans, or even of his own men.[89]

For his part, Bradley places the blame on Montgomery, quoting Canadian tardiness and his own reluctance to allow American forces to go forward for fear of colliding with the British. Montgomery, opines Bradley, was shifting his main effort westward to 'squeeze the enemy out toward the Seine' rather than increasing pressure on the pocket. Bradley insists that 'the vanguard of panzers and SS were sluicing back through it [the gap] toward the Seine', but provides no evidence to support that contention.[90] Indeed the reality is that SS and panzer forces were moving back to defend Argentan which was threatened by the Americans; no German divisions were 'stampeding', as Bradley suggests, to escape the trap but were doing exactly the opposite: fighting defiantly to prevent the Allies closing the trap. An opportunity to close the gap by pushing Patton's army towards Falaise was thus lost. In his *Memoirs* Montgomery makes no criticism of Bradley, referring instead to the decisive victory achieved by the Allies in Normandy.[91] Nor does he criticise Bradley in *Normandy to the Baltic* in which he is generous in his praise of the Americans.[92]

Both generals agreed finally that the pocket should be expanded eastwards, to lead to an Allied junction at Chambois. But the new plans were a compromise: Haislip's corps was launched on the drive to the Seine, the 'long envelopment' instead of being deployed in the 'short envelopment' through Argentan–Falaise, while Gerow's corps and the Canadians would try closing the gap along a line between the two groupings. First Canadian Army was now ready to re-open its offensive towards Falaise: Operation TRACTABLE would resume the push made in TOTALIZE; Simonds was again in command. However, Falaise was to be taken by Second British Army while the Canadians were to exploit to Trun, some dozen miles south-east.

Eighteen minutes before noon on 14 August the Canadians moved off under a smokescreen that was soon thickened by dust raised by their tanks and APCs and a heavy counter-battery programme from the corps artillery. Less than ten minutes earlier Allied medium bombers had dropped fragmentation bombs on the line of attack in the Laison valley while rocket-firing fighters had attacked artillery and other strongpoints farther back. The Jocks of 51st (Highland) Division, from I Corps, also attacked towards the Laison to protect the Canadian left flank. In spite of all Simonds' careful plans, the Germans were ready, had redeployed to meet the Canadian attack and were aware of the axes of advance that Simonds' men would be using. Only the day before German troops had killed the commander of a Canadian reconnaissance car and found on his body a copy of the corps commander's orders for TRACTABLE. To make matters worse the leading Canadian armoured brigade commander was fatally wounded in the first hour of the operation; this led to serious command problems in the ensuing engagements.

The leading troops were quickly on the Laison where some disoriented Germans surrendered. Fascine-carrying tanks from 79th Armoured Division then deployed to improvise crossing places – the Laison proved a better anti-tank obstacle than expected – while reconnaissance parties searched for other crossing points. By 3 o'clock much of the armour was across the stream and the infantry had dismounted to clear positions between Montboint and Ernes. True to form the Germans recovered quickly and, armed with exact information on the Canadians' lines of advance, soon began taking horrific toll of Canadian tanks. As the armour tried to gain the higher ground beyond the Laison their losses mounted but the arrival of more infantry later in the afternoon helped counter the enemy defence and the attack moved forward again.[93]

But, to add to Canadian woes that day, they had also been bombed by the RAF. Almost 400 casualties occurred, with sixty-five men killed, when heavy bombers, due to bomb seven points between Quesnay and Bons-Tassilly on the Falaise road, dropped their loads short. Some 805 bombers took part in the operation, beginning at 2 o'clock.[94] The majority bombed German positions and tank laagers but seventy aircraft dropped their bombs over as many minutes on a large quarry in which were sited some of 12th Canadian Field Regiment's guns.[95] This situation was caused by a lack of liaison between air forces and ground troops; the latter were using yellow flares to indicate their positions to the aircraft whereas the pathfinders were dropping yellow to indicate targets. Thus the more yellow smoke the soldiers used, the more the bombers targeted them; it took the Master Bombers over an hour to correct the mistake. This, the first time the RAF had bombed friendly troops in Normandy, caused considerable anger; some of the bombers were from Canadian squadrons. (The following day 12th Canadian Field were strafed by RAF Spitfires and USAAF Mustangs.[96]) Bomber Command's losses that day were two Lancasters.[97]

As night fell the Canadians and the Polish Armoured Division were closing on Falaise; orders were now changed to make the early capture of Falaise a Canadian task, although it was not to interfere with their advance on Trun. During the night Canadian patrols reached the road between Falaise and St Pierre sur Dives while the infantry brigades made some progress. With daylight the attack continued, but German resistance was stiffening and 4 Armoured Brigade was stopped by an anti-tank screen. Although 3rd Canadian Division gained some ground a counter-attack forced withdrawal from the village of Soulangy. During the afternoon and early evening German forces facing 2nd Canadian Division began to disengage and withdraw, allowing the Canadians to reach positions about a mile from Falaise. An order was then issued to the Canadian and Polish armour to push towards Trun while 2nd Canadian Division moved into the ruins of Falaise; the men who pushed into the town were from The South Saskatchewans and The Cameron Highlanders of Canada, supported by two squadrons of Shermans from The Sherbrooke Fusiliers. They were engaged in clearing the town of its last German defenders; some fifty of Hitlerjugend held out in the Ecole Supérieure of whom only four were believed to have escaped from the blazing building.[98] Not until the 17th did the Canadians finally clear Falaise. Those SS men who fought to the last in Falaise might be described as fanatical by British or American historians but others acknowledge both their courage and their dedication to a cause, irrespective of its corrupt nature. One would like to think that, had Britain been overrun in 1940, men of the Brigade of Guards would have fought to the end in the ruins of Buckingham Palace in similar fashion.

But now the Germans began retiring from the rapidly shrinking Falaise pocket. Von Kluge issued the retreat order on the 16th in one of the last acts of his life and certainly his last as C-in-C West. He had suffered Rommel's fate on the 15th, when, en route to visit Eberbach and Hausser, his car had been attacked by Allied aircraft. Although unwounded he was cut off for several hours because his wirelesses had been destroyed. Since he was also cut off from contact with OKW, Hitler, who had suspected von Kluge of trying to negotiate with the Allies, gave free rein to his imagination, decided that his C-in-C was a traitor* and called Field Marshals Model and Kesselring to decide on a successor. However, von Kluge turned up safe and well but, on the 16th, refused to order a counter-attack that OKW had demanded but which he knew was impossible.[99] Although Hitler later authorised a withdrawal, von Kluge had fallen completely out of favour and was relieved of his command. On his journey back to Germany to account for his stewardship to his Führer, he committed suicide, having written a letter to Hitler protesting his undying loyalty. That letter from a professional general of the German army is one of the starkest proofs of the degree to which the professionalism and

* Hitler had also suspected von Kluge of having some sympathy with the July plotters.

integrity of the officer corps had become corrupted by Hitler's regime.[100]

Field Marshal Walter Model was appointed to succeed von Kluge and his first act was to order Fifth Panzer and Seventh Armies to withdraw from the pocket while II SS Panzer Corps, now including what remained of 2nd SS, 9th SS, 12th SS and 21st Panzer Divisions, was to hold against the British and Canadians from the north and XLVII Panzer Corps, including the remains of 2nd and 116th Panzer Divisions, was to hold the Americans from the south.[101]

Hitler is said to have described 15 August 1944 as the worst day of his life[102] and one can see why: everywhere his armies were being hammered; the Soviets continued to push hard in the east and on the Mediterranean coast Operation DRAGOON had taken place that morning. In Normandy, Falaise was all but lost and I SS Panzer Corps, located thereabouts, was worn out; LXXXVI Corps was under attack by I British Corps and was being withdrawn across the Dives; 85th Division had almost ceased to exist; and 12th SS Panzer Division had but fifteen tanks left. French troops were racing towards the British end of the Falaise gap while a new American armoured division appeared to have arrived to join the battle and to advance northwards from Dreux.

During the fighting on 16 August Second Army's final Victoria Cross of the campaign was earned by a young officer of 1/5th Welch Regiment, in 53rd (Welsh) Division, Lieutenant Tasker Watkins. In recent days the Welsh Division had crossed the Orne at Grimbosq to capture Bois Halbout – 1st East Lancashire – and Fresney le Vieux – 1/5th Welch – after hard fighting, before advancing to within six miles of Falaise. The division was then assigned to cutting roads out of the town and while carrying out this task Lieutenant Watkins' B Company became involved in a brisk action during its advance near the railway at Barfour.[103]

B Company's line of advance was across open cornfields in which the enemy had placed booby-traps. It was still daylight and the company had not gone far before coming under fire from machine guns, mortars and artillery. Watkins, the sole officer left, took command and, against close-range enemy fire, charged two German posts in succession, killing or wounding the defenders with his Sten gun. When he reached his objective he found an anti-tank gun manned by an enemy soldier and, since his Sten had jammed, threw the weapon at the German's face, drew his pistol and shot the man before he could recover from the surprise of Watkins' unconventional use of a Sten. By now B Company was reduced to some thirty men but when it came under counter-attack from about fifty enemy soldiers Watkins directed his men's fire before leading a bayonet charge that completed the rout of the enemy. As dusk fell orders were given for a withdrawal but these did not reach B Company, which was then surrounded.[104]

Undaunted, Tasker Watkins decided to rejoin the battalion by leading his men round the flank of the enemy position through which he had so recently advanced. Whilst doing so the company was challenged at close range from an enemy post. Watkins ordered his men to disperse and, taking up a Bren, charged the post and silenced it. He then led the remnants of B Company back to the battalion. The citation for his Victoria Cross notes that:

> His superb gallantry and total disregard for his own safety during an extremely difficult period were responsible for saving the lives of his men and had decisive influence on the course of the battle.[105]

B Company's experience was not 'an isolated engagement. All units [of the division] met stiff resistance from an enemy who was fighting desperately to keep the escape route open.'[106] A few days later, as that stiff fighting continued, Tasker Watkins was wounded but survived to receive his Victoria Cross and be promoted to major.

It was on the 16th that 3rd Canadian Division reached the two road junctions in Falaise's northern outskirts while their comrades of 2nd Canadian Division entered the town from the west 'to face a night and morning of mopping up among the ruins of the old market town'.[107] Confident that the infantry would secure Falaise, Simonds now directed 4th Canadian Armoured Division on Trun, a move subsequently confirmed by Crerar who also made the cathedral city of Lisieux the first objective for Crocker's I Corps, which was to be reinforced during the day by the arrival of the Desert Rats from Second Army. That afternoon Montgomery telephoned Crerar to say that he believed that Trun should be captured quickly and held as strongly as possible since he considered that the panzer divisions west of Argentan would attempt to break out between there and Falaise in a north-easterly direction. Such a move would make Trun, hub of a network of several roads, and in the middle of the gap, a vital point at which to stop the enemy.

This was the day on which von Kluge turned up again at his headquarters to learn that the Canadians were almost in Falaise, Dempsey's leading formations at Condé sur Noireau and Flers, and Americans nearing Flers; Patton's Third Army was thrusting for Chartres and Orléans. He telephoned Field Marshal Jodl at Hitler's headquarters to say that it was impossible to implement Hitler's order for an attack through Argentan and Sées and recommended evacuation through the gap that was diminishing by the hour. Jodl gave von Kluge 'a certain freedom of action' which allowed the latter to order Army Group B's withdrawal. Later that day he confirmed the withdrawal but ordered that Falaise be 'held tenaciously'; Eberbach was to attack to the south-east while von

Kluge was to move to Fifth Panzer Army's battle headquarters. Before the day was out von Kluge had been replaced by Model as commander in chief. His career was over and his life was ticking into its final hours. However, in one of von Kluge's final acts as C-in-C West, Hausser was placed in command of all German troops inside the Falaise pocket and ordered to withdraw to the east.[108]

Fighting continued. As darkness fell, II Corps' armoured divisions – 4th Canadian and 1st Polish – had pushed the enemy back some two to three miles through close wooded country in which the Germans had contested every piece of ground. Canadian armour took a bridge over the Dives at Morteaux Couliboeuf; the Poles were almost there as well. To the north Crocker's I Corps, having taken St Pierre sur Dives, was closing on Lisieux to create a wedge between LXXXVI Corps on the coast and I SS Panzer Corps around Falaise. But still the fighting went on, with the Germans showing a steely determination to hold until as many of their men as possible could escape from the Falaise pocket. By now the gap was only fifteen miles wide, from Falaise to Argentan, and Seventh Army had been all but surrounded by the Allies while Fifth Panzer Army still had its strength within the pocket. Montgomery urged the Canadians on to Trun and thence the four miles to Chambois, to which Bradley was asked to order American troops to advance. The race was on to see whether von Kluge's last intention for his command could be realised or if Montgomery's hope to close the gap before Seventh Army could escape would come to pass.

As the Canadians fought their way into Falaise, four German divisions – 346th, 272nd, 85th and 12th SS Panzer – held a front from Cabourg on the Channel coast to Falaise; the front was pushed over the Dives by I Corps' bridgehead at St Pierre sur Dives and by II Canadian Corps at Jort, but from there it stretched to the south-west. From Falaise the German front continued westward to Condé sur Noireau, where it was opposed by Dempsey's Second Army, and then southward to some five miles beyond Flers where it turned to the east and faced First US Army. Seventh Army, reduced to four divisions and five divisional battlegroups,[109] held the line to the Rouvre; east of that river Eberbach's force still held Argentan and the front from the Rouvre to the Dives. Under Eberbach's command, XLVII Corps now faced First US Army's right wing and elements of Third US Army.* II SS Panzer Corps headquarters had also joined Eberbach with 9th SS Panzer Division and two heavy tank battalions.

After dark on the 16th, Seventh Army began withdrawing and was surprised to be able to do so with little interference from Allied air forces;

* This was Patton's command, the rest of which was now directed towards Dreux, Chartres and Orléans.

No. 2 Group's Mosquitoes were engaged against river crossings and railways between the enemy rear and the Seine. On the 17th it became clear to Second Army that a major withdrawal was underway on their front since opposition to their advance was almost non-existent until some rearguards were met that afternoon. As the army continued its advance towards the Rouvre, it was delayed by the usual German demolitions, mines and booby traps while all bridges had been destroyed. In the course of its night withdrawal Seventh Army had covered up to eight miles and was making ready for another bound back after dark. II SS Panzer Corps was falling back to act as army group reserve in the Vimoutiers area, far outside the steadily compressing pocket.[110]

In the area around Trun and Chambois the Germans were still escaping from the pocket, using the roads through both towns; these ran north-eastwards and Allied forces had not managed to seal off the area in spite of having made steady progress. Anxious to close the gap finally, Montgomery ordered the armoured divisions of II Canadian Corps – 4th Canadian and 1st Polish – to secure Trun but, as the day wore on, he modified his orders; the Poles were to bypass Trun and make for Chambois with all haste. The Polish tankmen were to ignore the possible cost of their advance since, argued Montgomery, 'it was absolutely essential . . . that the armoured divisions should close the gap between themselves and the Americans'.[111] But enemy resistance was still determined. North of Trun the land is broken and hilly, not ideal for tanks, and there I SS Panzer Corps had fought with such verve and doughtiness that Canadian tanks were still up to four miles short of Trun by nightfall. The SS men had been reinforced by elements of 21st Panzer that had escaped from the pocket and, even in their exhausted and weakened state, had played havoc with II Canadian Corps' advance. One Canadian regiment was about a mile short of the Vimoutiers road; the leading Polish squadrons, on the Canadian left, had also been brought to a stop short of that artery by enemy anti-tank guns. Some other factors had also worked to the Germans' advantage. Allied aircraft had been restricted by poor flying weather while the fluid situation on the ground forced Allied commanders to define a new bombline that prevented any air attacks closer than Vimoutiers.[112] Nor had the planned American attack towards Chambois begun; V Corps headquarters was coming up to organise the operation which its commander was not yet ready to begin. Thus the gap between Trun and Chambois remained open.

The skies cleared in the afternoon and Second Tactical Air Force's machines found targets plentiful between Vimoutiers and Lisieux. Here were great concentrations of vehicles presenting 'just the sort of targets the pilots had been waiting for since D-day'.[113] Like foxes in a chicken run the aircraft wreaked havoc on their victims; some 500 planes left many vehicles in flames and destroyed barges on the Seine. There was no let-up in these attacks until dusk when the aircraft returned to their bases. Even then the baton was taken up by bombers; some 200 machines from No. 2 Group hit river crossings and roads beyond Lisieux.

Allied troops were on the move again in the early hours of the 18th. At 2.00am a column from 1st Polish Armoured Division set off for Chambois. Moving too far east in the darkness they ran into a column of enemy vehicles. This proved no real impediment to the Poles and they may even have regarded it as a bonus as they switched on spotlights and opened fire on the enemy. Then it was back to their original task and, before long, the column was in les Champeaux on the Trun–Vimoutiers road where it turned south for Chambois. Orders to push on to Chambois had also been issued to 4th Canadian Armoured Division but the obstacle of I SS Panzer Corps remained firmly in place so that, by nightfall, the Canadians had taken Trun but were stalled at St Lambert sur Dives on the road to Chambois. Their Polish comrades were held up to the east around Coudehard. Both divisions were but three or four miles from Chambois. The American attack on Chambois had also been fought to a halt by XLVII Panzer Corps. With the Americans some three miles from Chambois the gap had been reduced to about six miles but the end of the day saw it still open.

The day had also seen considerable activity from Allied air forces. As soon as the sun had burned away the morning mist the planes were airborne and, by dusk, Second Tactical Air Force had flown 1,471 sorties, claiming the destruction of 1,100 vehicles and ninety tanks with a further 1,500 vehicles and 100 tanks damaged.[114] Undoubtedly these figures contain an element of duplication but, even allowing for this, massive damage had been wreaked on the retreating Germans. However, there had been attacks by Allied aircraft on Allied troops, especially those of I Corps. The greatest injury had been inflicted on 51st (Highland) Division.[115] Some forty such incidents were recorded. By contrast the Luftwaffe had been kept out of the battle area by aircraft from ADGB, the former Fighter Command, which mounted patrols along the Seine and forced Luftwaffe fighters away from the front; some sixteen Focke Wulf FW 190s were claimed as destroyed by RAF pilots.[116]

Those mid-August days also saw much action elsewhere on the front. Bradley's 12 Army Group was continuing its encircling movement to the Seine. While First US Army faced north along the southern flank of the Falaise pocket to complete the reduction of enemy forces in that salient, Patton's Third Army faced east to drive on Dreux (XV Corps), Chartres (XX Corps), and Orléans (XII Corps). Patton's men moved fast, so fast that airborne drops became redundant, and Orléans was liberated on the 16th, Dreux the following day and Chartres was also entered by US troops on the 17th.[117] Although maintenance difficulties slowed progress somewhat in the succeeding days, by 19 August 79th US Division had secured a bridgehead over the Seine below Mantes while US patrols were within a few miles of Paris.[118] On that same day 12 Army Group ordered XV and XIX Corps to advance along the Seine's southern bank on a front that stretched from Mantes to Dreux and Verneuil.

We have already seen how Second Army and First Canadian Army had made inroads into enemy-held territory during those same days so that Falaise was in Canadian hands and the battle for the pocket was into its final phase. On the 18th the Germans attempted to retrieve the situation by attacking towards Trun and Chambois with II SS Panzer Corps to secure the escape routes.[119] At much the same time V US Corps punched north towards Chambois from the Argentan sector to try to link up with the Canadian and Polish formations closing on the town while, on the western edge of the pocket, XXX Corps reached Poutanges and Ecouche and XII Corps made further inroads into enemy positions.

Describing the development of the battle in terms of the progression of armies and corps, or even divisions, tends to obscure the hard fighting that occurred at the very front where tank crews and infantry sections bore the brunt. There was no easing of the intensity of that fighting, especially where Canadians were pitted against SS soldiers; in extreme adversity the German soldier, whether army or SS, was at his toughest and many examples of this tenacity were doled out to Allied soldiers as the neck of the Falaise pocket came ever nearer to closure. Seventh Army continued its withdrawal from the Orne as Second Army closed in; the Germans intended to pull back to the Argentan–Falaise road and their rearguards were holding out against British and American pursuers. Both Second British and First US Armies were now operating on narrowing fronts; Second Army's front was on a three-divisional width (53rd (Welsh) and 59th (Staffordshire) Divisions of XII Corps and 11th Armoured of XXX Corps; VIII Corps had been pinched out as the front narrowed). German discipline remained good and their withdrawal during the night of 18–19 August

> was undisturbed from the air, for strong forces of 2 Group's [Mosquitoes] were again employed between Lisieux and the Seine, adding to the havoc on roads and among the ferries, pontoons and landing stages on the river.[120]

Next morning troops of 4th Canadian Armoured Division continued their advance on St Lambert sur Dives. The attack had begun on the 18th but met stiff enemy resistance at St Lambert, which included 88s. One battlegroup, including tanks, infantry and self-propelled anti-tank guns, was commanded by Major David Vivian Currie of 29th Reconnaissance Regiment (The South Alberta Regiment). As Currie's force moved on St Lambert, 88s knocked out two tanks, halting the advance. That evening,

Currie decided to go forward alone to reconnoitre the defences and rescue the crews of the crippled tanks. This he succeeded in doing under heavy mortar fire.[121]

On the morning of the 19th, Currie led an attack that had the advantage of surprise since it was executed without a preliminary artillery bombardment. Against determined opposition from tanks, infantry and anti-tank guns, Currie's men forced their way into the village and, by midday, had consolidated a position well inside St Lambert. Since St Lambert sat on a road vital to the escape of German forces from the pocket, a series of ferocious counter-attacks was launched on Currie's battlegroup. Each was repulsed. Attacks continued throughout that day and the next. The final, and probably the strongest, came as dusk fell on the 20th. This was beaten almost before it started as Currie's force wreaked havoc on the attackers as they deployed for their assault; enemy casualties were estimated at 300 dead and 500 wounded while another 2,100 men were captured. In spite of the state of exhaustion in which he and his men must have been, David Currie then continued his attack into St Lambert and secured the entire village, thus cutting off an escape route for many of those still trapped in the Falaise pocket.[122] Such was the achievement of Currie's small force that he was awarded the Victoria Cross.

> Throughout three days and nights of fierce fighting, during which all the officers in his command were either killed or wounded, Major Currie's gallant conduct and contempt of danger had set a magnificent example to all ranks of the force under his command.[123]

David Currie was the first Canadian soldier to earn the Victoria Cross in the campaign to liberate Europe.* His award was announced formally in November when Currie travelled to London to be decorated by King George VI.

As Currie and his men fought their battle in St Lambert the left flank of 4th Canadian Armoured Division crossed the Trun–Vimoutiers road to reach the high ground about Hordouseaux but Canadian tanks were unable to contact their Polish comrades who were engaged in a series of bloody skirmishes in the hilly country around Coudehard; no more than five miles separated the two formations but a meeting was denied by the tenacity of German opposition. The Poles were in a dire situation, having been isolated by the enemy and with low petrol stocks, much Polish petrol having been destroyed in an Allied air attack on the 18th.[124]

In spite of their travails the Poles fought doggedly and it is a measure of their courage and determination that, at about 7.00pm on 19 August, a

* Canadian airmen had already earned the Victoria Cross but Currie was the sole soldier and the sole survivor of the action that merited the Cross.

group of Poles finally succeeded in breaking through the enemy to reach and enter Chambois. There they met troops of 90th US Division who had reached Chambois just before them. The Falaise gap had been closed at last, the pocket sealed, at least partially, and many of the Germans remaining within it destined for prisoner-of-war camps. As the British Official History comments:

> By the capture of Trun and Chambois on the 19th roads running north-eastwards out of the pocket had at last been cut though, as Model realised, the Allied encirclement of Seventh Army was a loose one. The enemy formations retiring each night had inevitably kept on or near the roads. The Allied troops closing in on them had cut off and captured a bag of prisoners that grew larger each day, and Allied shelling and traffic break-downs led to the wholesale abandonment of destroyed and damaged vehicles and guns. Until the main forces reached the Falaise–Argentan road cohesion had been maintained. Now, it was largely lost.[125]

That the sealing was not perfect was known to both Germans and Allies and final efforts were being made by German formations to break out. Thus it was that the remnants of II Parachute Corps and Panzer Group Eberbach led the attempt by Seventh Army to break out to the north-east through an Allied ring that had not yet solidified. There were no guns or other heavy weapons to support Seventh Army and only a few tanks still survived. II SS Panzer Corps' two armoured divisions had been held behind Vimoutiers but had been unable to assist Seventh Army's breakout since Allied aircraft had destroyed much of their petrol. At about 8.00am on 20 August the German forces trying to break through ran up against the Canadians at St Lambert and an American regiment near Chambois. Weight of numbers carried German troops, led by 3rd Parachute Division, around the Canadians at St Lambert; there were simply not enough Canadian troops to arrest the movement, and those present were already engaged in that action in which David Currie earned the Victoria Cross.

Allied artillery fire wreaked havoc in the retreating forces and all control was lost as the large formation broke into smaller groups; with no wireless vehicles – all long since destroyed – there could be no communication or cohesion. Many Germans became prisoners at this stage. Others died as they ran into and engaged groups of Allied troops. The Poles near Coudehard were still under attack from the enemy, whose numbers were increased by tanks of II SS Panzer Corps, now replenished with fuel. As if to assist the enemy the weather prevented Allied aircraft from taking a hand in the battle. About mid-morning II SS Panzer Corps began counter-attacking in two main thrusts.[126] One was fought to a halt by the Poles at Coudehard and the other became enmeshed with the

Canadians. But the two Allied divisions had been split to create an opportunity, albeit fleeting, for German soldiers to escape; many took advantage of that opportunity.

Although Simonds ordered 4th Canadian Armoured to push forward to the south-east to link up with the Poles and seal the escape routes, the confusion of the fighting, with five armoured regiments engaged around Hordouseaux, contrived to prevent progress; in any case, there was no certainty about the Polish positions. Not until next day, the 21st, did the Canadians reach the Poles after some sharp fights en route. For their part the Poles, who had been re-supplied by parachute on the morning of the 21st, had fought with remarkable tenacity for three days during which they had been isolated by enemy forces. The British Official Historian comments that 'the Polish Armoured Division had fought with the greatest gallantry and stood its ground to a man'.[127]

From the west 53rd (Welsh) Division pushed forward to join the Canadians near Trun while battlegroups from 3rd and 4th Canadian Divisions linked up with their comrades at St Lambert to advance to Chambois. The last desperate attempts by German troops to escape the pocket came to naught as they ran into the Canadians. At last the gap was sealed firmly. The long battle for Normandy was over.

How successful had been the Allied attempt to encircle the German forces in the pocket? A contemporary account from Army Group B estimates that between forty and fifty per cent of those who attempted to break out reached II SS Panzer Corps' lines, which suggests that considerable numbers were lost. British returns of prisoners taken by those divisions engaged directly in the fighting to close the pocket indicate that Second Army took 7,500 prisoners between 16 and 21 August, inclusive, and II Canadian Corps took another 12,500. American records do not show separate figures for prisoners taken around the pocket but the British Official Historian believes that they would have been about the same; on 21 August US forces made some 9,000 enemy troops prisoner.[128] Material loss was more easily estimated: 21 Army Group sent specialists from No. 2 Operational Research Section into the battleground to examine the area and the section reported that, in one portion of the battlefield*, could be found the remains or wrecks of 344 tanks, SPGs or other armoured vehicles while there were also 2,447 lorries and cars with 252 towed artillery pieces. Since much German transport was horse-drawn – up to seventy-five per cent of the allocation of a standard infantry division – there were also many dead horses. But it was impossible to count the equine corpses, such was the stench that permeated the battlefields.

* This was the area bounded by Pierrefitte, midway between Argentan and Falaise, Argentan, Chambois, Vimoutiers, Trun and Pierrefitte.[129]

Veterans of Normandy all agree that the abiding memory of those days is the smell of death hanging in the air around them, a smell that rose from the bodies of dead men of both sides, of dead civilians who became victims of war, of dead cattle, on which many of Normandy's farmers depended, of dead horses, both those of the local farmers and of the German forces and even of dead goats, from whose milk some of the local cheeses were made. And there were airmen who flew above the battlefields who recalled that they could also smell that sickly, cloying aroma even hundreds of feet above the earth. No one who ever breathed it in can forget that smell.

> I'll never forget the Falaise gap. As we went through it, at each side of the road there were bodies piled up. You'd [have] thought it was [like], you know, the way you pile up sheaves of corn. There was dead bodies piled up [of] horses – there was a terrible stench from the dead bodies. That was one thing I'll never forget about the Falaise gap.[130]

Terrible damage had been inflicted on the German armies in Normandy but many survived to fight again. The Canadian historian is critical of his own countrymen for not achieving a more rapid closure of the gap between Trun and Chambois.

> Had our troops been more experienced, the Germans would hardly have been able to escape a worse disaster. They were especially fortunate in that the two armoured divisions available to the First Canadian Army – the 4th Canadian Armoured Division and the 1st Polish Armoured Division – had never fought before they were committed to battle in Normandy at one of the highest and fiercest crises of the war. Less raw formations would probably have obtained larger and earlier results.[131]

On 21 August the commander of 4th Canadian Armoured Division was relieved of his command to join a succession of senior officers, both British and Canadian, who were deemed to have failed the test of battle.[132]

Elsewhere, in the final phase of the battle, I Corps had pushed eastward in the area between II Canadian Corps and the coast. Strengthened by 1 and 4 Special Service Brigades and the newly-arrived 1 Belgian Infantry and Royal Netherlands (Princess Irene's) Brigades, 6th Airborne Division captured Troarn and pushed on towards the coast; in 6th Armoured Reconnaissance Regiment, Cromwell tanks had replaced the light tanks and proved useful in recce'ing for the advance.[133]

Naval guns helped bring about the surrender of the Houlgate battery, a persistent nuisance since D-Day, but the speed of advance was restricted by deliberate flooding of low ground by the Germans, while defences at Cabourg and around Dozule impeded the advance across the Dives delta. Nonetheless, by the 26th, 6th Airborne Armoured Recce and a Belgian reconnaissance squadron were leading the way to Pont Audemer; the regiment had also assisted infantry at Honfleur on the 23rd. On 27 August, and for the first time since D-Day, the men of 6th Airborne Division were able to rest, having been withdrawn from battle to return to Britain, their task in Normandy complete.[134]

While the British advance out of Normandy on the left flank along the coast was making slow progress, the Americans had a much clearer run and Patton's XV Corps had raced to the Seine while XIX Corps filled in between Gacé and Dreux. On 19 August troops of 79th US Division crossed the Seine by night.[135] Within twenty-four hours the entire division had followed. Hitler issued orders for resistance along the Seine and the defence of Paris which proved redundant as the speed of the Allied advance and the weakness of Model's command – Seventh Army had all but ceased to exist and its commander, Hausser, had been wounded – overtook the Führer's plans. Before long, British and Canadian troops were also en route for the Seine. So, too, were French troops under General Leclerc and, late on the 24th, French and American troops reached Paris. On 25 August the German commander, General von Choltitz, surrendered the city of light to General Leclerc.[136]

And the advance continued. Such was the speed of Allied progress in the later days of August as two army groups raced through France that veterans would look back on these as the days of the 'great swan'. Suddenly, after the attrition of Normandy, it seemed as if anything might be possible. Ahead lay the Low Countries and then the Reich itself. There were many who believed that the war might end by Christmas. Brussels fell to Second Army on 3 September, the fifth anniversary of the outbreak of war, and still there was much optimism. But, as the chill of autumn began biting into the evening air, cold reality also began to be felt. The Allied logistical chain was coming under greater strain as the advance moved eastward. New ports would be essential, especially Antwerp. But there was to be one final attempt to end the war in 1944 with plans to use the Allied Airborne Army to take the bridges over the Maas, Waal and Lower Rhine. This was to lead to Operation MARKET GARDEN and the battle of Arnhem in late-September. It would not achieve its aim and the onset of winter would see the Allies halted on the German frontier with The Netherlands occupied.

With the battle for Normandy over, Eisenhower brought SHAEF headquarters to France. On 1 September the Supreme Commander took over direct control of the ground battle. No longer was 12 US Army Group to be under Montgomery's operational command, even if the Americans had considered that command nominal in recent weeks. With Eisenhower in France at the helm, it was clear that the US was the senior partner. US forces continued building their strength in France whereas British forces were suffering severe manpower problems, as shown by the decision to break up 59th (Staffordshire) Division, the junior infantry formation in Second Army.[137] Before the year was out the Staffords' fate would be shared by 50th (Northumbrian) Division.[138]

As a form of compensation for his reduced stature within the Allied command structure, Montgomery was promoted to Field Marshal on 1 September. He received congratulations from many quarters, including General George Marshall, Chief of the US Army, and several of his British contemporaries. One letter commented that 'There could be no more appropriate recognition of what you and 21 Army Group have done for the world.'[139] What they had done was to help win the battle for Normandy, which led to the liberation of France and eventually to all occupied western Europe. It was no mean achievement.

NOTES

1 Bradley, *A Soldier's Story*, p. 342.
2 Fitzgerald, *History of the Irish Guards in the Second World War*, p. 396.
3 Ellis, *Victory in the West*, p. 420.
4 D'Este, *Decision in Normandy*, p. 386.
5 Quoted in Ellis, op cit, p. 375.
6 Ellis, op cit, p. 375.
7 Ibid, p. 304; D'Este, op cit, p. 408.
8 Bradley, op cit, p. 350–2.
9 Montgomery, *Memoirs*, p. 257; *Normandy to the Baltic*, pp. 250–3.
10 Hamilton, *Monty Master of the Battlefield*, pp. 745–6.
11 Ellis, op cit, p. 377.
12 Ibid, p. 378.
13 Ibid, p. 379.
14 Ibid.
15 D'Este, op cit, p. 401n.
16 Bradley, op cit, pp. 348–9.
17 D'Este, op cit, p. 404.
18 Ellis, op cit, p. 383; Bradley, op cit, pp. 358–67.
19 D'Este, op cit, p. 407.
20 Montgomery, *Memoirs*, p. 260.
21 Ellis, op cit, p. 386.
22 Quoted in Ellis, op cit, p. 386.
23 Ellis, op cit, p. 386.
24 Middlebrook & Everitt, *The Bomber Command War Diaries*, p. 553; Ellis, op cit, p. 388.
25 Ellis, op cit, pp. 388–9.
26 Ibid, p. 390.
27 Roberts, *From the Desert to the Baltic*, pp. 185–7.
28 Ibid, p. 187.

29 Doherty, *Only The Enemy*, p. 157.
30 Ellis, op cit, p. 391.
31 Ibid.
32 Ibid.
33 Ibid, p. 393.
34 Ibid.
35 Roberts, op cit, pp. 189–90.
36 Baynes, *The Forgotten Victor*, p. 220.
37 Daglish, *Operation Bluecoat*, pp. 105–6; Roberts, op cit, 191–2.
38 Ellis, op cit, p. 401.
39 Ibid.
40 Ibid, p. 402.
41 Ibid; Reynolds, *Sons of the Reich*, pp. 61–2; Verney (*The Desert Rats*, op cit) makes no mention of this rebuff, p. 214.
42 Ellis, op cit, p. 402; Verney, *The Desert Rats*, p. 215.
43 Ellis, op cit, p. 402; Horrocks, *A Full Life*, p. 180.
44 Taylor, *Record of a Reconnaissance Regiment: A history of the 43rd Reconnaissance Regiment (The Gloucestershire Regiment) 1939–1945*, p. 70.
45 Doherty, *Only The Enemy*, p. 163.
46 Middlebrook & Everitt, op cit, p. 555; Ellis, op cit, p. 410n.
47 Ellis, op cit, p. 405.
48 Quoted in Ellis, p. 405; sent by OKW at 2315 on 2 Aug and repeated to Army Group B HQ at 0020 on the 3rd..
49 Quoted in Ellis, p. 406.
50 Ellis, op cit, p. 407.
51 Montgomery, *Normandy to the Baltic*, p. 261.
52 Doherty, *Only The Enemy*, p. 160.
53 Ibid.
54 Ibid, p. 161.
55 Reynolds, *Steel Inferno*, p. 205.
56 NA, WO171/1351, war diary, 7 R Norfolk.
57 Ibid.
58 *London Gazette*, 26 Oct 44.
59 *London Gazette*, 2 Nov 44.
60 Military Historical Society, Lummis Files.
61 Reynolds, *Steel Inferno*, p. 210.
62 Bennett, *Ultra in the West*, p. 114.
63 Ibid.
64 Reynolds, *Steel Inferno*, p. 219.
65 Ibid, p. 227.
66 Lewin, *Montgomery as Military Commander*, pp. 227–8.
67 Ibid, p. 228.
68 Ellis, op cit, p. 421.
69 Ibid, p. 420.
70 Reynolds, *Steel Inferno*, p. 230.
71 Middlebrook & Everitt, op cit, p. 557.
72 Ibid.
73 Ellis, op cit, pp. 421–2; Salmond, *The History of the 51st Highland Division*, pp. 154–9.
74 Ellis, op cit, p. 422.
75 Reynolds, *Steel Inferno*, p. 233.
76 Ibid, p. 234.
77 Ibid, p. 237.

78 Tout, *Roads to Falaise*, p. 202.
79 Ibid, pp. 186–7.
80 Quoted in Reynolds, *Steel Inferno*, p. 237.
81 Ellis, op cit, p. 409.
82 Ibid; NA, WO171/1395, war diary, 5th Wiltshire Regt.
83 Ellis, op cit, p. 410.
84 Bradley, *A Soldier's Story*, p. 375.
85 Ibid.
86 Ibid, p. 425.
87 Quoted in ibid, p. 426.
88 Ellis, op cit, p. 427.
89 Hastings, *Overlord*, p. 290.
90 Bradley, op cit, pp. 376–7.
91 Montgomery, *Memoirs*, p. 263.
92 Montgomery, *Normandy to the Baltic*, pp. 269–70.
93 Ellis, op cit, p. 430.
94 Middlebrook & Everitt, op cit, p. 562.
95 Ibid; NA, WO179/3050, war diary, 12th Cdn Fd Regt.
96 Ibid.
97 Middlebrook & Everitt, op cit, p. 562.
98 Reynolds, *Steel Inferno*, p. 259. Reynolds points out that Kurt Meyer discovered in 1983 that eighteen other soldiers had escaped but had subsequently been captured.
99 Ellis, op cit, p. 433.
100 Ibid, p. 434.
101 Ibid.
102 Quoted in ibid, p. 431.
103 Ibid.
104 Military Historical Society, Lummis Files.
105 *London Gazette*, 2 Nov 44.
106 Barclay, *The History of the 53rd (Welsh) Division*, p. 68
107 Ellis, op cit, p. 432
108 Ibid, p. 439.
109 Ibid, p. 440.
110 Reynolds, *Sons of the Reich*, p. 79.
111 Ellis, op cit, p. 441.
112 Ibid.
113 Quoted in Ellis, op cit, p. 441.
114 Ibid, p. 443.
115 Salmond, op cit, p. 161.
116 Ellis, op cit, p. 444.
117 Ibid, p. 449; Bradley and Eisenhower give only brief summaries of 12 Army Group's advances at this stage..
118 Ibid, p. 440.
119 Reynolds, *Sons of the Reich*, p. 82.
120 Ellis, op cit, p. 445.
121 Ellis, op cit, p. 445; Military Historical Society, Lummis Files.
122 Military Historical Society, Lummis Files.
123 *London Gazette*, 27 Nov 1944.
124 Ellis, op cit, p. 445.
125 Ibid.
126 Reynolds, *Sons of the Reich*, p. 86.

127 Ellis, op cit, p. 447.
128 Ibid, pp. 447–8.
129 Ibid, p. 448; NA, WO106/4348.
130 Sam Anderson, 6 LAA Bty, i/v with author.
131 Stacey, *The Victory Campaign*, p. 276.
132 Ellis, op cit, p. 448.
133 NA, WO171/435, war diary, 6 A/b Armd Recce Regt.
134 NA, WO171/425, war diary, 6th A/b Div.
135 Ellis, op cit, p. 449; Bradley notes only that Third Army crossed the Seine, p. 385.
136 Bradley, op cit, p. 392.
137 Joslen, *Orders of Battle: Second World War*, p. 93.
138 Ibid, p. 81.
139 Hamilton, *Monty The Field Marshal*, p. 8.

CHAPTER XII

Normandy in retrospect

In bloody field doth win immortal fame

Whatever arguments persist about the Normandy campaign, one fact can never be disputed: the D-Day landings represent the greatest military operation ever. Planning, organising and executing such a mammoth undertaking demanded tremendous skills, resources and application and those who led the Allied nations and their armed forces met those demands when called upon. And the battle that followed the landings led to the destruction of Army Group B and a defeat that ranked with Stalingrad and 'Tunisgrad' in 1943 and the smashing of Army Group Centre in the same summer as Normandy.

The latter is probably one of the most severe defeats in history and yet, as Sir John Keegan argues, 'if strict comparisons are made between its results and those of Normandy, it may yet appear the Western Allies' victory was the greater'.[1] Keegan argues that the Western Allies committed only thirty-four divisions to Normandy against the 140 employed by the Soviets. Even allowing for the differences in divisional size – Russian divisions were smaller – and the larger proportion of corps and army troops in the Western armies, Keegan's argument stands: that in terms of effort the Allies in Normandy achieved a better result than the Soviets. Although the Soviet offensive saw Fourth and Ninth German Armies driven back some 250 miles to within fifty miles of Germany itself in only three weeks, an advance more spectacular than that in Normandy, losses inflicted on Germany and her allies were 300,000 dead or captured and twenty-eight divisions smashed. Yet in Normandy, German armies lost 500,000 men, half of them dead, while twenty-seven infantry divisions 'had been ground to dust'. On 6 June von Rundstedt had forty-eight infantry divisions of which only twenty-one remained in the order of battle in September. Of the twelve armoured divisions committed in Normandy, eleven had all but ceased to exist. German armoured formations lost 2,200 tanks in Normandy; by September those divisions could deploy only 120 tanks of the 1,800 that should have been available to them.

The Allied race through France and the liberation of both France and

Belgium was also a spectacular advance that removed an entire OKW theatre. Although the post of Supreme Commander West remained, the incumbent's responsibilities had reduced from those of early-June, when he oversaw the Mediterranean coast, France's Atlantic, Channel and North Sea coasts, the Low Countries, plus Germany itself, a huge reduction. And Keegan points out that losing France was more than symbolic to Germany since occupied France had supplied 'as much food to German tables as the . . . occupied east during 1941–44' as well as almost one-in-five of the 2,700,000 horses requisitioned for military use; the German army still relied largely on horse-drawn transport and artillery in 1945.[2] In addition, French industry and natural resources had been harnessed to Germany's war effort. Factories produced equipment for its army, Luftwaffe aircraft and material for all three services while much French coal, bauxite and iron ore was exported compulsorily to Germany. France was taxed to pay for the occupation and offset the cost of German military operations elsewhere. Keegan states that

> The total value of goods and services extracted in the last full year of occupation, 1943, equalled a quarter of Germany's whole national product in the last full year of peace, 1938.[3]

Interestingly, in view of the Allied destruction of France's rail system, eighty-five per cent of French rail movements in 1944 were dedicated to exporting French resources to Germany.[4]

Thus losing France was a huge economic and social blow to Germany as well as a great military defeat. That loss was due to the Normandy battles, which provided the springboard for the offensive that led Allied armies to the German frontier by the onset of winter. And those Allied armies now included a significant French element. By mid-August, Leclerc's division, the sole French formation on French soil in July, had been joined by four more in the French corps of Seventh US Army, which landed in southern France in Operation DRAGOON.* Although those latter divisions were largely colonial, by early-1945 the French army fielded seven divisions, almost entirely French in composition, against a shrinking German army, and would continue to grow to ensure a French zone of occupation in post-war Germany. And so the fall of France also strengthened the manpower of the armies aligned against Germany.

The Reich was much smaller in September 1944 than on 6 June. As Allied troops landed in Normandy, Allied armies were also advancing in Italy, passing Rome in pursuit of the retreating Army Group C. By the end of the Normandy campaign, the British Eighth and American Fifth Armies

* These would expand into First French Army, which formed 6 Army Group alongside Seventh US Army.

were preparing to smash the Gothic line with hopes that the Italian campaign would be over by Christmas 1944. That was not to happen, and nor would it happen in north-west Europe as the Allied advance stalled on the frontiers of Germany itself. In the east Red Army formations were re-organising for operations in Poland while, on 20 August, Malinovsky's Fifty-second Army broke through Germany's Army Group Ukraine, to be followed by Sixth Tank Army. Within four days these formations met up with two mechanised corps from Marshal Tolbukhin's armies near Leovo. Before long the Soviets were driving forward to link up with Tito's partisan forces in Yugoslavia and had crossed the border into Romania, threatening German forces in the Balkans; Romania accepted terms from the Russians and another partner had deserted Hitler. In southern France, French troops from Seventh US Army liberated Toulon on 20 August. Marseilles was liberated on 28 August, providing a Mediterranean port for the maintenance of Allied forces in southern France; convoys could sail to Marseilles directly from the USA.* Franco–American forces continued pushing north-westward with Soissons liberated and French troops across the Rhône on 29 August. General Jean de Lattre de Tassigny's French Corps then wheeled right to advance up the west bank of the Rhône and, on 12 September, near Dijon, 140 miles from Paris, a patrol of de Lattre's corps met another from Leclerc's 2nd Armoured Division.[5] Appropriately, the junction between OVERLORD and DRAGOON was made by Frenchmen, liberating their native land. This closing of the arms of the two invading forces in France underlines the strategic importance of the Normandy campaign; without it the liberation of western Europe would have been impossible. Without the wearing down of German forces in Normandy, DRAGOON could not have happened while the Germans might even have been able to reinforce and stabilise the eastern front. In turn that could have led to an armistice with the USSR, for Stalin might well not have been prepared to carry on against Germany if he believed that the Western Allies could not deliver their part of the bargain. Needless to say, the Italian campaign would still have bogged down; it had been deprived of resources to provide landing craft for Normandy and personnel for both OVERLORD and DRAGOON. Without the need to reinforce Normandy the Germans would have been able to reinforce Italy, thus making even more difficult the Allied task there.

Another question often posed about Normandy is: could the operation have taken place a year earlier? This brings us back to the differences between British and American commanders and politicians about the invasion's timing. When America entered the war the US President, his

* The failure to clear the Scheldt estuary before winter set in also meant that Marseilles was critical to the supply of 12 and 21 Army Groups.

Chiefs of Staff and political advisers were quick to adopt the 'Germany first' policy and, before long, Americans were advocating the earliest possible invasion of north-west Europe. General George Marshall, therefore, proposed concentrating British and US forces in Britain for a cross-Channel invasion. His plan fell into three elements: BOLERO, the build-up in the United Kingdom; SLEDGEHAMMER, an emergency invasion of the continent in autumn 1942 should the USSR appear to be about to collapse; and ROUNDUP, a cross-Channel assault in 1943. Although British and Americans agreed on the need for all three elements, differences began to appear on the timing of the third, with British chiefs concerned that a successful invasion would not be possible in 1943.

Winston Churchill at first favoured the concept of a 1943 invasion, although he opposed any such venture in 1942, realising that the main body of any invasion force that year would be British and that the chances of failure were high; British public opinion would not tolerate another Dunkirk. While he considered invasion possible in 1943, and promised Stalin as much, Churchill also wanted action elsewhere and was supported by Brooke. Brooke was a proponent of 'closing the ring' on Germany by defeating the Axis on the periphery before turning to Germany itself. Since significant British forces were already fighting in North Africa, it seemed logical to Brooke, and Churchill, that they should continue to be used there. In the event, Eighth Army was joined by First Army, which entered French north-west Africa in Operation TORCH in November 1942. Since American forces were also committed to TORCH they argued that, having cleared the Axis from North Africa, further Mediterranean operations should be undertaken to knock Italy out of the war. Unfortunately, and true to character, Hitler reinforced Tunisia in response to TORCH and the speedy German build-up, aided by much shorter lines of communication, ensured that the campaign did not end until May 1943. The lengthy fighting in Tunisia became a prime factor in ensuring that a cross-Channel invasion did not occur in 1943.

Most historians have accepted the argument that the invasion could not have happened in 1943, since all the requirements for victory were not in place until then. There have been exceptions to this school, chief among them John Grigg, whose book *1943 The Victory that Never Was* argues that the invasion could have occurred a year earlier.[6] Grigg suggests that OVERLORD could have happened in 1943 since the requirements already existed: overwhelming air superiority; sufficient Allied troops in Britain for a landing and subsequent build-up; the means to transport the force to France; and the ability to prevent concentration of enemy forces against the invasion force before the bridgehead was consolidated.

According to Grigg, the Allies had the potential for overwhelming air superiority in 1943 and could have executed the strategy of destroying German communications, bombarding positions immediately before the landing and providing air cover over the beachhead. Manpower, too, was available with sixteen British divisions in the UK in March 1943 preparing for an invasion as well as another eleven UK-based divisions; outside the UK were thirty-eight other British divisions. US manpower had reached seventy-three divisions by the end of 1942 with 5,397,000 men in the Army and Army Air Forces. Thus, opines Grigg, it would have been possible to have sufficient forces concentrated in Britain by summer 1943 to launch a cross-Channel invasion.

Could those men have been transported across the Channel in 1943? Grigg's answer is 'yes'; more landing craft were used to invade Sicily in July 1943 than in OVERLORD. Grigg argues that the craft were simply in the wrong place in 1943 and that British lack of enthusiasm for a cross-Channel invasion that year led the Americans to move craft from the Mediterranean to the Pacific towards the end of the year while US production of such vessels was cut back. Combined with the landing craft argument is the suggestion that the Atlantic Wall was so strong that 'any attempt to breach it before 1944 would have been suicidal lunacy'.[7] However, Rommel did not assume responsibility for the Wall until the end of 1943; he found it virtually non-existent in places; and one area where it was weak was in the Bay of the Seine. When we contemplate what happened on D-Day it is evident that the Wall was almost a chimera, that while it may not have vanished as the Allies landed, it was no great obstacle. There was no depth to the defences and Rommel's plan to counter-attack on the beaches was not carried out because he was absent and the invasion was not identified initially as the real thing. Nor were panzer divisions available to the local commander; what they might have done is illustrated only too well by 21st Panzer's penetration almost to the coast in the sole armoured counter-attack of D-Day. But the defences were weaker in 1943 than in June 1944 and Normandy was then still very much a backwater for the German garrison of France. All these factors support Grigg's argument.

What about the U-boats? The submarine fleet threatened to strangle Allied trans-Atlantic communications and deprive Britain of its lifeline to North America. Would the U-boats not have prevented an invasion in 1943? In March 1943 they took their heaviest toll of Allied shipping and, yet, by May the war at sea had turned against the Germans with Dönitz ordering his boats out of the north Atlantic to concentrate their efforts closer to home. Assuming that an invasion did not occur until August 1943 then the U-boat menace was under control, although there were new boats in production and new devices that could again increase their threat.

There is much in favour of Grigg's argument that the invasion could have occurred in 1943. But it is always easier to argue with the benefit of hindsight. In early-1943 the Allies did not know that the U-boats would be on the retreat by the end of May and, even when that happened, it took time for the scope of the change in German strategy to be appreciated. This would have weighed very strongly with the planners as they studied the possibilities for that year. Arguably, an invasion was possible in 1943 but, to paraphrase Wellington, it would have been a close run thing. Even in 1944, it was close run. Omar Bradley commented that the Allies succeeded 'by the slimmest of margins'. The degree of confidence needed to succeed was probably not there in 1943 and certainly not amongst the British chiefs, one of whom, Portal, continued to believe that bombing alone could win the European war. Paradoxically, had the operation taken place in 1943 then it almost certainly would have been under a British supreme commander who, in all probability, would have been Brooke. He is likely to have brought Montgomery home from Eighth Army to command ground forces but the presence of Brooke at the Allied helm would have been a very strong plus factor in achieving success.

To what degree was D-Day close run? Why did Bradley write that the Allies succeeded 'by the slimmest of margins'? There are several reasons, including the losses suffered in the night-time airborne attack, which were such that no further Allied airborne operations were carried out at night. Then there was the tragedy of Omaha Beach where American soldiers learned just how difficult Rommel's opposition would have been, had it been put into operation along the entire beachhead. This highlighted American failure to make use of the British 'Funnies' and the mistake of launching DD tanks too soon so that most were swamped on the run in to the beach. Success tends to obscure errors, of which there were several, all also conspiring to make the victory a narrow one. For all its achievements the naval bombardment had faults and did not eliminate all the German coastal batteries. There was a failure overall to note that embrasures on casemates faced the beaches rather than the sea. Aerial photos of defences had not been interpreted correctly and, since those embrasures were located to enfilade beaches and assaulting soldiers there rather than fire out to sea, the naval guns were firing not on the weakest part of the gun positions, i.e., where there was an opening, but on solid reinforced walls. At Sword Beach, there was also the failure to locate and assess the extent of the Hillman strongpoint that delayed 3rd Division's advance and was one reason why Caen was not taken on D-Day. Other errors included the fact that on Juno Beach insufficient consideration was given to tidal conditions.

Grigg's argument must be given some credibility, as must his consideration of the possible consequences of a successful 1943 invasion. These included the saving of many lives, including 600,000 Jews who died at Auschwitz between May and November 1944, as well as 250,000, at least, Hungarian Jews murdered in 1944.[8] Many civilians who died as a result of V1 and V2 attacks in 1944 and 1945 might have survived and, of course, the Soviets would not have broken out of Mother Russia so that the political map of post-war Europe would have been very different.

But, of course the invasion did not happen in 1943, for a variety of factors, considered in Chapter IV and summarised by stating that the Allies feared defeat, a repeat of Dieppe on an even greater scale, thereby ensuring that any further attempt to invade France would have been far in the future, if at all. And such a further attempt would have been very much in doubt had the USSR decided to make a separate peace with Hitler. The argument over a 1943 invasion could take an entire book – as it has done with Grigg's tome – and can only be summarised here. This author's view is that the situation must be considered, as far as possible, in the light of the circumstances of the time, with the knowledge and intelligence then available to Allied planners and with all the fears that those planners had, especially the British who had endured Dunkirk, Dieppe and a host of failures from an army of which they oftentimes despaired. In that light, the decision to delay until 1944 was one that can be understood as offering a greater chance for success. And since D-Day was close run in so many ways, who can say truly that the planners were wrong?

At the top of the planning table from January 1944 were Eisenhower and Montgomery, who would take so much of the responsibility for operations and, in Eisenhower's case, total responsibility for success or failure. Were they the right men for those positions? Perhaps the first question should be: why were they chosen? In Eisenhower's case, the answer is relatively easy; by late-1943 there could be no question but that the Supreme Commander would be American and Eisenhower's experience in Britain and North Africa made him a natural choice. Although consideration was given to selecting Marshall for the post this was ruled out since no one, including Eisenhower, was considered a suitable successor as head of the US Army. With an American as Supreme Commander, it was politic to have a British general as his ground commander in the initial phase, that is, until Eisenhower moved his headquarters to France. The commander of 21 Army Group was General Sir Bernard Paget, previously Commander-in-Chief, Home Forces and the man responsible for training the Army to the standard necessary for an operation such as the liberation of Europe. Paget had also played a significant part in planning OVERLORD and had given much careful study to the problems of combined operations, having experienced the Norwegian expedition of 1940. Although he played an important role in OVERLORD, Paget was not to see the operation through to execution. Instead he was appointed as Commander-in-Chief, Middle East, replacing Maitland Wilson, who succeeded Eisenhower as Supreme Allied Commander in the Mediterranean when the latter took overall command of OVERLORD. Thus it was that Montgomery was chosen to command 21 Army Group and the Allied armies in Normandy in the opening phase of the liberation.

With his diplomatic skills, his ability as a logistician and willingness to listen, Eisenhower was an excellent choice as Supreme Commander. Although lacking experience as a field commander and with little experience of battle, he was the American candidate for the post and his attributes were considered to outweigh his shortcomings. Brooke might have made a better all-round supreme commander but his appointment to fill the post could only have happened had the invasion occurred in 1943, when Britain's contribution would have been greater. The same argument applies to Alexander, a man who had all Ike's diplomatic skills – and more – and also possessed a true appreciation of the importance of logistics. In addition, his battlefield experience was greater than that of either Eisenhower or Brooke while he had the happy knack of choosing good staff and being able to inspire them without causing them to feel claustrophobic, a quality he shared with Eisenhower. But the balance of the alliance meant that no British commander would be considered, although the Deputy Supreme Commander, Naval and Air Commanders were all British. Eisenhower proved a good choice, using his diplomacy to best effect, even – or, especially – when dealing with the opinionated Montgomery. He certainly proved that he had the mettle of a great commander in postponing the assault for twenty-four hours. His decision to take advantage of a very brief spell of favourable weather was one of the greatest calculated risks of the Second World War. That decision alone made him the right man at the right time.

Bernard Montgomery has inspired more debate since the war than any other British commander. His appointment to command 21 Army Group was based on his reputation as the victor of El Alamein and his experience in the Sicilian and Italian invasions. His *Memoirs* suggest that all went according to his master plan, a claim that he also made for El Alamein. But this was far from the truth and, although Montgomery mentions the differences between himself and Eisenhower and the friction caused by Tedder's antipathy, he does not acknowledge any fundamental change in his master plan. He accepts that the schedule of times and phase lines was not adhered to and that plans and dispositions were adjusted 'to the tactical situation as it developed – as in all battles'.[9] In *Normandy to the Baltic* he makes the point that his target date for the Allied armies reaching the Seine was D+90 whereas the first Allied troops crossed that river on D+75, just over two weeks ahead of schedule. This point is made to counter those who talked about stalemate in Normandy and the slow pace of Allied operations. But while all this was happening, trust between Montgomery and the Americans was breaking down, as shown by the attitude of many modern American historians and by American veterans. (This author was present at a dinner in the US Marine Corps' Headquarters at Quantico, Virginia when a retired US general made it very clear that he had little or no respect for Montgomery, but was a great admirer of Omar Bradley. Nor could that general be described as anti-British. If anything, he was pro-British and included the late Lord Carver among his friends.)

Perhaps the best argued criticism of Montgomery in Normandy has been made by Carlo D'Este in his book *Decision in Normandy*. Discussing the development of American operations that culminated in COBRA and the exploitation of what was virtually an open flank south of the bocage, D'Este shows that this came about as a result of Bradley's planning – Plan B of LUCKY STRIKE – and not as the outworking of Montgomery's master plan. The latter states unequivocally that

> The strategy of the Normandy campaign was British, and it succeeded because of first class team-work on the part of all the forces engaged – British and American.[10]

D'Este contests this assertion.

> That Montgomery developed the framework of Allied strategy in Normandy is beyond dispute, but to mislead by suggesting that the operations now developing on the American front were that framework come to fruition is stretching the point. Assuredly it was the result of Anglo–American cooperation, but it must be pointed out that prior to COBRA Montgomery was directing the Third Army on Brittany while the First Army swung east through the bocage. It was only after COBRA had succeeded that Montgomery, too, began thinking in terms of a long, sweeping development to the Seine and Paris by US forces emerging from the confines of the bocage.[11]

While Eisenhower was probably 'more deeply committed to the concept of coalition warfare' than almost anyone else, the same cannot be said of Montgomery who was much more self-serving, arrogant and critical of others. That Montgomery played a major role in Allied victory in Normandy is not in dispute but his own assessment of his importance is. Modern American thinking, as D'Este points out, tends to portray Montgomery as 'a pretentious, egotistical general whose achievements never matched an inflated reputation'.[12] But was he the man for the hour in Normandy? That he kept his nerve in extremely difficult circumstances is very much in his favour. And Eisenhower credited him with the flexibility of thinking that allowed him to adapt quickly to the changing tactical situation when the Germans forestalled the capture of Caen. In earlier battles, especially at El Alamein and Mareth, Montgomery had also shown such flexibility but afterwards insisted that all had gone according to his plan. In that respect he was, as Nigel Hamilton writes, 'his own worst enemy'.[13] D'Este points out that it was Montgomery's perseverance, in spite of criticism, that allowed Bradley eventually to take the initiative and launch what became the breakout battle.

Was there an Allied alternative to Montgomery? Bradley might be seen as one but his reputation was not as high as that of the Irishman when the appointments were being made – and George Patton was almost an embarrassment at that time. Harold Alexander did not enjoy the confidence of Brooke, although Churchill would have been happy to see him commanding 21 Army Group and there is no doubt that he would have enjoyed better rapport with Eisenhower and the other commanders than did Montgomery. But Alexander was a non-starter, principally because of Brooke's attitude but also because he represented continuity in the Mediterranean. Other generals might have been called back from other theatres – Slim from Burma, for example, or Auchinleck; but the latter's reputation had been damaged greatly by Montgomery's comments about him and the former was not considered, at that time, in the same rank as Montgomery although, in the view of many, including this author, he was the best British field commander of the war. Richard O'Connor, Britain's first victor, was also a non-starter due to his incarceration in an Italian PoW camp; he did not return to the Allied lines until late-December 1943, much too late to be considered for such a senior appointment, especially as his last active command had been at corps level. Thus it can be argued that Montgomery, for all his faults and eccentricities, was probably the only suitable candidate for command of 21 Army Group when that appointment was made. He was Britain's best known general and had the aura of success and the confidence of those he commanded – although those who fought in tanks might have had less time for him had they been aware of his lack of knowledge on the limits of armour. Those Irish Guards who listened to him assert that German tanks were no match for British armour and anti-tank weapons were at the best bemused by him; they could see only too clearly what German tanks could do to armour such as their own Shermans. By default, therefore, Montgomery was the man to command 21 Army Group.

If there is one issue uniting those who commanded in Normandy, and who subsequently wrote about the campaign, it is the quality of Allied logistics. Wars are won as much by the logistic support provided to armies as by the equipment, training and courage of those in the field; the morale of the fighting soldier is sustained by those who provide his everyday needs, be that food, fuel, ammunition or clothing. Britain was the Allied logistical base for Normandy and the preparations made in Britain became the foundation for the greatest military expedition in history. To those preparations, and the work of British industry, was added American industrial muscle; the end result was a range of material and equipment for the Allied soldier unsurpassed in the Second World War. That included Mulberry harbours, fuel lines, including PLUTO, landing craft of all descriptions, amphibious craft that included the versatile and indispensable DUKW, the 'Funnies' of 79th Armoured Division, as well as the DD Shermans used by so many American and British armoured units, the Rhino ferries, rocket-firing Typhoon fighter-bombers and specially-adapted aircraft of the RAF's No. 100 Group. The list of innovative material is almost endless; the greatest brains in the free world had worked tirelessly to devise the wherewithal for its service personnel to defeat Hitler and the factories of the free world had kept production lines running around the clock to produce material for the battlefront.

From Detroit to Dagenham, from Seattle to Southampton, from California to Clydebank, the machinery of industry became geared to war and the armada that crossed the Channel on that June night in 1944 was the result of the efforts of all those workers in industry who had given the sailors, soldiers and airmen the means to land in Europe and prosecute the war to deliver Europe from Nazism. Normandy is probably the best example of how the Second World War was total war with civilian workers every bit as important as front-line soldiers. To pay proper tribute to those civilian workers would require a book in itself, as also would the work of the supply arms of the Allied nations who strove constantly behind the scenes with little recognition then, or since, to bring about victory. In the British Army the supply chain included the Royal Army Service Corps and Royal Army Ordnance Corps, which today have been amalgamated to form the Royal Logistic Corps. That corps also includes the Army Pioneer Corps and Army Catering Corps, both of which played important parts in Normandy and other campaigns; its motto, *We Sustain*, summarises its role, providing a brief mission statement as well as a motto. Without the sustainers there would have been no victory in Normandy.

History is often laced with myth and that of the Second World War is no exception. Wartime conditions demanded controlling information to the public, since the enemy could also have availed itself of that information and so truth was, in Churchill's words, often surrounded by a barricade of lies. One enduring myth is that the Second World War was one of movement in which casualties were not as severe as those of the Great War. Especially in the British psyche there were no killing fields, such as those of the Somme, in 1939–45. This is not true; although Britain's overall losses, including Commonwealth and Empire, were lower than between 1914 and 1918 this does not indicate that everyday casualties were substantially lower, that the risk to the individual soldier was less than that faced by his counterpart of an earlier generation. Comparing British casualties of the two world wars can be done only by taking account of a number of factors: the time that the Army spent in direct confrontation with the enemy; the nature of the standard British division; the numbers of men in those divisions involved in front-line combat.

Between 1914 and 1918 the greater part of the Army was engaged on the western front and, in the closing months of the war, from March to November 1918, faced the greater part of the German army; British losses in 1918 exceeded those of the Second World War.[14] However, between 1939 and 1945 the Army was only engaged against significant German forces in the campaign of 1940, really only a month of combat, and again between June 1944 and May 1945. The campaigns in North Africa and Italy did not involve large numbers of either British or German soldiers; in North Africa the opposing armies were initially quite small and only towards the end did either side commit a second army. And even while the Allies were fighting from Normandy to Germany itself, the greater part of the German army was fighting the Soviets. Thus British losses in the Second World War have to be considered in the light of British troops fighting large numbers of Germans for less than a year; even making allowances for the North African and Italian campaigns, it cannot be said that the British Army was engaged with significant German forces for any more than half the time it was so engaged in the earlier conflict. In the Great War, the majority of British divisions were infantry, each of three brigades, each disposing four battalions until February 1918 when losses brought about a reduction to three-battalion brigades; those battalions included 1,000 men each, giving the infantry division a total strength of 12,000 infantrymen, the majority of them riflemen. By contrast, in the Second World War there were fewer infantry divisions – cavalry divisions gave way to armoured divisions that saw more combat than their predecessors – and each division deployed fewer rifles in the line. Although the standard infantry division of the later conflict included three brigades each of three battalions, the strength of the battalions was considerably lower than those of the earlier generation with a maximum of thirty-five officers and 786 men. Overall divisional strength may have stood at 18,347 in 1944 but the division could deploy no more than the nominal strength of its rifle companies; this rarely exceeded 100 by the time of the Normandy campaign and meant that the rifle strength of a brigade might be no more than 1,200 men, with a division able only to deploy fewer than 4,000 riflemen in the attack. Battalions were later reduced to three companies as a result of losses in the infantry arm. A support company was also included; this numbered almost 200 and was responsible for heavy weapons, including mortars and anti-tank guns, as well as pioneers.[15] The division could also call on a support battalion with Vickers MMGs and 4.2-inch mortars; this battalion normally deployed one company to each infantry brigade.

But the greatest losses fell on the men of the rifle companies, many of which ceased to be effective after a short spell in action. In two weeks in

June, 1/6th Duke of Wellington's Regiment lost 373 officers and men killed, wounded or missing. The commanding officer, Lieutenant-Colonel R K Exham, was transferred to command another battalion and was succeeded by Lieutenant-Colonel A J D Turner MC. When Turner took over, on 25 June, he found few original officers left in the battalion. By the 30th he had lost two seconds-in-command as well as a company commander, leaving only a dozen officers who had landed with the battalion, all of them junior officers. The new CO wrote a 'lengthy report' on his battalion's state, noting that most men were 'jumpy' under shellfire and that there had been three cases of self-inflicted wounds in as many days. Since officers and NCOs had stopped wearing rank badges, new arrivals, of whom there were many, hardly knew who their seniors were and certainly did not know each other. He also noted that, on two occasions, he had had to threaten retreating soldiers with his revolver. He concluded that his battalion was no longer fit for front-line service and was 'in need of time for a thorough reorganisation and rest'. Montgomery chose to sack Turner for his alleged 'defeatist mentality'[16] and ordered that the battalion be disbanded to provide drafts for 1/7th Duke of Wellington's.[17]

Between D-Day and the end of the war, Britain lost 35,998 soldiers,[18] a figure representing almost a fifth of all Army fatalities during the war.* (Of these, more than half were infantrymen; 20,442 infantry of the line died with 1,777 members of the Army Air Corps (Parachute Regiment, Glider Pilot Regiment and Special Air Service) and 1,596 foot guards. Of the latter, many would have been serving in armoured battalions but it is impossible to ascribe the names in the Roll of Honour to either infantry or armour.) Almost three times as many were wounded and nearly 15,000 captured. Canadian deaths came to 10,740 with a further 30,910 wounded and 2,250 captured while American casualties were heaviest of all at 109,820 dead – exceeding the American death toll for the Great War – another 356,600 wounded and 56,630 taken prisoner.[20] Other Allies also suffered heavily: France had 12,590 dead, 49,510 wounded and 4,730 captured and Poland 1,160, 3,840 and 370.[21] All these figures represent army casualties and do not include sailors or airmen; and nor do they include the forces of Belgium and The Netherlands. Against this toll of Allied losses the German army sustained more than a half million dead or wounded, of whom 128,030 were killed and 399,860 were wounded. At the end of the war 7,614,790 German soldiers, including SS and foreign volunteers, went into captivity on the western front alone.

The cost to the Allies was great and this was especially true of British and Canadian forces. Although the British element was the majority in the

* These totalled 177,800.[19]

build-up to D-Day, Britain's Army was, by summer 1944, a wasting asset, as shown by the disbandment of divisions to make up losses elsewhere. Canadian losses, in an all-volunteer army, were similarly high and, although both combined do not constitute fifty per cent of the American deaths, the pool of manpower from which America was drawing its armies was not under the same strain as their British and Canadian Allies. White headstones, crosses and stars of David in innumerable war cemeteries tell their own story of the cost of the campaign. Liberation did not come quickly and cheaply. It was a hard struggle for which many paid with their lives.

There is a popular misconception that the liberation campaign was a fast-moving war once the Allies broke out of Normandy with armour playing a major part. This is not true; except for the period of the 'great swan' when the Germans pulled rapidly out of France and Allied forces raced through that country and into Belgium, the war was conducted at the pace of the infantryman, who continued to bear the brunt of battle. Whether American GI, British Tommy, Canuck or French Poilu, it was the infantryman who had to tackle his foe in close combat to take and hold ground. He had the support of his comrades in tanks and of the artillery, whose work was superb, with whom he worked much better than he had earlier in the war, but his war was still bloody and ferocious. That is not to say that the armoured soldier had an easy war. Far from it; there can be few more horrific ways to die than trapped in a blazing tank or in one with splinters of metal ricocheting throughout the crew compartment; but infantry often envied the tankmen their armoured steed.

There has been controversy over several aspects of the campaign, chief among those being the cooperation, or lack of it, between armour and infantry. Montgomery's strategy has also caused much discussion, as has the question of the relative capabilities of opposing soldiers. The first of these subjects, armour/infantry cooperation, has been the focus for several writers, most recently Roman Johann Jarymowycz, whose book *Tank Tactics from Normandy to Lorraine* is a comprehensive study of the armoured forces fielded by Britain, the United States, Canada, Germany, France, Poland and Russia. Jarymowycz, who served for thirty-five years in the Canadian reserve forces and commanded the Royal Canadian Hussars, concludes that the Germans continued to have a better understanding of armoured warfare and therefore deployed their tanks more effectively than the Allies in north-west Europe. He is especially critical of Montgomery whom he describes as a man who 'did not really understand what to do with tanks' and this in spite 'of his black beret'.[22] But even Montgomery eventually learned the lesson that 'we require one tank that will do both jobs', i.e., infantry and cavalry tanks. The division of armour used by both the British and French proved deeply flawed.

Jarymowycz is also critical of US armoured forces which were often too rigid in their command structure and used a flawed doctrine, the tank destroyer imposed on US armoured forces by General McNair; 'the M10 tank destroyer mounting a 90mm gun, was not effective against Panthers or Tigers and was so inadequately armored that both Pzkw IVs and mortars could stop them.'[23] US forces also refused to use the Sherman Firefly with its British 17-pounder anti-tank gun, even though this was the only Allied tank that could match the most modern German tanks in battle. This lacuna Jarymowycz attributes to American chauvinism and notes that when eventually Bradley decided to request Fireflies 'there were none to be had'.[24] Too much deference was given to Montgomery's thinking on armoured warfare. That he had conquered at El Alamein, Medenine and Mareth was allowed to obscure the fact that he had lost the fruits of victory in the pursuit through mishandling his armour; had Montgomery had a proper appreciation of the potential for mobile operations that his armour offered, Rommel's Panzer Armee Afrika might well have been destroyed in the first few days of its retreat from El Alamein. But Montgomery had not studied manoeuvre warfare, nor had the Americans. In contrast, Soviet armoured forces excelled at this type of fighting. Thus Montgomery's attempts to smash the Germans with massed armour, as evidenced in GOODWOOD, led to a battle of attrition rather than the deep battle that could have developed. Of the debacle that was the approach to GOODWOOD, the Irish Guards' historian has this to say:

> surprise had been lost. Instead of three armoured brigades attacking with one blow, it was the first one, then a long pause and finally the two others. The 11th Armoured Division afterwards said that they could have got through if only there had been someone on their left. But as it happened, the Reconnaissance Regiment, the Northamptonshire Yeomanry, were quite alone when they hit the German anti-tank screen . . . and an hour ahead even of their own armoured brigade.[25]

To understand whether Allied armour and infantry worked well together, we should also look at the infantryman. Allied infantry deployed less firepower than their German opponents, who also, invariably, had the advantage of fighting defensively, especially in the bocage. Both British and Canadian battalions lacked offensive firepower in their rifle companies. Each infantry section had a Bren gun which, while superbly engineered and reliable, was restricted by being magazine-fed with a maximum of thirty rounds; in practice, this was usually twenty-eight. Against this German infantry sections deployed an excellent belt-fed machine gun, the MG34, or its later, simpler stablemate, the MG42. The former could fire 800–900 rounds per minute (rpm) using a fifty-round belt, although a seventy-five-round drum magazine could be fitted instead, while the latter's rate of fire was up to 1,550 rpm with the fifty-round belt. Both had higher rates of fire than the Bren's 500 rpm and used a slightly heavier 7.92mm round; the Bren fired .303-inch (7.7mm) ammunition. As a squad weapon the Bren was more easily portable while the MG34 and MG42 were heavier and flapping belts could become entangled in undergrowth. In Normandy the German weapons were usually sited for defensive purposes, thereby giving their users an advantage over their opponents.

Because of the firepower to be expected from any German defensive position, Allied infantry relied on artillery and armour to keep their enemies' heads down.

The artillery was superb and German veterans testify that they feared British artillery more than any other arm. By 1944 the Royal Artillery had refined its role and training to such an extent that it gained a trust hitherto unknown. An excellent example of this trust occurred in the airborne bridgehead where both the CRA of 6th Airborne Division and the commanding officer of 1st Royal Ulster Rifles commented favourably on the support that they received from the artillery of 3rd Division, especially the speed and accuracy with which calls for fire support were answered. The former stated the support was 'very quick and generous and was instrumental in turning back at least one attack supported by tanks'.[26]

Armour/infantry cooperation improved as the campaign progressed and new lessons were absorbed that led to new tactics being developed, including the birth of battlegroups in both Second British and First Canadian Armies. Arguably, training in cooperation prior to the invasion had not been as rigorous as it might have been, especially as many lessons of the all-arms battle had been worked out in North Africa but ignored after Montgomery's accession to command of Eighth Army. Thus a level of cooperation that might have existed from D-Day onwards did not begin fully to develop until after GOODWOOD when both Dempsey and Montgomery thought that they could beat the enemy with massed armour and minimal infantry.

Montgomery's strategy has caused perhaps the greatest controversy in discussions of the Normandy campaign. Too often chauvinism enters into the equation, obscuring the real argument. This study of the campaign has indicated that Montgomery never really became an army group commander but continued to operate at corps or army level. Thus there are those who opine that Dempsey had Montgomery constantly gazing over his shoulder whereas the Americans were given a relatively free rein. Nor did Montgomery appear to pay much attention to the Canadians. When TOTALIZE was underway he failed to reinforce the Canadian effort with British divisions that could have been deployed to reinforce Simonds' corps. But Montgomery's greatest failing was not seeing the full strategic picture, because of his inability to think as an army group commander. He failed to make best use of his strategic resources and, as Jarymowycz argues

> He perpetuated doctrinal separatism – a democratic procession of regional initiatives with each commander inventing his own doctrinal solutions, which were then tested by U. S., British and Canadian offensives. Although he ruled with an iron fist and meddled in the most trivial affairs, once the armored pursuit began Montgomery left the Americans operationally alone and permitted incredible freedom of action late in the campaign.[27]

When Allied forces landed in Normandy there was the opportunity for a battle of such proportions that the enemy would be annihilated. But that would have required using much riskier strategy than Montgomery was prepared to do – by, for example, sending significant armoured forces deep into enemy positions to wreak havoc far beyond the coastal area while the Germans were still expecting a further landing in the Pas de Calais. With Allied air superiority and the reserves available this was possible; German armour was too widely dispersed to come together to meet such a thrust which could have left Rommel in disarray. But, as at El Alamein, Montgomery failed to make full use of his advantages and there was no expanding torrent of armour pouring through and out of Normandy. Instead Allied forces were committed to a steady war of attrition, fought by corps and divisions rather than by armies or the army group. In later years Montgomery would argue that all had gone according to his master plan of drawing enemy armour on to the British and Canadian forces on the left flank while allowing the Americans to begin their breakout and swing towards the Seine. His supporters have continued to make this argument, often quoting Bradley's comments which seem to back Montgomery's argument. Eisenhower's Chief of Staff, Bedell Smith told American historian Forrest Pogue in 1947 that

> Monty's talk of his original plan to hinge on Caen is absolutely balls. When he was checked in his original intent of taking Caen he had the idea of doing the other op. I believe the second shows greater insight. I don't see why he doesn't tell the truth.[28]

Of course, Eisenhower should have taken a firmer hand with Montgomery and he is, therefore, also guilty of the failures of the campaign, which resulted in the war in the west lasting into 1945 when there was potential for victory in 1944. Reflecting on our earlier consideration of whether they were the right men for the job, it would seem that the answer should be 'no' but that they were the best available, or likely to be made available. Both would continue to have adverse influence on the course of the war and their personal relationship – much more the dysfunctional Montgomery's fault than Ike's – could have done nothing positive for the Allied effort. There is an argument for saying that Montgomery should have been sacked in Normandy but the political implications of that were so great that Eisenhower would not risk it. Nor could Churchill be seen to dismiss Britain's most successful general, the man who had won El Alamein, cleared North Africa and led the invasions of Sicily and Italy. Montgomery was to remain at the head of 21 Army Group until the end of the war and to cultivate further the Monty legend in the years thereafter.

The final consideration mentioned above was the relative qualities of the opposing soldiers. Much has been written about the standard of the German soldier in Normandy and it sometimes seems that the Allies won only by sheer weight of numbers against an army of supermen. But it must be remembered that many German soldiers were reluctant warriors; Luftwaffe ground divisions and the battalions of foreign 'volunteers' are classic examples. Coast defence divisions were also of low quality with shaky morale. Not all German soldiers were highly trained fighters on a par with those of the SS divisions, or Panzer Lehr, or 21st Panzer. Their opponents, American, British and Canadian, were much better trained than they have generally been given credit for and the fact remains that these men beat what is often described as the best-trained army in the world. One can argue about the value of air power, of the murderous fire of Allied artillery, of the numerical superiority of Allied armour but so much fighting came down to infantry section, platoon or company against its equivalent that it may be stated that the campaign was made up of small-scale skirmishes in which the Allied soldier triumphed. He certainly suffered – of that there can be no doubt, but he triumphed in the end and that is what matters.

German soldiers and commanders were as capable of making mistakes as their Allied counterparts. One oft-quoted critic of the British in Normandy, Brigadier Hargest of the New Zealand forces, commented at length on British failings, including the perceived failure to cooperate between formations 'simply because they are in different divisions or corps'. In support of this he quoted a case where the enemy were able to drive a wedge 'nearly 2 miles deep' between VIII and XXX Corps.[29] The failure properly to liaise between armies also left a vacuum at Vire that assisted the Germans. But the latter were also capable of such errors. At the beginning of Operation BLUECOAT at the end of July, 2nd Household Cavalry, reconnoitring for 11th Armoured Division, discovered a track through the Forêt l'Evêque that led to an intact bridge over the Souleuvre river. That bridge was five miles into enemy territory and the penetration by the Household Cavalry was possible because they were moving on the new boundary set by von Kluge between Panzer Group West and Seventh Army. 'So it was an Army boundary, but neither Army had thought to guard it.'[30] In contrast to Hargest, who was killed on 12 August,[31] an Australian observer with 50th Division considered the Geordie soldiers to be outstanding and was especially admiring of British NCOs who were 'absolutely superb' with 'a terrific sense of responsibility'.[32]

One element of Allied operations that seems always to be praised is the cooperation of the air forces and yet this was far from perfect. Montgomery's biographer notes that 'less than forty-eight hours before the intended mounting of D-Day, the Allies were unable to agree on an air plan to support their armies'.[33] Although this applied especially to the use of bombers, the degree of cooperation that had grown up between Eighth Army and the Desert Air Force was not carried over into 21 Army Group. In part this was because Monty and the airmen had grown apart because of the former's attitude. But Montgomery did recognise the importance of close cooperation between ground and air forces and had tried to improve matters in the months before D-Day. But it was an imperfect system that was used at first, although it improved as the campaign progressed and many veterans to whom the author has spoken have nothing but praise for the airmen, one commenting that RAF Typhoon pilots were the bravest men he had ever seen: 'they would fly right into the barrel of an 88 to knock it out.'[34] In typical British fashion it might be said that the Allies muddled through – the Americans, as Bradley noted, were also guilty of this lack of appreciation of air cooperation – but muddle through they did, although that might be unfair to those who did so much work on the planning. A more accurate assessment might be that the Allies improvised when necessary. In doing so, the soldiers, sailors and airmen set the Allied Expeditionary Force firmly on the road to victory.

Above all, it must be remembered that the invasion was made possible only by the doughtiness of Britain's people who stood alone for freedom when Hitler overran Europe in 1940 and whose tenacity was epitomised by Winston Churchill. Omar Bradley recognised this and, in a generous tribute to those British people, he wrote of the fortifications at Plymouth which he saw as his ship left for Normandy:

> The British ought to leave them up to remind themselves and the world of the courage they showed when they built those things. That's something you can never take away from them.[35]

NOTES

1 Keegan, *Six Armies in Normandy*, p. 315.
2 Ibid, p. 316.
3 Ibid.
4 Ibid.
5 Breuer, *Operation Dragoon*, p. 247.
6 Grigg, *1943: The Victory that Never Was*, p. 3.
7 Ibid, p. 214.
8 Ibid, p. 232–3.
9 Montgomery, *Memoirs*, p. 254.
10 Ibid, pp. 261–2.
11 D'Este, *Decision in Normandy*, pp. 411–12.
12 Ibid, pp. 503–4.
13 Hamilton, *Monty Master of the Battlefield*, p. 606.
14 *IWM Book of 1WW*, p. 273.
15 Forty, *Handbook of the British Army*, p. 165.
16 Messenger, *For Love of Regiment*, p. 117; *Regimental History, Duke of Wellington's Regt*, p. 317.
17 *Regimental History, Duke of Wellington's Regiment*, p. 317.
18 Army Roll of Honour.
19 Ellis, *Victory in the West*, p. 254.
20 Ibid, p. 256.
21 Ibid.
22 Jarymowycz, *Tank Tactics from Normandy to Lorraine*, p. 323.
23 Ibid, p. 321.
24 Ibid.
25 Fitzgerald, *The History of the Irish Guards in the Second World War*, p. 376.
26 NA, CAB44/247, p. 239.
27 Jarymowycz, op cit, pp. 322–3.
28 Pogue papers, 12 Feb 47, Military History Institute, Carlisle Barracks, PA, quoted in ibid, p. 323.
29 NA, CAB106/1060.
30 Roberts, *From the Desert to the Baltic*, p. 189.
31 Baynes, *The Forgotten Victor*, p. 223.
32 NA, WO55/1803, 'With the 50th Division'.
33 Hamilton, op cit, op cit, p. 621.
34 Bob Balmer, 6 LAA Bty, i/v with author.
35 Bradley, *A Soldier's Story*, p. 265.

APPENDIX 1
Mulberry

In Chapters III and IV we saw that the creation of artificial harbours, or Mulberries, played an important part in assuaging worries about the maintenance of the invasion forces. The construction of the two Mulberry harbours absorbed much labour, concrete and steel in Britain where the harbours were built in sections ready for towing to the French coast. Although the concept appears simple the execution was complicated and required the skills of many engineers to put the harbours in place. That the entire project took only eight months from the moment that the plan was authorised until the equipment for the harbours was complete is signal testimony to the capacity of British industry to apply itself to the needs of a nation at war.

The first requirement in the project was for sheltered water for the five assault areas. This was to be provided by creating breakwaters from redundant ships, codenamed Corncobs, which sailed to Normandy to be sunk in line to form the breakwaters, known as Gooseberries. All five were to be complete by D+5. Seventy-four ships, including some obsolete warships, were used to form Gooseberries; fifty-nine were scuttled in the initial phase and another fifteen later. The Gooseberries off Gold and Omaha beaches were then to be expanded to form artificial harbours, each comparable in size to Dover harbour. This was to be done by sinking large ferro-concrete caissons to reinforce and extend the Gooseberries and continue them shoreward at either end. The codename applied to the caissons was Phoenix. Caissons varied in size according to the depth of water in which they were to be used; the largest measured 200 feet long by fifty-five feet wide by sixty feet high and weighed over 6,000 tons. There were 213 caissons.

Each harbour was designed to have two entrances from the sea while the berthing accommodation could cater for a small number of deep-draught ships and some twenty coasters, as well as large numbers of landing craft plus the various ancillary vessels essential to the operation of any harbour. The sheltered water thus created would allow the clumsy landing craft to move freely within the harbours in most weather conditions. Piers were also to be provided, built of articulated steel roadway, supported on pontoons anchored firmly to the bed of the sea but able to move up and down with the tide. Such piers were known as Whales. Small vessels could discharge at the pierheads irrespective of the tide state. For those deep-draught ships that could not be brought within the harbour complexes further breakwaters were provided. Constructed from floating steel components and known as Bombardons, these were located to seaward of the two harbours. Ninety-three Bombardons were built, each of cruciform section, 200 feet long and twenty-five feet high; each weighed about 2,000 tons when partially flooded. In all, the Mulberries required some two million tons of concrete and prefabricated steel.

All these components, except the Corncobs, which travelled under their own steam, had to be towed across the Channel having first been towed from the building yards to the assembly areas. Each part of the two harbours had then to be placed accurately and quickly, in tidal waters and with the possibility of attack by enemy aircraft or naval vessels.

APPENDIX 2
Landing Craft

One of the first requirements of the planners of NEPTUNE/OVERLORD was a range of specialised vessels that could carry the assault forces on to the beaches. Plans for such vessels were underway in the early stages of the war but were accelerated in late-1940.

These varied in size from the ocean-going LSTs, capable of carrying a squadron of tanks and landing them on a beach, down to the smallest LCAs that carried a number of tanks, or a complement of infantry to the beach, or were adapted for support roles. There was a range of Landing Craft, Tank, or LCT, capable of carrying up to eleven tanks of the Sherman class, each weighing thirty tons. Other LCTs were adapted for specific tasks to support a landing force: some were reclassified as Landing Craft, Tank (Rocket) Mk II, LCT(R) (2)s, and, as the designation suggests, were equipped to fire salvoes of rockets at a fixed range of 3,500 yards; each vessel was fitted with a false deck and carried 792 5-inch rockets. A further version, the LCT(R) (3) could carry up to 1,044 rockets. Some LCTs were converted to carry artillery, either medium guns or anti-aircraft guns. In the latter case, the vessels were then known as LCFs, or Landing Craft, Flak, of which there were three versions while there were two types of gun-armed landing craft, LCG(L)3 and 4, which mounted either one or two 4.7-inch guns; these weapons were surplus destroyer guns and some were superfiring and thus with a longer range.

Bigger even than the LSTs, commonly referred to as Large Slow Targets, were the LSCs, LSDs and LSGs, usually converted from merchant ships and each of which performed a specific role. The LSCs, Landing Ships, Carrier, were heavy cargo ships converted to carry up to thirty LCMs, Landing Craft Mechanised, each designed to carry either a single 30-ton tank or sixty soldiers. In operational mode, the LSCs could carry twenty-one LCMs and 323 troops. There were two such vessels, *Empire Charmain* and *Empire Elaine*, both weighing over 7,500 tons, although it appears that the former was never a Royal Navy ship.

HM Ships *Eastway*, *Highway*, *Northway* and *Oceanway* were Lend-Lease ships built in the United States as LSDs, or Landing Ships, Dock, developed from a British specification for an ocean-going vessel capable of carrying large numbers of vehicles as well as the craft that could put them ashore. In effect, they were floating, self-propelled dry-docks that could carry up to forty-one LVTs or forty-seven DUKWs. (The DUKW, pronounced Duck, was a US vehicle, capable of carrying two and a half tons and with an amphibious capability. It was to prove one of the most useful vehicles of the war.) The load could be increased to ninety-two LVTs or 108 DUKWs by the fitting of temporary decks. These ships weighed almost 8,000 tons laden, could reach a speed of over 15 knots and had a range of some 8,000 nautical miles at 15 knots. Even larger were the LSGs, Landing Ships, Gantry, which were Royal Fleet Auxiliary oil tankers converted on the slipway. Weighing almost 17,000 tons the LSGs – *Derwentdale*, *Dewdale* and *Ennerdale* – were fitted with gantries that could hoist LCMs weighing ten tons. The operational load of each vessel was fifteen LCMs with a maximum of 268 troops.*

A range of Landing Ships Infantry, classified into Large, Medium, Small and Hand (LSI(L)s, LSI(M)s, LSI(S)s and LSI(H)s) were converted merchant ships, two of which had been armed merchant cruisers, that could carry a variety of smaller landing craft and up to 1,631 soldiers, in the case of *Persimmon*. And two former railway ferries, *Daffodil* and *Princess Iris*, were converted to military use, but could still carry locomotives and rolling stock, as Landing Ships, Stern Chute, LSSs. *Daffodil* was sunk by a mine in 1945 while *Princess Iris* returned to its peacetime role in 1946.

These were the heavylifters that carried the smaller vessels close to their objectives or, in the case of LSTs, took their cargoes to the beach. Infantry generally went ashore in a variety of craft that included the Landing Craft, Assault (LCAs), (some, fitted with a 4-inch smoke mortar, were classified as LCS(M)s, which could carry thirty-five soldiers, or Landing Craft, Personnel** (LCPs), capable of carrying thirty soldiers, or Landing Craft, Vehicle (LCVs) with thirty-six soldiers or a 3-ton vehicle; there was another variant known as the LCV(P), Landing Craft, Vehicle and Personnel. A larger landing craft, the LCM, or Landing Craft, Mechanised, was produced in three types: LCM(1)s could carry a 16-ton tank or 100 soldiers; LCM(3) could carry a 30-ton tank or sixty troops; and LCM(7) could carry a 45-ton tank. Similarly, the Landing Craft, Infantry (Large), or LCI(L), could carry 188 men and put them onto a beach while the LCI(S), for 'small', had a complement of 102 soldiers; the former was an American vessel while the latter was British-built and a short-range craft.

* This was the complement of *Derwentdale*. *Dewdale* could carry 257 troops and *Ennerdale* 266.

** There were four variants of LCPs: LCP(2)s and LCP(S)s were British-built while LCP(L)s and LCP(R)s were American-built.

There were some other specialised vessels such as LSH(L)s, Landing Ships Headquarters (Large), which were fitted with an extensive suite of communications equipment and were also converted merchant ships, although one, *Bulolo*, had previously been an armed merchant cruiser. A number of ships, including some LSTs, were converted as LSFs, Landing Ships, Fighter Direction, from which aircraft protecting the assault force could be directed; as well as the LSTs, some merchant ships were also adapted for this role. Other small craft were used as smoke-laying vessels or for special, and often clandestine, duties, while barges were adapted to serve as floating bakeries to supply freshly baked bread to the men in the beachhead.

Almost all these vessels were designed and built, or adapted, during the war, often from specifications drawn up by the Admiralty in the early years of war, and were to prove invaluable in OVERLORD and other major assault operations. Without them the task of putting an attack force ashore, with artillery and armoured support, would have been so difficult as to have almost been impossible. Those who designed the various specialist craft used in OVERLORD made a very large contribution to the success of the operation.

Landing craft in action

Royal Marines' Captain Michael Previty commanded a flotilla of twelve LCIs that were ferried across the channel on LSIs and lowered close to the shore. Being lowered was a nerve-racking experience although there had been intense training, including exercises with troops, to prepare officers and crews for their task.

> There was quite a rough sea. The most alarming part of the whole business really was being lowered from the ship into the water with this considerable weight of boat and troops and there was a fairly good sea running at the time. I suppose the waves must have been going up and down about ten [or] twelve feet, up and down the side of the ship. You would unhook, hopefully, both ends of the boat at the same time and then you would set off . . . Going in was fairly simple: the waves would be forming behind you so that it was carrying you ahead, carrying you forward.[1]

Being low in the water the LCIs were hard to spot from shore. That also meant that they could be difficult to spot from vessel to vessel and so Previty's boat carried signal lights at the stern to assist the other LCIs maintain their positions. The flotilla would approach the shore in line-abreast formation so that all the vessels would land almost simultaneously.

> You would approach . . . in such a way as not to run up the shore so that you couldn't get off again. Usually, it was preferable to land on a slightly rising tide so that you could get off. If you were on a falling tide then, of course, if you did get stuck you were there for keeps, until the next tide came in.[2]

On the beach the crewmen had their first sight of Rommel's asparagus. Had their craft gone in at high tide, these obstacles could have caused many casualties among the assaulting soldiers.

Each landing craft discharged its soldiers and returned to the LSI, although 'one or two had to be pushed off' the beach. Previty described his own part in the operation in a matter-of-fact manner, as if it were purely routine. That part was rewarded with a Mention in Despatches while the French government awarded him a Croix de Guerre. He regarded the Croix de Guerre as recognition of the work of the flotilla and the LSI.[3]

NOTES

1 Previty, i/v with Miles Dungan.
2 Ibid.
3 Dungan, *Distant Drums*, op cit, p. 127.

Bibliography

Ambrose, Stephen E, *Pegasus Bridge D-Day: the daring British airborne raid* (London 1985)

Arthur, Max, *Men of the Red Beret: Airborne Forces 1940–1990* (London 1990)

Badsey, Stephen, *Normandy 1944* (Oxford 1990)

Barber, Neil, *The Day the Devils Dropped In. The 9th Parachute Battalion in Normandy – D-Day to D+6* (Barnsley 2002)

Barclay, C N, *The History of the 53rd (Welsh) Division in the Second World War* (London 1956)

Barker, A J, *Waffen SS at War* (London 1982)

Barnett, Correlli, *Engage the Enemy More Closely: The Royal Navy in the Second World War* (London 1991)

Baverstock, Kevin, *Breaking the Panzers. The Bloody Battle for Rauray, Normandy, 1 July 1944* (Stroud 2002)

Baynes, John, *The Forgotten Victor. General Sir Richard O'Connor KT GCB DSO MC* (London 1989)

Belchem, Major-General David, *Victory in Normandy* (London 1981)

Bennett, Ralph, *Ultra in the West. The Normandy Campaign of 1944–45* (London 1979)

Birt, Raymond, *XXII Dragoons 1760–1945. The story of a regiment* (Aldershot 1950)

Bishop, Chris and Drury, Ian (eds), *Combat Guns* (London 1987)

Blake, John W, *Northern Ireland in the Second World War* (London 1956 & Belfast 2000)

Bowman, Martin W, *USAAF Handbook 1939–1945* (Stroud 1997)

Boyd, F J George, *Boyd's War. The story of a Royal Navy Volunteer Reserve Fighter Pilot during the Second World War* (Newtownards 2002)

Bradley, Omar N, *A Soldier's Story* (New York, NY 1951)

Breuer, William B, *Operation Dragoon. The Allied Invasion of the South of France* (Shrewsbury 1988)

Bruce, Colin John, *War on the Ground 1939–1945* (London 1995)

Carruthers, Bob and Trew, Simon, *The Normandy Battles* (London 2000)

Carver, Michael (Field Marshal Lord), *The Apostles of Mobility. The Theory*

and Practice of Armoured Warfare (London 1979), *Out of Step. The Memoirs of Field Marshal Lord Carver* (London 1989)
Chandler, David G, & Collins, James Lawton, Jr (eds), *The D-Day Encyclopedia* (Oxford 1994)
Chesneau, Robert (ed), *Conway's All the World's Fighting Ships 1922–1946* (London 1980)
Churchill, Winston, *The Second World War* (London 1951)
Close, Major Bill, MC, *A View from the Turret. A history of the 3rd Royal Tank Regiment in the Second World War* (Tewkesbury 1998)
Compagnon, General Jean, *The Normandy Landings* (Rennes 1979)
Cooper, Matthew, *The German Army 1933–1945* (London 1978)
Cruickshank, C, *Deception in World War II* (Oxford 1979)
Daglish, Ian, *Operation Bluecoat* (Barnsley 2003)
Danchev, Alex and Todman, Daniel (eds) *War Diaries 1939–1945. Field Marshal Alanbrooke* (London 2001)
Daugherty, Leo, *The Battle of the Hedgerows. Bradley's First Army in Normandy, June–July 1944* (London 2002)
Dear, Ian, *Sabotage and Subversion. The SOE and OSS at War* (London 1996)
De Guingand, Major-General Sir Francis, *Operation Victory* (London 1947)
Delaforce, Patrick, *The Fighting Wessex Wyverns: from Normandy to Bremerhaven with the 43rd Wessex Division* (Stroud 1994), *Monty's Marauders: Black Rat and Red Fox* (Brighton 1997), *Taming the Panzers. Monty's tank battalions. 3RTR at War* (Stroud 2000)
D'Este, Carlo, *Decision in Normandy* (London 1983), *Eisenhower. Allied Supreme Commander* (London 2002)
Doherty, Richard, *The Sons of Ulster. Ulstermen at war from the Somme to Korea* (Belfast 1992), *Only The Enemy in Front. The Recce Corps at War 1941–46* (London 1994), *Irish Men and Women in the Second World War* (Dublin 1999), *Irish Volunteers in the Second World War* (Dublin 2001)
Dungan, Miles, *Distant Drums* (Belfast 1993)
Dunphy, Christopher & Johnston, Garry, *Gold Beach. Inland from King – June 1944* (Barnsley 1999)
Ehrman, John, *Grand Strategy, Vol V* (London 1956)
Ellis, John, *The Sharp End of War. The fighting man in World War II* (London 1980), *Brute Force. Allied strategy and tactics in the Second World War* (London 1990)
Ellis, L F, *Victory in the West. Vol I: The Battle of Normandy* (London 1962)
Fergusson, Sir Bernard, *Watery Maze: The story of Combined Operations* (London 1961)
Fitzgerald MC, Major D J L, *History of the Irish Guards in the Second World War* (Aldershot 1949)
Ford, Ken, *D–Day 1944: Gold & Juno Beaches* (Oxford 2002), *D–Day 1944: Sword Beach and the British Airborne Landings* (Oxford 2002)

Forty, George, *The Royal Tank Regiment. A Pictorial History* (Tunbridge Wells 1989), *World War Two Tanks* (London 1995), *The Armies of Rommel* (London 1997), *British Army Handbook 1939 –1945* (Stroud 1998), *Fortress Europe. Hitler's Atlantic Wall* (Shepperton 2002)

Fraser, David, *And We Shall Shock Them. The British Army in the Second World War* (London 1983), *Knight's Cross. A Life of Field Marshal Erwin Rommel* (London 1993)

French, David, *Raising Churchill's Army. The British Army and the War against Germany 1919–1945* (Oxford 2000)

Gethyn-Jones, Eric, *A Territorial Army Chaplain in Peace and War: a country cleric in khaki 1938–61* (East Wittering 1988)

Gorman, Sir John, *The Times of My Life* (Barnsley 2002)

Graves, Charles, *The Royal Ulster Rifles Vol III* (Belfast 1950)

Grigg, John, *1943. The Victory that Never Was* (London 1980)

Guderian, Heinz, et al (ed David C Isby) *Fighting in Normandy: The German Army from D-Day to Villers-Bocage* (London 2001)

Haining, Peter, *The Flying Bomb War* (London 2002)

Hamilton, Nigel, *Master of the Battlefield 1942–1944* (London 1983)

Hammerton, Ian C, *Achtung! Minen! The making of a flail troop commander* (Dartford 2000)

Handel, Michael I (ed), *Strategic and Operational Development in the Second World War* (London 1987)

Hart, Dr S Hart, Dr R and Hughes, Dr M, *The German Soldier in World War II* (Staplehurst 2000)

Harvey, Maurice, *The Allied Bomber War 1939–1945* (Tunbridge Wells 1992)

Hastings, Max, *Das Reich. The march of the 2nd SS Panzer Division through France, June 1944* (London 1981), *Overlord. D-Day and the battle for Normandy 1944* (London 1984)

Haswell, J, *The Intelligence and Deception of the D-Day Landings* (London 1979)

Hills, Stuart, *By Tank into Normandy* (London 2002)

Hinsley, F H et al, *British Intelligence in the Second World War Vol III Pt 2* (London 1988)

Hinsley, F H, *British Intelligence in the Second World War* (abridged edition, London 1993)

Hogg, Ian V, and Weeks, John, *The Illustrated Encyclopedia of Military Vehicles* (London 1980)

Horrocks, Sir Brian, *A Full Life* (London 1960)

How, Major J J, MC, *Hill 112. Cornerstone of the Normandy Campaign* (London 1984)

Howard, Michael, *British Intelligence in the Second World War. Vol V, Strategic Deception* (London 1990)

Jackson, W G F, *'OverLord' Normandy 1944* (London 1978)

Jarymowycz, Roman Johann, *Tank Tactics from Normandy to Lorraine* (Boulder, CO 2001)

Johnstone, Tom and Hagerty, James, *The Cross on the Sword. Catholic Chaplains in the Forces* (London 1996)

Joslen, Lieut-Col H F, *Orders of Battle Second World War 1939–1945* (London 1960)

Keegan, John, *Six Armies in Normandy* (London 1982), (ed), *Churchill's Generals* (London 1991)

Kershaw, R J, *D-Day: Piercing the Atlantic Wall* (Shepperton 1993)

Kilvert-Jones, Tim, *Sword Beach. British 3rd Infantry Division/27th Armoured Brigade* (Barnsley 2001)

Lacey-Johnson, Lionel, *Pointblank and Beyond* (Shrewsbury 1991)

Laffin, John, *British VCs of World War 2. A study in heroism* (Stroud 1997)

Latimer, Jon, *Deception in War* (London 2001)

Lewin, Ronald, *Montgomery as Military Commander* (London 1971), *Ultra Goes to War* (London 1979)

Liddell Hart, B H (ed), *The Rommel Papers* (London 1948), *The Other Side of the Hill* (London 1948)

Lucas, James, *Battle Group! German Kampfgruppen action of World War Two* (London 1993), *The Last Year of the German Army, May 1944–May 1945* (London 1994), *Hitler's Enforcers. Leaders of the German War Machine 1939–1945* (London 1996)

Lucas, James and Barker, James, *The Killing Ground. The battle of the Falaise Gap August 1944* (London 1978)

Lummis, Eric, *1 Suffolk in Normandy* (nd)

Mace, Paul, *Forrard. The story of the East Riding Yeomanry* (Barnsley 2001)

Macksey, Kenneth, *Rommel. Battles and Campaigns* (London 1979)

Massingberd, Hugh (ed), *The Daily Telegraph Second Book of Obituaries* (London 1996)

McKee, Alexander, *Caen. Anvil of Victory* (London 1964)

Mead, Peter, *Gunners at War 1939–1945* (London 1982)

Messenger, Charles, *The Commandos 1940–1946* (London 1985), *A History of British Infantry. Vol Two 1915–1994 For Love of Regiment* (London 1996)

Middlebrook, Martin and Everitt, Chris, *The Bomber Command War Diaries* (London 1985)

Miller, Robert A, *August 1944. The Campaign for France* (Novato, CA 1988)

Miller, Russell, *Nothing less than Victory* (London 1993)

Mitcham, Samuel W, Jr, *Hitler's Field Marshals and their Battles* (London 1988), *The Desert Fox in Normandy. Rommel's Defense of Fortress Europe* (New York, NY 1997)

Montgomery of Alamein, Field Marshal the Viscount, *El Alamein to the River Sangro. Normandy to the Baltic* (London 1973), *Memoirs* (London 1958)

Morgan, Lieutenant-General Sir Frederick E, *Overture to Overlord*, (London 1950)
Myatt, Frederick, *The British Infantry 1660–1945. The evolution of a fighting force* (Poole 1983)
Neillands, Robin, *The Desert Rats: 7th Armoured Division 1940–1945* (London 1991), *The Bomber War* (London 2001), *The Battle of Normandy 1944* (London 2002)
Neillands, Robin, and De Normann, Roderick, *D-Day 1944. Voices from Normandy* (London 1993)
Perrett, Bryan, *Seize and Hold: Master Strokes on the Battlefield* (London 1994), *Iron Fist: Classic Armoured Warfare Case Studies* (London 1995)
Pitt, Barrie (ed), *The Military History of World War Two* (London 1986)
Polmar, Norman and Mersky, Peter B, *Amphibious Warfare: An Illustrated History* (London 1988)
Powell, Geoffrey, *The History of The Green Howards: Three Hundred Years of Service* (London 1992)
Probert, Henry, *Bomber Harris. His Life and Times* (London 2001)
Reynolds, Michael, *Steel Inferno. I SS Panzer Corps in Normandy* (Staplehurst 1997), *Sons of the Reich. II SS Panzer Corps* (Staplehurst 2002)
Roberts, G P B, *From the Desert to the Baltic* (London 1987)
Rohmer, Richard, *Patton's Gap. An Account of the Battle of Normandy 1944* (London 1981)
Roskill, Stephen, *The Navy at War 1939–1945* (London 1960)
Routledge, Brigadier N W, OBE TD, *Anti-Aircraft Artillery, 1914–55. History of the Royal Regiment of Artillery* (London 1994)
Ryan, Cornelius, *The Longest Day* (New York, NY 1959)
Salmond, J B, *The History of the 51st Highland Division* (Bishop Auckland 1994)
Saunders, Tim, *Hill 112: Battles of the Odon* (*Gold Beach – Jig: Jig Sector and West – June 1944* (Barnsley 2002)
Shillito, Carl, *Pegasus Bridge Merville Battery* (Barnsley 1999)
Smith, Claude, *The History of The Glider Pilot Regiment* (London 1992)
Smyth, Sir John, *The Story of the Victoria Cross* (London 1963), *Great Stories of the Victoria Cross* (London 1977)
Shannon, Kevin and Wright, Stephen, *One Night in June* (Shrewsbury 1994)
Stacey, Colonel C P, *Official History of the Canadian Army in the Second World War, Vol. III, The Victory Campaign* (Ottawa 1960)
Stafford, David, *Roosevelt and Churchill. Men of Secrets* (London 1999)
Strawson, Major-General J M, CB, OBE, et al, *Irish Hussar* (London 1986)
Sutton, John (ed), *Wait for the Waggon. The Story of the Royal Corps of Transport and its Predecessors 1794–1993* (Barnsley 1998)
Taylor, Jeremy, *This Band of Brothers. A history of The Reconnaissance Corps of the British Army* (Bristol 1947), (ed), *Record of a Reconnaissance*

Regiment: A history of the 43rd Reconnaissance Regiment (The Gloucestershire Regiment) 1939–1945 (Bristol 1950)

Thompson, Julian (ed), *Victory in Europe. The North-West European Campaign 1944–45,* (London 1994), *The IWM Book of War behind Enemy Lines* (London 1998)

Tout, Ken, *A Fine Night for Tanks: The Road to Falaise* (Stroud 1998), *The Bloody Battle for Tilly* (Stroud 2000), *Roads to Falaise* (Stroud 2002)

Trevor-Roper, H R (ed), *Hitler's War Directives 1939–1945* (London 1964)

Turner, John Frayn, *Invasion '44. The full story of D-Day* (London 1959; Shrewsbury 1994)

Volunteers from Eire who have won distinctions serving with the British Forces: September 1939–February 1944 (np 1944)

Von Luck, Colonel Hans, *Panzer Commander* (New York, NY 1999)

Warner, Philip, *The SAS. The official history* (London 1971), *Phantom* (London 1982), *Horrocks. The general who led from the front* (London 1984), *World War Two. The untold story* (London 1988)

Whitaker, Brigadier General Denis, DSO and Bar, CM, ED, CD, and Whitaker, Sheelagh, *Dieppe. Tragedy to Triumph* (Barnsley 1992)

Willis, Leonard, *None Had Lances. The Story of The 24th Lancers* (Old Coulsdon 1986)

Wilmot, Chester, *The Struggle for Europe* (London 1952)

Unpublished

(National Archives, Kew)

A range of files was consulted at the National Archives, Kew (Public Record Office), including the official history series as well as war diaries of formations and units and other documents.

ADM202/99: 4 Special Service Brigade

AIR37/719: Overlord Transportation plan – evaluation of effectiveness of attacks on railway centres

AIR37/738: 2 TAF Operational Instruction No. 2/1943; Intentions for Operation RANKIN, Case C

CAB44/242 Section D, chapter I: operation 'Overlord', plans and preparations, 1940 to the 'touch-down' by Lieutenant-Colonel H G Pollock.

CAB44/243 Section D, chapter II: operation 'Overlord', D Day 1944 June 6; book I, the enemy; 30 Corps; 50 Division; 7 Armoured Division, by Lieutenant-Colonel A E Warhurst

CAB44/244 Section D, chapter II: operation 'Overlord', D Day 1944 June 6; book I, I Corps; 6 Airborne Division; 3 Canadian Division; 51 Division; 3 British Division, by Lieutenant-Colonel A E Warhurst

CAB44/245 Section D, chapter II: operation 'Overlord', D Day 1944 June 6; book III, United States corps; 5 United States Corps; headquarters

2nd Army; headquarters 21 Army Group; Supreme Headquarters Allied Expeditionary Force; administration, by Lieutenant-Colonel A E Warhurst

CAB44/246 Section D, chapter III: operations 1944 June 7–16 (D Day plus one to D Day plus ten); book I, Supreme Headquarters Allied Expeditionary Force and 21 Army Group; headquarters 2nd Army; headquarters 30 Corps, by Lieutenant-Colonels G S Jackson, G W Harris and W B R Neave-Hill

CAB44/247 Section D, chapter III: operations 1944 June 7–16 (D Day plus one to D Day plus ten); book II, I Corps; enemy reactions; administration; Royal Engineers, by Lieutenant-Colonels D F Cobourn, G S Jackson and W B R Neave-Hill

CAB44/248 Section D, chapter IV: 'break-out', advance and crossing the river Seine 1944 June 16–Aug 29; book I, the capture of Caen and the establishment of the Odon bridgehead, by Lieutenant-Colonels G S Jackson & W B R Neave-Hill

CAB44/249 Section D, chapter IV: 'break-out', advance and crossing the river Seine 1944 June 16–Aug 29; book II, operation 'Goodwood' the armoured thrust east of the river Orne to the Bourguébus ridge south of Caen by Lieutenant-Colonels G S Jackson and W B R Neave-Hill

CAB44/250 Section D, chapter IV, 'break-out' and crossing the river Seine 1944 June 16 – Aug 29; book III: the advance on Falaise and across the river Seine, by Lieutenant-Colonels G S Jackson, G W Harris and W B R Neave-Hill

CAB44/251 Section D, chapter IV: 'break-out', advance and crossing the river Seine 1944 June 16–Aug 29; book IV, administration 1944 June 16–July 23, by Lieutenant-Colonel W B R Neave-Hill

CAB44/271: Medical History of the War: The Campaign in North-West Europe

CAB44/295: Preliminary Planning for Operation *'Overlord'*

CAB44/309: The Campaign in North-West Europe: Information from German Sources

CAB65/46: War cabinet minutes

CAB106/969: History of COSSAC

CAB106/992: Administrative History of 21 Army Group 6 June 1944–8 May 1945

CAB106/1014: A Short History of XXX Corps in the European Campaign 1944–1945

CAB106/ 1060: Reports from Normandy 1944, 6 June–10 July by Brigadier James Hargest, New Zealand Army observer with XXX Corps

CAB106/1061: North-West Europe Campaign. Operation Goodwood 18 July 1944. Notes of conversations between General Dempsey, Commander Second British Army and (a) Lieutenant-Colonel G S

Jackson and (b) Captain B H Liddell Hart
CAB106/1062: Paper on command by Field Marshal Montgomery
FO371/41980: Effect of Overlord security measures on French communications
WO106/4348: Operational research in North West Europe
War Diaries
WO171/
20: HQ SHAEF
258–259: HQ I Corps
286–287: HQ VIII Corps
310: HQ XII Corps
336–340: HQ XXX Corps
376: Guards Armoured Div
439: 7th Armoured Div
409–411: 3rd Div
425: 6th Airborne Div
456: 11th Armoured Div
466–467: 15th (Scottish) Div
479–480: 43rd (Wessex) Div
499–500: 49th (West Riding) Div
513: 50th (Northumbrian) Div
527–528: 51st (Highland) Div
552–553: 53rd (Welsh) Div
571: 59th (Staffordshire) Div
583: 79th Armoured Div
591: 6th A/ldg Bde
593: 3rd Para Bde
595: 5th Para Bde
605: 5 Gds Armd Bde
613: 8 Bde
616: 9 Bde
619–620: 22 Armd Bde
627: 29 Armd Bde
638: 32 Gds Bde
646: 44 Bde
648: 46 Bde
651: 69 Bde
653: 70 Bde
658: 129 Bde
660: 130 Bde
662: 131 Bde
664: 146 Bde
666: 147 Bde
670: 151 Bde
673: 152 Bde
678: 153 Bde
680: 154 Bde
691: 159 Bde
702–703: 185 Bde
708: 214 Bde
712: 227 Bde
714: 231 Bde
837: 2nd H'hold Cav Rgt
838: 4/7 R Dgn Gds
839: 5th R Innisk Dgn Gds
840: 1st R Dgns
841: 22nd Dragoons
843: 8th King's R Ir Hussars
844: 11th Hussars
846: 15th/19th Hussars
847: 23rd Hussars
849: 24th Lancers
850: 2nd Derby Yeo
853: 2nd Fife & Forfar Yeo
854: Inns of Court Rgt
856: 4th County of London Yeo
859: 1st Northamptonshire Yeo
860: 2nd Northamptonshire Yeo
863: Staffordshire Yeo
864: Westminster Dgns
866: 3rd R Tank Rgt
877: 144 Rgt RAC
969: 7th Fd Rgt, RA
971: 33rd Fd Rgt, RA
976: 76th Fd Rgt, RA
1003: 190th Fd Rgt, RA
1015: 13th Rgt RHA
1017: 53rd A/ldg Lt Rgt, RA
1250: 1st Armd Cm Gds
1252: 5th Cm Gds
1253: 1st Mot Gren Gds
1254: 2nd Armd Gren Gds
1256: 2nd Armd Ir Gds
1257: 3rd Ir Gds
1259: 1st W Gds
1260: 2nd Armd W Gds
1262: 2nd Argyll & S'land Hldrs
1263: 7th Argyll & S'land Hldrs
1265: 1st Black Watch
1266: 5th Black Watch

1276: 7th Black Watch
1270: 5th Cameron Hldrs
1275: 9th Cameronians
1276: 2nd Cheshire
1278: 2nd Devons
1279: 12th Devons
1280– 1281: 5th Duke of Cornwall's LI
1284: 1st Dorset
1286: 4th Bn Dorset
1288: 7th Duke of Wellington's
1290: 6th Duke of Wellington's
1292: 10th Durham LI
1293: 11th Durham LI
1287: 5th Dorset
1297: 2nd Glasgow Hldrs
1299: 1st Gordon Hldrs
1301: 5th/7th Gordon Hldrs
1300: 2nd Gordon Hldrs
1302: 6th Green Howards
1303 7th Green Howards
1304: Hallamshire Bn
1305: 1st Hampshire
1306: 7th Hampshire
1313: 10th Highland LI
1314: 2nd Kensington
1318: 1st King's Own Scottish Bdrs
1322: 6th King's Own Scottish Bdrs
1324: 1/4th King's Own Yorks LI
1325: 2nd King's Shropshire LI
1326: 4th King's Shropshire LI
1332: 1st S Lancs
1334: 2nd Lincolns
1335: 4th Lincolns
1340: 1st Middx
1341: 2nd Middx
1347: 8th Middx
1349: 3rd Monmouth
1350: 1st R Norfolk
1351: 7th R Norfolk
1357: 2nd Ox & Bucks LI
1359: 8th Rifle Bde
1362: 8th R Scots
1364: 6th R Scots Fus
1366: 1/5th Queen's
1367: 1/6th Queen's
1368: 1/7th Queen's
1371: 7th Somerset LI
1372: 4th Somerset LI
1383: 1st R Ulster Rifles
1382: 1st Tyneside Scottish
1384: 2nd R Ulster Rifles
1386: 1/5th Welch
1387: 2nd R Warwickshire
1396: 1st Worcester
1397: 2nd E Yorks
1398: 5th E Yorks

WO179/
258–259: I Can Corps
2700: II Can Corps
2768–2769: 3rd Can Div
2872: 6 Can Bde
2879: 7 Can Bde
2886–2887: 8 Can Bde
2893–2894: 9 Can Bde
2927: Queen's Own Cameron Hldrs of Can
2936: Hld LI of Can
2941: Le Regt de la Chaudière
2944: Les Fusiliers Mont Royal
2947: North Shore Rgt
2948: N Nova Scotia Hldrs
2957: Cameron Hldrs of Can
2958: Queen's Own Rifles of Can
2960–2961: Regina Rifle Rgt
2965: R Winnipeg Rifles
2968: S Saskatchewan Rgt
2969–2970: Can Scottish
2974: Stormont, Dundas & G'garry Hldrs
2990: 7th Recce (17th D of York's R Can Hussars)
2991: 8th Recce (14th Can Hussars)
2998: 18th Can Armd Rgt (12th Manitoba Dgns)
3012: 29th Recce Rgt (S Alberta)
3024: 2nd Can AGRA
3028: 3rd Can A/tk Rgt
3050: 12th Can Fd Rgt
3051: 13th Can Fd Rgt
3052: 14th Can Fd Rgt
3045: 4th Can Fd Rgt
3046: 5th Can Fd Rgt
3047: 6th Can Fd Rgt
3085: 3rd Can LAA Rgt
3086: 4th Can LAA Rgt

The Military Historical Society
The Lummis Files, held at the National Army Museum, Chelsea

Files on Stanley Hollis VC, The Green Howards; Andrew Mynarski VC, RCAF; Ian Bazalgette VC, RAF; Sidney Bates VC, Norfolk Regiment; David Jamieson VC, Norfolk Regiment; Tasker Watkins VC, Welch Regiment; David Currie VC, 29th Armoured Reconnaissance Regiment (The South Alberta Regiment).

Private accounts

Bassam, F J, Seaforth Highlanders	Imperial War Museum ref: 94/41/1
Devlin, Patrick, Royal Ulster Rifles, *Reminiscences of a Rifleman in Normandy*	
Wingfield, Brigadier A D R, DSO MC, 10th Royal Hussars	Imperial War Museum ref: PP/MCR/353

Newspapers

The Times
The Manchester Guardian
The Daily Telegraph
Evening Telegraph
Evening Despatch
Daily Mail
London Gazette
The Irish Times

Other

Kiltimagh Life and Times – various issues

Websites

US Army Rangers:
http://www.benning.army.mil/rtb/history/wwiidieppe.htm
Mulberry Harbours:
http://www.gnometech.freeserve.co.uk/html/mulberry_harbour.html
John Desmond Bernal:
http://www.spartacus.schoolnet.co.uk/Jbernal.htm
Tank Museum, Bovington: http://www.tankmuseum.org
Tank Museum, D-Day website: http://www.d-daytanks.org.uk

Index